ds Trinity

Individual Differences and Personality

Third edition

Individual Differences and Personality

Third edition

School of Psychology, Queen's University, Belfast

HODDER
EDUCATION
AN HACHETTE UK COMPANY

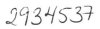
First published in Great Britain in 2010 by
Hodder Education, An Hachette UK Company,
338 Euston Road, London NW1 3BH

Hachette UK's policy is to use papers that are natural, renewable and
recyclable products and made from wood grown in sustainable forests.
The logging and manufacturing processes are expected to conform to the
environmental regulations of the country of origin.

The advice and information in this book are believed to be true and
accurate at the date of going to press, but neither the author nor the publisher
can accept any legal responsibility or liability for any errors or omissions.

British Library Cataloguing in Publication Data
A catalogue record for this book is available from the British Library

Library of Congress Cataloging-in-Publication Data
A catalog record for this book is available from the Library of Congress

ISBN 978 1 444 10859 0

1 2 3 4 5 6 7 8 9 10

Cover credit: © Dougal Waters/Photographer's Choice/Getty Images

Typeset in 11 on 13pt Minion by Phoenix Photosetting, Chatham, Kent
Printed and bound in Italy

What do you think about this book? Or any other Hodder Arnold title?
Please send your comments to educationenquiries@hodder.co.uk

http://www.hoddereducation.com

To Wesley

Contents

Preface

This book is all about personality, intelligence, mood and motivation – the branches of psychology that consider how (and, equally importantly, *why*) people are psychologically very different from one another. It also considers how such individual differences may be measured using psychological tests and other techniques. The book is primarily aimed at undergraduate students in psychology departments who are taking courses such as individual differences, personality, intelligence and ability, psychometrics or the assessment of individual differences. However, students in other disciplines (such as education) and at other levels (e.g. postgraduate courses in occupational psychology) are also likely to find much to interest them – as is anyone else who is interested in the nature, causes and assessment of personality and intelligence.

The book sprang from a course of lectures that I have taught at Queen's University, Belfast, and it was written largely out of a sense of frustration with existing texts. There are plenty of excellent textbooks covering personality theory, but using one of these in isolation has always seemed to me to be inadequate, since students graduating in psychology should surely also know something about the psychology of abilities, mood, motivation, and so on.

Moreover, several texts confine themselves to a historical survey of theories and are remarkably non-evaluative – they offer a selection of theories and leave it to the reader to try to discover which are useful. Several theories are now recognized as deadends and I think that it is important that students should be aware of promising modern work, rather than what seem now to be ancient follies. Furthermore, few texts consider how individual differences can be assessed or how tests can be evaluated. Given that a statistical method (factor analysis) underpins most modern attempts to describe personality and mental abilities and that theories can only be tested through the use of well-designed psychological tests to measure personality, mood, mental abilities and so on, it is also necessary to consider how these characteristics should best be measured. It is otherwise quite possible to draw wrong conclusions from studies based on ill-conceived tests. In addition, most readers of this book are likely to use tests in some shape or form (e.g. as a part of their project work or in their professional careers).

The book, therefore, comprises two sections, as such: the first deals with theories and applications of individual differences and the second with the necessary methodology. However, this is *not* a psychometrics textbook, so readers will search the second section in vain for the mathematical formulae that are fundamental to this branch of psychology. Given psychology students' notorious dislike of matters mathematical, I have instead tried to provide a conceptual understanding of the important issues. However, I do explore the topic of factor analysis in some detail because of the fundamental importance of this technique for many theories of personality and ability, with one chapter providing a conceptual understanding of the topic and another showing readers how to perform (and interpret the results obtained from) such analyses.

As well as being updated, this new edition includes a chapter on emotional intelligence, a considerably expanded treatment of reinforcement sensitivity theories of personality, more coverage of fascinating recent work on the influence of intelligence on health and wellbeing in later life and a chapter on the applications of individual differences to real-life problems.

My criteria for including theories and methodologies should also be made explicit. I have included theories if they are well supported by empirical evidence, important for historical reasons or useful in applied psychology. I have not included much information about the development of personality and ability, social learning theory or constructivist models, since these are traditionally taught in other branches of the discipline. The psychometrics chapters consider the usual theoretically and practically important issues (reliability, validity, etc.), but also progress to more advanced topics which will be important for those who will use, commission or interpret the results of psychological tests during their professional careers.

I must thank many people for their help and support during the preparation of this book. Past and present undergraduates and longsuffering graduate students have given useful feedback on draft chapters. My head of department, colleagues and friends (the distinction is often blurred) at Queen's have been more than supportive. Jasmin Naim and Liz Wilson, my editors, were immensely helpful during the writing and rewriting process. Wesley Moore supported me throughout and showed me that there is more to life than psychology. And, finally, thanks to Pip the cat, for playing with me during coffee breaks.

Colin Cooper
Belfast
January 2010

Introduction to individual differences

Introduction

Most branches of psychology examine how people (or animals) behave in different settings or under different experimental conditions: they assume that people are all much the same. Thus when developmental psychologists talk about 'stages of development', the tacit assumption is that all children develop in broadly similar ways. Likewise, social psychology produces theories to explain why people *in general* may show obedience to authority, prejudice and other group-related behaviours. Cognitive psychologists have shown that people recognize the meaning of a word more quickly when it is preceded by a semantically related 'prime'. Physiological psychologists often assume that everyone's nervous system has much the same sort of structure and will operate in much the same way. So much of psychology involves finding rules that describe how people *in general* behave.

Yet this is only part of the story, for there is also significant variation *between* people. Some children develop more quickly than others, some individuals seem more obedient to authority or more prejudiced than others. Some people will recognize all types of words quickly while others will take far longer; drugs such as caffeine and alcohol seem to have much more of an effect on some individuals than on others, and many psychophysiological measures (such as the sweatiness of the skin and patterns of electrical activity in the brain) show marked variation from person to person. The psychology of individual differences seeks to understand how we should best describe the ways in which people vary and to understand how and why such variations in behaviour come about. These individual differences are extremely important in everyday life. Employers seek out those who have the attitudes, abilities, skills and motivation required for a particular post. Most of us do the same sort of thing when making friends and seeking partners – perhaps enduring loud music, boring parties and dating agencies rather than simply marrying the person who lives next door.

Given that the aim of psychology is to describe, explain and predict the behaviour of organisms (people), it is clear that neither of these two approaches is sufficient on its own. It is necessary to understand both the setting in which the behaviour occurs and relevant individual differences. For example, in order to predict whether a jailed psychopath will re-offend if released, it is necessary to understand both the general law (the statistical probability that a jailed psychopath taken at random will re-offend), and individual differences that are related to re-offending behaviour (for example, the extent to which the person shows remorse or empathy for his victims). This book focuses on individual differences.

I believe that there are four main reasons for studying individual differences:

- *It is of interest in its own right.* The examples given earlier show that we attach considerable importance to individual differences and so studying how and why some individuals are different from others is an intriguing issue in its own right.

- *Psychological tests are useful in applied psychology.* The study of individual differences almost invariably leads to the publication of psychological tests. These measure abilities, knowledge, personality, mood and many other characteristics and are of immense value to educational, occupational and clinical psychologists, teachers, nurses, careers counsellors and others who may want to diagnose learning difficulties, dyslexia or outstanding mental ability or seek to assess an individual's suitability for promotion, level of depression or suitability for a post that requires enormous attention to detail. The proper use of psychological tests can thus benefit both society and individuals.

- *Tests are useful 'dependent variables' in other branches of psychology.* Psychologists make extensive use of psychological tests when conducting experiments. A clinical psychologist may suspect that feelings of hopelessness often lead to suicide attempts. In order to test this hypothesis, it is obviously necessary to have some way of measuring hopelessness in suicidal and non-suicidal people and by far the simplest way of doing so is to look for an appropriate psychological test. Cognitive psychologists studying the link between mood and memory must be able to assess both mood and memory in order to be able to test whether a particular theory is valid and so they need sound mood questionnaires.

- *Other branches of psychology can predict behaviour better when they consider individual differences.* We saw earlier that other branches of psychology rely on broad laws to predict behaviour, e.g. 'behaviour therapy', in which the principles of conditioning are used to break some undesirable habit. The therapist may know that a certain percentage of his or her patients may be 'cured' by this technique, but is unlikely to be able to predict whether any *one individual* is more or less likely than average to benefit from the therapy. However, it might well be found that the effectiveness of a particular type of treatment is affected by the individual's personality and/or ability – a treatment that is successful in some individuals may be much less successful in others. By taking such individual differences into account, statistical tests become more sensitive. For example, instead of using analysis of variance to determine whether patients who are given behaviour therapy for a particular problem tend to show fewer symptoms than those who are assigned to a control condition, it is far better also to measure relevant personality and ability traits. One can then perform what is known as an 'analysis of covariance' instead. This shows whether the personality and ability traits are related to the number of symptoms shown *and* whether the two groups differ in the number of symptoms shown. It can show whether individual differences and/or the experimental condition influences behaviour.

Main questions

Any attempt to understand the nature of individual differences must really address two quite separate questions. The first concerns the *nature* of individual differences – how individual differences should be conceptualized. There is a wide range of answers to this question, as will be seen in the following chapters. Indeed, it has been suggested that personality does not exist and that how we behave may be determined entirely by the situations in which we find ourselves rather than by anything 'inside us' and the evidence for such claims must be scrutinized carefully.

The second main question concerns how and why individual differences in mood, motivation, ability and personality arise. It should be clear that research into the 'how' of individual differences can really only start once there is general agreement about their structure. It would be a waste of time to perform experiments in order to try to understand how 'sociability' (or 'creativity', 'depression', 'the drive for achievement', etc.) works if there is no good evidence that sociability is an important dimension of personality in the first place. Thus studies of processes must logically follow on from studies of structure. Process models of individual differences address questions such as the following. Why should some children perform much better than others at school? Why should some people be shy and others outgoing? Why do some individuals' moods swing wildly from depression to elation and back again? Why are some individuals apparently motivated by money to the exclusion of all else?

We cannot hope to answer all of these questions in the following chapters, but we shall certainly explore what is known about the biological (and to some extent the social) processes that underlie personality, mood, ability and motivation.

There is, however, one problem. Unless it is possible to measure individual differences accurately, it will be completely impossible either to determine the structure of personality, intelligence, etc. or to investigate its underlying processes. The development of good, accurate measures of individual differences (a branch of psychology known as *psychometrics*) is an absolutely vital step in developing and testing theories about the nature of individual differences and their underlying processes. For this reason, this book contains several chapters (14 to 19) that focus on measurement issues.

How can we discover individual differences?

What sort of data should we use to discover individual differences? This is not an easy question to answer, for there are several possibilities.

Clinical theories

Several theories have grown out of the experiences of clinical psychologists, who realized that the ways in which they conceptualized 'abnormal behaviour' (particularly conditions such as anxiety, depression and poor self-image) might also prove useful in understanding individual differences in the 'normal' population. Some have probably been rather quick to do this. Freud, for example, saw really rather small samples of upper middle-class Viennese women (many

Photo credit: © Cultura RM Alamy

of whom showed symptoms that are so unusual that they do not appear in modern diagnostic manuals), refused to believe some of what they told him (such as memories of sexual abuse) and built up an enormous and complex theory about the personality structure and functions of humankind *in general.*

Detailed studies of individuals

Many people claim to have a rather good understanding of 'what makes others tick' – for members of their families and close friends, at any rate. For example, we may believe that we know through experience how to calm down (or annoy) others to whom we are close and may feel that we have a good, intuitive understanding of the types of issue that are important to them, thereby allowing us to 'see the world from their point of view' and predict their behaviour. For example, we all have some intuitive feeling about when to mention difficult issues to those close to us. Perhaps this type of 'gut feeling' should be the mainstay of individual difference research?

There are several difficulties with this approach, even if it can be proved that this approach leads to accurate prediction of behaviour. First, it will (presumably) take a long period of time to know anyone well enough to be able to make accurate predictions. Second, it is not particularly scientific, as it will be difficult to quantify the measurements that are obtained. Third, the vagaries of language will make it

Photo credit: © anshuca-fotolia.com

very difficult to determine whether different people operate in different ways. Two people could describe the same characteristic in an individual in two quite different ways and it would be impossible to be *sure* that they were referring to precisely the same characteristic. However, the greatest problem of all is self-deception. It is very easy to overestimate how well one can predict someone else's behaviour and there is good evidence that most observers will see and remember the 1% of behaviours that were correctly predicted and ignore or explain away the 99% of predictions that were incorrect – a phenomenon called 'confirmatory bias'. Davies (2003) discusses this in the context of personality assessment. All these difficulties also apply to attempts to discover the roots of personality through introspection – there is no guarantee that the theories that emerge from such a process will be true in any scientific sense of the word.

Armchair speculation

If one has made good, unbiased observations of how individuals behave in many situations, it might be reasonable to generate and test some hypotheses about behaviour. For example, someone may notice that some individuals tend to be anxious and jumpy, worry, lose their temper more easily than most and so on. That is, the observer may notice that a whole bundle of characteristics seem to vary together and suggest that 'anxiety' (or something similar) might be an interesting aspect of personality. Of course, there are likely to be all sorts of problems associated with such casual observations. The observations may simply be wrong, or they may fail to take account of situations. For example, the people who were perceived as being anxious might all have been in some stressful situation – it may be that the *situation* (rather than the person) determines how they react. Moreover, the ideas may be expressed so vaguely that they are impossible to test, as in Plato's observation that the mind is like a chariot drawn by four horses. Literature contains several testable hypotheses about personality, e.g. when Shakespeare speaks through Julius Caesar as follows:

> Let me have men about me that are fat,
> Sleek-headed men and such as sleep o' nights,
> Yond' Cassius has a lean and hungry look.
> He thinks too much; such men are dangerous.

(Shakespeare: *Julius Caesar* I:ii)

This quotation suggests some rather interesting (and potentially empirically testable) process models of 'dangerousness'.

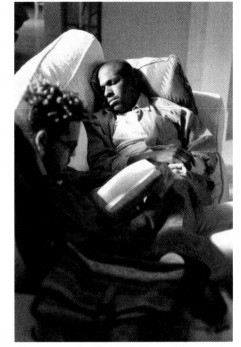

Photo credit: © 1997 Doug Menuez/ PhotoDisc, In Getty Images

Scientific assessment of individuals using mental tests

Because of the problems inherent in other approaches discussed already, many psychologists opt for a more scientific approach to the study of personality and other forms of individual difference. One popular approach involves the use of statistical techniques to discover consistencies in behaviours across situations and to determine which behaviours tend to occur together in individuals. The raw data of such methods are either behaviours (such as performance on test items that require certain skills or knowledge), ratings of behaviour (obtained by trained raters who note well-defined behaviours and so very different from the clinical approach just mentioned) or self-ratings on questionnaires that are constructed using sound statistical techniques. Much care is taken to ensure that the measurements are both accurate and replicable.

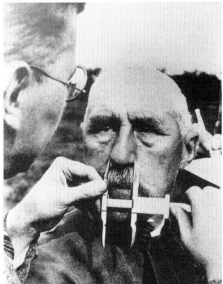

Photo credit: © akg-images/Alamy

Summary

This brief chapter has introduced the general area of individual differences and has suggested that the topic is worth studying because of its inherent interest, the many practical applications of tests designed to measure individual differences, the need to measure individual differences in order to test theories in other branches of psychology and the ability to make more accurate predictions from theories that consider both individual differences and the impact of experimental interventions on behaviour. We have also considered some methods for studying individual differences, each with its own advantages and drawbacks and have introduced the distinction between structural models ('how do people differ?') and process models ('why/when/where?') and laid the foundations for discussing the assessment of individual differences.

References

Davies, M. F. (2003). Confirmatory bias in the evaluation of personality descriptions: positive test strategies and output interference. *Journal of Personality and Social Psychology 85*(4), 736–44.

2 Kelly and Rogers

Background

The theories of George Kelly and Carl Rogers are included in this book because they are both simple and highly influential in counselling psychology. They suggest that personality should be understood by obtaining a detailed understanding of how individuals function, based on sympathetic clinical interviews and techniques such as the repertory grid and Q-sort.

Recommended prior reading

Chapters 1 and 14.

Introduction

The theories of George Kelly and Carl Rogers are treated together because they are both *phenomenological* in nature – they assume that a person's conscious experience can reveal their basic personality. More specifically, they suggest that an individual's personality can be understood by knowing how they understand and experience the world, both emotionally and cognitively. Thus both Kelly and Rogers focus on how the *individual* perceives him- or herself and other people. The aim is to understand each individual's unique view of the world, through exploring his or her thoughts, feelings and beliefs. This technique (known as introspection) is perhaps the most obvious and simple way of investigating personality, which is why we consider these theories first.

As will be shown later, other theorists tend to disagree with the view that asking people to 'look inside' and describe their views and feelings can reveal their basic personality. Freud and his followers suggest that the main determinants of personality lurk in areas of the mind that are usually completely unconscious and so are not accessible to introspection. Furthermore, since they believe that people have an almost infinite capacity for self-delusion, 'remembering' events that did not happen and forgetting those that did take place, the approach of simply asking people to think about how they feel about themselves or others may be doomed to failure. According to Freud, only the clear-minded and dispassionate analyst can see the true nature and origins of behaviour and symptoms and the client has to be persuaded of the veracity of the analyst's interpretations. Trait theorists also have problems with this approach because they are suspicious of the use of Q-data: they prefer not to make the assumption that what a person says about themselves is necessarily accurate.

Both Rogers and Kelly maintain that our *subjective* view of ourselves, other people and events is of paramount importance. Since we can all choose to view events from a variety of standpoints (losing one's job may be viewed as a personal rejection, a minor inconvenience or a great opportunity to change one's lifestyle), any such theory of personality must focus on how we view and interpret events. Kelly once suggested that 'the individual's views of themselves and other people provides the only sensible basis for understanding how the individual's personality system operates'.

Because of this belief in the ability of the individual to communicate his or her thoughts, feelings and experiences and potentially to *alter* 'unhelpful' views of the world, the theories described in this chapter have had a substantial impact on counselling and clinical psychology. Rogers' theory, in particular, is almost indistinguishable from the practice of 'client-centred therapy' that is the cornerstone of counselling techniques.

Self-assessment question 2.1

What is meant by the phenomenological approach to personality study?

An introduction to George Kelly's personal construct theory

George Kelly trained as a clinical psychologist and ran a mobile psychological service in Kansas in the 1920s. He had a background in psychoanalytical theory, but gradually became convinced that his clients were 'paralyzed by prolonged drought, dust-storms and economic concerns, not by overflowing libidinal forces' (Rykman 1992: 338). He felt that what was lacking from traditional theories of personality was any account of the way in which individuals conceptualized, or tried to make sense of, the world. Indeed, such theories appeared to ignore what seemed obvious to Kelly – that people strive to understand what is happening in their lives and to predict what will happen next. He noted that:

A typical afternoon might find me talking to a graduate student at one o'clock, doing all those familiar things that thesis directors have to do – encouraging the student to pinpoint issues, to observe, to become intimate with the problem, to form hypotheses either inductively or deductively, to make some preliminary test runs, to relate his data to his predictions, to control his experiments so that he will know what led to what, to generalize cautiously and revise his thinking in the light of experience.

At two o'clock I might have an appointment with a client (i.e. patient). During that interview I would not be taking the role of scientist but rather helping the distressed person work out some solutions to his life's problems. So what would I do? Why, I would try to get him to pinpoint issues, to observe, to become intimate with the problem, to form hypotheses either inductively or deductively, to make some preliminary test runs, to relate outcomes to anticipations, to control his ventures so that he will know what led to what, to generalise cautiously and to revise his dogma in the light of experience.

(Kelly 1963b, quoted in Bannister and Mair 1968: 3)

Kelly's cognitive theory thus suggests that each person operates rather like a scientist – making observations (of people), using these observations to formulate rules that explain how the world works, then applying those rules to new people and observing whether they behave as expected. If the rules do indeed seem to explain behaviour, the 'model' thus created is useful. If not, it needs to be refined or discarded in favour of an alternative. Different individuals will develop quite different models to predict how others will behave – a principle that Kelly termed 'constructive alternatism'. The theory therefore how focuses on how our perception of others and not how they really are. As a result of this we each develop our own informal theories about how others behave – 'people who laugh a lot are probably sad and unhappy inside', 'bigoted people are not in touch with their own feelings' and so on. Each of these theories may be useful in helping us to understand how certain individuals will react in certain situations and we are constantly trying to determine the types of person for whom these theories make accurate predictions and the settings in which the predictions work. For example, we test our theory of bigotry when we meet new people by trying to gauge how bigoted and how in touch with their feelings each person is and estimating whether there is a negative correlation between these two characteristics.

Why different people develop different systems of constructs

There are several possible reasons why different individuals produce different constructs when completing repertory grids. First, not everyone is interested in predicting the same set of outcomes. A salesperson will have a financial interest in distinguishing those who will make a purchase from those who are browsing and will therefore probably notice features of people's behaviour that are not at all obvious to the rest of us.

Second, people differ in the way in which they use language – by 'antisocial' I may mean 'quiet and reserved', but someone else may mean 'aggressive or destructive'. So even if it is possible to find out what words people use to categorize others, it does not follow that two individuals who use the same word are actually referring to the same thing (i.e. the same psychological or behavioural characteristic) by using that word. Similarly, it is possible that two people who use two *different* words to describe a characteristic might be referring to precisely the same thing – one person's 'aloof' might refer to exactly the same psychological characteristics as another person's 'shy'.

Third, people's own backgrounds and values will influence the way in which they construe behaviours. Suppose two individuals witness a third placing a traffic cone on top of a lamppost. One might construe the person as 'criminal' (as opposed to law abiding) and another might construe them as 'high spirited' (as opposed to boring).

> **Self-assessment question 2.2**
>
> Why do people generally use different constructs to describe the same element(s)?

When construct systems fail

Our predictions about people's behaviour are not always accurate. Suppose we believe that the three ideal ingredients for a pleasant night's socializing involve other people whom we construe as talkative, relaxed and generous. We would expect a stranger whom we construed in this manner to be good company. Suppose that the prediction is completely wrong and the night turns out to be a disaster. Faced with a discrepancy between their mental model of what *should* happen and the actual behaviour and feelings of all concerned, the individual doing the construing has several courses of action open to them:

- They can re-evaluate the person with regard to each of the characteristics. Perhaps the stranger was not quite as generous/talkative/relaxed as was first thought. This implies that the model for the kind of person who makes good company may still be correct, as it was the initial construing of the stranger's character that was faulty.

- Perhaps the whole ghastly evening shows that some *other* characteristics (such as extreme political views or a penchant for lechery or practical joking) can *also* influence whether a person makes good company. The model can be extended to take these constructs into account. The stranger would not have performed well against some of these new criteria and so this accounts for the unenjoyable evening.

- They may conclude that the model is a failure and that they need to consider quite different characteristics of people in order to predict their behaviour. Abandoning one's mental model of how people work and having to construct a new one is thought to be associated with feelings of threat and fear, as we shall see.

Discovering personal constructs: the repertory grid

Each person classifies objects and people ('elements') by means of 'personal constructs'. These can be represented by two terms that have opposite meaning to that individual, e.g. good/bad, lively/boring. If we can find a way to determine the nature of these dimensions ('constructs') that the person uses to impose some structure on the world, four interesting questions immediately arise:

- *What constructs does an individual use?* In other words, what aspects of other people seem to matter most to this individual? What characteristics does he or she find useful in attempting to predict how others will behave? Are there any obvious features that simply do not seem to be considered? Are there any very idiosyncratic constructs?

- *How does the individual construe certain key 'elements' in his or her life?* In particular, how does the person construe him- or herself, as well as their family and their friends? The technique offers yet another method for exploring feelings about the person's self.

- *What are the relationships between the constructs?* It is quite possible that the constructs will be correlated. For example, we may find that a patient views 'lively' (rather than 'dull') people as 'untrustworthy' (rather than 'honest') – which may open up all kinds of fruitful avenues for clinical enquiry.

- *What are the relationships between the elements?* For example, do men choose for their wives people whom they construe in much the same way as they do their mothers? What if a woman construes her husband in much the same way as she construes sex criminals?

The *repertory grid technique* can help to address all of these issues. The basic idea is very simple and you will find it useful if you try the technique on yourself. A participant is given a 'role title' (e.g. 'brother') and is asked to write down the name of one real person ('element') who occupies this role in their life. This is then repeated for about a dozen role titles. They would typically include the participant, their mother, father, partner, a particular brother, a particular sister, someone whom the participant dislikes, someone for whom they feel sorry, their boss at work, a close friend of the same sex, a well-liked teacher etc. and are usually chosen so as to cover the main relationships in the participant's life, with disliked as well as liked individuals featuring on the list.

The role titles may be specially chosen for clinical applications. For example, a therapist who wanted to understand a person's self-concept might include 'myself as I would like to be', 'myself as I am now', 'myself as my family see me', 'myself 5 years ago'. One who wanted to understand a client's addiction might include 'me before drinking', 'me after drinking', 'me as I believe I will be after quitting drink'. Being able to tailor the repertory grid to the circumstances of any individual is one of the great strengths of the technique.

The participant taking the grid shown in Figure 2.1 has filled in the names of five appropriate individuals under their 'role titles' in the first row of the grid. They are then given just three of these names ('triads'), which have been chosen more or less at random, and are asked to think of one important *psychological* way in which any one of these individuals differs from the other two. For example, they might see one characteristic as being 'mean' – this is the 'emergent pole' of the first construct. They would then be asked to describe the opposite of 'mean'. It could be 'generous', 'helpful' or many other possibilities; it does not have to be a *logical* opposite in the sense of a dictionary definition. However, let us suppose that our participant decides that the opposite of 'mean' is 'generous' – this is the 'contrast pole' of the construct. The words describing the emergent and contrast poles of the construct are entered into the first row of the repertory grid, as shown in Figure 2.1. The process is then repeated using another three elements, until sufficient constructs have been generated or until the participant is unable to produce any new constructs. Few people can produce more than a dozen or so different constructs. If someone finds it difficult to think of a new construct, it is useful to encourage them to group the elements differently. Rather than looking for a construct which differentiates one's boss from oneself and one's brother, one could reflect on how one differs from one's brother and one's boss, how one's brother differs from one's boss and oneself and so on.

	Father Peter	Mother Fiona	Self David	Boss Mark	Friend Fred	
Mean						Generous
Happy						Miserable
Lively						Quiet
etc.						etc.

Figure 2.1 Example of a repertory grid.

Two points need to be borne in mind when encouraging someone to reveal their constructs. First, they should be encouraged to produce constructs that are psychological characteristics and not (for example) physical features (e.g. tall vs. short, male vs. female) or anything to do with an individual's background or habits (e.g. poor vs. wealthy, drinker vs. teetotaller). The second important principle is that each construct should be different from those given previously. Gentle questioning is necessary to ensure that the participant feels that this is the case.

Once the participant's constructs have been discovered, it is necessary to find out how they view ('construe') each of the elements. There are several ways of doing this. The simplest is to ask the participant to rate each element on a five-point scale. A rating of 1 indicates that the phrase in the left-hand column (the 'emergent pole') of the construct describes the element very accurately – for the first construct in Figure 2.1 this is 'mean'. A rating of 5 indicates that the phrase in the right-hand column (the 'contrast pole' of the construct) describes the element very accurately – 'generous' in this case. A rating of 2 would show that the element was fairly mean, a rating of 4 that they were fairly generous, and a rating of 3 that they were of average generosity. Each person or 'element' is rated in this way and one then moves on to the next construct. The repertory grid eventually looks something like that shown in Figure 2.2.

	Father Peter	Mother Fiona	Self David	Boss Mark	Friend Fred	
Mean	1	4	5	1	2	Generous
Happy	4	5	1	5	3	Miserable
Lively	5	4	2	5	3	Quiet
Hedonistic	5	4	3	5	4	Moral
Friendly	4	1	1	3	1	Aloof
etc.						etc.

Figure 2.2 Completed repertory grid.

Self-assessment question 2.3

What is meant by:

1. a construct

2. a role title

3. an element

4. a triad?

Analysis of repertory grids

Whole books have been written about how to analyse these grids and the possibilities are virtually endless. Simply looking at the grids can help one to obtain a general impression of how an individual construes him- or herself, and some clinical work relies on this approach. However, most analyses explore two main areas – patterns of similarities between the constructs and similarities between the elements.

Similarities between the constructs are interesting because they reveal the 'stereotypes', which are discussed later. You can see this for yourself from the grid shown in Figure 2.2. If an element has a rating of 1 or 2 on the 'happy vs. miserable' construct, then they also tend to have a rating of 1 or 2 on the 'lively vs. quiet' construct. The same is true for ratings of 4 and 5. This shows that the individual perceives happy people as being lively and miserable individuals as being quiet, which is really rather an interesting finding. The obvious way to analyse these relationships is to correlate the rows of the matrix together.

The second way of analysing grids is to look for similarities between its *columns*. This shows whether the participant sees two *elements* as being similar. For example, look at the columns representing the participant's father and their boss (Mark) in Figure 2.2. You can see that this participant tends to place these two individuals in similar positions on each of the constructs. When one has a rating of 1 or 2 the other is likely to have a similar rating. This shows that the participant regards these two individuals as having much the same type of personality. However, there is a problem when correlating elements. A large positive correlation indicates that two columns are almost directly proportional, not that they are the same. For example, if two elements are given ratings of 1, 2, 2, 1 and 2, 5, 5, 2 on four constructs, these elements will correlate perfectly, although it is clear that the ratings given to the elements are very different. You may wish to invent your own statistics for comparing the *absolute* similarity of the ratings given to two elements. You could, for example, add up the differences between two columns, ignoring any minus signs – e.g. $4 + 1 + 1 + 4 = 10$. Alternatively, you could take the square root of the average squared difference between the pairs of ratings.

Some psychologists perform much more complex analyses on the data from repertory grids. One popular technique, called 'factor analysis', will be discussed in Chapters 16 and 17. My view is that most such analyses should be avoided, since the data rarely if ever meet the statistical assumptions for these analyses. The small amount of data produced by the repertory grids means that each of the correlations has a large amount of error associated with it – so that a small change to one of the numbers in a grid will have quite a dramatic effect on the size of the correlations and thus on the results from the factor analysis. It is really much safer to keep the analyses simple.

Repertory grids have a very wide range of uses, since they can be designed for specific applications as diverse as understanding how individuals categorize works of art and eliciting experts' knowledge which can then be used as the knowledge base for 'expert system' computer programs (e.g. Chao, Salvendy and Lightner 1999). They are also useful in occupational psychology: for example, if one uses role titles such as 'productive colleague', 'lazy colleague', 'someone who works hard but ineffectively', 'good manager', one can discover how workers construe colleagues who perform well – something that may be fed into the personnel selection system.

Self-assessment question 2.4

How might you use repertory grid techniques to discover how individuals categorize complex stimuli, such as works of art?

Fixed role therapy

As well as using the repertory grid, Kelly suggested that if one wanted to learn what a particular person was like, he or she should be invited to write a short self-description *as if it were written by a close friend*. His books contain several examples of this. The therapist then deduces the constructs that have been used. For example, if someone wrote: 'Marvin was a sad child, unlike the rest of his friends who were contented' the therapist would infer the sad/contented construct. Once a person's constructs are known, they may be used therapeutically in what is known as 'fixed role therapy'. Here the therapist asks that person to 'playact' being a very *different* person. For example, if a person construed him- or herself as being 'quiet', 'unemotional' and 'anxious', the therapist might ask them to try *acting* as if they felt the opposite (normally for a period of some weeks) so that they could explore what it felt like to construe themselves differently and to try to develop their construct systems.

Methods of construing

Kelly argued that the development and elaboration of a construct system is a vitally important aspect of mental health. If an individual employs relatively few constructs, then they will simply not have the cognitive apparatus for perceiving the fine distinctions between people that are necessary to predict their actions. At the other extreme, an individual could have a vast and unwieldy system of constructs that are not well organized and that can provide conflicting suggestions as to how the other person should behave. Instead, Kelly considered that a system of constructs should be relatively small, but constantly refined.

Kelly suggested that constructs can be applied to elements in three ways. *Pre-emptive* construing simply enables us to categorize others without allowing for further elaboration. For example, by applying the construct 'criminal/honest' to someone and deciding that they are at the 'criminal' pole, pre-emptive construing would imply that all criminals are exactly the same and they have no other interesting features. The person is (quite literally) 'just a criminal'.

A *constellatory* construct is little better. It basically works in terms of crude stereotypes – if an individual is construed in a certain way (e.g. as a criminal), then he or she will automatically be assumed to possess a number of other characteristics. For example, a person perceived as a criminal might automatically be construed as violent (rather than gentle), unintelligent (rather than intelligent) and so on – a description that hardly fits the average City fraudster.

It is much better for the individual to use constructs in a *propositional* manner, in which he or she evaluates the individual along each of their available constructs – some criminals might be viewed as intelligent and others as unintelligent, some would be construed as violent and others as gentle. In other words, the person tries to construe each element as an *individual* rather than in terms of packages of constructs (as with constellatory construing), or by simply not trying to develop their understanding (as with pre-emptive construing).

Self-assessment question 2.5

Why are propositional constructs thought to be the most useful?

It should be obvious that not all constructs will apply to all elements. The 'good/bad' construct can be applied to most things, but 'friendly/unfriendly' cannot really be applied to cheeses (except perhaps for the pepper-covered ones that burn your mouth) and 'representational/abstract' cannot really be applied to anything other than visual art. Thus we say that each construct has a 'range of convenience', that is, a range of elements to which it applies.

Emotion

One very important group of constructs consists of those that are used to describe one's self – constructs that are used to understand what sort of person one is and to predict one's future actions. These are called *core constructs*, and since it is important that we should be able to understand and predict our own behaviour, any disruption of these constructs is associated with several unpleasant emotional experiences. *Guilt* is experienced when we construe ourselves as behaving in ways that are inconsistent with our previous self-construction. For example, if someone who has previously used the construct 'honest/dishonest' as a core construct (rating themselves as 'honest') is forced to construe some of his or her behaviours as 'dishonest' (e.g. stealing from a shop in order to keep in with his or her peer group), then Kelly claimed that such an individual will experience guilt.

Feelings of *threat* may arise when one realizes that one's core constructs are about to change radically. For example, anyone would feel threatened when diagnosed with some terrible illness (e.g. AIDS, Alzheimer's disease) which inevitably meant that the 'self' would have to be radically reconstrued. *Fear* is similar, but involves things about which we know less. I know something about the symptoms of AIDS and Alzheimer's disease, but relatively little about the effects of being bitten by an adder or being involved in a car crash – I feel threatened by the former pair and fear the latter pair. Children feel *threatened* if they feel that their parents may separate, but they *fear* ghosts.

Hostility arises when one continues to try to use a construct that is manifestly not working – our hostile actions attempt to coerce others into giving us evidence that our construing is, after all, correct. Football supporters whose team has tumbled to the bottom of the league will want to continue to construe their team as 'excellent' (as opposed to useless) and will react with hostility whenever they realize this is inappropriate.

Anxiety is felt whenever it is realized that one's construct system is unable to deal with events – that is, that the events which occur fall outside the *range of convenience* of the construct system. Feelings of anxiety may well then be followed by attempts to extend the construct system in order to understand the novel situation. If a person has few constructs that are useful in helping them to predict how people will behave in groups, it should follow that they experience anxiety in group situations.

Kelly's view of *aggression* is, surprisingly, diametrically opposed to his view of hostility. Whereas hostility is seen to be the result of clinging to constructs that simply fail to predict events, aggression accompanies experiments that are performed to check the validity of one's construct system. We may literally 'play games' with people to see if they react as expected, or test out our construct system in new settings, by performing new activities or by assuming some other persona. This constant testing of the construct system is a vitally important aspect of personal growth, since it is only through finding the weaknesses of one's construct system that one can usefully develop it.

Issues arising from Kelly's theory

Kelly's theory is not currently popular in psychology, although computer scientists use it extensively in order to discover how experts distinguish between objects ('knowledge elicitation'). This   **15** is unfortunate, as the repertory grid technique can be extremely useful in clinical and occupational psychology, experimental aesthetics, psychophysics and social psychology – indeed, in any area in which it may be useful to try to understand how an individual discriminates between several different objects or people. Before leaving this theory, I shall briefly mention some issues that may be worth thinking about when reading the literature:

- Kelly's theory relies on language to describe the constructs and this can be problematical. It would be a brave therapist who claimed she could view her world through the construct system of another person, whose subtle nuances of meaning may elude her.

- The technique is not useful for comparing individuals. If a company wants to recruit salespeople, then sociability is one obvious requirement – the organization wants a salesperson who will go and talk to potential customers. While it would be possible to attempt to understand the phenomenal (personal) world of each applicant and to deduce from this how outgoing each person perceives him- or herself there is absolutely no guarantee that the self-reports will be accurate. I can think of several rather dull individuals who are firmly convinced that they have a first-rate sense of humour!

- Third, the utility of a construct in predicting behaviour is confounded with the accuracy with which judgements about elements can be made. A construct will only be useful for predicting behaviour if (a) the construct is related to the behaviour and (b) the individual is able to accurately assess peoples standing on the construct. If the person doing the construing makes extremely bad judgements when attempting to assess people on the 'trustworthy/ devious' construct, then the construct will clearly be useless for helping them to predict behaviour, although if they could only learn how to evaluate people better it could be extremely helpful. Thus finding that a person lacks a particular construct could mean that they have a 'blind spot' for that characteristic or that they are unable to accurately assess people's level of the construct and so do not find it useful in predicting behaviour.

- There are also several areas that are *not* covered by Kelly's theory. There is no good theory of personality development apart from the belief that we all seek to expand and extend our construct systems. How, when and why we learn to construe is something of a mystery.

- Some may also feel that it is all rather mechanistic – classifying individuals and making coldly logical decisions about how they may behave (with emotions popping up as a sort of by-product) does not sound like a very warm, human activity. And given that personal experience plays such an important part in this theory, it is slightly odd that we rarely seem to perceive ourselves *using* constructs consciously.

- What are the criteria used to determine whether the construct system requires revision?

- What determines *how* this is done (e.g. the introduction of new constructs or the re-evaluation of certain elements)?

- How could one determine whether Kelly's view of 'man-the-scientist' is correct? The theory may 'feel right' to individuals, but, as we argue in Chapter 14, subjective reactions are really a rather poor way of establishing the worth of a theory.

- It is difficult to make specific predictions on the basis of the theory. If a person construes himself as being tough, hostile and determined to get his own way, then it seems reasonable to suspect that he may be somewhat aggressive – but how? Engaging in heated debate, partner beating, playing sport? The theory cannot tell us.

It should be clear if you have tried administering and interpreting another person's repertory grid that phenomenology is both the greatest strength and the greatest weakness of Kelly's theory. What we *need* in order to evaluate this theory are hard, empirical studies of precisely how ordinary people decide that their construct systems are failing and then revise them – that is, we need to check whether our construct systems are indeed used and revised as Kelly suggested.

The person-centred theory of Carl Rogers

Whereas Kelly believed that people form hypotheses and behave analytically in forging a useful construct system, Carl Rogers focused closely on the meanings of the *feelings* experienced by each individual. As we shall see in Chapter 3, a Freudian would dismiss emotional experiences as mere by-products of some more fundamental unconscious conflict and a personal construct psychologist would regard them as interesting indicators of how well the construct system was working. For Rogers, the subjective experience of reality was by far the most interesting source of data. According to Rogers' view, a psychologically healthy individual is one who is in touch with their own emotional experiences, who 'listens' to their emotions and can express their true feelings openly and without distortion.

Rogers was a clinical psychologist by training. His theories developed gradually from the 1940s to the 1980s and the basic principles of his approach have been adopted enthusiastically by counsellors and clinical psychologists who believe that a careful, empathic study of what a person thinks and feels is the most valuable way of gaining an insight into their nature. He believed that open honest communication between individuals is an exceptionally rewarding experience for both parties, and his method of therapy is primarily concerned with creating a safe, supportive environment in which the client feels comfortable enough to remove any barriers and to explore his or her true feelings about him or herself and others. For Rogers, therapy is not about a therapist 'doing things to' a client but instead about giving the client the space and support to verbalize their thoughts and feelings and eventually to work out their own solutions.

The most important concept in Rogers' personality theory is the 'self'. This concept sprang from his clinical work, in which clients would use expressions such as 'I'm not my usual self today', implying that they had a unified mental picture of themselves which could be consciously examined and evaluated. This is known as the 'self-concept'. Rogers' clinical work further led him to believe that his clients basically wanted to get to know their true self – to stop behaving as they felt they *ought* to behave and just fulfilling the demands of others:

As I follow the experience of many clients in the therapeutic relationship which we endeavour to create for them, it seems to me that each one is raising the same question. Below the level of the problem situation about which the individual is complaining – behind the trouble with studies or wife or employer, or with his own uncontrollable or bizarre behavior, or with his frightening feelings – lies one central search. It seems to me that at the bottom each person is asking 'Who am I, really? How can I get in touch with this real self, underlying all my surface behavior? How can I become myself?'

(Rogers 1967: 108)   **17**

Having done so, individuals become less defensive and more open to their own attitudes and feelings and can see other people and events as they truly are, without using stereotypes. The over-all picture is similar to Kelly's view of using constructs in a propositional rather than a pre-emptive manner. The individual also gets to *like* him or herself, and to stop fearing his or her emotions:

Consciousness, instead of being the watchman over a dangerous and unpredictable lot of impulses, of which few can be permitted to see the light of day, becomes the comfortable inhabitant of a society of impulses and feelings and thoughts, which are discovered to be very satisfactorily self-governing when not fearfully guarded.

(Rogers 1967: 119)

When he or she becomes aware of the self, the individual becomes much less dependent on the views and opinions of others. What matters now is to do what seems right for them, rather than looking to others for approval. 'Unconditional positive regard' is thought to be of paramount importance in allowing the individual to explore him- or herself. By this is meant a relationship with another person in which the individual feels that it is they themselves who is valued and loved. This love would hold whatever terrible thing they were to do (or admit to in the course of exploring their self-concept) – it is not *conditional* on how they behave.

In addition to the self-image, we can all envisage several other types of 'self', e.g. 'self as I was when I left school' and 'self as I would like to be' and it can sometimes be useful to consider the ways in which these memories and ideals differ from the current view of the self.

Self-assessment question 2.6

What is the self-concept? How can it be discovered?

The suggestions just discussed have implications for therapy and Rogers (1959) listed several conditions that should be met if the therapist is to be able to help the client to explore their self-concept. These requirements are as follows:

- that the client and therapist are in *psychological contact* – that is, that they are 'on the same wavelength'

- that the client's behaviour is not at odds with his or her self-image (a situation known as 'a state of *incongruence*'), which results in feelings of anxiety

- that the *therapist is congruent* – that is, that the therapist's self-image accurately reflects the way in which he or she behaves

- that the therapist shows *unconditional positive regard* for the client

- that the therapist experiences an empathic understanding of the client's *internal frame of refer-ence* – that is, that he or she can sense the person's feelings

- that the client *perceives* the therapist's unconditional positive regard and empathic under-standing – the therapist successfully communicates his or her unconditional regard and empa-thy to the client.

Thus, in Rogerian therapy, the therapist will at times disclose his or her own feelings towards the client, even though these may sometimes be rather negative. However, care will be taken to ensure that the client realizes that this is just the therapist's *impression* of the client and does not indicate that there is anything *wrong* with the client.

Rogers believes that people behave in a manner that is consistent with their self-image. For example, someone who views him- or herself as shy and retiring will try to behave in a manner consistent with this view. It is almost as if the individual uses the 'self-concept' as a kind of Delphic oracle – a source to be consulted in times of uncertainty that will tell the individual how they should behave. We try to ensure that our behaviour is congruent with our self-image. Whenever an incongruence does arise (for example, when someone who views himself as mild mannered loses his temper), feelings of tension and anxiety are experienced that are most unpleasant. In fact, these feelings are so unpleasant that the person may try to distort reality (e.g. by telling himself that he was an innocent victim of someone else's aggression), thereby denying any incongruence between his self-image and his behaviour. The problem is that such distortions make it difficult for the person to perceive his true self: it is much better, in the long run, for an individual to recognize and accept the behaviour than to use 'defences' such as this.

Rogers suggests that each individual 'has one basic tendency and striving – to actualize, maintain and enhance the experiencing organism' (Rogers 1951). Self-actualization is a term that basically describes how we each fulfil our human potential – we learn to know, accept and like our true selves, we can form deep relationships with others, we can be sensitive to others' needs and view others as individuals (rather than in terms of stereotypes) and we can learn to break free from the demands of conformity. The term (coined by Abraham Maslow) is highly abstract and it is not at all obvious how it can be assessed. However, the idea that we become wiser, more sensitive, more in touch with our true selves and less concerned with convention as we get older does have some intuitive appeal. What is less obvious is that this is a 'basic tendency and striving' – it could, arguably, be a mere by-product of having had more experience of other people as one ages.

The clinical method and Q-sort

Measuring attitudes to the self by clinical interview can be a long, difficult process. However, there are other techniques for measuring attitudes towards the self, ideal self, etc. The Q-sort is a measure designed by Stephenson (1953) to do just this. The client is given a pile of approximately 100 cards, on each of which is a self-descriptive statement such as 'I usually like people', 'I don't trust my emotions', 'I am afraid of what other people may think of me' and so on. The client is asked to sort these into several piles (about five) ranging from statements that are most characteristic of them to those that are least characteristic. The number of cards to be placed in each pile is usually specified.

The placement of each card is recorded and the exercise is repeated under other conditions, e.g. after several sessions of therapy or after asking the client to sort the cards according to his or her 'ideal self' rather than actual self. It is a simple matter to track changes in the way in which the cards are sorted and thus to build up a picture of how the self-concept is evolving or the precise ways in which the self is seen to be rather different from the ideal self and these can be usefully explored during the therapeutic interview.

A clinician could make up their own cards and this might be useful for exploring particular issues that may have been raised or hinted at, but not fully explored. There also seems to be no reason why the items in any standard personality questionnaire could not be transferred on to cards and administered in this way, but the tendency is to use a standard set of items (the Cali- **19** fornia Q-set) to cover most of the standard feelings about the self. Block (1961) gives full details on the use of the Q-sort technique in various settings. This measure provides a quick method of allowing individuals to express their feelings about themselves in a quantifiable manner.

Several questionnaires have also been developed to measure self-concept. They are quite widely used in clinical and social psychology and Kline (1999) discusses them in some detail. They are certainly popular, with just one test, the 'Self-Esteem Scale' (Rosenberg 1965) being cited well over 1000 times in the literature. The items in this ten-item scale are very similar to each other and basically they just ask 'do you like yourself?' in ten different ways. The test also shows *very* high correlations with other tests measuring anxiety and depression (–0.64 and –0.54, respectively) and, as Kline points out, the evidence that either this scale or alternative measures that he discusses actually measure self-esteem itself is rather flimsy. We return to this in Chapter 6.

Self-assessment question 2.7

How might you test whether the Q-sort gives an accurate assessment of self-concept?

Evaluation

It is difficult to evaluate Rogers' theory, since it is more of a philosophical view of the person than a formal, concrete psychological theory. It evolved from Rogers' own experiences as both therapist and man, rather than from any formal empirical data that can be independently scrutinized. In addition, it may not be a scientific theory in that it would be difficult to show that the self-concept does *not* exist. We all think about work colleagues, family members, mass murderers and cabinet ministers from time to time and make some attempts to understand why they act in the various bizarre ways in which they do: it would be amazing if we never thought about ourselves at all. Likewise, perhaps I have an 'integrated self-concept' (see myself as a single individual) since this is what I *am*. Thus it could be argued that we are all *bound* to have an integrated self-concept, much as Rogers described.

A great deal of what Rogers says about the development of self-concept and the search for the true self certainly feels true to many people. However, as discussed in Chapter 14, this does not necessarily mean that it is correct. Many people presumably feel convinced that they have a good chance of winning a fortune whenever they buy a lottery ticket or back a horse. More empirical evidence is needed to back up these claims.

The next problem is the source of data. In Rogers' theory (along with that of Kelly) there is a total reliance on self-report: the clients' self-insights are assumed to be correct. What if the client is unwilling or unable to introspect in detail, perhaps because of poor verbal skills or problems dealing with abstract concepts?

That said, the theory has some strengths. Like Kelly's personal construct theory it attempts to explain how the whole person functions, rather than concentrating on just one or two aspects of personality. It has also made some very specific suggestions about the necessary conditions for therapeutic change and empirical studies have shown that the client's experience of warmth, unconditional positive regard and empathy are indeed crucial factors in determining the success of some forms of psychotherapy (Truax and Mitchell 1971). However, the problem is that many of the concepts are rather vaguely defined – the accurate assessment of 'empathy' and 'genuineness' is a nontrivial problem and patients cannot agree as to what the terms mean (Bachelor

1988). Nonetheless, some aspects of the theory can be tested, e.g. the assumption that psychological health is marked by congruence between self and experience.

Rogers and Kelly's theories are similar in many respects. They are both phenomenological, based on clinical experience and weak on developmental theory. However, they differ drastically in terms of therapy. While Rogers focuses on helping the client grow, mature, discover and accept their true self, Kelly's method fixed role therapy encourages people to try out new selves (e.g. becoming spontaneous rather than cautious) to see whether this improves their ability to predict behaviour.

Suggested additional reading

Two excellent summaries of Kelly's work have recently been published. Walker and Winter (2007) provide a comprehensive overview of Kelly's work, although many readers will want to consult some of the original sources that they cite to obtain a more in-depth understanding of the issues that they discuss. Benjafield (2008) gives an more historical and philosophical view of Kelly's theories and places them in context. Personal construct theory is developed in the two volumes of Kelly (1955), the first three chapters of which are reprinted as Kelly (1963a). Kelly's work was particularly influential in the UK, probably because of the efforts of the late Don Bannister through books such as Bannister and Fransella (1989) and Bannister and Mair (1968), which reproduce and discuss some of Kelly's unpublished writings. More recent sources include Fransella and Thomas (1988) and the work of Neimeyer and Neimeyer (1990, 1992) with much of the literature being published in the *Journal of Constructivist Psychology* and the *International Journal of Personal Construct Psychology*. There are also several good personal construct sites on the internet.

Rogers (1967) provides a humble and very *personal* account of his theory and clinical methods that makes compelling reading. Other useful sources include Rogers, Kirschenbaum and Henderson (1989) and the chapter by Raskin and Rogers (1989). Papers by Bozarth and Brodley (1991) and two reprints of early papers by Rogers (1992a, 1992b) may appeal to those who are interested in the therapeutic implications of these theories. The obvious source of information on Q-sort methodology is Block's (1961) book and also his account of a large longitudinal study in which Q-sort methodology was used to tame an unruly mass of qualitative data (Block 1971).

Answers to self-assessment questions

SAQ 2.1

This involves trying to discover and understand each person's unique view and interpretation of the world in which they live. For example, when examining family dynamics, a phenomenologist would be interested in the *implications* of a child's belief that her mother was cruel and unkind and not particularly interested in whether the mother really *was* unkind.

SAQ 2.2

I suggest three main reasons. First, different observers may be trying to predict different outcomes and so may pay attention to rather different aspects of people's behaviour. Second, the vagueness of language makes it possible that two observers might use two different phrases when they are actually referring to precisely the same characteristic in another person. Third, all kinds of social values are likely to colour the way in which we interpret behaviour.

SAQ 2.3

1. A construct is a psychological dimension that an individual finds useful when classifying a certain set of elements (usually people).

2. A role title is the name of a type of person with whom the individual is likely to be well acquainted (e.g. a brother). A wide range of role titles is used to ensure that the individual considers a wide range of people when completing the grid.

3. An element is a particular individual who fills one of the role titles (e.g. John, who is 'a brother').

4. A triad is a group of three elements used to elicit constructs by asking the individual to name one psychological way in which any one of the elements in the triad is very different to the other two.

SAQ 2.4

Either provide or elicit a list of elements, e.g. paintings, smells, faces or pieces of music. Present three of these and ask the individual to describe how one differs from the other two – then continue and analyse as before. The ratings given to the constructs can perhaps be correlated with features of the stimuli (e.g. the year in which they were painted or written) in order to help to identify the constructs.

SAQ 2.5

Propositional constructs are useful because they do not force people to use any of their other constructs in certain stereotyped ways that may not be appropriate for a particular individual. If pre-emptive or constellatory constructs are used (e.g. saying 'Alan is nothing but a student'), this forces the rest of the construct system to attribute certain characteristics to Alan, rather than allowing him to be evaluated *as an individual* on each of the constructs following observations of his behaviour. Thus the construct system is unlikely to be able to predict the individual's behaviour very accurately, with unpleasant emotional consequences, as will be discussed later.

SAQ 2.6

The self-concept is our view of our personality, abilities, background, etc., *as it really is*, and not as it is modified by the demands of society or our own aspirations. It is a coherent mental image of the type of person that we really are, deep down. It can best be explored in the context of a supportive relationship with another person.

SAQ 2.7

There is no simple way of testing this. After all, the individual is the only person who can really comment on some of his or her deepest, most personal feelings. However, it might be possible to attempt some experiments. One approach could involve giving the Q-sort twice, after a gap of, say, a week or two, and checking that the person produces roughly the same arrangement of cards. If there *is* a marked discrepancy (and the client cannot think of any reason why their self-image may have altered), then it may be unwise to proceed with the technique. Alternatively, the cards (and particularly those towards the extremes of the distribution, which best and least describe the individual) could be put into a questionnaire and other people (e.g. partner, parents, close friends) could be asked to rate the client on each quality, thereby showing whether the client's self-image was consistent with other people's impressions. Or the therapist could be asked to describe the person's self-concept and this could be compared with the results of the Q-sort.

References

Bachelor, A. (1988). How clients perceive therapist empathy: a content analysis of 'received' empathy. *Psychotherapy 25*, 227–40.

Bannister, D. and Fransella, F. (1989). *Inquiring Man: The Psychology of Personal Constructs*. London: Croom Helm.

Bannister, D. and Mair, J. M. M. (1968). *The Evaluation of Personal Constructs*. London: Academic Press.

Benjafield, J. G. (2008). George Kelly: cognitive psychologist, humanistic psychologist, or something else entirely? *History of Psychology 11*(4), 239–62.

Block, J. (1961). *The Q-sort Method in Personality Assessment and Psychiatric Research*. Springfield, IL: Thomas.

Block, J. (1971). *Lives through Time*. Berkeley, CA: Bancroft Books.

Bozarth, J. D. and Brodley, B. T. (1991). Actualization: a functional concept in client-centered therapy. *Journal of Social Behavior and Personality 6*(5), 45–59.

Chao, C.-J., Salvendy, G. and Lightner, N. J. (1999). Development of a methodology for optimizing elicited knowledge. *Behaviour & Information Technology 18*(6), 413–30.

Fransella, F. and Thomas, L. F. (eds) (1988). *Experimenting with Personal Construct Psychology*. London: Routledge.

Kelly, G. A. (1955). *The Psychology of Personal Constructs* (Vols I and II). New York: Norton.

Kelly, G. A. (1963a). *The Autobiography of a Theory*. Columbus: Ohio State University Press.

Kelly, G. A. (1963b). *A Theory of Personality*. New York: Norton.

Kline, P. (1999). *The Handbook of Psychological Testing* (2nd edn). London & New York: Routledge.

Neimeyer, G. J. & Neimeyer, R. A. (eds) (1990). *Advances in Personal Construct Psychology: A Research Annual* (Vol. 1). Greenwich, CT: JAI Press.

Neimeyer, R. A. & Neimeyer, G. J. (eds) (1992). *Advances in Personal Construct Psychology* (Vol. 2). Greenwich, CT: JAI Press.

Raskin, N. J. & Rogers, C. R. (1989). Person-centred therapy. In R. J. Corsini and D. Wedding (eds), *Current Psychotherapies* (4th edn). Ithaca, NY: F. E. Peacock.

Rogers, C. R. (1951). *Client-centered Therapy*. Boston, MA: Houghton-Mifflin.

Rogers, C. R. (1959). A theory of therapy, personality and interpersonal relationships, as developed in the client-centered framework. In S. Koch (ed.), *Psychology: A Study of a Science* (Vol. 3). New York: McGraw-Hill.

Rogers, C. R. (1967). *On Becoming a Person*. London: Constable.

Rogers, C. R. (1992a). The necessary and sufficient conditions of therapeutic personality change. *Journal of Consulting and Clinical Psychology 60*(6), 827–32.

Rogers, C. R. (1992b). The processes of therapy. *Journal of Consulting and Clinical Psychology 60*(2), 163–4.

Rogers, C. R., Kirschenbaum, H. and Henderson, V.-L. (eds) (1989). *The Carl Rogers Reader*. Boston, MA: Houghton-Mifflin.

Rosenberg, M. (1965). *Society and the Adolescent Self-image*. Princeton, MA: Princeton University Press.

Rykman, R. M. (1992). *Theories of Personality* (5th edn). Belmont, CA: Wadsworth.

Stephenson, W. (1953). *The Study of Behavior*. Chicago: University of Chicago Press.

Truax, C. B. and Mitchell, K. M. (1971). Research on certain therapist interpersonal skills in relation to process and outcome. In A. E. Bergin and S. L. Garfield (eds), *Handbook of Psychotherapy and Behaviour Change*. New York: Wiley.

Walker, B. M. and Winter, D. A. (2007). The elaboration of personal construct psychology. *Annual Review of Psychology 58*, 453–77.

3 Depth psychology

Background

Oddly, perhaps, the earliest personality theories are among the most complex. Sigmund Freud and his followers developed theories of personality from their experience of treating patients suffering from psychological disorders and suggested that the same principles should also apply to 'normal' people. These theories are sometimes called depth *psychologies* because they propose that our behaviour can be traced back to deep-seated memories and wishes of which we are normally unaware. These theories have been included in this book for several reasons. They were some of the first that claimed to be based on empirical data. They are still influential in some disciplines (although not, these days, in mainstream psychology). Their suggestion that events of which we are unaware can influence our behaviour now receives some support from cognitive psychology. Furthermore, these are very *broad* theories: they attempt to explain a whole range of interesting human behaviours.

Recommended prior reading

None.

Freud's theories

Introduction

Sigmund Freud (1856–1939) is one of the giant figures in personality psychology. His theories set out to explain every interesting aspect of human behaviour – from child development to religion, from sexual behaviour to wit and humour – and it provided a method for treating many psychiatric disorders. It is still one of the very few theories that proposes that people may be motivated and influenced by factors of which they are completely unaware. There is no substitute for reading translations of Freud's original works, especially as several of them were written to educate non-expert readers, such as his medical colleagues.

Freud began studying medicine in Vienna in 1873. After qualifying, he concentrated on physiological and neurological research, including some pioneering work on the effects of cocaine and the testes of the eel.

In the nineteenth century, psychiatric disorders that had no obvious physiological basis were dismissed out of hand as being impossible. Some patients who showed symptoms as varied as memory failure, paralysis, nervous tics (twitching), tunnel vision, blindness, loss of speech and convulsions were diagnosed as suffering from various forms of *hysteria*; that is, symptoms without a good physiological cause. Freud's interest in psychiatry began in the 1880s when he travelled to Paris to study with Charcot, the celebrated neurologist. Charcot was researching how hypnotic suggestion could be used to implant a suggestion in the mind of a normal volunteer who would then perform some activity (or experience some feeling, such as a numb leg) even after being released from the hypnotic trance.

Freud saw some similarity between the behaviour of Charcot's hypnotized subjects and that of patients who suffered from hysteria. In both cases, the behaviour or symptom had no physical cause – the numbing of the leg resulting from a hypnotic suggestion had a purely psychological origin. In addition, subjects who were hypnotized were unaware of the *source* of their behaviour or motivations to perform certain actions, in much the same way that hysterical patients claimed to be completely ignorant of the origins of their symptoms. Thus Freud speculated that some kind of precipitating mental event may explain the symptoms of hysterics. As both the hypnotized subject and the hysterical patient seem to have no memory for such an event, it must be located in an area of the mind that is not normally accessible to consciousness, but from where it can nevertheless influence behaviour and bodily and mental symptoms.

Perhaps hysterical symptoms might be cured through appropriate psychological manipulations in much the same way as a hypnotic suggestion can be cancelled through the instructions of the hypnotist? On returning to Vienna, Freud set himself up as a specialist in the treatment of 'nervous diseases' and collaborated with Josef Breuer. They jointly published *Studies in Hysteria* (1893/1964), which is the basis of Freud's theory of psychoanalysis. They reported some remarkable cures of hysterical symptoms through the use of hypnosis. Patients were hypnotized and were then encouraged to believe that their symptoms would disappear and to speculate about the causes of the symptoms (as in Freud's analysis of Emmy von N). Freud considered that the careful probing of the patients' reminiscences (rather than hypnotic suggestion) was the ultimate cause of these cures. He claimed that:

Each individual symptom immediately and permanently disappeared when we had succeeded in bringing clearly to light the memory of the event by which it was produced, and in arousing its accompanying affect [a word that Freud uses synonymously with 'emotion'], and when the patient had described that event in the greatest possible detail and had put the affect into words.

(Freud and Breuer 1893/1964: 57)

This is the first description of the technique known as *free association*. It involved the patient's reclining on a couch, while the psychoanalyst asked her to say the very first thing that came to mind in response to occasional words spoken by the psychoanalyst. The patient was particularly urged not to omit any detail, no matter how trivial, unimportant, embarrassing or irrelevant it appeared to be. The psychoanalyst paid careful consideration to these reminiscences and noted in particular those occasions when the patient found it difficult to produce an association in response to a word or phrase. This might indicate that some psychological mechanism, known as a *repression*, was interfering with the patient's ability to respond. As the patient had been urged to say whatever came to mind, a failure to produce an association was not due to self-censorship. Instead, it suggested that there was some unpleasant, emotionally charged memory that had been pushed into an unconscious part of the mind and that might be the cause of the hysterical symptom.

Freud's patients were eventually able to recall events (often from childhood) that had been completely forgotten for many years and that had been associated with some strong and unpleasant emotional experience. When they both recalled the painful event and re-experienced the emotion that was felt at the time, the physical symptom simply disappeared. Freud claimed to have cured symptoms such as an inability to drink, paralysis, blindness, nervous tics and loss of memory using this technique, which he termed *psychoanalysis*. Here is a description of one of Breuer's early attempts to probe the unconscious mind using hypnosis in an attempt to cure a young woman who used to enter trance-like states, similar to some forms of epilepsy:

It was observed that, when the patient was in her states of '*absence*' [altered personality accompanied by confusion], she was in the habit of muttering a few words to herself which seemed as if they arose from some train of thought that was occupying her mind. The doctor, after getting report of these words, used to put her into a kind of hypnosis and repeat them to her so as to induce her to use them as a starting point. The patient ... in this way reproduced in his presence the mental creations which had been occupying her mind during the '*absences*' and which had betrayed their existence by the fragmentary words which she had uttered. They were profoundly melancholy phantasies – 'daydreams' we should call them – sometimes characterised by poetic beauty, and the starting point was as a rule the position of a girl at her father's sick-bed. When she had related a number of these phantasies, she was as if set free, and she was brought back to normal mental life … It was impossible to escape the conclusion that the alteration in her mental state which was expressed in the '*absences*' was a result of the stimulus proceeding from these highly emotional phantasies.

(Freud 1959: section IV)

Self-assessment question 3.1

Try to explain the following terms:

a. free association

b. resistance

c. repression.

Analyses of dreams, 'slips of the tongue', wit and similar everyday experiences led him to conclude that the mental structures that he deduced from the analysis of hysterical patients were universal. Thus his theory sought to become a general theory of personality, rather than an explanation for hysterical behaviour alone.

Freud's theories of the mind

As memories and fantasies can be dragged reluctantly back into consciousness:

- It seems that there are two main areas of the mind – one that is susceptible to conscious scrutiny through introspection and another whose contents are normally unconscious.

- It is also important to discover how the contents of the unconscious region of mind influence behaviour, as in the case of hysterical symptoms.

- Finally, it is necessary to understand how memories pass from the conscious to the unconscious regions of the mind and why memories that have been transferred into the unconscious region usually stay there, except in the case of psychoanalytical treatment.

Freud suggested that the mind could be divided into two basic sections. One of these, the *ego*, is conscious and capable of logical, rational thought. He identified another, unconscious area of mind, which he called the *id*. This contains the basic instincts (sex and aggression), satisfaction of which leads to feelings of pleasure and which therefore motivate behaviour – the 'pleasure principle'. Memories and thoughts that have become associated with these instincts have also been pushed into the id. The instincts, memories and fantasies in the Freudian id affect day-to-day behaviour and experience, without the individual's being aware that they even exist.

The analysis of hysterical patients led Freud to a conclusion that shocked Vienna. The unconscious memories and fantasies of his proper, well-to-do female patients were almost invariably sexual. Psychoanalysis revealed that the emotional content of a thought or memory (or the emotion that became attached to it through association, a process now known as *classical conditioning*) determined its destiny. Painful memories or unacceptable thoughts were banished to the unconscious mind (the id), where they joined the seething lusts and aggressive drives that are found there and somehow strived to force themselves back into consciousness. The id therefore contains two basic instincts, namely *eros*, also known as the *life instinct*, which is satisfied through sexual activity, and a self-destructive force known as *thanatos* or the *death instinct*, which can also be turned outwards against the world, resulting in aggressive or sadistic behaviour. Freud believed that we always seek to satisfy these deep-seated (but unconscious) instincts for sex and aggression – the *pleasure principle*. The id demands their immediate and complete satisfaction, no matter how inappropriate, impractical or unreasonable this may be and without consideration of social conventions or other people. Freud called this *primary process* thought, which is also characterized by its illogicality and tolerance of ambiguity. For example, the id would have no difficulty in simultaneously desiring and wishing to destroy a person. Melanie Klein claims to have identified terrifying destructive and aggressive fantasies in very young infants, which are thought to be typical of the way in which the id operates.

Freud believed that the ego splits off from the id as the child grows older, as a result of its experiences of the outside world through sight, touch, hearing and the other senses. A part of the mind becomes conscious, aware of the outside world, self-aware and capable of rational thought. The basic aim is still the satisfaction of the drives from the id, but these can be assuaged far more effectively through postponement and the use of social conventions. Satisfying the sexual instinct immediately and completely with the first person one encountered (as the id would demand) would probably not be a good idea. It would result in a prison sentence (segregated from members of the opposite gender!) and so would fail to provide a long-term solution. It would also run counter to the moral standards of one's conscience (the *superego*). It will be far more effective in the long term to act rationally under the control of the ego and develop a relationship.

There are also other ways in which the drives can be satisfied, such as by reading or other activities (e.g. art, humour, gastronomy), in which basic drives are being satisfied in socially acceptable ways. These are sometimes known as *derivatives* of the original drives, that is, ideas that are connected to the basic instincts of sex and aggression, but whose satisfaction is more acceptable to the ego. As Fenichel (1946) observes, most neurotic symptoms are derivatives of the two basic instincts (p. 143).

Childhood experiences are thought to be all important for adult development. According to Freud, childhood is a battleground between the two major instincts and the attempts of parents to ensure that they are satisfied in socially acceptable ways. Derivatives of the sexual and aggressive instincts are formed and the ego develops defence mechanisms.

Defence mechanisms

It is also necessary to understand why some painful memories are 'forgotten', why they result in a physical symptom and why the symptom disappears when the memory is relived. Freud noted with interest that the key forgotten memories tended to be dismissed as unimportant by the patient. Only as a result of careful listening and prompting by the analyst could they eventually be recalled. This suggested that there were some forces (of which the patient was unaware) that tried to keep the painful memory out of consciousness. They were called *defence mechanisms* and over a dozen of them have been proposed by Freud and his followers. The most well known is called *repression* and this term is used interchangeably with 'defence mechanism' in Freud's early writings. It implies a purposeful forgetting of an emotion-laden wish or memory. However, once it reaches unconsciousness, fuelled by libido it constantly tries to re-enter consciousness with the result that there is a perpetual battle taking place between the wish (which has been repressed into the id) and the defence mechanisms. When a repressed wish or memory tries to re-enter consciousness, anxiety levels supposedly rise and this triggers the defence mechanisms into operation. Disguised and unrecognizable substitutes for the original wish may, however, enter consciousness. These may emerge as dreams, daydreams, fantasies or as neurotic symptoms.

The more memories an individual banishes into the id, the stronger the defence mechanisms that are required to keep them there. Thus everyone is to some extent neurotic, because we have all dealt with painful memories by forcing them into unconscious regions of the mind, from where they continue to exert a malevolent influence on our feelings and behaviour. Freud, therefore, believed that the model of personality drawn up from the study of hysterical patients should also apply to 'normal' people. At night the defence mechanisms relax and the contents of the id can infiltrate the ego in a disguised form, often as symbols in dreams. Many of these are sexual in nature – for example, the penis may be represented by sticks, daggers, telescopes, watering cans, fishing rods, feet, etc.

Repression is the crudest, most primitive type of defence mechanism. It blocks all memory of the threatening memory or instinct and forces it back into the id. Others include *isolation*, in which an instinct or memory may be allowed into consciousness because the all-important emotion associated with the drive is stripped away: aggressive instincts may be neatly satisfied through becoming a surgeon.

Projection involves attributing one's own unacceptable fantasies, impulses, etc. on to other people. For example, an aggressive person may see others as being aggressive. *Displacement of object* involves the expression of a sexual or aggressive wish, but against a substitute person, animal or object. *Reaction formation* occurs when one's ego reacts as if a threat (from the id) is always present. Thus someone who has strong sexual urges may show extreme prudery, famously obvious in 'clean-up-television' campaigners. If one decides that it is one's duty to monitor the airwaves for signs of filth and depravity, then one is (reluctantly, of course) exposed to rather a lot of it – which conveniently satisfies the demands of the id, while keeping the ego in ignorance of one's *true* motives for campaigning.

There are more defence mechanisms than those discussed here, several of which were suggested by followers of Freud. Descriptions of some of the more popular ones may be found in Kline (1984) or in any of the texts mentioned at the end of this chapter.

Neurotic symptoms

Freud identified several different types of neurotic symptom in his patients. These include *anxiety hysteria*, in which excessive anxiety is attached to certain people or situations, *anxiety neurosis*, in which the feeling of anxiety is powerful but diffused and not linked to any particular individuals or settings, and *conversion hysteria*, in which unconscious fantasies are acted out as emotional outbursts. Freud believed that physical illnesses such as muscle pains, breathing irregularities and even short-sightedness could sometimes be traced back to psychological causes – the so-called *organ neuroses*. Depression, the choice of unusual sexual objects, compulsive actions, addictions and compulsions (such as shoplifting) are also perceived as having an underlying psychological cause.

Despite the highly varied nature of these symptoms, Freudians believe that they have several features in common. First, as Fenichel reminds us (1946: 18), the patient experiences some unusual symptom – a feeling of anxiety, a compulsion to steal, bodily pains or whatever – but is unable to determine its cause through introspection. Second, Freudians believe that all these symptoms have their roots in some conflict between the id and the ego, which has activated defence mechanisms. They therefore stem from the blocking of one of the powerful instincts by the ego. The exact form that the symptom takes depends on childhood experiences and the techniques the infant used to deal with threats from the id. Third, the symptom is always thought to have some special sexual or aggressive significance to the individual.

Consider a man who obtains sexual excitement from viewing and touching female footwear. A foot may symbolize a penis, so if the man is (unconsciously) afraid of being castrated; it may prove less threatening to obtain sexual excitement from a woman's shoes than from sexual relationships. Intercourse will raise fears of castration, as it reminds men that women do not possess a penis – foot fetishists endow women with a symbolic penis in an attempt to reduce castration anxiety (Fenichel 1946). Alternatively, castration fears may emerge as a phobia, as in the case of 'Little Hans', who became anxious that a horse would bite him. The 'horse' was, of course, the boy's father.

According to Freud, all symptoms thus result from some powerful emotion, wish or thought which is repressed or otherwise defended against. These are usually sexual and often involve the memory of childhood sexual abuse. Freud took the conventional view of his time that abuse was unlikely to have occurred and he proposed that the 'memory' of these events instead revealed a fantasy about something for which the child longed:

Almost all my women patients told me that they had been seduced by their father. I was driven to recognise in the end that these reports were untrue, and so came to understand that hysterical symptoms are derived from phantasies and not from real occurrences.

(Freud 1932: 154)

These 'screen memories' are really fantasies that are superimposed on to our early memories and so become indistinguishable from them. This is why Freud formed the view that some form of sexual instinct is present even in children and that the 'blocking' of this instinct could result in neurotic symptoms later in life.

Psychoanalysis seeks to undo the defence mechanisms that lock a particular thought or wish in the unconscious. It will release it into consciousness, which should also remove the symptom that emerged as a derivative of the original impulse. Thus the therapist must first find a link between the symptom and some unconscious mental process, e.g. through noting 'blockages' in the free association process or free associating to dream contents. Once the analyst has a clear picture of the source of the neurotic symptom, this underlying fear or wish is explained to the patient, together with examples of the defence mechanisms used and the nature of the derivative(s) of the original impulse. The patient will generally object that what the analyst said never took place: their objections are brushed aside by the analyst because they represent a feeble attempt to use defence mechanisms to avoid recognizing the truth. When the ego eventually faces up to these childhood memories and fears and appreciates the nature of the resistance that has been applied, there is no need to defend further, as the ego is fully aware of the 'threat'. Thus all of the derivatives of the threat should disappear, including the troublesome symptoms.

Freud's theory of infantile sexuality

Fenichel (1946) reminds us that Freud believed that the newborn infant is essentially id – demanding total and immediate satisfaction of all instinctual demands. Freud (1923/1955) postulated that, in the early years of life, the sexual instinct was satisfied through oral contact with objects – exploring, sucking and later biting the nipple and other objects. Abraham (1952) later divided the oral stage into two phases, one involving oral incorporation, or sucking, and the other involving oral sadism, or biting. Following the oral phase, the focus of sexual satisfaction shifts to the anus during potty training. Presenting the parents with 'gifts' (or, alternatively, withholding the faeces) at this stage is the child's first real opportunity to exercise control over the environment and faeces are thought to have strong symbolic links to money, babies and the penis. Phrases such as 'stinking rich', 'filthy lucre', 'rolling in it' and 'where there's muck there's money' do, after all, crave explanation.

The penis and clitoris become the focus of the libido during what is known as the 'phallic' phase, but at the age of about 5 years young boys suffer the 'Oedipus complex' and the 'castration complex' – arguably the most important and traumatic event in one's life. The Oedipus complex is named after the hero of Sophocles' play who unknowingly kills his father and then commits incest with his mother. It occurs when the young boy lusts after his mother and so views his father as a sexual rival. He realizes through observation that girls do not possess a penis and will come to a terrible realization – that a girl's penis has been cut off by a jealous father. Anxious to avoid this catastrophe, the young boy will repress all lustful feelings for his mother, and will 'identify' with his father. Identification is a form of defence mechanism into which threatening objects are incorporated – in this instance, the father's moral values are adopted to form the 'superego' or **31** moral conscience. As girls do not possess a penis they blame their mother for this inadequacy and identify with their father in order to have a penis at their disposal (the 'Electra complex'). Following these traumas, both sexes enter what is known as the 'latency period' in which there is no focus of sexual activity, then puberty (the 'genital phase').

The degree of satisfaction or frustration that the infant encounters at each psychosexual stage is thought to determine his or her adult personality type. Kline (1981) compiled some lists of the adult characteristics that Freud and his followers have linked to overindulgence or frustration at various stages of psychosexual development. Those fixated at the oral incorporation phase are optimistic, dependent and curious and would love soft and milky foods. Oral sadists would be bitter, hostile, argumentative and jealous. Those fixated at the anal phase would become obstinate, excessively tidy and stingy. Accountants, perhaps.

Testing Freud's theories

There are several reasons why it is difficult to tell whether any parts of Freud's theories are actually correct:

- Many of the concepts used (e.g. 'Oedipus conflict', 'penis envy') cannot easily be operationalized or quantified.

- The theory can suggest several different 'explanations' for the same event. For example, cynicism may be (a) be an acceptable way of expressing aggressive feelings about an object or (b) it could stem from a strong sexual desire that is converted into its opposite through the defence mechanism of reaction formation. A cynical view could indicate unconscious feelings of either love or hatred.

- Psychoanalysis is not an effective form of therapy (Eysenck 1957) and some of the patients whom Freud claimed to have cured remained highly disturbed (Sulloway 1979).

- Freud's theories were based on a very small, rather strange sample of people, taken over 100 years ago and so may not nowadays have general applicability.

- Finding that obsessional neurosis is linked to the defence mechanism of isolation (for example) in just one or two patients does not imply that this is invariably the case.

- What took place during Freud's clinic was not recorded and so cannot be verified by independent observers.

- The theories are *post hoc* – that is, possible explanations of past events that cannot easily be used to predict future behaviour.

What sources of data are useful in evaluating Freud's theories? We discount patients' and therapists' accounts of the effectiveness of treatment, as neither of these will be objective; having invested thousands of pounds (or a lifetime's work) in psychoanalysis, it would be difficult to admit to oneself that it is completely useless (Festinger 1957). Scientific studies of the effectiveness of psychoanalysis offer another possibility, although proper control groups are needed, since if patients do get better this may be because of 'spontaneous remission'. However, evaluating *psychoanalysis* is not sufficient to test the veracity of Freud's theories. Farrell (1981) has observed that Freudian theory is not a single theory, but a collection of loosely linked subtheories. Thus even if psychoanalysis is shown to be of little value, other aspects (e.g. psychosexual personality types, structure of mind, defence mechanisms) may possibly be correct.

Having said that, certain aspects of Freud's theories are clearly of central importance, since they are used as explanations in virtually all the subtheories. If it could be shown that behaviour is completely unaffected by unconscious factors (i.e. that the id is an unnecessary concept), that there is no evidence that defence mechanisms filter memories or perceptions on the basis of their emotional content or that the Oedipus complex does not exist, then many aspects of Freudian theory would collapse. Hence it makes sense to concentrate on such issues.

Several books summarize the hundreds of studies that have been performed to scientifically test some aspects of Freud's theories, for example, Fisher and Greenberg (1996). Kline (1981) is one of the better ones because it is evaluative. Clearly, if an experiment has been poorly designed (perhaps not having control groups, valid tests, a large sample of participants) and/or is based on a misunderstanding of Freudian theory (for example by asking children which parent they prefer in an attempt to discover *unconscious* Oedipal wishes), then its failure to show anything interesting says nothing about the merits of Freudian theory. Even though Kline's book reports several experiments that do appear to give some support to some aspects of the theory, very few of them appear to have been successfully replicated by independent research groups. For example, Hammer's (1953) work on symbolism showed that when men who were about to be surgically sterilized were asked to draw a house, a tree and a person, their trees were more often shown as being cut down and their houses lacked chimney pots when compared with control groups. But no one appears to have replicated this work. Likewise a finding that people sweated more (showing anxiety) when exposed to symbols of death rather than to other shapes (Meissner 1958) does not appear to have been replicated. So one cannot have great confidence that these are solid, reliable effects. Most of the literature described later is elderly, because these days very few psychologists see any point in attempting to test Freud's theories.

Self-assessment question 3.3

What three qualities are required in any experiment designed to put part of Freud's theory to the test?

Perceptual defence

The defence mechanism of repression seems to be very close to the phenomenon of perceptual defence as studied by Bruner and Postman (1947). They claimed that individuals find it harder to recognize emotionally threatening words than neutral or positively toned words. A typical experiment might involve the establishment of 'recognition thresholds' for various words, which are basically the minimum duration for which a word has to be exposed for it to be correctly recognized. The words would be displayed for a very brief period using a piece of equipment called a tachistoscope. The person being tested would guess what the word was. If they guessed incorrectly, the word would be shown again for a slightly longer duration, this process being repeated until it was correctly identified.

It was found that words with negative associations (e.g. 'whore', 'rape', 'death') had to be shown for longer periods of time than other words in order to be correctly recognized; they had longer recognition thresholds. This suggested that some type of psychological mechanism monitored the emotional content of the words as they were being perceived and could in some way affect the visibility of the words in an attempt to keep threatening words from being consciously perceived. These studies were extremely controversial and raised a stream of protests and alternative explanations, ranging from philosophical objections to the idea of a homunculus – a 'little man inside the head' who monitors what enters consciousness – to sound methodological criticisms of the early experiments. The old perceptual defence experiments were flawed because they failed to control for word length and word frequency, both of which can affect the ease with which words are recognized. Short, common words are recognized much more rapidly than long or unusual words. One would have to be very certain that the word 'penis' really was present before calling it out, whereas one would guess neutral words quite freely, which would result in the 'taboo word' appearing to have a higher recognition threshold than the neutral word ('response suppression'). There are other problems with perceptual defence experiments, some of which are discussed by Brown (1961) and Dixon (1981).

Since the paradigms were developed by experimental psychologists, the emphasis has been on proving that the perceptual defence effect exists, rather than on examining its correlates. Thus while many studies claim to show (or not to show!) that the emotional meaning of a stimulus is related to its detectability, hardly any of them examine individual differences. It would be simple to calculate scores indicating how pronounced the perceptual defence effect is for each individual, e.g. by subtracting the individual's mean threshold for neutral words from their threshold for threatening words. One could then test whether individuals who show a massive difference are anxious, rated by their therapists as 'repressors', and in other ways examine the correlates of perceptual defence. (Such studies are extremely rare, but see Watt and Morris 1995.) These days cognitive scientists are happy to accept that the emotional words of which a person is apparently unaware can influence both their physiological reactions and their cognitions (Gibbons 2009). Perception without consciousness is alive and well: the idea that our lives may be influenced by wishes of which we are unaware is less controversial than it has ever been. However, even if one accepts that the words in such experiments are presented so dimly or so quickly that they truly cannot be recognized, such experiments provide scant support for Freud's theories: the key thing about the *Freudian* unconscious is that its contents motivate just about all our behaviours and are at the heart of neurotic conflicts.

Psychosexual development

If Freud's theory of psychosexual development is correct, one would expect to find that:

- the adult personality characteristics that Freud described (e.g. the 'anal character', with its blend of orderly, obstinate and stingy characteristics) would be found in adults

- adults who show these characteristics to an extreme extent would have been either over- or under-indulged at the appropriate psychosexual stage.

The oral and anal character types were studied by Kline (1967, 1968, 1969; Kline and Storey 1977) who developed questionnaires to measure the adult personality characteristics of the oral and anal characters. The anal character was found – the characteristics of orderliness, obstinacy and stinginess do seem to tend to occur together in adults, suggesting that they have a common cause, just as Freud suggested. Not one but two oral characters were found – the oral optimist (talkative with a cheerful outlook and a liking for sweet, milky things) and the oral pessimist (jealous, sarcastic and pessimistic, with a liking for crunchy and spicy foods). Thus the three main adult personality types do seem to exist, much as Freud suggested, and Kline has developed three questionnaires, namely the Oral Optimism Questionnaire (OOQ), the Oral Pessimism Questionnaire (OPQ) and the Anal Interests Questionnaire (Ai3Q) to measure them.

This does not mean that the adult personality characteristics arose for the reasons that Freud outlined. Some workers have attempted to perform longitudinal or retrospective studies in order to determine whether people who are over- or under-indulged at the oral or anal stages of infancy go on to develop extreme levels of the corresponding adult personality characteristics, but without much success. However, the methodology was often weak (using unreliable scales to assess the adult personality trait, or using such tiny samples that the studies lacked statistical power) and in any case it has been found to be very difficult to obtain accurate retrospective data about how, precisely, children were weaned and potty trained – parents simply cannot remember the detail. So, as Kline (1981) observes in his detailed discussion of these studies, while they do not confirm Freud's theories, this is as likely to be because of their methodological difficulties as it is to be due to the fact that the theory is incorrect.

Summary

Freud's theory represents an attempt to build a huge, all-encompassing theory of personality from meagre data – unstandardized clinical observations. Very few people now accept that classical psychoanalysis is effective in curing neurotic symptoms, so one major aspect of Freud's theory appears to be flawed. Some aspects of Freudian theory can, perhaps, be tested empirically – although are rarely successfully replicated. As Erdelyi (1974, 1985) has pointed out, many of Freud's notions can mesh quite well with modern information processing and cognitive theories – indeed, there has been a distinct resurgence of interest in a cognitive unconscious (Kurthen, Grunwald and Elger 1999). Priming experiments suggest that the meaning of a word *can* be extracted and understood before the word itself can be consciously recognized, which used to be one of the main arguments against perceptual defence experiments. However, at present there is no conclusive evidence that any part of Freud's theory is correct, although the experimental literature offers some support for a repression-like process.

Psychoanalysis has not stood still since the time of Freud and developments such as object relations theory (Fairbairn 1952) and Lacanian psychoanalysis (Lacan and Wilden 1968) have proved popular with some, even though their basic tenets seem even more abstract and less open to scientific scrutiny than does the work of Freud. For example, Lacan's approach is deeply philosophical and rooted in the meaning of language: discourses on 'the real' (in a lecture Lacan gave in 1953) for example seem to produce few hard propositions that are amenable to scientific scrutiny. Fairbairn stresses the importance of relationships (either with other people or one's own thoughts and fantasies) in development. His view was that we are motivated not by the drives from the id, but by relationships, and suggests that the unconscious mind develops from the ego (rather than vice versa) when repression of intolerable guilty thoughts effectively splits the ego into several parts. I know of no attempts to test such theories empirically and suspect that their proponents would be generally unsympathetic to the idea of doing so.

Carl Jung

Carl Jung, a Swiss psychiatrist, corresponded and worked with Freud between 1905 and 1913. He developed an alternative approach to psychoanalysis, one which emphasized the role of mysticism, fantasy, symbolism and spirituality in human behaviour and which played down the role of sexual instincts as a motivating force. Jung believed that there were two, quite different, aspects of the unconscious mind. The 'personal unconscious' held memories that had been repressed or forgotten – but without the life and death instincts that so dominate the Freudian id. The personal unconscious played a minor role in Jung's theories. Pride of place was given to the *collective unconscious* – a storehouse of wisdom and experience that is (somehow) passed down from generation to generation and which contains the wisdom and experiences of humankind. Although Jung maintained that we are not aware of this region of our mind, he maintained that it predisposes us all to be sensitive to certain images and themes in life. For example, whereas Freud's view of symbols was limited to a rather crude set of analogies between sexual organs and various objects (guns and penises, for example), Jung was fascinated by shapes called *mandalas* (see Figure 3.1). These are abstract shapes, representing wholeness or completeness: they are circular, fairly symmetrical and have significance in both Buddhist and Hindu religions where they signify wholeness or the universe: 'It is the path to the centre, to individuation ... I knew

Figure 3.1 An example of a mandala. Photo credit: © Philippe Lissac/Godong/Corbis

that in finding the mandala as an expression of the self I had attained what was for me the ultimate' (Jung 1963).

As well as the mandala, Jung proposed that various types of character are represented in this collective unconscious. They are known as *archetypes*. Thus he suggests that we are predisposed to recognize characters such as the hero, wise old man, caring mother, the shadow (the darker, evil side of the self), the anima (the feminine side of a man) or the animus (the masculine side of a woman), the persona (the mask we present to the world, hiding our true self behind it). This might explain why similar characters play a part in myths and legends from around the world – although, of course, a simpler explanation is that mothers feature large in myths and legends because we are drawing on the personal experiences of having had a mother and not because of any inherited predisposition at all. It is very difficult to see how one could possibly tell whether this part of Jung's theory is correct. Neither is there any obvious physiological mechanism that would allow memories to be passed on directly from generation to generation, thereby perpetuating the archetypes.

Jung paid much attention to apparent coincidences and believed that that visions and dreams could be genuinely informative, rather than just representing some horrible sexual urge from the id. For example, in 1913 and 1914 Jung experienced the following vision on two occasions:

I saw a monstrous flood covering all the northern and low-lying lands between the North Sea and the Alps. When it came up to Switzerland I saw that the mountains grew higher and higher to protect our country. I realized that a frightful catastrophe was in progress. I saw the mighty yellow waves, the floating rubble of civilization, and the drowned bodies of uncounted thousands. Then the whole sea turned to blood.

(Jung 1963: 175)

The First World War began shortly afterwards. This is an example of *synchronicity* – the idea that two events, one of which is external and the other internal (the war and the vision) occur at the same time without there being any clear causal link between them. Rather than treating the vision as a psychotic episode, Jung suggests that visions and dreams carry important messages from the unconscious and should be interpreted using symbolism.

According to Jung, some people were thought to focus more on events external to themselves; other people, events in the world and so on. He coined the term 'extraverts' for these individuals and contrasted them with 'intraverts', who are much closer to their own inner self and who are far more interested in inner, spiritual and psychological experiences than the outer world. Neuroses, according to Jung, came about because a flawed relationship with another person, adverse life events or some similar cause, for example, having a dominating mother may affect one's ability to form relationships with other women. They were not the result of repressed sexual desires bubbling up from the id. Instead, such a relationship may affect the individuation process – the period of psychological maturation during which the person learns to embrace and understand their unconscious minds (e.g. through dream interpretation), they become aware of the archetypes such as the shadow and anima/animus and ultimately understand themselves as whole people.

Jung likewise identified four different types of thought: he called them 'psychological orientations':

[W]e must have a function which ascertains that something is there (sensation); a second function which established what it is (thinking); a third function which states whether it suits us or

37

not, whether we wish to accept it or not (feeling), and a fourth function which indicates where it came from and where it is going (intuition).

(Jung 1963: 396)

It should be clear that if Freud's ideas were difficult to test, Jung's are almost impossible to scrutinize scientifically. First, many of the concepts are vague in the extreme. For example, it is not entirely clear what represents a mandala and what does not. Second, we have already observed that the notion of archetypes is almost impossible to test. Even if it could be shown that archetypes such as the 'wise old man' or 'all-embracing mother' exist and influence our psychological development, it is not clear whether these figures stem from the depth of our collective unconscious or from our memories of our own parents which have accumulated through childhood. Third, there is no evidence that the interpretations of dreams, visions and other inner experiences or accounts to explain the origins of neurosis are either accurate or consistent. Would two Jungian analysts come to the same interpretation? There appears to have been no attempt to find out in the research literature. Even if the interpretations were consistent, how could one tell whether or not they were actually correct?

Most of Jung's theories are clearly problematic from a scientific point of view. However, one idea that comes out of it – the notion of extraversion – has been extensively researched, as discussed in Chapter 7.

Alfred Adler

Adler was another disciple of Freud's who, like Jung, rejected Freud's theories because of their emphasis on sexual motivation. A Marxist doctor who worked with working-class patients, Adler (see Adler and Jelliffe 1917) noticed that someone with a physical disability might strive to excel in an area in which they might have thought it would be impossible. For example, people with artificial legs have climbed Everest (Wainright 2006); Winston Churchill stuttered but sought out a career that involved extensive public speaking and oratory (Begbie 1921: 105). Adler himself had been crippled in childhood, which may be part of the reason for his interest in this phenomenon. Whatever the reason, Adler believed that the main motivating factor was not sexual, but a striving for superiority. This model, in which personality has its roots in social factors rather than biological drives, ties in with his Marxist beliefs. The principle can apply to psychological factors as well as physical ones. We all start as weak, powerless children and seek to develop our skills. If this does not happen (when a child does not perform well at school or at sports for example) an *inferiority complex* can develop if, because of a poor self-image, the person introspects too much and obsesses about this issue. Such individuals will feel that they are a failure. By way of contrast, some others who obsess about it may develop a *superiority complex*, whereby they cover up for their perceived psychological weaknesses and 'lord it' over others.

Adler's model of personality, *individual psychology*, takes a holistic view of the individual, rather than breaking the person down into components such as the id and the ego:

- society (friendships, humanitarian interests)

- work (cooperative activity benefiting others)

- love (caring more for another than oneself).

Suggested additional reading

The shortest summary is the *Five Lectures on Psycho-Analysis*, with the *Introductory Lectures on Psychoanalysis* (originally published between 1915 and 1917) (Freud 1917/1964) offering slightly more detailed treatment, and the *New Introductory Lectures on Psychoanalysis* (Freud 1932) providing an updated and extended summary of Freud's main theories. All are, or have been, published in paperback. There are also some useful summaries of Freud's theories, such as those by Brown (1964), Kline (1984), Stafford-Clarke (1965) and Stevens (1983), but it would be a shame to consult these without first reading some original Freud. Kline's (1981) *Fact and Fantasy* critically discusses the methodological problems associated with the various experiments and tries to ignore the technically flawed literature when drawing some broad conclusions about how well Freud's theories have stood up to empirical testing. Other useful texts are Erdelyi's (1985) *Psychoanalysis: Freud's Cognitive Psychology* (but only for those with a good background in cognitive psychology) and Fisher and Greenberg's (1996) *Freud Scientifically Appraised*, which covers much of the more recent work, although sometimes less critically than one might expect. Westen (1998) argues that, despite many problems (e.g. measurement and quantification), modern revisions of Freud's work may be of some contemporary relevance. It is not always clear to me that the data that are discussed owe much to Freud's input: for example, to argue that models of associative memory based on stimuli that are neither emotion laden nor of personal relevance provides support for the Freudian unconscious seems to me to be facile.

Jung's theory does not seem to generate so many research papers: those that are published in the *Journal of Analytical Psychology* are usually deeply theoretical and/or clinically based and written by practitioners who are largely committed to the broad principles of Jung's theories. They tend not to be based on empirical evidence and so do not really allow for the scientific evaluation of Jung's theories: they do not (perhaps cannot) seek to falsify the basic tenets of Jungian theory. For example, how *could* one research synchronicity? That said, the Society for Analytical Psychology offers a number of short papers for download on their website (http://jungian-analysis.org/) which may be of interest.

Adlerians publish in the *Journal of Individual Psychology* and once again, the material tends to be clinically based or suggests how the theory could be applied in other settings (e.g. education). But to my eye at any rate, it is all rather uncritical. There is, however, one (rather tangential) area of Adler's theory that has received considerable attention, namely the links between birth order and personality, which turn out to be quite small. (See Jefferson, Herbst and McCrae 1998 or Saroglou and Fiasse 2003.)

Answers to self-assessment questions

SAQ 3.1

a. Free association is one of the main features of psychoanalysis. The patient agrees simply to say whatever comes into his or her mind, no matter how trivial, fleeting or shocking it may be. The analyst speaks a word and observes the patient's response and in particular notes any difficulty in producing an association. Such difficulties may suggest that the word is linked to some traumatic memory and so an unconscious mental process (called a 'repression' in Freud's early work) strives to keep all associations with this event out of consciousness.

b. A resistance is an unconscious force that prevents the patient from producing free associations with words which touch on unresolved conflicts. The resistance prevents these associations from becoming conscious – it is the force that opposes free association.

c. Repression is one example of a defence mechanism. It is a process by which a memory, wish or impulse (generally sexual in nature) is kept out of conscious awareness.

SAQ 3.2

a. Any psychological mechanism whose aim is to prevent the contents of the id from reaching the ego.

b. Isolation.

c. The feeling of love would be turned to hate (by reaction formation), so that the unconscious feeling 'I love him' becomes 'I hate him'. Projection turns this into 'he hates me'. Freud suggested that these two defence mechanisms occurred in homosexuals, who were supposed to feel paranoid for this reason.

SAQ 3.3

First, a sound understanding of the theory is the first prerequisite – sometimes experiments are performed to test hypotheses that Freud never really suggested. Second, there has to be a good way of assessing ('operationalizing') the concept that is being tested. One cannot test Freud's hypothesis that 5-year-old girls develop penis envy unless one can find some way of measuring penis envy! It would not be unfair to say that most questionnaires that have been developed to measure Freudian concepts simply fail to measure what they claim to assess and so it is not possible simply to look through a catalogue of questionnaires and choose one that assesses the concept of interest, since it will almost certainly not prove adequate for the job. Finally, careful attention must be paid to experimental design, statistical analysis, ensuring that the number of subjects is large enough to give the experiment reasonable statistical power, ensuring that competing hypotheses are identified and eliminated, checking that control groups are well chosen and so on.

References

Abraham, K. (1952). The influence of oral eroticism on character-formation. In *The selcted papers of Karl Abraham*. London: Hogarth Press.

Adler, A. and Jelliffe, S. E. (1917). *Study of Organ Inferiority and its Psychical Compensation: A Contribution to Clinical Medicine*. New York: The Nervous and Mental Disease Publishing Company.

Begbie, H. (1921). *The Mirrors of Downing Street: Some Political Reflections*. New York & London: G. P. Putnam's Sons, Knickerbocker Press.

Brown, J. A. C. (1964). *Freud and the Post Freudians*. Harmondsworth: Penguin.

Brown, W. P. (1961). Conceptions of perceptual defence. *British Journal of Psychology Monograph Supplements 35*.

Bruner, J. S. and Postman, L. (1947). Emotional selectivity in perception and reaction. *Journal of Personality 16*, 69–77.

Dixon, N. F. (1981). *Preconscious Processing*. New York: Wiley.

Erdelyi, M. H. (1974). A new look at the New Look. *Psychological Review 81*(1), 1–25.

Erdelyi, M. H. (1985). *Psychoanalysis: Freud's Cognitive Psychology*. New York: Freeman.

Eysenck, H. J. (1957). *The Dynamics of Anxiety and Hysteria: An Experimental Application of Modern Learning Theory to Psychiatry*. New York: Frederick A. Praeger. Fairbairn, W. R. D. (1952). *Psychoanalytic Studies of the Personality*. London: Routledge & Kegan Paul.

Farrell, B. A. (1981). *The Standing of Psychoanalysis*. Oxford: Oxford University Press.

Fenichel, O. (1946). *The Psychoanalytic Theory of Neurosis*. London: Routledge & Kegan Paul.

Festinger, L. (1957). *A Theory of Cognitive Dissonance*. Stanford, CA: Stanford University Press.

Fisher, S. and Greenberg, R. P. (1996). *Freud Scientifically Appraised*. New York: Wiley.

Freud, S. (1917/1964). *Introductory Lectures on Psychoanalysis* (J. Strachey, trans., Vol. 1). Harmondsworth: Penguin.

Freud, S. (1923/1955). *Historical and Expository Works on Psychoanalysis: Two Encyclopedia Articles: Libido theory* (J. Strachey, trans. Vol. 15). Harmondsworth: Penguin.

Freud, S. (1932). *New Introductory Lectures on Psychoanalysis* (J. Strachey, trans. Vol. 2). Harmondsworth: Penguin.

Freud, S. (1959). *An Autobiographical Study* (J. Strachey, trans. Vol. 15). Harmondsworth: Penguin.

Freud, S. and Breuer, J. (1893/1964). *Studies in Hysteria*. Harmondsworth: Penguin.

Gibbons, H. (2009). Evaluative priming from subliminal emotional words: insights from event-related potentials and individual differences related to anxiety. *Consciousness and Cognition 18*(2), 383–400.

Hammer, E. F. (1953). An investigation of sexual symbolism: a study of HTPs of eugenically sterilised subjects. *Journal of Projective Techniques 17*, 401–15.

Jefferson, T., Jr., Herbst, J. H. and McCrae, R. R. (1998). Associations between birth order and personality traits: evidence from self-reports and observer ratings. *Journal of Research in Personality 32*(4), 498–509.

Jung, C. G. (1963). *Memories, Dreams, Reflections* (R. A. C. Winston, trans.). London: Routledge & Kegan Paul.

Kline, P. (1967). Obsessional traits and emotional instability in a normal population. *British Journal of Medical Psychology 40*(2), 153–7.

Kline, P. (1968). Obsessional traits, obsessional symptoms and anal erotism. *British Journal of Medical Psychology 41*(3), 299–305.

Kline, P. (1969). The anal character: a cross-cultural study in Ghana. *British Journal of Social and Clinical Psychology 8*(2), 201–10.

Kline, P. (1981). *Fact and Fantasy in Freudian theory*. London: Methuen.

Kline, P. (1984). *Personality and Freudian Theory*. London: Methuen.

Kline, P. and Storey, R. (1977). A factor analytic study of the oral character. *British Journal of Social and Clinical Psychology 16*(4), 317–28.

Kurthen, M., Grunwald, T. and Elger, C. E. (1999). Consciousness as a social construction. *Behavioral and Brain Sciences 22*(1), 197.

Lacan, J. and Wilden, A. (1968). *The Language of the Self: The Function of Language in Psychoanalysis*. Baltimore, MD: Johns Hopkins Press.

Meissner, W. W. (1958). Affective response to death symbols. *Journal of Abnormal and Social Psychology 56*, 295–9.

Saroglou, V. and Fiasse, L. (2003). Birth order, personality, and religion: a study among young adults from a three-sibling family. *Personality and Individual Differences 35*(1), 19–29.

Stafford-Clarke, D. (1965). *What Freud Really Said*. Harmondsworth: Penguin.

Stevens, R. (1983). *Freud and Psychoanalysis*. Milton Keynes: Open University Press.

Sulloway, F. (1979). *Freud, Biologist of the Mind*. London: Burnett.

Wainright, M. (2006). A double amputee, several grandparents and a Playboy model ... it's been a busy week on Everest. *The Guardian*, 20 May: 1.

Watt, C. A. and Morris, R. L. (1995). The relationships among performance on a prototype indicator of perceptual defense vigilance, personality, and extrasensory perception. *Personality and Individual Differences 19*(5), 635–48.

Westen, D. (1998). The scientific legacy of Sigmund Freud: toward a psychodynamically informed psychological science. *Psychological Bulletin 124*, 333–71.

4 Broad trait theories of personality

Background

In our everyday lives, we often explain people's behaviour through ascribing to them characteristics that are consistent across both time and situations (so-and-so is 'nervy' or 'talkative', for example). Trait theory develops this idea scientifically, using factor analysis to discover the main ways in which people differ from one another and to design tests to measure these traits. It also checks whether people's behaviour really is consistent. Trait theories are now widely believed to be the most useful means of studying personality – although there is less agreement about precisely which trait theory is the most appropriate. Several questionnaires have been developed to provide reliable and valid measures of the main personality traits, many of which have been found to have a biological basis, as discussed in Chapters 9 and 15. This chapter considers just three highly influential trait theories; some others are discussed in Chapter 9.

Recommended prior reading

Chapters 1, 14, 15 and 16.

Introduction

The personality theories considered so far have attempted to understand the nature of personality and its underlying processes through detailed analyses of individuals. The pattern of free associations generated by Freud's small sample of patients led to elaborate and speculative theories about the structure of mind, child development, motivation and other aspects of personality structure and process. Kelly sought to understand each person's unique pattern of personal constructs – the unique cognitive framework that each individual uses to anticipate and model events in the world. Rogers' theory is still less analytical, viewing people as whole individuals who grow and develop over time, coming to like and accept themselves as they are.

One problem that is common to all three theories is the difficulty of measuring personality. 'Self-actualization' remains a vague abstraction. There is no clearly valid way of assessing unconscious mental processes such as the extent of an individual's Oedipal fixation. Moreover, while the use of repertory grids may be particularly useful for understanding the number and nature of the constructs used by individuals, it cannot easily allow individuals to be compared. Three individuals might complete three different repertory grids, but ultimately there is no easy way of deciding how, precisely, their personalities differ.

It may, therefore, be useful to approach the problem from another direction. Instead of considering each individual's phenomenological world (as Kelly and Rogers did), it may be useful to develop techniques that will allow people's personalities to be compared, i.e. to map out the main ways in which people differ from one another. Once the main dimensions of personality have been established, it should be possible to develop tests to show the position of each person along each of these dimensions – thus allowing people's personalities to be compared directly.

Trait theories of personality follow precisely this approach. They assume (then later test) that that there is a certain constancy about the way in which people behave – that is, they propose that behaviour is to some extent determined by certain characteristics of the individual, and not *entirely* by the situation. This seems to tie in well with personal experience. We very often describe people's behaviour in terms of adjectives ('bossy', 'timid') implying that some feature of *them*, rather than the situations in which they find themselves, determines how they behave. (We shall discuss the role of situations in a little more detail later.) Describing people in terms of adjectives may sound a little reminiscent of Kelly's theory; after all, one use of the repertory grid is to find out which individuals are construed in similar ways. However, the crucial difference lies in the type of data used. According to Kelly's theory, an individual's *perception* of other people is what is important – it does not matter whether these perceptions are accurate. However, trait theories attempt to map out the ways in which people really *do* differ from one another and so depend on accurate (i.e. reliable and valid) techniques for measuring personality.

The basic aims of trait theories are therefore simple:

- To discover the main ways (dimensions) in which people differ. Once this is achieved then it is necessary to develop valid tests to measure these traits. One can then describe a person's personality merely by noting their scores on all of these personality dimensions, in much the same way that the position of a ship may be defined by specifying its latitude and longitude.

- To check that scores on these dimensions do, indeed, stay reasonably constant across situations – for, if not, situations must determine behaviour, people have no personality and we should all retrain as social psychologists.

- To discover how and why these individual differences come about – for example, whether they are passed on genetically, through crucial events in childhood (as Freud would have us believe), through the examples of our parents (as suggested by Bandura) or because of something to do with the biology of our nervous systems.

The present chapter deals with the first two issues, a discussion of personality *processes* being left until Chapters 7 and 11.

Factor analysis applied to personality

You will recall from Chapter 1 that the main purpose of measuring traits is to describe how an individual will behave most of the time – hence personality descriptions such as 'John is an anxious type' may lead us to suspect that John will be more likely than most to leap into the air when startled, to worry about examinations, to be wary of bees and so on. Using one word – 'anxious' – allows us to predict how John will *probably* behave in a whole range of situations. But how should one decide which words one should pluck from the dictionary in order to describe personality?

The first problem is that there are just too many words. Allport and Odbert (1936) found over
4500 words that described personality traits and so it would be impossible to assess people on all

of them. Second, if different investigators choose different adjectives, it will be difficult to prove that these mean the same thing – for example, if one individual says that 'Elizabeth is retiring', while another says that she is 'shy', are they describing precisely the same personality characteristic? It is impossible to be certain just by looking at the meaning of the words, since language tends to be imprecise, with many adjectives having subtle nuances and/or multiple meanings (perhaps you thought initially that Elizabeth was coming to the end of her working life). Thus different people may use different words to describe the same feature of personality and may perhaps use the same words to describe different aspects of behaviour. This does not bode well for reliable, valid measurement. Third, it is possible to develop scales that describe trivial aspects of behaviour, while leaving important aspects of behaviour unmeasured. For example, it would probably be easy to develop a scale to measure the extent to which individuals feel paranoid, even though paranoia is probably not an important determinant of most people's behaviour.

Fourth, this approach only lets us describe personality. It cannot indicate what might *cause* people to have different personalities. As mentioned in Chapter 14, circular definition involves deducing presence of a trait from some behaviour and then using it explain that behaviour. Doctors do this all the time. You might feel pain from swollen tonsils, visit your local doctor and be told that your throat hurts because you have tonsillitis. Except, of course, that your doctor has not explained anything to you. He or she has just translated your symptom into Latin (tonsillitis = swollen tonsils) and offered it to you as an explanation. Similarly, in the previous paragraph we noted that Elizabeth was quiet and retiring and deduced from this that she is less *sociable* than other people. It is very tempting to then try to *explain* these behaviours by means of the trait of sociability – to assert that Elizabeth avoids parties is *because* she is low on the trait of sociability.

To avoid falling into this trap it is vital to ensure that traits are far broader than the behaviours that are used to define them. 'Tonsillitis' can be used as explanation only if the doctor understands that it implies an acute bacterial infection that will probably last a few days and might be treated with penicillin. 'Sociability' would be a useful trait if (and only if) it has broader implications than a liking for parties, etc. If it could be shown to have a genetic basis, to be heavily influenced by some actions of one's parents or related to some aspect of brain or neuronal functioning, then we could be confident that the trait of sociability is a real characteristic of the individual. The behaviour that we observe (the swollen tonsils, the lack of socializing) arises because of some real biological/social/developmental/cognitive peculiarity of that person. It is a 'marker' for some broad 'source trait' that *leads* the person to avoid social gatherings and is not just a convenient label to summarize a person's behaviour. Without such evidence, traits are only convenient descriptions of behaviour – they cannot be used to explain it.

Discovering the origins of personality

How, then, can we go about discovering these 'source traits' – these broad dispositions that cause people to behave in certain ways? In Chapter 16, we observe that factor analysis can sometimes show up the *causes* of behaviour. We show there that if we factor analyse various pieces of data from people, some of whom have been drinking, the technique of factor analysis tells us that one factor corresponds to the alcohol-induced behaviours (slurring, staggering, etc.). This obviously represents true causal influences on behaviour: the three behaviours have a common origin (alcohol in the bloodstream). Thus the technique of factor analysis is able to show both how many causal influences are at work and which behaviours are influenced by which substance.

45

This situation is remarkably similar to that facing personality psychologists. Trait theory assumes that individuals differ in the extent to which they possess certain personality traits, the only problem being that we do not know in advance how many of these traits there are, or what they are like. However, we also assume that these traits influence behaviour. So, in order to determine what these personality traits are, it is simply necessary to measure the behaviour of a large number of people, to correlate these behaviours together and to carry out a factor analysis as described in Chapter 17. The factors that emerge from this analysis should show which behaviours tend to occur together as a result of certain causal influences – influences that are termed 'personality traits'. If people's scores on these traits can be shown to be influenced by genetic, biological, social, developmental or cognitive variables, then we can be confident that a true 'source trait' has been identified, which can then be used to explain behaviour. (For a contrary view, see Buss and Craik 1983.)

In the remaining sections, we shall consider various attempts to reveal the main personality traits through the use of factor analysis.

Self-assessment question 4.1

What are the four main problems involved in selecting trait descriptors?

The lexical hypothesis and Cattell's theory

In the previous section, I suggested (somewhat glibly) that, in order to discover the main personality factors, it is merely necessary to measure huge numbers of behaviours, correlate them together, and factor analyse the results. The problem is, of course, that deciding how to quantify human behaviour is a remarkably difficult task. Those with experience in comparative psychology will know that logging the behaviour of mere rodents can be very difficult and time consuming. To do this for humans would be a mammoth undertaking and it would probably be necessary to monitor hundreds if not thousands of aspects of behaviour in order to capture the full richness of a person's personality. Measuring hundreds of behaviours of thousands of people in myriad different situations is an almost impossible task. There is another problem, too, in that measures of behaviour often contain dependencies. For example, it is not easy for a person to eat, drink and talk simultaneously, so if an individual is eating, he or she will not be drinking or talking. We shall note in Chapter 16 that such dependencies can play havoc with factor analyses – they can produce entirely spurious factors.

Cattell (1946) argued that, instead of measuring behaviours, we should focus on adjectives. Specifically, he argues that every interesting aspect of personality would probably have been observed during the course of evolution and a term describing it would have entered the language. Thus the dictionary should contain words that describe every conceivable personality characteristic – generally in the form of adjectives such as 'happy', 'bad tempered', 'anxious', 'uptight', 'phlegmatic' and so on. Suppose a sample of these adjectives were to be extracted from a dictionary. It would probably be the case that some of these words mean the same as others – 'anxious' and 'uptight', for example. Wherever this happens, one or other of the adjectives could be dropped. This would produce a sample of words that describe *different* aspects of personality. Suppose now that these words were put into a questionnaire (so that people could rate themselves on each adjective) or that trained raters assessed people's behaviour on the basis of these adjectives. It would then be possible to collect data and correlate all of the responses to the various adjectives in order to find out whether 'happy' people also tend to be 'phlegmatic', etc. Factor analysis can be used to determine which of these ratings tend to group together. The factors that emerge should be the main personality 'source traits'. The assumption, that the factor analysis of correlations between adjectives that differ in meaning will reveal all of the main personality traits, is sometimes referred to as the 'lexical hypothesis'. It has the advantage of being largely atheoretical: the contents of the language are distilled down into a list of traits and there is no need for psychologists to make arbitrary (and perhaps incorrect) prior assumptions about what the main dimensions of personality are.

Cattell drew heavily on the work of Allport and Odbert (1936) when attempting to identify the main personality factors. These authors extracted a list of adjectives that could be used to describe people from the 1925 edition of Webster's New International Dictionary. Cattell eliminated synonyms from this list in order to avoid the problem of interdependent variables and added in some specialized terms from the psychological and psychiatric literature. When this was done, the original list of 4500 adjectives was reduced to 180 and then to 42–6 (Cattell 1957). These terms were used to rate the behaviour of a group of people, whereupon the correlations between the 45 trait descriptors were computed and factor analysed, yielding some 23 factors.

The assessment of behaviour through ratings is time consuming. Furthermore, there may be some personality traits (such as feelings and attitudes) that, except in pathological cases, may not be obvious to someone who is rating behaviour – someone may feel frightened when walking down a lonely road at night, but step out bravely. Moreover, the very presence of the rater may alter some behaviours – our pedestrian may not feel as anxious as usual because of the presence of the rater. Thus Cattell has attempted to measure personality traits by methods other than observers' ratings – most notably through the use of questionnaires and 'objective tests'. The hope is that many of the personality factors identified in one medium will also appear in others.

The crucial assumption of the lexical hypothesis is that single adjectives in the dictionary can describe all types of behaviour. Can you think of any patterns of behaviour that are not described by a single word? You might like to discuss some with your friends, to ensure that you all agree that the patterns of behaviour do actually exist. To get you started, I cannot think of any English word that describes taking pleasure in others' misfortunes (as in the German *Schadenfreude*). If you can think up many such patterns of behaviour, this may indicate that the lexical hypothesis is unlikely to be able to cover the full range of behaviours (or, of course, it may just be that the behaviours that you notice in other people are illusory – you may *think* that you notice characteristics that do not, in fact, exist).

Self-assessment question 4.2

How do you think that one can tell whether a personality factor derived from a rating scale is the same as a factor that appears in ratings of behaviour?

Cattell's most famous tests for measuring personality are the Sixteen Personality Factor Questionnaires, the 16PF (Cattell and Cattell 1995; Cattell, Eber and Tatsuoka 1970; Cattell and King   **47**

2000). I refer to these questionnaires in the plural because there is a whole series of different forms of these self-report questionnaires that yield scores on 15 personality traits plus intelligence. An 'industrial version' was published in 2000, otherwise the fifth edition (1993 in the USA, 1995 in the UK) is the most recent, with scales that are somewhat more reliable than in previous editions. However, the correlation between some of the scales in the fifth edition and their supposedly equivalent predecessors is sometimes less than 0.4!

The scales of the 16PF are shown in Table 4.1. Two words are given to describe each trait and these show the characteristics of a low and high scorer. However, it is important to remember that these are traits (not personality types) and so the questionnaire does not categorize someone as either 'warm' or 'reserved' for example. Instead, for each person, the questionnaire will produce a score that will usually be somewhere between the two extremes.

A	Warm/reserved	**L**	Suspicious/trusting
B	[Intelligent]	**M**	Imaginative/practical
C	Unemotional/emotional	**N**	Shrewd/forthright
E	Assertive/cooperative	**O**	Guilty/self-assured
F	Cheerful/sober	**Q1**	Radical/conservative
G	Conscientious/expedient	**Q2**	Self-sufficient/affiliative
H	Socially bold/shy	**Q3**	Controlled/impulsive
I	Self-reliant/sensitive	**Q4**	Tense/tranquil

Table 4.1 Scales of the 16PF

You will notice that the scales start at A, B etc. but that there are some gaps (no factor D, for example). This is because Cattell found that not all traits could be measured through self-report questionnaires. For example, how could you write questionnaire items to measure modesty? Anyone who *said* they were modest would surely not be! Traits such as these, however, could perhaps be assessed through other means – e.g. observer ratings, or objective tests (see later). Contrariwise, some traits may possibly show up in self-report questionnaires but not through behaviour ratings etc. and these are prefixed Q in Table 4.1. So 'radical/conservative views' (Q1) can only supposedly be detected via questionnaires – and I would suggest that it is reasonable to claim that this would not be obvious to someone who just observed one's behaviour.

Cattell has always championed the use of oblique rotations in factor analysis and so these scales can themselves be intercorrelated and factored, producing second-order factors, of which there now seem to be four or five, including 'extraversion' (characterized by sociability, enthusiasm, risk taking and needing the company of others) and 'anxiety' (nervousness, guilt, timidity, suspicion and compulsiveness). There is also a variant of this test designed for adolescents (the High School Personality Questionnaire), 8 to 14 year olds (the Children's Personality Questionnaire), 6 to 8 year olds (the Early School Personality Questionnaire) and 4 to 6 year olds (the Preschool Personality Questionnaire). There is some variation in the number and nature of the factors measured by these questionnaires, which Cattell (e.g. Cattell 1973) explains by suggesting that some traits develop later than others. He also explored personality in clinical groups and developed the Clinical Analysis Questionnaire, which measures (among other things) some seven distinct factors of depression.

It seems that Cattell's work is well founded in theory, care has been taken in sampling the variables that could describe personality, the scales have been factor analysed and many questionnaires have been developed. So why consider any alternative? The problem is that no one apart from Cattell and his colleagues can find anything approaching 16 factors in the 16PF. If the questionnaires do, indeed, measure 16 distinct personality traits, it should be possible to administer these to a large sample of people, correlate the items together, perform the factor analysis as described in Chapter 16 and discover that the items load 16 factors precisely as claimed by Cattell. The literature on this really is definitive – for whatever reason, the 16PF simply does not measure 16 factors (Barrett and Kline 1982a; Byravan and Ramanaiah 1995; Howarth 1976; Matthews 1989; Wells and Good 1977). This is important as the factor analysis shows which items belong to which scales. It indicates which particular items should be added together when the test is scored. The discovery that the instructions for scoring the 16PF are not even remotely similar to the factor structure obtained when the items are factor analysed indicates that everyone who has been using the test has been scoring it in a meaningless fashion. Despite this fundamental problem, the test is still widely used, particularly in occupational psychology.

Cattell's attempts to measure personality by means of 'objective tests' were, if anything, even less successful. The 'Objective Analytic Test Battery' (Cattell and Schuerger 1978) was an attempt to measure some of the main personality factors by means of objective tests. However, Kline and Cooper (1984) showed that the factors resolutely refused to emerge as expected and that the test appeared to measure *ability* rather better than it assessed *personality*.

Cattell (1986; Cattell and Krug 1986) disagrees with the studies that failed to demonstrate the expected structure in the 16PF. He argues that the tests that were used to determine the true number of factors were inappropriate (although these included his own 'scree test'). He also expressed concerns about the adequacy of rotation to simple structure, preferring his own subjective methods to those used and trusted by virtually every other psychometrician. The simplest way to rebut the criticisms would be for Cattell to produce a clear, 16-factor matrix arising from his studies with the 16PF. The 1970 handbook for the 16PF did not include such a table and when one was eventually published it did not show the clear factors that everyone expected.

The reasons for these flaws are uncertain. Recall that the 16PF was constructed through factor analyses performed by hand – a laborious and error-prone process. It may be that errors crept in here. Block (1995) suggested another possibility. Remember that the 'personality sphere' as mapped out by Cattell included not only the lexical trait descriptors, but also descriptions of personality traits arising from other psychological theories, to ensure that nothing was left out. Hence the personality descriptions used by Cattell were not *just* an exhaustive list of all trait descriptors, since several variables were included that he believed to be of theoretical importance, even though they did not seem to appear in the word sample. It is not, therefore, surprising that some of these hypotheses were borne out. (See also John 1990.)

Thus, although Cattell is one of the few psychologists to appreciate the need for careful sampling of the domain of trait descriptors, the inclusion of items from previous theories presents a problem. It also seems that there are fewer personality traits than suggested by Cattell and that tests designed to measure Cattell's personality traits are flawed. Given these problems, it is hardly **49** worthwhile discussing the nature of Cattell's factors or considering the evidence for the validity of the 16PF. Instead, we shall consider a more modern lexical approach to personality measurement.

Self-assessment question 4.3

When a test is factor analysed, why is it important to check that the items that form factors correspond to the instructions for scoring the test that are given in the test handbook?

The 'big five' model of personality

Several researchers have developed slightly different models of personality based on five (rather than 16) factors. Tupes and Christal (1992) became interested in reapplying the behaviour rating scales for personality devised by Cattell and described in the previous section. As before, the aim was to correlate and factor analyse the correlation between the adjectives in order to reveal the fundamental dimensions of personality. By using large samples of people and more modern methods of factor analysis they hoped to discover a factor structure that was more replicable than Cattell's. They found five personality factors, which they named, although (alarmingly) Passini and Norman (1966) discovered that when people were asked to rate the behaviour of complete strangers (whose behaviour they had not observed), the same factors emerged as when people rated individuals whom they know well. It is therefore probable that the method of rating used by Tupes and Christal was flawed; raters may not have recorded how people actually behaved, but instead how they *thought* the people being rated should behave (Lassiter and Briggs 1990). Thus the factors may reflect social stereotypes, rather than accurate assessments of behaviour.

Norman (1967) sought to update Cattell's 'personality sphere' by producing a list of 1431 terms that could describe personality. These he sorted into 75 clusters in accordance with the Tupes and Christal factors. Note that these traits were *subjectively assigned to a pre-existing model* (the five-factor model proposed by Tupes and Christal) rather than emerging through a process of factor analysis. Goldberg (1990) reports studies showing that five factors emerge when the 75 'Norman clusters' are used as the basis of a self-rating scale, which is perhaps less than surprising given that Norman *designed* the 75 clusters in order to yield five factors.

Much is made of the fact that the Norman/Goldberg five-factor model is not restricted to the English language, which may perhaps indicate that they are tapping a fundamental feature of human behaviour. Trait descriptors can be grouped according to the five-factor model in languages as diverse as German and Filipino (Angleitner, Ostendorf and John 1990; Church, Katigbak and Reyes 1996). I am not entirely convinced that this demonstrates the universality of the five-factor model, since these sortings of adjectives show how individuals *believe* behaviours group together and not how they actually *do* intercorrelate.

The strongest proponents of a five-factor model are Paul Costa and Robert McCrae (see Table 4.2). They began by using cluster analysis (a rough and ready approximation of factor analysis) to investigate correlations between items in Cattell's 16PF (Costa and McCrae 1976). They found two clear clusters of items that appeared to measure 'extraversion' (sociability, confidence, optimism, cheerfulness, etc.) and 'neuroticism' (worrying, guilt proneness, anxiety, etc.), plus a tiny third cluster. More items were added and three clusters were then derived (Costa and McCrae 1978) the third being known as 'openness to experience' and measuring the ways in which people deal with novel events, such as fantasy, aesthetics, feelings and actions.

Trait	Description of someone scoring high
Openness	Imaginative, moved by art, emotionally sensitive, novelty seeker, tolerant
Conscientiousness	Competent, orderly, dutiful, motivated to achieve, self-disciplined, thinks before acting
Extraversion	Warm, gregarious, assertive, active, excitement seeker, positive emotions
Agreeableness	Trusting, straightforward, altruistic, cooperative, modest, tender minded
Neuroticism	Anxious, angry, hostile, depressed, self-conscious, impulsive, vulnerable

Table 4.2 Costa and McCrae's five personality factors

They then decided, quite arbitrarily, that each of these three factors should be measured by six aspects of behaviour that they termed 'facets'. These represent lower level forms of behaviour which, taken together, define the factor. For example, 'angry hostility' is one facet of neuroticism – it could be assessed by expressions such as 'I am quick to anger', 'it doesn't take a lot to make me mad' and so on. The obvious objections to this technique are that (a) there is no earthly reason why there *should* be six facets per factor and (b) the facets are often so narrow in content that their items are *guaranteed* to form scales. For example, someone who says 'yes' to one of the above items is *bound* to say 'yes' to the other; you may like to reread Chapter 15 to remind yourself of the problems that result from constructing scales by paraphrasing the same item several times. Undeterred by all this, Costa and McCrae developed $6 \times 3 = 18$ sets of eight items, which eventually managed to form factors much as they were designed to. However, by this stage all attempts to keep to a lexical sampling model had been abandoned – the items were designed to measure a particular set of facets and factors.

Two further factors were later added to this three-factor model in order to allow Goldberg's two factors of 'agreeableness' and 'conscientiousness' to be measured, although some violence was done to Goldberg's five-factor model in the process. No one argued about the basic factors of extraversion and neuroticism, but Goldberg's third factor (previously identified as 'intellect') was altered so that it more closely resembled 'openness to experience'. The five factors shown in Table 4.2 (acronym OCEAN), constitute the currently popular five-factor model of personality, whose factors are usually measured using the NEO-PI(R) questionnaire (Costa and McCrae 1992b).

Considerable work has now gone into validating the NEO-PI(R) factors, generally by:

- establishing their existence in a variety of languages (e.g. DeRaad, Perugini and Szirmak 1997; McCrae and Costa 1997)

- correlating them with other questionnaires (e.g. Ferguson 2000)

- directly validating the factors against behaviour; for example, determining whether personality can predict 'risky' sexual behaviour (Trobst et al. 2000)

- examining the origins of these factors (genes, family environment or extra-familial influences; (e.g. Jang, McCrae, Angleitner, Riemann and Livesley, 1998).

There have, of course, been other attempts at explaining the processes that cause people to show a particular level of neuroticism, openness, conscientiousness, extraversion and agreeableness.

There may however be some problems with the theory. Costa and McCrae's model hinges on the work of Tupes and Christal, since this is what led Norman to categorize his traits in the way that he did and this (via Goldberg's work) led to the five-factor model that they took up. Is the Tupes and Christal work really adequate? It certainly has a great many technical problems, not least the quality of the ratings performed. In addition, one might expect the NEO-PI(R) to yield five factors when its facets are subjected to a confirmatory factor analysis (described in Chapter 17), whereas some evidence suggests that it does not (Parker, Bagby and Summerfeldt 1993; Vassend and Skrondal 1997). McCrae and his colleagues (1996) then suggested that the reason for this was that the standard statistical method used, rather than anything to do with the construction of the NEO-PI(R). The debate rumbles on.

Facets that supposedly belong to quite different factors can turn out to be quite highly correlated, as shown in the NEO-PI(R) manual For example, assertiveness (a facet of extraversion) correlates −0.42 with self-consciousness (a facet of extraversion). This correlation is actually larger than four out of the five correlations between assertiveness and the other facets of extraversion! And this is not an isolated example. A related problem is that some of the five factors are themselves highly correlated. Block (1995) mentions a correlation of −0.61 between neuroticism and conscientiousness in a female sample. It really does not seem that the five factors are truly independent, as Costa and McCrae originally supposed. Thus, although 'big five' models are enormously popular (even the fifth edition of the 16PF allows these variables to be assessed as second-order factors) there are still some real doubts as to whether all of the scales of the NEO-PI(R) actually measure what they claim to. One of the problems with this model is that has become highly commercialized: the questionnaires are commercial products and so there may be pressures on developers to produce evidence for their validity to boost sales.

The work of Eysenck

Whereas Cattell's approach to exploring the main personality traits has been essentially data-driven – a 'bottom-up' process – Hans Eysenck has instead advocated a 'top-down' method of analysis in which likely personality traits are identified from the clinical and experimental literature. He spent 50 years investigating the three main aspects of personality described in the book *Dimensions of Personality* (1947), namely intraversion vs. extraversion (Eysenck spells this word with an 'a'), neuroticism vs. emotional stability, and psychoticism (or tough mindedness) vs. tender mindedness. The first two terms, in particular, have a long history. Eysenck and Eysenck (1985) have shown that these stretch back over 2000 years to Galen and Hippocrates, were subsequently adopted in 1798 by Kant and surfaced again in the writings of Swiss psychoanalyst Jung during the 1920s. The basic premise of all these writers is that there are two basic dimensions of personality, rather as shown in Figure 4.1.

The vertical line in Figure 4.1 represents the personality dimension of emotional instability, or 'neuroticism'. Highly neurotic individuals are moody, touchy and anxious, whereas those low on neuroticism are relaxed, even tempered and calm. The second dimension is that of extraversion. Extraverts are hearty, sociable, talkative and optimistic individuals – the types who insist on talking to you on train journeys. Intraverts are reserved, pessimistic and keep themselves to themselves. The fact that these two lines are at right angles suggests that these two dimensions

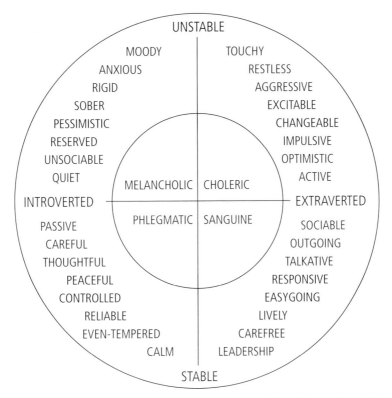

Figure 4.1 Personality dimensions of neuroticism and extraversion. (Reproduced from Eysenck and Eysenck (1985), with the kind permission of Plenum Publishing.)

of personality are independent (uncorrelated). Figure 4.1 also shows the four 'Galen types' (melancholic, choleric, phlegmatic and sanguine) relative to these axes and around the outside are descriptions of behaviours that might be observed from various combinations of these dimensions. Thus someone who is neither particularly stable nor unstable, but very intraverted, might be described as quiet or passive, a stable extravert might be described as responsive and easygoing and so on.

Figure 4.1 does not show Eysenck's third major dimension of personality, which was only formally added to the theory in 1976. Eysenck's dimensions of extraversion and neuroticism could not differentiate between schizophrenics, or borderline schizophrenics, and normal subjects. A third dimension, psychoticism, was introduced to the model in an attempt to achieve this. Individuals scoring high on psychoticism would be emotionally cold, cruel, risk taking, manipulative and impulsive. They are more likely than low scorers to develop schizophrenia (Chapman, Chapman and Kwapil 1994). Those scoring low on psychoticism would be warm, socialized individuals. Psychoticism is thought to be largely uncorrelated with either extraversion or neuroticism and so Eysenck's model of personality can be represented by three, mutually orthogonal personality dimensions – extraversion, neuroticism and psychoticism.

Over the years, Eysenck has devised several techniques to measure these three dimensions of personality, using scales such as the Maudsley Medical Questionnaire (MMQ), the Eysenck Personality Inventory (EPI) and, most recently, the Revised Eysenck Personality Questionnaire **53**

(EPQ-R). Some sample items are given by Eysenck and Eysenck (1985: 84). Unlike some of the other questionnaires considered earlier, the items in Eysenck's scales do form three clear factors precisely in accordance with expectations (e.g. Barrett and Kline 1982b). A version of the test for children is also available.

Eysenck has thus concentrated on two of the personality traits that emerge from the five-factor theorists and as 'second-order' factors from the 16PF (Hundleby and Connor 1968), together with a dimension of psychoticism that he finds to be appreciably negatively correlated with Costa and McCrae's 'agreeableness' and 'conscientiousness'. According to Eysenck (1992), Goldberg found a correlation of –0.85 between psychoticism and these two measures (combined), indicating that agreeableness and conscientiousness may well be components of psychoticism, rather than factors in their own right. Later studies have shown rather smaller correlations (e.g. McCrae and Costa 1985) and since Eysenck's death, Costa and McCrae's five-factor model has become more dominant. My own view is that Eysenck's model of personality is at least as useful as that of Costa and McCrae or Cattell, not least because the questionnaire designed to measure these traits clearly does its job.

Dissenting voices

Before we leave this chapter, it is necessary to consider some criticisms that have been levelled against all types of trait theory. Conley (1984), Mischel (1968) and other social psychologists have argued that it is situations, not traits, that determine behaviour. They argue that although we choose to *believe* that individuals behave in consistent ways (corresponding to personality traits), such beliefs are at odds with the data. However, three pieces of evidence show that this view is untenable. First, if personality were determined purely by situations, personality traits simply would not exist and so measures of these traits (such as scores on personality questionnaires) would be unable to predict any aspects of behaviour. However, sources such as Herriott (1989) show that personality traits can predict a range of behaviours. Second, if personality were determined by situations, then personality could not be influenced by our genetic makeup. Several are, as described in Chapter 11. Finally, studies such as those by Conley (1984) and Rushton, Brainerd and Preisley (1983) show a considerable consistency in behaviour. Indeed, Conley has shown that after correcting for the use of unreliable tests, the consistency of personality traits over time is of the order of 0.98.

> **Self-assessment question 4.4**
>
> Using the data in Table 4.3, plot a graph showing how each individual's level of anxiety varies from one situation to another. What would you expect this graph to look like if:
>
> a. situations, not personality, determine behaviour
>
> b. personality, not situations, determines behaviour
>
> c. behaviour is determined by the interaction of situation and personality?
>
> Which of these best describes what is going on in your graph?

Other theories such as learning theory and social learning theory have been proposed as alternatives to traits. For if our actions are determined by our reinforcement history and/or the behaviour of our role models, then personality traits certainly cannot be said to *cause* behaviour. One

In lectures	Coffee with friends	In a statistics practical class	Watching a horror film	Reading Dickens
8	7	18	14	6
3	2	16	4	2
7	8	17	8	7

Table 4.3 Hypothetical anxiety scores of five people in five situations

way of addressing this issue is to consider the effects of such processes on personality traits. If role modelling and reinforcement techniques are all important in determining how a child or adult behaves, one would expect brothers and sisters to have similar personalities, by virtue of their having been brought up according to the same family ethos. To anticipate Chapter 11, the influence of this 'shared environment' on children's personalities is minuscule and there is enormous variation in personality within families. This makes it unlikely that such learning theories will be of value as explanations for behaviour.

A third criticism of trait psychology comes from social psychologists with an interest in the 'construction process' (e.g. Hampson 1997). Rather than viewing personality as a characteristic of the individual, these theorists delve into the processes whereby personality attributions are made – that is, how behaviours are identified, categorized and attributed to either the person ('John is a snappy person') or the situation ('John is under stress'). Personally, I have no problem with this work, except that it is social psychology rather than anything to do with individual differences! For if we view traits as being real, internal characteristics of the individual, then it matters not one jot how others view them. This approach may be useful in fostering awareness of some measurement problems inherent in personality questionnaires, but once again the acid question is whether or not scores on personality questionnaires can predict anything. If they can, then there is more to personality than a social construction process.

Summary

This chapter has covered a lot of ground and has outlined the most promising approaches to the measurement of personality. You should now be able to define traits and discuss the problem of 'circularity' in using traits to describe behaviour, and discuss Cattell's lexical hypothesis for sampling personality traits from the language – you may have your own views on the adequacy of this method. The personality models of Cattell, Costa and McCrae, and Eysenck have been discussed in some detail (as has the quality of their associated psychometric tests) and you should be familiar with some criticisms of trait theory that are sometimes levied by social psychologists and learning theorists.

Suggested additional reading

Suggesting additional reading for this chapter is somewhat more problematic than for other chapters, because the literature is developing so rapidly in this area that anything that I mention here is soon likely to be superseded. The best solution would be to consult the papers and books cited in the text, perform a literature search, browse the journals *Personality and Individual Dif-*

ferences or *Journal of Personality and Social Psychology* or visit William Revelle's excellent website, the 'Personality Project', at Northwestern University. The old papers by Costa and McCrae and Eysenck (Costa and Mccrae 1992a; Eysenck 1992) are still well worth reading for two conflicting accounts of the advantages of the five-factor model over the three-factor model, while Matthews, Deary and Whiteman (2003) provide an excellent account of the nature and background of modern personality theory.

Answers to self-assessment questions

SAQ 4.1

First, there are a great many adjectives in the language and so it is difficult to know how to choose between them. Second, if different investigators happen to choose different samples of words, it is going to be difficult to ascertain whether their tests actually measure the same underlying psychological dimensions of personality. Third, it is difficult to ensure that *all* potential personality traits have been examined – that is, that the model is comprehensive. Finally, it is necessary to show that any concept (trait) measured by a set of adjectives is broader in scope than the adjectives that are used to measure it, before it can be used as an explanation for behaviour.

SAQ 4.2

There are two possibilities, both of which require that the same large ($n > 100$) sample of people have their behaviour assessed by raters *and* fill in the questionnaire. One can either correlate the two measures together or factor analyse the correlations between all of the items (both ratings and questionnaire items). Factoring is the better approach, as this will also identify any items that fail to measure the trait(s) in question.

SAQ 4.3

The factor analysis shows which items measure the same underlying trait. Suppose that a ten-item test is factored, and the analysis shows that items 1 to 5 load on one factor and items 6 to 10 load on another quite different factor. Obviously the test *should* be scored so that items 1 to 5 form one scale and items 6 to 10 form another. If, by way of contrast, the test handbook recommends adding together scores on items 1, 2, 3, 7, 8 and 9, the resulting total score will be a mixture of two quite different traits – and quite meaningless. (Consider, for example, how you would interpret a person's score from a test in which five of the items measured nervousness and five items measured vocabulary – it is impossible.)

SAQ 4.4

a. Very jagged – each person's score would vary enormously from situation to situation, and there would be no differences in the *average* score of each person (computed across situations).

b. The graphs would be entirely flat – people would yield precisely the same score in every situation.

c. A mixture of the two.

56   Your graph is best described by (c).

References

Allport, G. W. and Odbert, H. S. (1936). Trait names: a psycho-lexical study. *Psychological Monographs 47*, whole issue.

Angleitner, A., Ostendorf, F. and John, O. P. (1990). Towards a taxonomy of personality descriptors in German: a psycholexical study. *European Journal of Personality 4*, 89–118.

Barrett, P. and Kline, P. (1982a). An item and radial parcel factor analysis of the 16PF questionnaire. *Personality and Individual Differences 3*(3), 259–70.

Barrett, P. and Kline, P. (1982b). Personality factors in the Eysenck Personality Questionnaire. *Personality and Individual Differences 1*, 317–33.

Block, J. (1995). A contrarian view of the five-factor approach to personality description. *Psychological Bulletin 117*(2), 187–215.

Buss, D. M. and Craik, K. H. (1983). The act frequency approach to personality. *Psychological Review 90*(2), 105–26.

Byravan, A. and Ramanaiah, N. V. (1995). Structure of the 16PF 5-ed from the perspective of the five-factor model. *Psychological Reports 76*(2), 555–60.

Cattell, R. B. (1946). *Description and Measurement of Personality*. New York: World Book Company.

Cattell, R. B. (1957). *Personality and Motivation Structure and Measurement*. Yonkers, NY: New World.

Cattell, R. B. (1973). *Personality and Mood by Questionnaire*. San Fransisco: Jossey-Bass.

Cattell, R. B. (1986). The 16PF personality structure and Dr. Eysenck. *Journal of Social Behavior and Personality 1*(2), 153–60.

Cattell, R. B. and Cattell, H. E. P. (1995). Personality structure and the new 5th edition of the 16PF. *Educational and Psychological Measurement 55*(6), 926–37.

Cattell, R. B., Eber, H. W. and Tatsuoka, M. M. (1970). *Handbook for the Sixteen Personality Factor Questionnaire*. Champaign, IL: IPAT.

Cattell, R. B. and King, J. (2000). *16PF Industrial Version (Revised)*. Henley-on-Thames: The Test Agency.

Cattell, R. B. and Krug, S. E. (1986). The number of factors in the 16PF: a review of the evidence with special emphasis on methodological problems. *Educational and Psychological Measurement 46*(3), 509–22.

Cattell, R. B. and Schuerger, J. M. (1978). *Personality Theory in Action*. Champaign, IL: IPAT.

Chapman, J. P., Chapman, L. J. and Kwapil, T. R. (1994). Does the Eysenck Psychoticism Scale predict psychosis – a 10-year longitudinal study. *Personality and Individual Differences 17*(3), 369–75.

Church, A. T., Katigbak, M. S. and Reyes, J. A. (1996). Towards a taxonomy of trait adjectives in Filipino: comparing personality lexicons across cultures. *European Journal of Psychology 10*, 3–24.

Conley, J. J. (1984). The hierarchy of consistency: a review and model of longitudinal findings on adult individual differences in intelligence, personality and self-opinion. *Personality and Individual Differences 5*, 11–25.

Costa, P. T. and McCrae, R. R. (1976). Age differences in personality structure: a cluster-analytic approach. *Journal of Gerontology 31*, 564–70.

Costa, P. T. and McCrae, R. R. (1978). Objective personality assessment. In M. Storandt, I. C. Siegler and M. F. Elias (eds), *The Clinical Psychology of Aging*. New York: Plenum.

Costa, P. T. and Mccrae, R. R. (1992a). 4 ways 5 factors are basic. *Personality and Individual Differences 13*(6), 653–65.

Costa, P. T. and McCrae, R. R. (1992b). *NEO-PI(R) Professional Manual.* Odessa, FL: Psychological Assessment Resources.

DeRaad, B., Perugini, M. and Szirmak, Z. (1997). In pursuit of a cross-lingual reference structure of personality traits: comparisons among five languages. *European Journal of Personality 11*(3), 167–85.

Eysenck, H. J. (1947). *Dimensions of Personality: A Record of Research.* London: Routledge & Kegan Paul.

Eysenck, H. J. (1992). 4 ways 5 factors are not basic. *Personality and Individual Differences 13*(6), 667–73.

Eysenck, H. J. and Eysenck, M. W. (1985). *Personality and Individual Differences.* New York: Plenum.

Ferguson, E. (2000). Hypochondriacal concerns and the five factor model of personality. *Journal of Personality 68*(4), 705–24.

Goldberg, L. R. (1990). An alternative 'description of personality': the big-five structure. *Journal of Personality and Social Psychology, 59,* 1216–29.

Hampson, S. (1997). The social psychology of personality. In C. Cooper and V. Varma (eds), *Processes in Individual Differences.* London: Routledge.

Herriott, P. (1989). *Assessment and Selection in Organisations.* Chichester: Wiley.

Howarth, E. (1976). Were Cattell's personality sphere factors correctly identified in the first instance? *British Journal of Psychology 67*(2), 213–30.

Hundleby, J. D. and Connor, W. H. (1968). Interrelationships between personality inventories: the 16PF, MMPI and MPI. *Journal of Consulting and Clinical Psychology 32,* 152–7.

Jang, K. L., McCrae, R. R., Angleitner, A., Riemann, R. and Livesley, W. J. (1998). Heritability of facet-level traits in a cross-cultural twin sample: support for a hierarchical model of personality. *Journal of Personality and Social Psychology 74*(6), 1556–65.

John, O. P. (1990). The 'big five' factor taxonomy: dimensions of personality in the natural language and in questionnaires. In L. A. Pervin (ed.), *Handbook of Personality: Theory and Research).* New York: Guilford Press.

Kline, P. and Cooper, C. (1984). A construct validation of the Objective-Analytic Test Battery (OATB). *Personality and Individual Differences 5*(3), 323–37.

Lassiter, G. D. and Briggs, M. A. (1990). Effect of anticipated interaction on liking – an individual difference analysis. *Journal of Social Behavior and Personality 5*(5), 357–67.

Matthews, G. (1989). The factor structure of the 16PF: 12 primary and 3 secondary factors. *Personality and Individual Differences 10,* 931–40.

Matthews, G., Deary, I. J. and Whiteman, M. C. (2003). *Personality Traits* (2nd edn). New York: Cambridge University Press.

McCrae, R. R. and Costa, P. T. (1985). Comparison of EPI and psychoticism scales with measures of the five-factor model of personality. *Personality and Individual Differences 6*(5), 587–97.

McCrae, R. R. and Costa, P. T. (1997). Personality trait structure as a human universal. *American Psychologist 52*(5), 509–16.

McCrae, R. R., Zonderman, A. B., Costa, P. T., Bond, M. H. and Paunonen, S. V. (1996). Evaluating replicability of factors in the Revised NEO Personality Inventory: confirmatory factor analysis versus Procrustes rotation. *Journal of Personality and Social Psychology 70*(3), 552–66.

Mischel, W. (1968). *Personality and Assessment*. New York: Wiley.

Norman, W. T. (1967). *2800 Personality Trait Descriptors: Normative Operating Characteristics for a University Population*. Ann Arbor: University of Michigan, Department of Psychological Sciences.

Parker, J. D., Bagby, R. M. and Summerfeldt, L. J. (1993). Confirmatory factor analysis of the revised NEO personality inventory. *Personality and Individual Differences 15*(4), 463–6.

Passini, F. T. and Norman, W. T. (1966). A universal conception of personality structure? *Journal of Personality and Social Psychology 4*(1), 44–9.

Rushton, J. P., Brainerd, C. J. and Preisley, M. (1983). Behavioral development and construct-validity: the principle of aggregation. *Psychological Bulletin 94*, 18–38.

Trobst, K. K., Wiggins, J. S., Costa, P. T., Herbst, J. H., McCrae, R. R. and Masters, H. L. (2000). Personality psychology and problem behaviors: HIV risk and the five-factor model. *Journal of Personality 68*(6), 1233–52.

Tupes, E. C. and Christal, R. E. (1961). *USAF ASD Technical Report No. 61–97*. Lackland Air Force Base, Texas.

Tupes, E. C. and Christal, R. E. (1992). Recurrent personality-factors based on trait ratings. *Journal of Personality 60*(2), 225–51.

Vassend, O. and Skrondal, A. (1997). Validation of the NEO Personality Inventory and the five-factor model. Can findings from exploratory and confirmatory factor analysis be reconciled? *European Journal of Personality 11*(2), 147–66.

Wells, W. T. and Good, L. R. (1977). Item factor structure of the 16 PF. *Psychology: A Journal of Human Behavior 14*(2), 53–5.

Emotional intelligence

Background

Emotional intelligence (EI) has become a very popular topic in the last decade. Emotional intelligence reflects how sensitive a person is to their own and other people's emotional states and their skill with dealing with other people. It seems that practically everyone from employers and teachers to self-help gurus believe that such 'people skills' are vitally important and that they should be developed and trained – without ever considering basic issues such as whether emotional intelligence actually exists or whether it is different from the personality and ability traits that we have already examined. Science is now catching up with practice and many of these issues are now starting to be resolved.

Recommended prior reading

Chapters 4, 6, 8, 15 and 16.

Introduction

Why are some individuals 'good with people' – by which I mean able to identify their emotional state, work out the right thing to say and demonstrate social awareness? Likewise, why do some people fly into passionate rages and appear to be at the mercy of their emotions, while others seem to be able to understand and manage their feelings? Being sensitive to one's own and others' emotional states is known as 'emotional intelligence'. It has long been recognized that general intelligence, g, as described in Chapter 8, may not be the only thing that affects people's performance (e.g. at work) and some mention of this was made as early as the 1920s (Thorndike 1920). However, the first real experimental studies of emotional intelligence took place in the late 1980s when researchers such as Salovey and Mayer (1990) reviewed the literature and started to develop a more detailed model of how the concept of emotional intelligence should look.

They defined emotional intelligence as the 'ability to monitor one's own and others' feelings and emotions, to discriminate among them, and to use this information to guide one's thinking and actions' and link it to the concept of 'social intelligence'. Crucially, they suggest that there are three main components to emotional intelligence. Recognizing and expressing emotions in self and others are, surprisingly perhaps, grouped together as one component. The second component is the regulation of emotion – doing things (such as listening to music) because they induce a particular emotional state in oneself and managing the moods of others (e.g. by choosing which emotions to expose to them). Finally, they argue that it possible to use emotions effectively – for example, they suggest that the literature shows that it may be useful to induce a sad mood if one wants to think about one's self.

The area received a massive burst of publicity in 1995 following the publication of *Emotional*

Intelligence by Daniel Goleman, a journalist with a PhD in psychology (Goleman 1995). It was written for a popular audience and made several far-reaching claims: for example, the sub-title of the book is 'why it [emotional intelligence] can matter more than IQ'. Because this work is so well known (and often accepted uncritically by non-psychologists), it is important to outline its merits and its shortcomings.

Goleman's contribution

Throughout the book Goleman argued that mainstream psychology has paid insufficient attention to recognizing and managing emotions. Goleman argues that the being able to recognize one's own and other people's emotions and learning how to regulate one's own emotional state is important in understanding why the most successful people are not (he claims) always the most intelligent. He suggests that problems in these areas can have important implications for everyday life (e.g. our dealings with others; high school shootings) and points to the importance for psychological and social wellbeing of controlling impulses and negative feelings such as rage, or worry. Only then can we reach the 'flow' – a condition in which we are able to focus completely on what we are doing, with little awareness of events in the outside world: this produces a feeling of great satisfaction or joy. Goleman argues that making passionate love can exemplify what is meant by this state.

The limbic system and amygdala are thought by Goleman to be of prime importance in determining how we express our emotions, along with cognitive techniques that modify the nature and strength of the emotions that we experience. This does not sound very different from Eysenck's theory of personality. As outlined in Chapters 4 and 7, Eysenck's factor termed *neuroticism* describes, at one extreme, people who are at the mercy of their negative feelings, such as worry, guilt, anxiety and depression and mood swings and, at the other, people who are sanguine, in touch with their inner emotional life and emotionally stable. So is 'emotional intelligence' the same as neuroticism? Unfortunately, it is impossible to tell this from reading Goleman's book, as it does not contain a single reference to Eysenck's work (or, come to that, to the work of any other personality theorists who have studied anxiety/neuroticism, such as Cattell, Costa or Spielberger). Neither does Goleman give any hints as to how we should go about assessing emotional intelligence and this makes the theory difficult to test. How can it be shown that emotional intelligence is (or is not) more important than general ability in predicting performance if there is no way of assessing emotional intelligence or even any evidence that it is indeed a single entity?

Goleman also relates emotional intelligence to cognitive abilities. This is important, because part of his thesis is that 'continual emotional distress can create deficits in a child's intellectual abilities' (1995: 27) – which should, if true, imply some correlation between emotional intelligence and general cognitive ability. Brebner and Stough (1995) reviewed the substantial early literature in this area and reported that the correlations are typically near zero, at best in the order of –0.2. However, Goleman's view of the psychology of cognitive abilities is slightly unusual. The book contains no mention of the structure of abilities now generally recognized by most psychologists (see Chapter 8) and does not even mention the work of Carroll, Spearman or Thurstone. Instead, the chosen model of abilities is that of Howard Gardner and, we will argue in Chapter 8, this is an idiosyncratic view that is not always related to the mainstream literature and is not at all well supported by empirical evidence.

Goleman also sometimes ignores alternative explanations for phenomena. For example, he cites Mischel, Shoda and Rodriguez (1989) on delay of gratification. Here young children are given the choice of taking one small reward (a marshmallow) immediately or being promised that they will receive two when the experimenter returns in 20 minutes. Goleman argues that delay of gratification is an early attempt at emotional control and so children with higher scores on emotional intelligence will be more likely to opt for two marshmallows. However, there is also a substantial literature relating performance on this task to general intelligence (Mischel and Metzner 1962), which shows that 'smart' and older children delay gratification: finding that some children delay gratification while others do not is not, on its own, sound evidence for emotional intelligence. Indeed, one could argue that an emotionally aware child who is well aware of the fickle nature of adults should take the marshmallow immediately, given there is no guarantee that the experimenter will ever return! So it could be argued that children who are emotionally intelligent should take the one marshmallow, rather than risking getting none – the very opposite of Goleman's claim.

Goleman recounts how children who delay gratification when aged 4 also tend to show higher scores on mental ability tests, are better adjusted as adolescents and are far superior as students to those who act on a whim. This he attributes to the power of being able to manage one's emotions. However, there is no evidence that this is because the task reflects willingness to delay gratification: it could just as well be because it reflects general intelligence. Empirical evidence tends to favour the latter explanation. For example, Mehrabian (2000) factor analysed several measures, including delay of gratification, emotional sensitivity and general intelligence. Delay of gratification fell out on the same factor as did general intelligence factor; it did not have a large loading on the emotional intelligence factor.

It is therefore necessary to move on from Goleman's book to examine some more recent research into the nature (and correlates) of emotional intelligence and to devise effective ways to assess it.

The nature of emotional intelligence

Petrides and Furnham (2000) make an important point about the structure and nature of emotional intelligence. They point out that recognizing emotions, and deciding how to utilize them, is a cognitive skill – a mental ability – because there are clear right and wrong answers. Does that grimace indicate amusement, disgust or fear? Should I listen to gentle relaxing music if I want to 'brainstorm' and come up with creative ideas? Contrariwise, some aspects of emotional intelligence sound more like personality traits. Being sensitive, well adjusted, assertive, optimistic, happy etc. (all qualities that have been identified as components of emotional intelligence) can hardly be viewed as abilities: they are instead descriptions of how a person usually behaves across most situations – personality traits, in other words. Thus 'emotional intelligence' (EI) actually has two quite different meanings. The first, sometimes known as *ability EI*, describes how well a person can use information about emotional states: how well they can identify emotions in themselves and others, how well they can manipulate others' emotions and so on. *Trait EI* is the term that Petrides and Furnham use to describe the personality-like aspects of EI. This strikes me as a somewhat unfortunate choice of words – after all, ability EI is a trait too! But the term has now become engrained in the literature and there it will remain.

Self-assessment question 5.1

What is the essential distinction between trait EI and ability EI?

Models of emotional intelligence

If EI is viewed as an ability, then it should be assessed like any other ability – by compiling a test containing items that have been shown to be correct or incorrect and assessing how well the indi-

Figure 5.1 shows a photograph of Lynne Spence taken by Margaret McRorie (McRorie and Sneddon 2007) as part of a research project designed to capture real (rather than acted) emotions, and study the way in which they change over time. To test your emotional intelligence, what emotion do you think Lynne is experiencing?

Figure 5.1 Spot the emotion. (Reproduced from McRorie and Sneddon (2007), with permission.)

vidual can identify the correct answers. For example, if there is agreement between experts that a particular facial picture denotes anger, one item in a test of ability EI could well involve showing someone that picture and asking them which of five different emotions it depicted. By the same token, those who favour the trait EI (personality-like) approach would ask people to rate how well statements such as ('I am good at gauging others' emotions') apply to them. The obvious problems with this second approach are that respondents may have poor self-knowledge and/or may try to give a good impression of themselves. More worryingly, if a person's responses to a self-report test of trait EI are biased in this way, it seems likely that their responses to personality questionnaires are likely to be similarly affected. These 'instrument factors' (Cattell 1973) are therefore likely to cause scores on trait EI scales to correlate with scores on other personality tests. Since one way of validating a trait EI scale is to correlate it with personality scales, this is may be a substantial problem. However, it is an empirical issue and we will consider it when we turn to the measurement of EI.

Ability EI

Mayer, Salovey and Sluyter (1997) argued that there are four main areas in which people can demonstrate skills at using abilities: the 'four-branch model' (see Figure 5.2). They claim that scores on these four abilities are correlated and so that it is also possible to combine scores in these four areas and use an overall measure of ability EI.

Perceiving emotion is perhaps the most obvious way of assessing a person's ability EI. For example, how well can a person perceive the emotion in someone's face, tone of voice, posture and so on? In the exercise based on Figure 5.1, Lynne was experiencing great fear – she was teetering on top of a high and (she thought) extremely unsafe stack of crates and the rope round her waist was (she thought) only loosely attached to a tree branch.

The literature shows that there are substantial individual differences in people's ability to 'read' the emotional state of others, although these skills are also affected by cultural factors, group membership etc. (Reich, Zautra and Potter 2001). Factors other than EI seem to matter when recognizing emotions. It is perhaps unsurprising to discover that emotional recognition can be learned; what is most surprising is that it is learned very early in life. Dunn, Brown and Beardsall (1991) assessed the extent to which parents, children aged 36 months and a sibling used 'feeling state terms' (words such as 'sad' or expressions such as 'that's disgusting') when interacting normally at home. The 36-month-old infants were followed up and it transpired that there was a significant correlation between the amount of emotional talk at 36 months and these children's ability to recognize emotions when they were 6 years old – and this did not just seem to happen just because some children were more verbally fluent than others.

The second branch of emotional ability concerns how well people recognize the links between emotions and thought. For example, there is a considerable literature showing that a person's emotional state (both natural and induced) influences the way in which they tackle problems and the quality of thought. Isen's (2001) review demonstrates that positive feelings (she describes these as 'positive affect' but I think she probably means low negative affect: see Chapter 12) increase creativity and improve problem solving in both laboratory-style tasks and more practical tasks, such as resolving disputes between people and even making accurate medical diagnoses. It has been suggested (Spering, Wagener and Funke 2005) that false feedback about performance on an intelligence test (which produces negative affect) seems to lead to a change in the way in

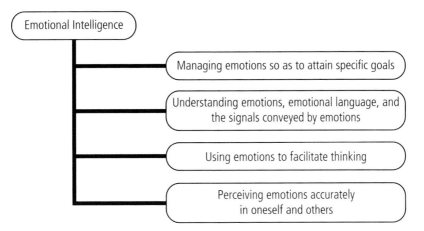

Figure 5.2 Four-branch model of ability EI (Mayer, Salovey and Sluyter 1997).

which information is processed, with more low-level information gathering and careful analysis. However, to my mind, it is uncertain whether this change in cognitive style is really due to negative affect. It seems just as likely that it occurs because of the (sensible) realization that because one has apparently performed poorly on an intelligence task, it would be prudent to slow down and take care in future. Whatever the fine details of such relationships, someone with high levels of emotional intelligence should be sensitive to the ways in which their moods affect their cognitive processes.

The third aspect of ability EI involves the understanding of emotions: for example, knowing what the emotional impact of a particular event is likely to be for oneself or others. This can be assessed by presenting people with various scenarios and asking them to assess their likely emotional impact. This too seems to have a surprisingly early onset. Denham, Zoller and Couchoud (1994) asked preschool children (aged approx. 48 months) to identify the emotions shown by four puppets (happy, sad, angry and afraid). The children were asked to describe events that could have made the puppet feel like this. For example, the child might feel that a puppet may feel happy because it had been given an icecream. These authors were mainly interested in the origins of such skills (socialization), but from our perspective the interesting thing is that such young children were able to identify sensible causes of emotion at all. The presence of autistic traits and the development of theory of mind are both likely to affect performance on this aspect of trait EI. For adults, this ability is likely to be more analytical: for example, to be able to appreciate the distinction between liking and loving, to understand complex feelings such as awe and to appreciate the possibility of feeling love and hate simultaneously.

The final area of trait EI is the management of emotion in one's self and in others. Sometimes emotional feelings just happen as a consequence of life events (for example, sadness following a tragedy) but at other times it may be possible to manage or manipulate emotions. For example, an emotionally intelligent individual may know which activities will help them to manage their anger or depression or what to say to bring about a particular mood change in another person. The use of coping strategies (Folkman and Lazarus 1980) would seem to be one obvious example of how individuals may manage their own moods and emotions, although curiously while there are a number of papers examining links between trait EI (i.e. the personality-like aspect of EI) and **65** coping strategies (Saklofske, Austin, Galloway and Davidson, 2007), little appears to have been done to check the link between coping and ability EI.

Self-assessment question 5.2

What are the four branches of ability EI proposed by Mayer, Salovey and Sluyter (1997)?

Ability EI is almost invariably assessed using the Mayer–Salovey–Caruso Emotional Intelligence Test, the MSCEIT (Mayer, Salovey and Caruso 2002), a good description of which is given by Mayer et al. (2003). This test is not without its controversies. First, what are the correct answers to the questions? Two approaches have been followed: consensus scoring and expert scoring. Consensus scoring simply means administering the items to a large sample of people and identifying which answer is the most popular. This is assumed to be 'correct', which appears to be a very major assumption, given that we know the extent to which individuals are susceptible to socially desirable responding etc. Expert scoring involves a panel of expert researchers making essentially the same decision. Although there is some disquiet in the literature about the merits of these approaches and concern that they may sometimes produce very different results (Roberts, Zeidner and Matthews, 2001), if just a few items have been wrongly scored as a result of this procedure, this should be detected via the factor analysis/item analysis procedure and so such items are likely to be removed from the test.

Trait EI

Several models of the personality-like trait emotional intelligence have emerged since the 1980s and we will consider just two of them – one because it is widely used, and the other because it is well supported by academic research. One problem with the trait EI approach concerns the sampling of items. Precisely what types of question should go into a questionnaire measuring emotional intelligence? Theorists cannot take a global approach like Cattell and the early five-factor theorists did, identifying all the words in the language that could possibly describe emotional intelligence – because by definition, no one knows at the outset what emotional intelligence actually is! Some theorists (and I will deliberately not include a reference to their work or speculate about why they do so) view traits such as 'conscientiousness' and 'achievement drive' as components of emotional intelligence, which is odd considering they are well-studied traits in their own right. There is a real danger that the concept of emotional intelligence may have been over-extended by 'pop psychologists' and those wish to sell tests to occupational psychologists under this flag of convenience.

Many authors take the lead from Salovey and Mayer's (1990) list of facets of emotional intelligence (see Table 5.1) which includes several non-ability facets that were dropped from the 1997 'ability model'. However, there is no guarantee that this model is correct.

Bar-On's model

Reuven Bar-On, an, Israeli clinical psychologist, initially studied factors associated with feelings of wellbeing and developed 15 scales/133 items to measure 15 factors of emotional intelligence. These 15 scales, each of which is supposed to indicate an aspect of successful emotional function-

Original label	Current label	Abbreviation	Definition	Sample item
Emotion in the self: verbal	Recognition of emotion in the self	RecSlf	Being in touch with one's feelings and describing those feelings in words	If I am upset, I know the cause of it
Emotion in the self: nonverbal	Nonverbal emotional expression	NvExp	Communicating one's feelings to others through bodily (i.e. nonverbal) expression	I like to hug those who are emotionally close to me
Emotion in others: nonverbal	Recognition of emotion in others	RecOth	Attending to others' nonverbal emotional cues, such as facial expressions and tone of voice	I can tell how people are feeling even if they never tell me
Emotion in others: empathy	Empathy	Emp	Understanding others' emotions by relating them to one's own experiences	I am sensitive to other people's feelings
Regulation of emotion in the self	Regulation of emotion in the self	RegSlf	Controlling one's own emotional states, particularly in emotionally arousing situations	I can keep myself calm even in highly stressful situations
Regulation of emotion in others	Regulation of emotion in others	RegOth	Managing others' emotional states, particularly in emotionally arousing situations	Usually, I know what it takes to turn someone else's boredom into excitement
Flexible planning	Intuition versus reason	IvR	Using emotions in the pursuit of life goals; basing decisions on feelings over logic	I often use my intuition in planning for the future
Creative thinking	Creative thinking	CrTh	Using emotions to facilitate divergent thinking	People think my ideas are daring
Mood redirected attention	Mood redirected attention	MRA	Interpreting strong – usually negative – emotions in a positive light	Having strong emotions forces me to understand myself
Motivating emotions	Motivating emotions	MotEm	Pursuing one's goals with drive, perseverance and optimism	I believe I can do almost anything I set out to do

Table 5.1 Salovey and Mayer's (1990) ten facets of emotional intelligence

ing, are supposed to form five 'dimensions' as shown in Figure 5.3. There is also a short (51-item) version of the test and versions designed for younger participants.

Although it claims to be based on a comprehensive survey of the literature, very little of Bar-On's work has been published in academic journals. It is very much a commercial (rather than an academic) enterprise and the test has reached the marketplace without the usual processes of peer commentary, debate over the soundness of the underlying theory, statistical methods and so on. Whether this matters or not is a moot point.

There are several points of interest about this model. First, the definition of emotional intelligence is very broad. Reality testing, for example, is supposedly the ability to recognize whether one's impressions accurately correspond with the real world: problem solving is the ability to define and solve problems. It is not at all obvious to this author why these are included. Neither is it clear why happiness and optimism are thought to be indices of emotional intelligence. But even if it can be successfully argued that happiness and optimism should be included, my second point is that there could well be explanations other than EI that account for some people being happier than others: lifestyle and dopamine levels being two obvious contenders. Third, some of the concepts seem rather similar: happiness and optimism again, for example. Fourth, as Palmer, Manocha, Gignac and Stough (2003) observe, Bar-On's own empirical evidence for the 15-factor/ five dimension structure of the test is less than convincing: he sometimes suggests that other models fit the data better.

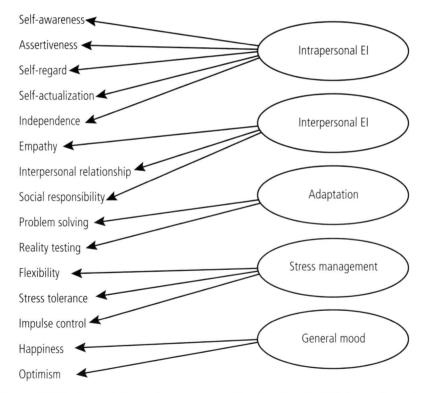

Figure 5.3 Scales and dimensions measured by the Bar-On EQ-i questionnaire.

Palmer et al. (2003) factor analysed the items of the EQ-i using an Australian sample. Their analyses, which were methodologically far superior to those used by Bar-On, showed just six (not 15) scales. The most important factor found in their analysis comprised items that should, in theory, have formed two quite different scales: self-regard and happiness items, together with a scatter of items from other scales. The impulse control, problem solving and emotional self-awareness factors were found to emerge cleanly, while items that should have formed two separate flexibility and independence factors all loaded on the same factor. Items that should have formed three distinct factors, viz. interpersonal relationship, social responsibility and empathy are all loaded substantially on one factor, suggesting that no meaningful distinction can be made between these concepts. All this is hardly convincing evidence for the structure of the EQ-i. When just one factor was extracted, most of Bar-On's items showed substantial loadings on the factor, suggesting that it might be safer to talk in terms of a general factor of EI rather than Bar-On's 15-factor/five-dimensional model.

Schutte's model

Schutte et al. (1998) developed a short self-report measure of trait EI, the Emotional Intelligence Scale, which was designed to assess a single factor of emotional intelligence. Subsequently, others such as Petrides and Furnham (2000) and Keele and Bell (2008) showed that its items in fact measured four factors of EI labelled 'optimism/mood regulation', 'appraisal of emotions', 'social skills' and 'utilization of emotions'. The Schutte scale is widely used, not least because it is not a carefully protected commercial test: the items are reproduced in the original 1998 article.

Petrides and Furnham's model

Petrides and Furnham, at University College London, have developed and tested a four-factor model of emotional intelligence. The four factors of emotional intelligence that they propose are wellbeing, self-control skills, emotional skills and social skills. Petrides and Furnham (2003) have developed a most useful measure of trait emotional intelligence, which has been extensively peer reviewed, is available free of charge for academic and clinical use, is available in both a long and a short form (153 or 30 items) and has been translated into more than 20 languages.

The basic structure of the Trait Emotional Intelligence Questionnaire (TEIQue) is not dissimilar to the Bar-On model. It consists of 15 facets of trait emotional intelligence, which load onto four factors (wellbeing, self-control, emotionality and sociability). These four factors then intercorrelate to produce a second-order factor of trait emotional intelligence. Table 5.2 shows the detailed structure of this scale.

The structure of the TEIQue has received empirical support from other researchers. For example, Mikolajczak, Luminet, Leroy and Roy (2007) find good support for the structure shown in Table 5.2, while Petrides, Stough, Saklofske and Parker (2009) consider other evidence that demonstrates that this model shows good psychometric properties. It seems that if one wants to measure trait intelligence, the TEIQue certainly seems to show good measurement properties. A website maintained by Petrides also contains much useful information about EI, as well as links and offprints.

Facets	High scorers perceive themselves as …	Factor
Self-esteem	successful and self-confident.	
Trait optimism	confident and likely to 'look on the bright side of life'.	Well-being
Trait happiness	cheerful and satisfied with their lives.	
Assertiveness	forthright, frank, and willing to stand up for their rights.	
Emotion management (others)	capable of influencing other people's feelings.	Sociability
Social awareness	accomplished networkers with excellent social skills.	
Emotion perception (self and others)	clear about their own and other people's feelings.	
Emotion expression	capable of communicating their feelings to others.	Emotionality
Relationships	capable of having fulfilling personal relationships.	
Trait empathy	capable of taking someone else's perspective.	
Emotion regulation	capable of controlling their emotions.	
Impulsiveness (low)	reflective and less likely to give in to their urges.	Self-control
Stress management	capable of withstanding pressure and regulating stress.	
Adaptability	flexible and willing to adapt to new conditions.	–
Self-motivation	driven and unlikely to give up in the face of adversity	–

Table 5.2 Structure of the Trait Emotional Intelligence Questionnaire (TEIQue) (adapted from Petrides (2003)).

Can tests of emotional intelligence predict behaviour?

There is such a substantial literature in this area that it is not possible to summarize it all here. In any case, the inferences that are drawn about the relationship between EI and behaviour depend crucially on:

- the *quality* of the test. A test that is a feeble measure of trait EI is unlikely to correlate significantly with behaviour, but this does not preclude their being a relationship between EI and behaviour if a better test were used.

- the *theoretical relevance* of the study. There are plenty of published papers that seem to lack a clear theoretical rationale. If one would not really expect EI to be strongly related to a particular behaviour, then nothing of much importance can be deduced from the findings. There are plenty of studies in the literature which appear to lack a decent theoretical rationale and so when these fail to show a link between EI and behaviour, it cannot really say anything about the usefulness of the EI construct.

- the *accuracy* with which the other behaviour is measured. It goes without saying that if the behaviour with which the EI measure is correlated is not measured with precision, the study cannot be expected to show anything useful.

- the *influence of other variables*. This is probably the greatest problem in EI research. Just because a test measuring EI correlates with some behaviour, it does not follow that EI itself is the cause of that relationship. It could well be that other variables (perhaps intelligence or personality traits) are correlated with both EI and the behaviour being measured and this may cause the correlation to emerge.

Cartwright and Pappas (2008) provide an excellent overview of EI research and also demonstrate some relationships between scores on EI scales and various occupational/industrial criteria. Van Rooy and Viswesvaran (2004) perform a meta-analysis on 60 independent studies in this area. Several substantial correlations are found: for example, that there is a correlation of 0.23 between scores on EI measures (they combined both ability EI and trait EI scales for this analysis). The tests predicted academic performance only modestly (with a validity of approximately 0.1) but fared better when predicting success in employment or other areas (e.g. sport), with validity coefficients of approximately 0.23.

Self-assessment question 5.3

What other sorts of experiment might you run to check whether a test claiming to assess emotional intelligence really did assess this trait?

Validity of measures of trait EI

There are two important questions in emotional intelligence research. The first is whether scores on ability EI tests and/or trait EI questionnaires can actually predict whether people demonstrate good emotional skills: for example, whether trained counsellors and therapists score better than **71** the general population or whether people rated as emotionally unskilled by their friends will show low scores on the various scales. The second question explores why this occurs. For is there any firm evidence that emotional intelligence is anything other than a mixture of the old, well-researched personality traits? The title of a paper by Schulte, Ree and Carretta (2004) gives an idea of the scepticism that some researchers feel.

As far as the first question is concerned, a full review of the literature is out of the question in a book such as this: there are just so many studies to consider. In addition, it should be remembered that whether a test measuring EI correlates with real-life behaviour will, of course, depend on the quality of the test itself! A test that is a feeble measure of EI cannot be expected to correlate substantially with behaviour, but this failure does not mean that EI *as a concept* is valueless. Another, better, test could have shown a relationship. Likewise, the nature of the criterion is important. Finding that emotional intelligence is (or is not) related to month of birth, burnout in student volunteers etc. would seem to be fairly weak evidence for the usefulness of the concept: it is necessary to ensure that the criterion variable has some theoretical link to emotional intelligence. All too often, tests of emotional intelligence seem to have been correlated with other variables on the offchance that something interesting may emerge. For example, it is not completely clear to me why one would expect EI to be related to academic performance. One would need some sort of convincing theoretical model spelling out what aspects of study etc. should be facilitated by EI, so that these can be explored and tested in detail. Otherwise there is little point in performing an experiment – and any failure to find a relationship – that cannot say anything about the utility of the concept of EI.

The predictive power of tests of EI

Cartwright and Pappas (2008) provide a good overview of EI research and also describe some relationships between scores on EI scales and various occupational/industrial criteria. Van Rooy and Viswesvaran (2004) performed a meta-analysis on 60 independent studies in this area: some of their results are summarized in Table 5.3.

The first section shows the correlations between overall EI and the 'big five' personality factors. It can be seen that these correlations are quite substantial and it is clear that EI is by no means independent of conventional personality traits. However, the correlations are rather smaller than might be expected: some studies (Dawda and Hart 2000) show correlations between trait EI and the big five personality factors all in excess of 0.4 before correcting for unreliability. It is unfortunate that van Rooy and Viswesvaran do not show results for trait EI and ability EI measures separately. It could be that trait EI has a stronger correlation with personality than is shown in Table 5.3, while the lower correlations of ability EI and personality have brought down the overall estimate. It is likewise probable that the overall modest correlation between EI and cognitive ability may represent a large correlation with ability EI and a near zero correlation with trait EI, as discussed later. The EI measures predicted academic performance only modestly (with a validity of approximately 0.1), which makes one wonder why such tests seem to be used extensively in this context. They fared better when predicting success in employment or other areas (e.g. sport), with validity coefficients of approximately 0.24.

Incremental validity studies

Van Rooy and Viswesvaran (2004) also looked at the incremental validity of ability EI measures. In other words, if one administers a test of general intelligence to try to predict performance,

Variable	Correlation	Correlation corrected for measurement error
Agreeableness	0.19	0.23
Conscientiousness	0.25	0.31
Emotional stability	0.27	0.33
Extraversion	0.28	0.34
Openness	0.19	0.23
Cognitive ability	0.15	0.22
Employment	0.22	0.24
Academic success	0.09	0.10
Other performance	0.22	0.24

Table 5.3 Relationships between overall EI (mixture of trait EI and ability EI) and other variables (adapted from van Rooy and Viswesvaran (2004))

how much better will the prediction be if a test of ability EI is also used? They conclude that 'the increase is minimal' (an extra 2% of the variance). This makes it hard to argue that ability EI is a novel and useful concept for predicting this sort of behaviour: another analysis led these authors to conclude that 'the claims that EI can be a more important predictor than cognitive ability … are apparently more rhetoric than fact'.

Schulte, Ree and Carretta (2004) also cast doubt on the utility of the MSCEIT. They administered the MSCEIT alongside a Big Five personality questionnaire and a test of ability and found that scores on the MSCEIT correlated 0.45 with general cognitive ability (g). Their analysis showed that scores on the MSCEIT add little to what could be predicted from a test of general intelligence and the big five inventory (the multiple correlation was over 0.8: as these authors had a restricted range of ability in their student sample, the value that one might expect in the general population could be even higher).

The correlations between trait EI and intelligence were much lower (in the order of 0.09). When the relationships with personality were considered, van Rooy and Viswesvaran (2004: 93) concluded from their meta-analysis that:

Our results also indicate that emotional intelligence and personality appear to be more highly correlated than many researchers would prefer. Indeed, three of the Big Five factors of personality had correlations with EI in excess of .31; the lowest correlation was .23 with agreeableness and openness to experience. This suggests that the distinctiveness of EI and personality may not be as clear-cut as it needs to be.

73

One problem with these meta-analyses is that they may combine scores from good and not-so-good tests of emotional intelligence. It is therefore telling that Petrides et al. (2009) established some rather substantial relationships between the TEIQue measure of trait emotional intelligence and a number of outcomes, such as life satisfaction and depression, even after controlling for the effects of the big five personality factors. In other words, the TEIQue does seem to 'add value' when predicting such criteria, whereas some other measures may not. This measure of emotional intelligence may have considerable potential.

Suggested additional reading

Very little of the literature in this area is particularly technical (although some does require a basic grasp of multiple regression techniques) and so any of the references cited in this chapter can safely be recommended. For a broad overview of the area coupled with a discussion of how EI is related to performance at work, Cartwright and Pappas (2008) is hard to beat. Mayer, Salovey and Caruso's (2008) upbeat overview of the status of EI is well worth reading – although perhaps in conjunction with Schulte, Ree and Carretta, as it is possible that the reason that ability EI predicts performance is because it is correlated with general cognitive ability, g. (See also Chapter 8 of this book.) Finally, Petrides, Furnham and Frederickson (2004) offer a well-balanced overview of the area circa 2004 and some background about the development of their TEIQue questionnaire.

Answers to self-assessment questions

SAQ 5.1

Trait EI refers to personal characteristics – personality traits, if you like – that describe how 'emotionally intelligent' a person is – but where the assessment method does not require them to *demonstrate* how good they are at perceiving, managing, regulating or using emotions. Trait EI is typically assessed by asking someone to rate how well various statements such as 'It is important for me to keep in touch with my true emotions', 'People have told me that I am "genuine"', 'I am good at calming other people down', for example, apply to them.

Ability EI requires people to *demonstrate* how effectively they can use emotions. For example, someone might be asked to identify which emotions they would experience in a particular situation or what emotion another person is experiencing in a video clip (where there is a strong consensus from experts as to what the 'correct' answers are). The answers here can be scored as correct or incorrect, as in a traditional ability test.

SAQ 5.2

Mayer, Salovey and Sluyter's four branches of ability EI refer to:

1. perceiving emotions accurately in others and oneself

2. being able to use emotions to facilitate thought

3. grasping the meaning of emotions, recognizing how your actions may affect other people's emotional state and being able to talk about emotions

4. managing emotions where necessary – e.g. preventing anger leading to road rage.

SAQ 5.3

In order to test whether EI is the *cause* of a particular relationship – for example, to test whether high levels of EI result in greater happiness – it is necessary to also measure other variables which could affect EI and happiness: for example, the big five personality traits and perhaps general intelligence. Then one can perform some statistical analyses that essentially determine how well the big five personality traits and *g* (but *not* EI) predict happiness. Finally, one can consider whether adding EI to this selection of tests significantly improves the overall level of prediction. If so, then it is clear that the correlation between EI and happiness does not just come about because some other traits (the big five and *g*) influence both happiness and scores on the trait EI questionnaire. It is instead likely that there is something 'special' about EI, which causes it to influence happiness, quite independently of the other traits. Hierarchical regression analysis, path analysis and partial correlations are some of the types of analysis that can be used to test this.

References

Brebner, J. and Stough, C. (1995). Theoretical and empirical relationships between personality and intelligence. In D. H. Saklofske and M. Zeidner (eds), *International Handbook of Personality and Intelligence.* New York: Plenum.

Cartwright, S. and Pappas, C. (2008). Emotional intelligence, its measurement and implications for the workplace. *International Journal of Management Reviews 10*(2), 149–71.

Cattell, R. B. (1973). *Personality and Mood by Questionnaire.* San Francisco: Jossey-Bass.

Dawda, D. and Hart, S. D. (2000). Assessing emotional intelligence: reliability and validity of the Bar-On Emotional Quotient Inventory (EQ-i) in university students. *Personality and Individual Differences 28*(4), 797–812.

Denham, S. A., Zoller, D. and Couchoud, E. A. (1994). Socialization of preschoolers' emotion understanding. *Developmental Psychology 30*(6), 928–36.

Dunn, J., Brown, J. and Beardsall, L. (1991). Family talk about feeling states and children's later understanding of others' emotions. *Developmental Psychology 27*(3), 448–55.

Folkman, S. and Lazarus, R. S. (1980). An analysis of coping in a middle-aged community sample. *Journal of Health and Social Behavior 21*, 219–39.

Goleman, D. (1995). *Emotional Intelligence.* New York: Bantam Books.

Isen, A. M. (2001). An influence of positive affect on decision making in complex situations: theoretical issues with practical implications. *Journal of Consumer Psychology 11*(2), 75–85.

Keele, S. M. and Bell, R. C. (2008). The factorial validity of emotional intelligence: an unresolved issue. *Personality and Individual Differences 44*(2), 487–500.

Mayer, J. D., Salovey, P. and Caruso, D. R. (2002). *Mayer–Salovey–Caruso Emotional Intelligence Test (MSCEIT) User's Manual.* Toronto, ON: MHS Publishers.

Mayer, J. D., Salovey, P. and Caruso, D. R. (2008). Emotional intelligence – new ability or eclectic traits? *American Psychologist 63*(6), 503–17.

Mayer, J. D., Salovey, P., Caruso, D. R. and Sitarenios, G. (2003). Measuring emotional intelligence with the MSCEIT V2.0. *Emotion (Washington DC) 3*(1), 97–105.

Mayer, J. D., Salovey, P. and Sluyter, D. J. (1997). What is emotional intelligence? In *Emotional Development and Emotional Intelligence: Educational Implications.* New York: Basic Books.

McRorie, M. and Sneddon, I. (2007). *Real Emotion is Dynamic and Interactive*. Paper presented at the Second International Conference on Affective Computing and Intelligent Interaction (ACII2007).

Mehrabian, A. (2000). Beyond IQ: broad-based measurement of individual success potential or 'motional intelligence'. *Genetic Social and General Psychology Monographs 126*(2), 133–239.

Mikolajczak, M. R., Luminet, O., Leroy, C. and Roy, E. (2007). Psychometric properties of the Trait Emotional Intelligence Questionnaire: factor structure, reliability, construct, and incremental validity in a French-speaking population. *Journal of Personality Assessment 88*(3), 338–53.

Mischel, W. and Metzner, R. (1962). Preference for delayed reward as a function of age, intelligence, and length of delay interval. *Journal of Abnormal and Social Psychology 64*(6), 425–31.

Mischel, W., Shoda, Y. and Rodriguez, M. L. (1989). Delay of gratification in children. *Science 244*(4907), 933–8.

Palmer, B. R., Manocha, R., Gignac, G. and Stough, C. (2003). Examining the factor structure of the Bar-On Emotional Quotient Inventory with an Australian general population sample. *Personality and Individual Differences 35*(5), 1191–210.

Petrides, K. V. and Furnham, A. (2000). On the dimensional structure of emotional intelligence. *Personality and Individual Differences 29*(2), 313–20.

Petrides, K. V. and Furnham, A. (2003). Trait emotional intelligence: behavioural validation in two studies of emotion recognition and reactivity to mood induction. *European Journal of Personality 17*(1), 39–57.

Petrides, K. V., Furnham, A. and Frederickson, N. (2004). Emotional intelligence. *Psychologist 17*(10), 574–7.

Petrides, K. V., Stough, C., Saklofske, D. H. and Parker, J. D. A. (2009). Psychometric properties of the Trait Emotional Intelligence Questionnaire (TEIQue). In *Assessing Emotional Intelligence: Theory, Research, and Applications*. New York: Springer Science + Business Media.

Reich, J. W., Zautra, A. J. and Potter, P. T. (2001). Cognitive structure and the independence of positive and negative affect. *Journal of Social and Clinical Psychology 20*(1), 99–115.

Roberts, R. D., Zeidner, M. and Matthews, G. (2001). Does emotional intelligence meet traditional standards for an intelligence? Some new data and conclusions. *Emotion (Washington DC) 1*(3), 196–231.

Saklofske, D. H., Austin, E. J., Galloway, J. and Davidson, K. (2007). Individual difference correlates of health-related behaviours: preliminary evidence for links between emotional intelligence and coping. *Personality and Individual Differences 42*(3), 491–502.

Salovey, P. and Mayer, J. D. (1990). Emotional intelligence. *Imagination, Cognition, and Personality 9*, 185–211.

Schulte, M. J., Ree, M. J. and Carretta, T. R. (2004). Emotional intelligence: not much more than *g* and personality. *Personality and Individual Differences 37*(5), 1059–68.

Schutte, N. S., Malouff, J. M., Hall, L. E., Haggerty, D. J., Cooper, J. T., Golden, C. J. et al. (1998). Development and validation of a measure of emotional intelligence. *Personality and Individual Differences 25*(2), 167–77.

Spering, M., Wagener, D. and Funke, J. (2005). The role of emotions in complex problem-solving. *Cognition & Emotion 19*(8), 1252–61.

Thorndike, E. L. (1920). Intelligence and its uses. *Harper's Magazine 140*, 227–35.

van Rooy, D. L. and Viswesvaran, C. (2004). Emotional intelligence: a meta-analytic investigation of predictive validity and nomological net. *Journal of Vocational Behavior 65*(1), 71–95.

6 Narrow personality traits

Background

The theories described in Chapter 4 sought to map out the whole of personality: that is, discover (and measure) all the important personality traits along which people vary. However, not everyone has approached the study of personality in this way. Some have chosen to focus on one particular trait – perhaps based on something that has been identified from the clinical literature, such as autism or self-concept. By writing items and analysing them as described in Chapters 15 and 18 it is possible to determine whether such a trait exists. An important part of this validation process involves establishing how the trait relates to the 'standard' personality traits described in Chapter 4 as there is always the risk that a supposedly 'new' trait is in fact identical to an existing trait or a mixture of existing traits.

Recommended prior reading

Chapters 4, 5 and 18.

Introduction

Chapter 4 considered models of personality that were intended to identify all the major personality traits and suggest how they should best be assessed. The advantages of this approach are several. First of all, it allows for the proper sampling of variables. The lexical hypothesis (on which Cattell's model and perhaps the five-factor model are based) should, in theory, ensure that all possible traits have been considered when mapping personality. What is more, because synonyms were removed from the list of trait names, we can be reasonably sure that the traits are not trivial. Trivial personality traits – Cattell calls them 'bloated specifics' – emerge when the words or phrases used in a personality scale are essentially paraphrases of each other or all refer to the same very narrow aspect of behaviour. For example, Table 6.1 shows a scale that might measure happiness. At first sight the items look reasonable, but on closer inspection it is clear that they all just ask the same question in different ways: how happy are you?

So why is this an issue? It is a major problem because the way in which a person answers one item should pretty much guarantee how they will answer the others. For example, could anyone who 'agrees' with Question 3 possibly agree to Question 4 or Question 5? Could someone who strongly agreed with Question 5 conceivably do anything other than strongly agree with Question 4 and strongly disagree with the rest? My point is that if we assume that people behave consistently when answering this questionnaire, the response they give to one item determines what the responses to the rest of the items must be. There is no need to gather data to prove this point: it follows inevitably from the meanings of the words in the scale. So finding that such items form a factor is not a finding of any scientific interest.

	Strongly agree	Agree	Neutral	Disagree	Strongly disagree
1 I am extremely happy					
2 Life is pretty good, on the whole					
3 The number of days I feel good is similar to the number when I feel down					
4 I am unhappy much of the time (reverse scored)					
5 I feel desperately miserable all the time (reverse scored)					

Table 6.1 Items in a putative happiness scale

It is, however, possible to ask participants to complete questionnaire such as this – and these scales will show the most wonderful psychometric properties. The items will form a clear factor. The reliability (coefficient alpha) is likely to be very high, even from short scales. But rather than measuring different aspects of some important concept, all this scale has done has 'inflated' one item and modified its difficulty (the score that most people would give if they were asked it).

In Chapter 16, we show that factor analysis can be used to identify source traits. If we measure several quite different aspects of behaviour, the discovery that some of them correlate together suggests that there is some interesting common cause. For example, should your stomach feel queasy and you should suffer symptoms of vomiting and diarrhoea, you would quite reasonably conclude that you probably have food poisoning. You infer that these different symptoms have a common cause (a bacterium) because these three quite distinct symptoms occur together.

If we put together questionnaire items asking people about their mood, whether they wake early, their ability to think clearly, eating habits and so on and administered these to a sample of people, we would find that they correlate together because depressed individuals will show all of these symptoms. But there is no *a priori* reason to suppose that sleep patterns should be related to thinking clearly. If there were no such thing as depression, we would not expect sleeping patterns to be related to early waking, etc. Only if the items are genuinely independent, like this, can we infer the presence of a source trait from a factor analysis. If the items are bound to correlate together because they all mean much the same thing, they will form a factor – but that factor is of no real interest.

Self-assessment question 6.1

Suppose that participants were asked to rate how accurately each word or phrase described them. Suppose too that factor analysis showed each item had a loading above 0.4 on the one factor that emerged. How might you investigate whether these items form a 'bloated specific'?

- certain of myself
- self-assured
- confident
- in control of myself
- unsure of myself (reverse scored).

The remainder of this chapter will introduce some of the many narrow personality traits that have been developed by researchers who are interested in exploring specific aspects of personality, rather than trying to discover the broad structure of human personality. One thing may have occurred to you if you have read Chapters 16 and 17 by this stage. It is quite possible that a 'narrow' personality factor is simply a combination of two or more well-established personality traits (e.g., from the five-factor model, or Eysenck's model of personality). For example, suppose we have some test that claims to measure a new trait – Trait X. We will also make the assumption that the tests that we use allow peoples scores on extraversion (E), neuroticism (N) and Trait X to be measured perfectly accurately. Suppose that we gave tests measuring Trait X, E and N to a sample of people and found that the correlation between E and N was 0.0, that E correlated 0.866 with Trait X and N correlated 0.5 with Trait X. This would indicate that Trait X was, in fact, nothing more than a combination of extraversion and neuroticism. How can we tell? You will remember from your knowledge of statistics that the square of the correlation tells you how much variance is shared by two variables. As 0.866 squared plus 0.5 squared equals 1.0, this tells us that a person's score on Trait X can be predicted with perfect accuracy if one knows their scores on E and N. Trait X is not novel at all and is therefore not worth studying.

Of course, in real life we cannot measure peoples scores on personality traits with perfect accuracy, the main personality traits are somewhat correlated (the correlation between N and E is approximately -0.3, for example) and we also need to take into account more than two personality factors when performing the analysis. But the same basic principles can be extended to take account of these issues and it is possible to discover whether any allegedly novel personality trait is anything other than a mixture of the traits that we already know and love. This is sometimes known as locating a trait within personality factor space. Unfortunately, ideas for novel personality traits invariably come from humans, who may wish to carve out careers for themselves on the basis of this discovery: they will not want to find that their favourite trait is nothing new at all and so not all narrow personality traits have been checked in this way.

Self-assessment question 6.2

What does 'locating a trait within factor space' mean and why is it important?

There are vast numbers of tests that claim to number huge numbers of narrow personality traits and choosing which to include in this chapter is inevitably arbitrary. I have included those that are widely used, currently being cited frequently in the literature or are of some theoretical or practical importance.

Sensation seeking

This personality trait has an unusual origin, stemming from military psychologists' attempts to determine how susceptible individuals would be to 'brainwashing' techniques of interrogation supposedly used during the 1960s. These techniques involved putting people into environments that were as unstimulating as possible: for example, they might be immersed in a tank of water in a dark, silent room, so receiving no stimulation from touch, sight, hearing, smell or taste. It was found that this was a most unpleasant sensation and people often became disoriented (for example, losing track of time) and hallucinating. People in these settings try to stimulate themselves (e.g. by tapping or singing; Jones 1969) in order to reduce the monotony of the environment. Such activity is not confined to humans. Sensory stimulation acts as a positive reinforcer for animals who are kept in unstimulating surroundings, who will learn to press a bar if this leads to stimulation (Kish 1966). Thus it seems that people are hungry for stimulation when placed in monotonous environments.

This effect may not be limited to unstimulating laboratory studies. There may also be important individual differences in the extent to which people seek out novel, thrilling behaviour. Some people thrive on driving fast, having varied sex lives and forever seeking exciting new experiences (e.g. bungee jumping, parascending) while others may actively avoid novelty and risk and prefer an unstimulating, routine lifestyle, enjoying the same routine at work each day and travelling to the same hotel at the same time each year to read safe, unexciting books. Sensation seeking may thus be a personality trait.

Marvin Zuckerman has researched individual differences in sensation seeking for over 30 years and his books (Zuckerman 1979, 1994) offer the best available treatment of the topic. He defines sensation seeking as 'the seeking of varied, novel, complex and intense sensations and experiences, and the willingness to take physical, social, legal and financial risks for the sake of such experience' (Zuckerman 1994: 27) and has developed several scales to measure this trait, two of which are reproduced along with norms, scoring keys, reliability and validity data and details of foreign translations (see Zuckerman 1994).

Factor analysis of items written to assess sensation seeking suggests that it comprises four distinct facets:

- *Thrill and adventure seeking* involves seeking out frightening physical activity.

- *Experience seeking* involves stimulation through travel, the arts and trying alternative lifestyles.

- *Boredom susceptibility* implies a dislike of a fixed routine or of dull people.

- *Disinhibition* involves stimulation from social activities: casual sex, getting drunk or using drugs socially.

The correlations between these facets are all positive, but vary drastically in size depending on which version of the test is being used. For Form IV of the scale the correlations usually range from 0.28 to 0.58, whereas for Form V of the scale they vary from about 0.14 to about 0.41 (Zuckerman 1994: 52). Confirmatory factor analyses (e.g. Haynes, Miles and Clements 2000) certainly suggest that the factor structure of Form V is less than satisfactory.

Sensation seeking and the main personality factors

The four subscales from Form V of the sensation-seeking scale and the scale scores from a short form of Eysenck's EPQ were jointly factored by Glicksohn and Abulafia (1998). These researchers extracted three factors; extraversion, neuroticism and psychoticism. Three of the sensation-seeking subscales (experience seeking, boredom susceptibility and disinhibition) all had substantial loadings (above 0.6) on the P factor. Thrill and adventure seeking loaded on both P and E. A factor analysis of the items in the SSS and EPQ-R-S revealed a similar story and almost the same thing was earlier reported by Zuckerman, Kuhlman and Camac (1988). Zuckerman, Kuhlman, Thornquist and Kiers (1991) found that *all* the sensation-seeking scales fell onto the P factor.

It is therefore clear that sensation seeking is highly correlated with psychoticism and, to a lesser

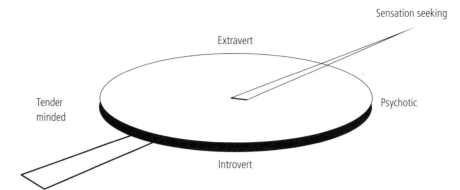

Figure 6.1 Sensation seeking (SS) located relative to Eysenck's factors of extraversion (E) and psychoticism (P).

extent, extraversion. Figure 6.1 shows Eysenck's dimensions of psychoticism and extraversion (c.f. Figure 4.1 for extraversion and neuroticism) and how sensation seeking relates to these two factors.

This figure shows that sensation seeking is not simply a mixture of psychoticism and extraversion: if this were the case it would be of little psychological interest, because there would be no need to develop a questionnaire to measure sensation seeking; instead, one could just estimate it by (for example) multiplying someone's psychoticism score by 3 and adding it to their extraversion score. Instead, the line representing sensation seeking in Figure 6.1 slants up through the plane of the paper into a third (sensation-seeking) dimension. Sensation seeking is a dimension of personality that *is* correlated with P (and to some extent with E) but one that also has some special meaning of its own; scores on a sensation seeking scale cannot be perfectly estimated from P and E alone, as shown by Glicksohn and Abulafia (1998).

> **Self-assessment question 6.3**
>
> What are the main characteristics of sensation seeking?

Correlates of sensation seeking

Scores on the various sensation-seeking scales have been found to correlate significantly with such a huge range of variables that it is not possible to summarize them all here; summaries are given in Zuckerman (1994). High sensation seekers take part in risky activities, ranging from climbing Everest to bomb disposal (Breivik 1996; Glicksohn and Bozna 2000). The higher someone's level of sensation seeking, the more they self-stimulate themselves through movement when undergoing sensory deprivation (Zuckerman et al. 1966). They are more likely to use drugs and explore sex at an early age (Stanton, Li, Cottrell and Kaljee, 2001), enjoy abstract art (Furnham and Avison 1997) and find rude and incongruous jokes funny (Ruch 1988).

An obvious problem with this work is that some of the items in the sensation seeking questionnaire may relate directly to the criterion behaviour. For example, if we count alcohol as a drug then five of the items in the SSS-V scale relate directly to drug use, with others (e.g. admitting to sometimes doing things that are a little frightening, illegal) having more tangential relevance. If you ask someone whether they take drugs and then include several drug-related questions in a personality questionnaire, then there is *bound* to be a link between the two measures. To combat this researchers sometimes omit the drug-related items in the SSS when looking at sensation seeking and drug use; drop the sex-related items when exploring sensation seeking and sexual behaviour or attitudes and so on. It is worthwhile checking that this sort of precaution has been taken when interpreting any study – not just those involving sensation seeking. For if only five out of 40 items relate perfectly to drug taking while the other 35 have no relationship whatever to it, the correlation that is obtained will be in the order of 0.35–0.40, which can easily get mistaken for a genuine finding instead of a statistical artefact.

Psychobiology of sensation seeking

As discussed in Chapter 4, in order to use any trait description ('sensation seeking', 'intelligence' etc.) as an explanation for why a person behaves in a certain manner, it is necessary to ensure that scores on the trait reflect one some fundamental process: e.g. the expression of certain genes or some maturational or social influence. This explains why Zuckerman has spent much time exploring the origins of the sensation seeking trait. If:

1. there is a close correspondence between sensation-seeking scores and levels of some hormone, neurotransmitter, etc. and

2. this relationship is so strong that scores on the sensation-seeking scale may be used as a cheaper alternative to biologically assaying levels of these chemicals

then it may be reasonable to conclude that sensation seeking (which is really the behavioural consequence of certain hormonal levels, or whatever) *causes* the individual to behave in certain ways – for example, driving recklessly.

Monoamine oxidases (MAOs) are enzymes that destroy various types of neurotransmitter in the synapse between neurones; monoamine oxidase inhibitors (MAOIs) are chemicals (some being well known as antidepressants) that reduce the depletion of neurotransmitters. A substantial literature shows that reduced levels of MAO are associated with increased motor activity, social activity and antisocial behaviour (e.g. Klinteberg 1996) – male sex hormones also reduce MAO levels. The behaviours associated with low levels of MAO certainly sound as if they may be related to sensation seeking and this model even explains the sex difference that is commonly observed in sensation-seeking behaviour – and indeed there is a significant negative correlation between MAO levels and scores on sensation-seeking questionnaires (Bardo, Donohew and Harrington 1996).

However, although frequently significant, this correlation is not large enough to suggest that MAO levels are the sole determinant of sensation-seeking behaviour and so Zuckerman has expanded the theory to look in more detail at the serotenergic, dopaminergic and noradrenergic systems. Several of these seem to control behaviour relevant to sensation seeking. For example, sertotonergic systems are related to behavioural inhibition and dopaminergic systems to seeking out reward and novelty. Zuckerman also weaves in cortisol levels and the interaction between these systems and stress to create a complex theory of the biological basis of sensation seeking (Netter, Hennig and Roed 1996).

Overview

The factor analytic results clearly show that sensation seeking is a component of psychoticism. It has also been related to alternative personality systems, such as that of Costa and McCrae, and to Zuckerman's own five-factor model of personality, but there is not space here to consider these linkages in detail. There is also good evidence for some association between sensation seeking and levels of MAO and neurotransmitters. However, it is less clear whether all these variables can be combined to predict a person's level of sensation-seeking behaviour accurately.

Schizotypy

Several researchers (e.g. Claridge 1985; Meehl 1962) have developed the argument that there is no real discontinuity between 'normal' and 'abnormal' behaviour; those who have depressive personalities may be more likely to suffer bouts of clinical depression than those who do not. Likewise, those who have higher than average scores on anxiety inventories are more likely to develop a full-blown anxiety disorder than are phlegmatic individuals. This idea (sometimes known as the *continuity hypothesis*) becomes of particular interest to personality theorists when applied to schizophrenia.

Schizophrenia is psychiatric condition that will affect about 1% of us at some time in our lives. Its symptoms can include hallucinations (seeing or hearing things that are not physically present, voices being particularly common), delusions (believing things that are unlikely to be true; for example, that their thoughts are being stolen or that they are being controlled by aliens via televisions), lack of emotion, illogical thought processes and inability to concentrate. The person becomes increasingly more eccentric, isolated and apathetic. (The idea that schizophrenia is anything to do with 'Jekyll and Hyde' or multiple personalities is an unfortunate myth that is without foundation.)

If the continuity hypothesis holds true for psychoses (such as schizophrenia) as well as for neuroses such as anxiety and depression, it might be possible to find 'normal' individuals who show milder signs of these symptoms of schizophrenia and who might be at above average risk of developing the condition in the future. For example, are normal people who believe in flying saucers also more likely to show shallow emotional responses, have problems concentrating and occasionally see or hear things that are not really present? Schizotypy is the term that refers to people who function completely normally, but show low levels of the cognitive, emotional and attentional problems that are found in aggrandized form in schizophrenics.

The concept of schizotypy therefore has much in common with Eysenck's idea of psychoticism. Both of these traits are thought to predict risk of developing schizophrenia, but researchers such as Claridge have tried to extrapolate all the main symptoms of schizophrenia from the clinical to the non-clinical population. Eysenck focused more on impulsive, sensation-seeking, cruel and solitary behaviours – with little mention of perceptual distortions or cognitive or attentional problems. Thus although the traits have something in common, they are unlikely to be identical.

Measurement of schizotypy

Several different scales have been developed to measure schizotypy, generally by factor analysing the responses that people make to a set of items that have been designed to measure the concept.

The problem is that researchers differ in the way in which they conceptualize it. For example, it is common for researchers to use a 'magical ideation' scale (Chapman, Edell and Chapman 1980) as if it measured schizotypy – yet this really only assesses strength of unusual beliefs. Others show better evidence of construct validity, being constructed by examining the symptoms that constitute the clinical definition of schizophrenia and generating items which may tap milder versions of these symptoms. Tests that have been constructed using factor analysis include Raine's (1991) Schizotypal Personality Questionnaire, the Schizotypal Trait Questionnaire, Form A (Claridge and Broks 1984), known as the STA, and the Oxford–Liverpool Inventory of Feelings (Mason, Claridge and Jackson 1995), the O-LIFE.

Several correlated facets are usually found when the items on these questionnaires are factor analysed. For example, the 37 items of the STA questionnaire generally produce three correlated factors; 'unusual perceptual experience', 'paranoid ideas' and 'magical thinking', although one study indicates that there may also be a factor comprising items concerned with social anxiety and sensitivity to criticism (Rawlings, Claridge and Freeman 2001). The O-LIFE questionnaire assesses 'positive' symptoms of schizophrenia, by which is meant those unusual symptoms of schizophrenia such as unusual perceptual experiences and magical thought. Deficits associated with schizophrenia (withdrawal) form another scale, cognitive and attentional problems a third and aggressive nonconformity a fourth The correlations between these facets of schizotypy are generally substantial (in the order of 0.4 to 0.7) and define a factor of schizotypy. The reliability of the facets is entirely satisfactory and different scales correlate well together (Mason et al. 1995). There is thus good evidence that 'watered- down' symptoms of schizophrenia form a trait within the normal population. But is this trait related to schizophrenia?

Schizotypy and schizophrenia

A huge amount of research has been performed in this area and it is impossible to do it justice in just a few paragraphs. Claridge (1997) summarizes much of the research literature and Lenzenweger (2006a) gives an excellent overview of the development of the concept and the relationship between schizotypy and schizophrenia. There are two important questions that can be asked:

1. Are high scores on schizotypy scales linked to schizophrenia? For example, via longitudinal studies or studying the 'normal' relatives of schizophrenics?

2. Much is now known about which cognitive, attentional and other processes are affected by schizophrenia and about which remain intact. Do individuals who score high on measures of schizotypy show similar patterns of deficits to schizophrenics?

The problem with any longitudinal study to determine whether schizotypy is linked to the development of schizophrenia in later life is that initial testing would have to be performed quite early (as schizophrenia commonly manifests itself in adolescence) and as less than 1% of the population will ever develop schizophrenia, huge samples will have to be screened. Thus most research uses less precise techniques for determining whether schizotypal personality traits really do predispose people to developing schizophrenia. Chapman et al. (1994) describe a study in which 500+ individuals were identified as being at high risk of developing psychosis and were followed up 10 years later. Those showing unusually high scores on perceptual aberration and magical ideation scales were more likely than controls to show signs of psychoses, have psychotic relatives, show schizotypal symptoms and psychotic-like experiences. The study does provide some suggestion that schizotypy predicts later psychosis – although it does not show that it predicts full schizophrenia.

Relatives of schizophrenics (who may therefore have shared some genes/family environment with the schizophrenic relative) are sometimes found to have elevated scores on measures of schizotypy. For example, it has been found that schizotypy in relatives is related to positive symptoms of schizophrenics (Mata et al. 2000) yet these authors could find no evidence that the schizophrenics' childhood levels of schizotypy (estimated by retrospective report from the mothers) were above average. However, this may just reflect the unreliability of the mothers' memories.

Turning to the second type of evidence, it is possible to measure eye movements and therefore discover whether a person moves their eyes smoothly when following a moving object with their eyes or whether the eyes make a number of jumps (saccades). It is well known that schizophrenics and their relatives find it harder to follow a smoothly moving dot around the screen than do control groups and this has been used as a marker for proneness to schizophrenia (Iacono et al. 1992). A substantial literature shows that poor ability to follow a moving object smoothly with the eyes is also linked to schizotypy (Gooding, Miller and Kwapil, 2000). This suggests that schizotypy and schizophrenia may have a common neurophysiological makeup.

Several other studies also find similarities between schizotypy and schizophrenia. Schizophrenic men are poor at identifying odours (though not at discriminating between them) – a finding of some interest, as the brain pathways involved in olfaction are reasonably well understood, and are known to involve brain areas (just behind the eyes) which are also implicated in other tasks at which schizophrenics perform poorly (Seidman et al. 1991). Interestingly, men with high scores on schizotypy questionnaires also show impaired odour-naming performance (e.g. Park and Schoppe 1997), once again suggesting that schizotypy and schizophrenia may share common neurophysiological processes.

It is well known that schizophrenics find it hard to ignore irrelevant information; unattended, irrelevant information is more likely to break through into consciousness. This may result in some positive symptoms: for example, schizophrenics may consciously recognize rhymes for words and say these, even when they are not appropriate or relevant, whereas non-schizophrenics will not even consciously notice rhyming associations. One common task asks people to read out words from a card as quickly as possible: these words are all names of colours (e.g. 'red', 'green') but they are printed in different colours: the word 'green', for instance, may be printed in red ink. Negative priming involves two trials where the answer to one trial becomes the irrelevant stimulus for the next trial: for example, 'blue' written in green ink followed by 'red' written in blue. The participant should read out 'blue, red'. Schizophrenics with 'positive symptoms' (delusions, etc.) show reduced inhibition and so less of a negative priming effect than do non-schizophrenics (Williams 1996) and so do people with high scores on the 'positive' aspects of schizotypy (Moritz, Mass and Junk 1998; Steel, Hemsley and Jones 1996).

Self-assessment question 6.4

Why is it important to perform experiments such as those described in the previous paragraphs?

Conservatism and authoritarian attitudes

There are a number of personality traits assessing conventional attitudes, authoritarian behaviour and dogmatic beliefs. The concepts have a long history, stretching back to the work of Adorno, Frenkel-Brunswick, Levinson and Sanford (1950) with more recent developments by Wilson and Patterson (1968) and Ray (1979) although the proliferation of names given to the concept caused confusion: it was not generally recognized that a number of different theories were all measuring the same thing. The scales fall together on one factor (Kline and Cooper 1984) known as the authoritarian personality.

Conservatism is not just related to voting behaviour, but to more fundamental cognitive processes, such as a preference for simple, unambiguous and familiar routines and to a respect for 'institutions' (e.g. the monarchy, religion, the family), conventional morality (e.g. regarding sexual activity and drug use), strong views about crime and punishment and a belief that seeking pleasure is wrong (Adorno et al. 1950). Because authoritarian attitudes show themselves in so many ways, as mentioned earlier, we can be confident that authoritarianism is more than a 'bloated specific'.

Measurement of conservatism/authoritarianism

A number of scales have been developed to measure conservative and/or authoritarian attitudes. Widely used measures include the Wilson–Patterson Conservatism Scale (Wilson and Patterson 1970) the Balanced Dogmatism Scale (Ray 1970), the Authoritarianism Scale (Ray 1979) and the Altemeyer (1988) Right Wing Authoritarianism scale. There are some theoretical debates about the precise nature of conservatism and authoritarianism: for example, some left-wing governments are extremely authoritarian and so it may be unwise to measure authoritarianism by looking solely at conservative or right-wing opinions. However empirically, studies in the western world usually show all of these variables loading onto the same factor.

The nature of authoritarianism

Surprisingly perhaps, it seems that authoritarianism is a true personality factor rather than just an attitude that develops as a consequence of one's upbringing and experience: authoritarian/ conservative attitudes are quite strongly heritable: for example, Bouchard et al. (2003) looked at the conservatism scores of pairs of identical and non-identical twins, all of whom had been reared apart. Identical twins showed conservatism scores that correlated 0.59: they were appreciably more similar than pairs of non-identical twins (who correlated just 0.21) indicating that increased genetic similarity results in increased similarity in conservatism. (See Chapter 11 for more details of how to interpret these data.) Likewise, the behaviour of preschool children was found to correlate substantially with conservatism, assessed two decades later (Block and Block 2006), which suggests that conservative attitudes are a result of some very early or genetic influences. The heritability of conservatism seems to be in the order of 0.57, which is also in accordance with a number of earlier studies employing different methodologies. Political attitudes do not seem to be mostly determined by one's upbringing, which must come as something of a shock to students of politics and sociology (Block and Block 2006)!

Still more surprisingly, authoritarianism/conservatism is also linked to rather low-level aspects of brain function. Suppose that participants in an experiment are asked to press a button every time that a cross appears on a screen. This is a very simple task to learn and soon becomes automatic. However, suppose that a second condition is now introduced: for example, if a sound is played when the cross appears, the person should not make any response. Most trials in the experiment involve the cross appearing in the absence of sound (a 'go' trial) and just a few involve the inhibition of this response, indicated by the sound ('no-go' trials). So from the participant's point of view, the 'normal' response is to push the button when the cross appears, except when the presence of the sound indicates that no response should be made. This task is quite difficult to perform accurately and everyone sometimes pushes the button even though the presence of a sound indicates that they should not do so. Performance on just these trials was analysed by Amodio, Jost, Master and Yee (2007). The authors recorded electrical activity from the bran during this task and focused on the peak of electrical activity which occurred approximately 50ms after the incorrect response (see Figure 6.2).

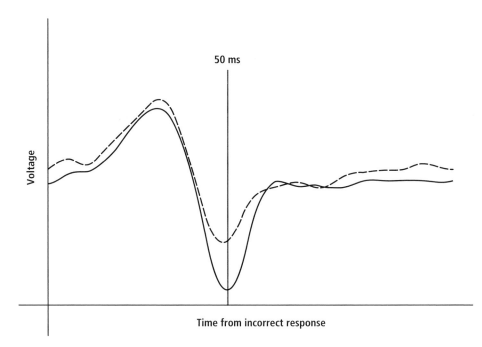

Figure 6.2 Brain electrical activity of liberal (solid) and conservative (dashed) personality types following an incorrect response. (Adapted from Amodio, Jost, Master and Yee (2007).)

The voltage recorded 50ms after the incorrect response was correlated with conservatism ($r = -0.59$, $N = 43$, $p < 0.001$) with the more liberal individuals showing the largest drop in voltage. The authors' analyses suggest that this electrical activity originates in the dorsal anterior cingulate cortex. Thus it seems that this aspect of personality is surprisingly strongly linked to a rather basic neural process – where more conservative individuals showed a smaller response than liberals when they fail to inhibit a response.

Conclusions

Conservatism/authoritarianism is an aspect of personality that is largely distinct from extraversion and neuroticism (Kline and Cooper 1984), but related to openness to experience (van Hiel, Kossowska and Mervielde 2000). It is indeed surprising that this trait shows such a substantial heritability (one of the highest that has so far been discovered) and clear links to neural activity. This evidence shows how the methods of psychology can exorcise myths about the social origins of attitudes.

Morningness

Rumour has it that some of us love to get up early, wake quickly and produce our best work early in the day, whereas others are slow to wake up, prefer to stay up late at night and work well in the late evening. These extreme personality types are sometimes known as 'larks' and 'owls', but most researchers believe that people fall along a continuum – a trait with extreme morningness at one end and eveningness at the other. Unsurprisingly, this trait is of particular interest to those working with circadian rhythms and there is a substantial literature linking this trait of morningness–eveningness to various aspects of behaviour. For example, a literature review by Cavallera and Giudici (2008) shows that questionnaire scores have been linked to performance at shift work and various physiological variables such as the time at which body temperature reaches its maximum (which is earlier for 'larks' than for 'owls') and so on. Morningness–eveningness is supposed to reflect individual differences in circadian clocks, which seem to involve neural oscillators in the ventral hypothalamus. One would therefore expect this trait to have substantial heritability: it would be surprising if the genes that determine the structure and function of the brain do not influence this rather simple behavioural outcome. Cavallera and Giudici point to literature suggesting that this trait has a heritability of at least 50%. Much of this morningness–eveningness literature is rather specialized and not particularly relevant for this book, but it does seem that scores on the various questionnaires relate as expected to physiological responsiveness and behaviour.

Matthews (1988) examined the links between morningness–eveningness, mood and other personality traits. He found that morningness–eveningness was linked to two circadian rhythms, one related to negative emotions, such as depression, and the other linked to arousal. These are essentially positive affect and negative affect, as described in Chapter 12. However, sex differences were quite marked and complicated the interpretation of the data (for example, morningness was correlated with anxiety for males, but not for females) and gender also interacted with time of day and mood. All in all the picture is fairly complicated – but one can be fairly sure that morningness–eveningness does not correspond closely to other, well-known personality traits.

Randler (2008) explores how scores on a morningness–eveningness questionnaire relate to the five-factor model of personality. Our behaviour is often determined by external factors. For example, employers may not allow individuals to start work late, and so would-be 'owls' may be forced to go to bed earlier than they would wish in order to obtain enough sleep to function the following day. Thus rather than just correlating scores on morningness–eveningness questionnaires and sleeping habits with personality, these authors also considered when individuals woke up on their days off and the difference between the hour of waking on their days off and their hour of waking during the working week.

Their results showed a significant but small correlation ($r = 0.11$) between morningness and the big five agreeableness factor in adolescents (there was no significant relationship for adults). Conscientiousness correlated approximately 0.37 with morningness. Several correlations between sleeping habits and personality reach statistical significance, but as this study was based on a large sample ($n > 1000$) many of the significant correlations are rather small and indicate only a very weak relationship between the variables. The exception is once again conscientiousness, which correlates 0.23 with hours of sleep taken at weekends, and it also seems that the more conscientious individuals are less likely to stay in bed for a long time at weekends. But the most interesting finding is probably that there is no evidence at all for any relationship between morningness–eveningness and the two main personality traits, extraversion and neuroticism. Morningness–eveningness seems to be a narrow trait that correlates somewhat with conscientiousness, but which is otherwise quite distinct from the main personality factors.

Self-esteem

Self-esteem is an enormously popular topic in social psychology: it essentially reflects the extent to which an individual likes him- or herself and Kline (1999) has been one of those who has observed that the most commonly used test that measures self-esteem, the Rosenberg Self-Esteem (RSE) Scale (Rosenberg 1965), is deeply flawed by being a bloated specific. The ten items essentially all ask the same question over and over. Thus rather than being a 'source trait', a personality factor that could be a genuine causal influence on behaviour, the items that constitute the Rosenberg scale are bound to form a factor because they all have the same meaning. This makes the entire concept of self-esteem of dubious use as an explanation for behaviour even advocates of this approach to measuring personality have stated:

In our experience, even when the RSE items are interspersed with items from other scales, participants frequently write comments such as, 'I have already answered this question!' Such reactions may lead participants to skip questions, respond randomly, and engage in other test-taking behaviors that contribute to invalid protocols.

(Robins, Hendin and Trzesniewski 2001: 157)

These authors go on to demonstrate that a single question – 'I have high self-esteem' – is as effective as the longer Rosenberg scale for measuring self-esteem: it shows similarly sized correlations with other variables, such as personality traits. From this analysis, it seems that self-esteem should not be regarded as a source trait. However, as self-esteem is an attitude rather than a personality trait, perhaps one should not apply the same criteria as for personality traits. However, it seems that there is another major problem with the whole concept of self-esteem.

Robins et al. (2001) report correlations as shown in Table 6.2 between the Rosenberg Self-Esteem Scale and personality; their results are broadly in line with other similar studies.

Some of these correlations are exceptionally large. Summing and squaring these correlations (which gives an estimate of the size of the overlap between self-esteem and personality, assuming that the big five personality factors are uncorrelated) gives 0.82. So well over 80% of the variation in self-esteem scores can be explained by the big five personality factors. It could be argued that this analysis is flawed. As the big five extraversion and neuroticism factors are known to be negatively correlated, this will overestimate the overlap between self-esteem and personality. By the same token, none of the tests is perfectly reliable (see Chapter 15) and this will tend to under-

NEO extraversion	0.41
NEO agreeableness	0.23
NEO conscientiousness	0.28
NEO neuroticism	−0.70
NEO openness to experience	0.16

Table 6.2 Correlations between self-esteem and personality (from Robins, Hendin and Trzesniewski (2001))

estimate the true value of the correlations, so the figure of 0.82 is unlikely to be too far from the truth.

Given that Robins et al. (1981) remind us that 'in a recent review, Gray-Little et al. (1997) concluded that the RSE is a reliable and valid measure of global self-worth and "deserves its widespread use and continued popularity"', it is clear that this is not just a problem with some obscure scale, but a major issue for those who research in this area. The finding seems to suggest that "self-esteem" (as measured by the Rosenberg inventory) is a redundant concept. It is little more than a mixture of high neuroticism and low extraversion. My evaluation of the importance of self-esteem is something of a minority view (albeit one based on hard evidence); most social psychologists stress the prime importance of the concept, although it is good to see that some working in that field (e.g. Baumeister, Campbell, Krueger and Vohs 2003; Krueger, Vohs and Baumeister 2008) are developing awareness of some of the problems with this concept.

Summary

I suggest that for any narrow personality trait to be valuable, it should:

- have a clear theoretical rationale: for example, the schizoptypy scale containing items that reflect milder versions of symptoms of schizophrenia

- have an effective method of assessing each individual's position along the trait, without which it is impossible to test any hypotheses associated with the theory

- be demonstrably distinct from the global personality models, such as those of Eysenck or Costa and McCrae

- have some literature exploring the processes that cause individuals to differ on their levels of the trait, for example, the surprising literature on the importance of genetic influences on conservative attitudes or the link between schizotypy and negative priming.

This chapter has considered some of the many personality traits that have been developed for rather specific research purposes. The choice of what to include has inevitably been subjective: traits such as mindfulness and religiosity are increasingly cited in the literature and it would also be possible to make a case for considering impulsivity, optimism, perfectionism, self-efficacy, rumination and yet other traits. However, those that I have included seem to me either to have a particularly interesting theoretical rationale or to have continued importance. The exception is self-esteem, **91** a concept that is hugely popular in social psychology and which is discussed here because its advocates often do not appreciate the problems associated with this trait and its measurement.

Suggested additional reading

Lenzenweger (2006b) gives a good account of the nature of schizotypy and its relationship to schizophrenia and discusses a model for genetic and environmental influences. A good account of conservatism/authoritarianism research is given by Altemeyer (1998), while Baumeister et al. (2003) discuss whether it is right to regard self-esteem as a causal influence on behaviour.

Answers to self-assessment questions

SAQ 6.1

Identifying bloated specifics is not easy. The first stage should be to look at the items and determine whether answering one item in a certain way forces a respondent to give a particular answer to another question. If this is widespread, then the scale is probably a bloated specific. Second, if the scale has unusually high reliability given its length (say reliability above 0.80 for a ten-item test) this can be a warning sign that the test is a bloated specific. This is because if the test items are sampled from a wide domain (as they should be) two items will only correlate because they share common variance because of the trait they both measure: if they measure a bloated specific, they will share specific variance, too, which will increase the reliability of the scale. The next step is to determine how scores on this scale relate to other source traits – locating the trait in factor space. It may be the case that scores are closely related to one or more well-known source traits.

SAQ 6.2

'Locating a trait within factor space' means determining how this trait relates to the main source traits described in Chapter 4. It involves administering some measure of the trait alongside standard personality questionnaires, such as the Eysenck Personality Questionnaire (Revised) to a good-sized, representative sample of people. You then have several options: you could factor analyse the responses to all of the items in the questionnaires together, to find whether the items in the novel trait form a distinct factor that is different from E, N and P; you could use confirmatory factor analysis to test this hypothesis. Either way, this analysis will also show the correlations between the standard personality factors and the novel trait. Or, if your sample is not large enough for factor analysis, you could correlate scale scores together: you might discover that the trait is moderately related to neuroticism (r = 0.4, for example), but not at all correlated with extraversion or psychoticism. If sample size permits, you should use multiple regression (using the novel scale as the dependent variable and E, N and P as independent variables) to extend this analysis and show whether scores on the novel scale are largely predictable from the well-known personality factors. This tells you whether the trait is worth measuring – or whether it is just a mixture of well-studied personality traits.

SAQ 6.3

Sensation seeking involves individuals seeking stimulation in a variety of ways – through aesthetics and lifestyle choices, avoidance of routine, hedonistic activities such as casual sex and seeking out thrilling physical activities.

SAQ 6.4

This work is important as it seeks to determine whether schizotypy is, indeed, a mild form of schizophrenia. It is easy to write some items that may assess mild psychotic symptoms, factor analyse them and try to interpret the factors in terms of the high-loading items. However this is only face validity: it is necessary to use the techniques of construct validity (Chapter 15) to determine whether high scores on this scale are associated with the low-level cognitive and emotional aberrations that characterize schizophrenia.

References

Adorno, T. W., Frenkel-Brunswick, E., Levinson, D. J. and Sanford, R. N. (1950). *The Authoritarian Personality*. New York: Harper.

Altemeyer, B. (1988). *Enemies of Freedom: Understanding Right-wing Authoritarianism* (1st edn). San Francisco: Jossey-Bass.

Altemeyer, B. (1998). The other 'authoritarian personality'. In *Advances in Experimental Social Psychology* (Vol. 30). San Diego, CA: Academic Press.

Amodio, D. M., Jost, J. T., Master, S. L. and Yee, C. M. (2007). Neurocognitive correlates of liberalism and conservatism. *Nature Neuroscience 10*(10), 1246–7.

Bardo, M. T., Donohew, R. L. and Harrington, N. G. (1996). Psychobiology of novelty seeking and drug seeking behavior. *Behavioural Brain Research 77*(1–2), 23–43.

Baumeister, R. F., Campbell, J. D., Krueger, J. I. and Vohs, K. D. (2003). Does high self-esteem cause better performance, interpersonal success, happiness, or healthier lifestyles? *Psychological Science in the Public Interest 4*(1), 1–44.

Block, J. and Block, J. H. (2006). Nursery school personality and political orientation two decades later. *Journal of Research in Personality 40*(5), 734–49.

Bouchard, T. J., Jr., Segal, N. L., Tellegen, A., McGue, M., Keyes, M. and Krueger, R. (2003). Evidence for the construct validity and heritability of the Wilson–Patterson Conservatism Scale: a reared-apart twins study of social attitudes. *Personality and Individual Differences 34*(6), 959–69.

Breivik, G. (1996). Personality, sensation seeking and risk taking among Everest climbers. *International Journal of Sport Psychology 27*(3), 308–20.

Cavallera, G. M. and Giudici, S. (2008). Morningness and eveningness personality: a survey in literature from 1995 up till 2006. *Personality and Individual Differences 44*(1), 3–21.

Chapman, L. J., Chapman, J. P., Kwapil, T. R., Eckblad, M. and Zinser, M. C. (1994). Putatively psychosis-prone subjects 10 years later. *Journal of Abnormal Psychology 103*(2), 171–83.

Chapman, L. J., Edell, W. S. and Chapman, J. P. (1980). Physical anhedonia, perceptual abberation, and psychosis proneness. *Schizophrenia Bulletin 6*, 639–53.

Claridge, G. S. (1985). *Origins of Mental Illness*. Oxford: Blackwell.

Claridge, G. S. (1997). *Schizotypy: Implications for Illness and Health*. Oxford: Oxford University Press.

Claridge, G. S. and Broks, P. (1984). Schizotypy and hemisphere function. 1. Theoretical considerations and the measurement of schizotypy. *Personality and Individual Differences 5*(6), 633–48.

Furnham, A. and Avison, M. (1997). Personality and preference for surreal paintings. *Personality and Individual Differences 23*(6), 923–35.

Glicksohn, J. and Abulafia, J. (1998). Embedding sensation seeking within the big three. *Personality and Individual Differences 25*(6), 1085–99.

Glicksohn, J. and Bozna, M. (2000). Developing a personality profile of the bomb-disposal expert: the role of sensation seeking and field dependence–independence. *Personality and Individual Differences 28*(1), 85–92.

Gooding, D. C., Miller, M. D. and Kwapil, T. R. (2000). Smooth pursuit eye tracking and visual fixation in psychosis- prone individuals. *Psychiatry Research 93*(1), 41–54.

Haynes, C. A., Miles, J. N. V. and Clements, K. (2000). A confirmatory factor analysis of two models of sensation seeking. *Personality and Individual Differences 29*, 823–39.

Iacono, W. G., Moreau, M., Beiser, M., Fleming, J. A. E. and Lin, T. Y. (1992). Smooth-pursuit eye tracking in 1st episode psychotic-patients and their relatives. *Journal of Abnormal Psychology 101*(1), 104–16.

Jones, A. (1969). Stimulus-seeking behavior. In J. P. Zubeck (ed.), *Sensory Deprivation: Fifteen Years of Research*. New York: Appleton Century Crofts.

Kish, G. B. (1966). Studies of sensory reinforcement. In W. K. Honig (ed.), *Operant Behavior*. Englewood Cliffs, NJ: Prentice-Hall.

Kline, P. (1999). *The handbook of psychological testing* (2nd edn). London and New York: Routledge.

Kline, P. and Cooper, C. (1984). A factorial analysis of the authoritarian personality. *British Journal of Psychology 75*(2), 171–6.

Klinteberg, B. (1996). The psychiatric personality in a longitudinal perspective. *European Child & Adolescent Psychiatry 5*, 57–63.

Krueger, J. I., Vohs, K. D. and Baumeister, R. F. (2008). Is the allure of self-esteem a mirage after all? *American Psychologist 63*(1), 64–5.

Lenzenweger, M. F. (2006a). Schizotaxia, schizotypy, and schizophrenia: Paul E. Meehl's blueprint for the experimental psychopathology and genetics of schizophrenia. *Journal of Abnormal Psychology 115*(2), 195–200.

Lenzenweger, M. F. (2006b). Schizotypy: An organizing framework for schizophrenia research. *Current Directions in Psychological Science 15*(4), 162–6.

Mason, O., Claridge, G. S. and Jackson, M. (1995). New scales for the assessment of schizotypy. *Personality and Individual Differences 18*(1), 7–13.

Mata, I., Sham, P. C., Gilvarry, C. M., Jones, P. B., Lewis, S. W. and Murray, R. M. (2000). Childhood schizotypy and positive symptoms in schizophrenic patients predict schizotypy in relatives. *Schizophrenia Research 44*(2), 129–36.

Matthews, G. (1988). Morningness–eveningness as a dimension of personality: trait, state, and psychophysiological correlates. *European Journal of Personality 2*(4), 277–93.

Meehl, P. E. (1962). Schizotaxia, schizotypy and schizophrenia. *American Psychologist 17*, 827–38.

Moritz, S. H., Mass, R. and Junk, U. (1998). Further evidence of reduced negative priming in positive schizotypy. *Personality and Individual Differences 24*(4), 521–30.

Netter, P., Hennig, J. and Roed, I. S. (1996). Serotonin and dopamine as mediators of sensation seeking behavior. *Neuropsychobiology 34*(3), 155–65.

Park, S. and Schoppe, S. (1997). Olfactory identification deficit in relation to schizotypy. *Schizophrenia Research 26*(2–3), 191–7.

Raine, A. (1991). The SPQ – a scale for the assessment of schizotypal personality based on DSM-III-R criteria. *Schizophrenia Bulletin 17*(4), 555–64.

Randler, C. (2008). Morningness–eveningness, sleep–wake variables and big five personality factors. *Personality and Individual Differences 45*(2), 191–6.

Rawlings, D., Claridge, G. S. and Freeman, J. L. (2001). Principal components analysis of the Schizotypal Personality Scale (STA) and the Borderline Personality Scale (STB). *Personality and Individual Differences 31*(3), 409–19.

Ray, J. J. (1970). The development and validation of a balanced dogmatism scale. *Australian Journal of Psychology 22*(3), 253–60.

Ray, J. J. (1979). Does authoritarianism of personality go with conservatism? *Australian Journal of Psychology 31*(1), 9–14.

Robins, R. W., Hendin, H. M. and Trzesniewski, K. H. (2001). Measuring global self-esteem: construct validation of a single-item measure and the Rosenberg Self-Esteem Scale. *Personality and Social Psychology Bulletin 27*(2), 151–61.

Rosenberg, M. (1965). *Society and the adolescent self-image.* Princeton, NJ: Princeton University Press.

Ruch, W. (1988). Sensation seeking and the enjoyment of structure and content of humor – stability of findings across 4 samples. *Personality and Individual Differences 9*(5), 861–71.

Seidman, L. J., Talbot, N. L., Kalinowski, A. G., McCarley, R. W., Faraone, S. V., Kremen, W. S. et al. (1991). Neuropsychological probes of fronto-limbic system dysfunction in schizophrenia – olfactory identification and Wisconsin Card Sorting Performance. *Schizophrenia Research 6*(1), 55–65.

Stanton, B., Li, X. M., Cottrell, L. and Kaljee, L. (2001). Early initiation of sex, drug-related risk behaviors, and sensation-seeking among urban, low-income African-American adolescents. *Journal of the National Medical Association 93*(4), 129–38.

Steel, C., Hemsley, D. R. and Jones, S. (1996). 'Cognitive inhibition' and schizotypy as measured by the Oxford–Liverpool inventory of feelings and experiences. *Personality and Individual Differences 20*(6), 769–73.

van Hiel, A., Kossowska, M. and Mervielde, I. (2000). The relationship between openness to experience and political ideology. *Personality and Individual Differences 28*(4), 741–51.

Williams, L. M. (1996). Cognitive inhibition and schizophrenic symptom subgroups. *Schizophrenia Bulletin 22*(1), 139–51.

Wilson, G. D. and Patterson, J. R. (1968). A new measure of conservatism. *British Journal of Social & Clinical Psychology 7*(4), 264–9.

Wilson, G. D. and Patterson, J. R. (1970). *Manual for the Conservatism Scale.* Windsor: NFER Publishing Company Ltd.

Zuckerman, M. (1979). *Sensation Seeking.* London: Wiley.

Zuckerman, M. (1994). *Behavioral Expressions and Biosocial Bases of Sensation Seeking.* Cambridge: Cambridge University Press.

Zuckerman, M., Kuhlman, D. M. and Camac, C. (1988). What lies beyond E and N – factor-analyses of scales believed to measure basic dimensions of personality. *Journal of Personality and Social Psychology 54*(1), 96–107.

Zuckerman, M., Kuhlman, D. M., Thornquist, M. and Kiers, H. (1991). 5 (or 3) robust questionnaire scale factors of personality without culture. *Personality and Individual Differences 12*(9), 929–41.

Zuckerman, M., Persky, H., Hopkins, T. R., Murtaugh, T., Basu, G. K. and Schilling, M. (1966). Comparison of stress effects of perceptual and social isolation. *Archives of General Psychiatry 14*, 356–65.

7 Biological, cognitive and social bases of personality

Background

At the start of Chapter 4, we stressed that merely identifying the main factors of personality does not imply an *understanding* of the underlying concepts and that trying to use such factors as explanations for behaviour is dangerously circular. We suggested that in order to use factors to *explain* behaviour it is necessary to show that the traits are much broader in scope than the specific questions posed in the questionnaires – for example, to show that a trait measured by a particular personality questionnaire is just one manifestation of some rather fundamental biological or social process that also affects other aspects of our behaviour.

Recommended prior reading

Chapter 4, perhaps Chapter 11.

Introduction

We have seen in Chapter 4 how there is now quite good agreement between theorists about two of the main personality factors (extraversion and neuroticism) – few would now disagree that these are the two main personality traits. However, merely establishing the *structure* of personality is only the first step in any scientific study of individual differences. Doctors have known a lot about the structure of the human body (the location of the main organs) for millennia, but it is only fairly recently that medical science has begun to understand how the organs operate and interact. So it is with personality. The main dimensions having been identified, the really interesting questions involve trying to understand:

- what causes certain behaviours to vary together to form these traits
- what causes an individual to develop a particular personality.

One possible answer to the second question is that personality traits (or rather the *potential* to show certain patterns of behaviour in certain situations) may, to some extent, be inherited from our parents. Because exactly the same techniques are used to find the extent to which intelligence is typically influenced by genes, the family environment or other aspects of our environment, these two issues are considered together in Chapter 11.

What, then, are the obvious possible determinants of personality? There are two main types of theory. Social theories stress the importance of the environment in personality development. For these theories, the prime determinant of the child's adult personality is the nature of the home in which children are raised. Such theories assume that newborns really are fairly similar in their biological makeup and potential for personality development. They also have to suggest that the environment (including social processes) is all important in maintaining adult personality. Biological theories, by way of contrast, suggest that all children are not equal at birth, if only because of their genetic makeup. They stress the importance of genetic factors and biological mechanisms (sometimes directly related to the amount of electrical activity in certain regions of the brain) in determining behaviour – or rather for creating the propensity for certain types of behaviour to be manifested, given the appropriate environmental conditions in both childhood and adult life.

Unfortunately, these two schools of personality theorists rather rarely talk to one another, they hold separate conferences and they tend to publish in rather different journals, so remarkably few studies consider the influence of both biological/genetic makeup and social processes on behaviour. This is a pity, since there is no logical reason why social theories have to assume that all individuals have functionally identical nervous systems (that is, nervous systems that operate in precisely the same way). Likewise, although biologically/genetically inclined theorists have to add the proviso 'given suitable environmental conditions' to all of their predictions about behaviour, they generally assume that people's environments (and developmental experiences) were rather similar.

Social determinants of personality

Perhaps childhood experience is all important, as Freud, Rogers and Kelly (and also theorists such as Bandura and Skinner) maintain. Freud would argue that the child's psychosexual development (overindulgence or frustration at a particular developmental stage) will lead to the emergence of certain adult personality traits, as might the particular pattern of defence mechanisms used, degree of Oedipal conflict, degree of identification with a parent, as well as specific childhood experiences. Thus the personality traits that we observe in questionnaires may simply reflect the adult consequences of different childrearing practices. The problem is, of course, that these concepts are difficult or impossible to assess, and so it is difficult or impossible to test this theory. Attempts to assess the main adult psychosexual personality types by means of questionnaires such as the Ai3 have only limited success and attempts to tie in adult personality types to critical events during children's psychosexual development have foundered, possibly (but not necessarily) because of the difficulties encountered in obtaining good, clear data about how individual children are weaned, potty trained, etc. (Kline 1981).

For Rogers, the person's view of their self, ideal self, etc., their self-consistency, congruence and the extent of self-actualization is all important. If a child is brought up in an environment in which it feels that it is loved *unconditionally* by its parents (when bad behaviour is followed by the message 'I don't like what you have just done', rather than 'I don't like you'), then the child will view itself as lovable and will grow up congruent and self-actualizing. Thus it seems reasonable to ask whether the main personality traits are themselves affected by parental attitudes.

At first glance, the evidence seems to suggest that they are. For example, Coopersmith (1967) found that children's self-esteem depended on unconditional, loving acceptance of the children by their parents, control using reward rather than punishment and clear indications of what was and was not acceptable behaviour. Thus it does seem clear that self-esteem is affected by the parents' behaviour and since scales measuring self-esteem correlate with extraversion and neuroticism (Kline 1993), these two personality factors may also affected by such social processes.

Of course, there is a flaw in these arguments. Suppose that self-esteem has a substantial genetic component. In that case it is possible that children of parents who have high self-esteem will also grow up to have high self-esteem because a predisposition to behave in this way has been transmitted genetically and not because of the way in which parents with high self-esteem behave towards their children. Contrariwise, if the family environment is all important (as assumed in Coopersmith's interpretation), then a social explanation is entirely appropriate. Unfortunately, this is a broad criticism of virtually all studies that attempt to assess the impact of parental behaviour on personality (or ability, for that matter). It is vital that such studies should consider the possibility that genes can influence both the parents' behaviour and the eventual behaviour or personality of the children.

Kelly's theory is less than explicit about how and why a particular individual develops a particular set of constructs and comes to construe him- or herself in a particular way. We know that children's construct systems become more complex and differentiated (Honess 1979), but how and why children develop rather different construct systems does not seem to be at all well understood – although I would be surprised if this was unrelated to the variety of people and events to which the child were exposed (a stimulating environment) and the perceived consistency of the behaviour of others (so allowing useful predictions to be made).

Self-assessment question 7.1

What is the main problem with any experiment that seeks to determine the effects of upbringing on behaviour – for example, by using surveys to determine whether certain forms of childrearing (e.g. loving acceptance of children by their parents) lead to certain personality traits (e.g. high self-esteem) in childhood or later life?

It is thus clear that determining the social influences on personality is a remarkably difficult research question, for the following reasons:

- It is often very difficult to collect accurate, quantitative information about the types of social interaction experienced by children.

- Some theories (e.g. that of Kelly) never really attempt to explain how personality develops. The notion that this is a social process is more of an assumption than a testable proposition.

- Just because certain forms of parental behaviour are found to be associated with certain personality characteristics in the offspring, it cannot be assumed that the parental behaviour *causes* the personality characteristic to emerge. It is possible that some genetically transmitted personality traits might generally lead to certain types of parenting behaviour, but that the genes, rather than these behaviours, will cause similar traits to emerge in the children. Which of these explanations is the correct one can only be determined by the experiments discussed in Chapter 11.

- Quantifying social influences is a particularly difficult process. Those that will have most effect on personality will (presumably) be those that take place over a long period of time with the parents and other members of the family – in young children, at any rate. Fortunately, the methods of behaviour genetics allow us to determine the extent to which the 'family ethos' influences personality without having to assess the interactions in detail. If it is assumed that parents generally treat their children fairly equally (an assumption that research does show to be reasonably true), then the 'family ethos' should cause all children in a family to develop similar personalities. By assessing the similarity of the personalities of children within a family and comparing this with the similarity of personalities *between* families it is possible to estimate the extent to which the family ethos moulds personality.

However, there is another way of quantifying the effect of social variables, namely by attempting to determine the extent to which *biological* variables can account for individual differences in personality and assuming that the remainder is due to various types of social factor.

Biological bases of personality: Eysenck's theory

The biological approach suggests that all nervous systems are not the same – there may be individual differences in the structure and function of people's nervous systems and this can account for the emergence of personality traits. That is, any group of behaviours that vary together (and are identified as traits by factor analysis) do so because they are all influenced by some brain structure(s). The useful thing about such an approach is that it is much easier to test empirically than are social theories. With modern psychophysiological techniques – including exotica such as functional magnetic resonance imaging (fMRI) – it is easier to check whether individual differences in personality are reliably associated with individual differences in structure and function of the nervous system than it is to attempt to analyse social interactions that may have taken place years previously.

Of course, this begs the question of how and why individual differences in nervous system structure and function themselves come about. It is not impossible that such factors may affect the development of the nervous system, in which case social factors might affect personality through the mediation of neural mechanisms. However, most proponents of the biological approach do not address this question directly.

Self-assessment question 7.2

What I have painted here is a fairly 'reductionist' view of personality and one with which some readers may feel uneasy. What are the objections to looking for the roots of personality in the physiology and biochemistry of the nervous system?

Hans Eysenck (1967) put forward a general biological theory to explain the origins of extraversion and neuroticism, with Eysenck and Eysenck (1985) summarizing much of the empirical work that followed the publication of this theory. Matthews and Gilliland (1999) provide an excellent summary of this theory and a similar animal-based model of Jeffrey Gray. The theory has been updated and modified somewhat by David Robinson (1996) but I shall not consider these modifications as they are rather complex and not, as yet, supported by a great deal of data.

Biological basis of neuroticism

Eysenck viewed neuroticism as a factor of 'emotionality' – highly neurotic individuals will tend to give extreme emotional responses (tears, fear) to life events that may well leave more stoic, low-neuroticism individuals emotionally unmoved. Thus if some brain structure is known to control the extent of such emotional reactions, it is possible that neuroticism may simply reflect individual differences in the sensitivity of this system to external stimuli. If temperature is used

99

as an analogy for the degree of emotional content of a thought, perception or memory, we can view neurotic and stable individuals as having their thermostats set to different levels. For highly neurotic people, a small increase in emotional temperature is enough to trigger the thermostat and activate a full emotional response. For stable individuals, the emotional response is activated only in response to a gross increase in emotional temperature.

The limbic system is one of closely linked structures (including the hippocampus, hypothalamus, amygdala, cingulum and septum) towards the base of the brain – Eysenck sometimes refers to this system as the *visceral* brain. It has long been known to be involved in the initiation of emotional activity. It affects the sympathetic branch of the autonomic nervous system, which is often known as the 'flight or fight' mechanism, since its activation can be viewed as preparing the organism for either of these two behaviours. Activation of the sympathetic nervous system results in faster heart rate, increased respiration rate, increased blood flow to the limbs, increased sweating and a closing down of the blood supply to the gut and other organs that are not involved in urgent physical activity. Unpleasant emotional feelings, such as fear, anxiety or anger, are also experienced. The terms anxiety and neuroticism are closely linked, with anxiety being a mixture of neuroticism and low levels of extraversion (Eysenck 1973; Eysenck and Eysenck 1985). However, in the discussion that follows I shall use the terms 'anxiety' and 'neuroticism' interchangeably, since they correlate together with a value of about 0.7 (Eysenck and Eysenck 1985). We know that anxiety can be assessed by questionnaires and that activity in the autonomic nervous system can be assessed by a number of techniques. These include the psychogalvanic response (PGR), in which the skin resistance is measured on a part of the body that is well endowed with sweat glands. The burst of sweating that follows increased activity of the autonomic nervous system leads to a decrease in electrical resistance, which can be measured. Thus it is possible to test this theory directly, as people with high levels of anxiety should produce more emotional physiological responses to moderately stressful stimuli (unpleasant pictures, perhaps) than individuals with low anxiety levels.

Biological basis of extraversion

Eysenck's theory of extraversion involves another structure at the base of the brain, known as the ascending reticular activating system (ARAS). This fearsome-sounding structure simply controls the amount of electrical activity that takes place in the cortex – it is a kind of 'dimmer switch' for the electrical activity in the cortex. It should also be mentioned here, for completeness, that there are nerve fibres linking the ARAS with the limbic system, so the two systems are not entirely neurologically independent. Perhaps as a consequence of this, most workers find a correlation of about –0.3 between the extraversion and neuroticism scales of the Eysenck Personality Questionnaire (EPQ). Eysenck proposed that:

- the ARASs of intraverts and extraverts operate at different levels, as a result of which the cortices of intraverts are habitually much more electrically active ('aroused') than those of extraverts

- a moderate degree of cortical arousal is experienced as being pleasurable, whereas very high or very low levels of cortical arousal are experienced as being unpleasurable.

Of course, factors other than the ARAS can arouse the cortex, the most obvious of which is sensory stimulation. Looking at changing images, listening to music and talking to people can all lead to increases in cortical electrical activity. Eysenck argues that, under quiet conditions (e.g. working in a library), extraverts – whose cortices are normally not very highly aroused – may experience unpleasurable feelings since their level of cortical arousal is considerably below the point that is felt as pleasurable. Therefore they do something about it – talking to others, listening to music on headphones, taking frequent break for caffeine and conversation, and generally behaving in ways guaranteed to infuriate intraverts. For intraverts are *naturally* highly aroused and any further increase in arousal level is distinctly unpleasurable. Extraverts need a constant environmental 'buzz' to arouse their cortices to pleasurable levels, whereas intraverts would find any such stimulation over-arousing and hence unpleasurable.

It has been found that drugs that increase or decrease the level of arousal in the cortex also affect the ease with which animals learn a conditioned response. This suggests another extension of the theory and Eysenck claims that intraverts should therefore condition more easily than extraverts because of their higher levels of cortical arousal. For example, if an intravert has several unpleasant emotional experiences in a particular setting (e.g. turning over an examination paper and not knowing any of the answers), he or she should be more likely than an extravert to develop feelings of fear, depression or anxiety when entering that room or to show avoidance behaviour. These symptoms are conditioned emotional responses, which naturally suggests that behaviour therapy is the technique of choice for removing them.

This is Eysenck's theory of extraversion and it is clearly empirically testable. Measuring electrical activity in the ARAS is admittedly difficult (because of its position at the base of the brain), but assessing the electrical activity of the cortex and the ease with which classical or operant conditioning takes place is straightforward. Other techniques are possible, too, as will be seen in the next section.

Biological basis of psychoticism

Psychoticism is much less well understood and some researchers have suggested alternatives to this trait: for example, conscientiousness and agreeableness in the five-factor model (Chapter 4) and the discussion of sensation seeking in Chapter 6. However, Eysenck noted that levels of psychoticism were much higher in males than in females and that criminals and schizophrenics (both of whom tend to have high P scores) also tend to be male. Therefore Eysenck suggested (Eysenck and Eysenck 1985) that psychoticism is linked to levels of male hormones (e.g. androgens) and perhaps to other chemicals (e.g. serotonin and certain antigens). Again, this theory (albeit rudimentary) is clearly testable.

Self-assessment question 7.3

How might one test whether Eysenck's theory of psychoticism is correct?

Problems with Eysenck's theory

Eysenck therefore suggests that the three main personality dimensions may be directly linked to the biological and hormonal makeup of the body. We may display certain patterns of personality because our nervous systems work in slightly different ways and it is these individual differences that are picked up by factor analysis and interpreted as personality traits. It is tempting to argue that certain people 'just are' extraverted because of the level of arousal which their ARAS imparts to their cortex and that there is no need to consider any environmental explanations at all.

However, even if individual differences in cortical activity were found to explain completely the individual differences in extraversion, this begs the question of why one person's ARAS works at a rather different level from that of another. Could *this* be influenced by life events? This is where genetic studies of personality (discussed in Chapter 11) are so useful, as they can indicate the relative importance of biological and environmental determinants of personality at any age.

Our understanding of brain structure and function has changed considerably since Eysenck's book was published in 1967. The theory also fails to take into account other important phenomena, e.g. lateralization. Zuckerman (1991) points to a huge body of evidence from brain-damaged patients showing that personality change following damage to the cortex depends on whether the left or the right hemisphere is affected and it seems that neuroticism is modestly related to difference in activation between the mid portion of the left and right frontal lobes (Minnix and Kline 2004). However, Eysenck's theories do not distinguish between the left and right hemispheres.

However, the great advantage of the biological theories is that they can be shown to be incorrect. This is in stark contrast to many (one is tempted to say 'most') of the mechanisms suggested by other theorists – terms such as self-actualization, id processes, defence mechanisms, self-congruence and so on, are difficult to define and assess, and belong to models that are so complex that they cannot easily be verified. The simplicity of Eysenck's model probably means that it will be unable to explain the origins of personality *perfectly*, although one should surely always prefer a simple but empirically verifiable model to a complex model that cannot be falsified.

Eysenck's biological theory of personality: empirical results

Extraversion

Eysenck and Eysenck (1985) consider a number of hypotheses that flow naturally from the cortical arousal theory of extraversion, together with a discussion of the main research findings and this section owes much to their work.

If extraversion is biologically based, it seems reasonable to suggest that individual differences in the underlying brain structures may be genetically transmitted. Hence studies of the genetics of extraversion may be valuable for testing the broad idea that extraversion may have a biological basis. This does *not*, of course, test the specific arousal hypothesis already discussed. However, if extraversion could be shown to be determined entirely by the way in which children are reared, it is perhaps less likely that it would be related to individual differences in neurology than if it could be seen to have a strong genetic component. This entire issue is covered in some depth in Chapter 11, which concludes that there is evidence that individual differences in extraversion have a substantial genetic component.

Extraversion and the electroencephalogram (EEG)

By comparison with extraverts, one would expect intraverts with higher levels of arousal to show:

- greater habitual levels of cortical arousal

- stronger responses to novel stimuli.

The electroencephalogram (EEG) is a technique for analysing electrical activity in the brain by attaching metal electrodes to the surface of the scalp in carefully standardized positions and measuring the differences in voltage between each electrode and a neutral point (such as the ear-lobe). The electrical signals travel around inside the head in a fairly complicated manner, but it is possible to measure the electrical activity in several of the main brain structures by this method and, fortunately, the cortex is one of these areas (just beneath the skull). The EEG is usually plotted as a graph of electrical voltage against time and is often analysed (using a mathematical technique known as *Fourier analysis*) in order to determine whether there are regular, periodic variations in the electrical activity and, if so, their frequency.

For example, Figure 7.1 (a) shows regular low-amplitude, high-frequency electrical activity. 'Low amplitude' means that the changes in voltage from peak to trough in the graph are fairly small, of the order of 25 to 100 microvolts (millionths of a volt). 'High frequency' means that the voltage changes direction quite often. Low-amplitude brainwaves that change direction with a frequency of between eight and 13 cycles per second are known as *alpha activity*. Alpha activity is typically found when people are wide awake and alert, so the simplest possible test of Eysenck's cortical arousal hypothesis would merely involve assessing how cortically aroused people were (as indicated by the EEG) and correlating this with their scores on the extraversion scale of the EPQ(R).

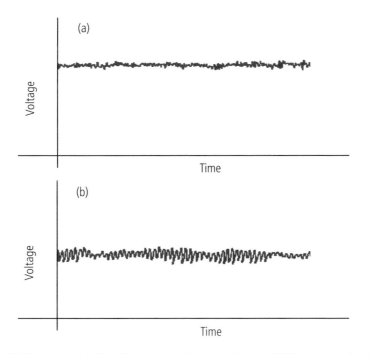

Figure 7.1 Two EEG traces: (a) high-frequency, low-amplitude EEG trace, indicative of alertness; (b) low-frequency, high-amplitude EEG trace, indicative of relaxation.

Gale (1983) reviewed the literature and found that intraverts were more aroused than extraverts in 22 out of 38 studies, thus providing evidence in support of Eysenck's theory. He felt that methodological problems with several of the studies probably muddied the picture; when particularly careful studies are performed relationships between EEG activity and extraversion can be found (e.g. Hagemann et al. 2009). Tran, Craig and McIsaac (2001) designed a study that took on board Gale's methodological comments and found that far fewer extraverts than intraverts showed high arousal in the frontal cortex (the trend was not significant for the posterior parts of the cortex).

PET scans and extraversion

The easy (but expensive!) way to check what is going on in the brain is to throw away the electrodes and examine how much energy each part of the brain is metabolizing. Positron emission tomography (PET) scans examine this directly and involve injecting radioactively labelled glucose into a vein and monitoring which part(s) of the brain eventually use it. Do intraverts' cortices really seem to use more glucose than those of extraverts? One study suggests so, but two find that some regions of extraverts' cortices are more active than those of intraverts (Deckersbach et al. 2006; Haier et al. 1987; Kim et al. 2008). A similar technique (again using a radioactive tracer) that examined the amount of blood flow in various parts of the brain did, however, reveal significant correlations of between -0.21 and -0.41 between the amount of blood flow and extraversion, in several different areas of the cortex (Mathew, Weinman and Barr 1984). Johnson et al. (1999) managed to partially replicate this effect, with intraverts showing significantly greater cerebral blood flow in the frontal cortex. These studies are rather inconclusive.

Classical and operant conditioning

You will recall that drugs which affect cortical arousal also affect the ease with which animals form conditioned responses. If extraversion is linked to cortical arousal, one might therefore expect ease of conditioning to be related to scores on extraversion in humans. The main problem here is that cognitive factors (e.g. conscious awareness of the reinforcement contingencies – the nature of the reinforcement schedule being used) are thought to complicate matters whenever conditionability is being assessed in humans, as can the precise detail of the conditioning task (e.g. the strength of the unconditioned stimulus).

The most commonly used paradigm for humans is classical conditioning of the eye-blink response to a tone. A tone is followed by a puff of air to the eye, which elicits the eye-blink response. After several such pairings, the tone alone will produce the eye blink and the number of trials before this is achieved is a measure of the person's conditionability. However, the problem is that when speed of conditioning is measured in the same individuals using a number of different experimental paradigms, the results simply do not show substantial correlations between the different paradigms. So, for humans, there is probably no such thing as general 'conditionability' (Eysenck and Eysenck 1985). That said, a recent study on acquisition of the fear response by Pineles, Vogt and Orr (2009) found that the warmth and activity facets of Costa and McCrae's extraversion factor correlated as expected, but the positive emotion facet correlated in the wrong direction.

Sedation thresholds

One rather crude way of assessing the activity of a cortex involves determining the amount of a sedative drug required to make individuals unconscious (as assessed by the EEG or lack of responsiveness to words). As intraverts are more cortically aroused, they may require higher doses than extraverts to make them unconscious (although many other factors may also affect the required dosage). This is so – but only for moderate or high-level neurotics (Claridge, Donald and Birchall 1981).

Self-assessment question 7.4

Why is it important to discover the processes that cause personality?

Neuroticism

There are several problems with Hans Eysenck's (1967) biological theory of neuroticism. First, the genetic component is not nearly as large as for extraversion, which suggests that a purely biological model may be inappropriate (see Chapter 11). Second, empirical evidence suggests that 'arousal' in the autonomic nervous system is not nearly as simple as was previously thought. Different individuals express signs of autonomic arousal in different ways. When frightened, some people may sweat, others may show muscle activity (twitching or trembling), some will show increased heart rate and others may show an increase in pupil size. Very few individuals show all these responses. Thus, although almost all neurotic people *claim* to feel sweaty hands, churning stomachs, pounding hearts and so on, when the electrodes are attached, the psychophysiological measures do not form a factor. Some of the reasons why this might be the case have been discussed by Lacey and Lacey (1970) and Pennebaker (1982). Thus consistent differences between the EEG measures (etc.) of low- and high-neuroticism individuals are rarely found (Fahrenberg, Schneider and Safian 1987). Finally, the model ignores cognition: as anxiety is a highly unpleasant emotion, it seems reasonable to suppose that people will develop strategies for dealing with warnings of threat or danger. Thus an information-processing theory might offer a useful alternative.

Michael Eysenck (Hans Eysenck's son) has developed such a theory and there is now good evidence that highly anxious people are hypervigilant. They explore the environment with their senses and so show more eye movements, look out for threat-related stimuli in the environment and, when they find them, process them more deeply. For example, Eysenck and Byrne (1992) gave their volunteers a switch to hold in each hand. They were shown stimuli consisting of three words. One of these words was always 'left' or 'right' and the participants were simply asked to look for this word (ignoring the others) and press the appropriate button. The dependent variable was the time taken to press the button from the onset of the display. A range of distractor words was used. As well as various control conditions, various types of threatening words ('failure', 'murder') were also shown. Highly anxious individuals (a) responded more slowly overall to words (indicating that they were processing them more deeply than the stable individuals) and (b) were particularly badly distracted by physically threatening words. In another experiment, Byrne and Eysenck (1995) found that highly anxious individuals were better able to search through a screenful of faces and detect the threatening (angry) ones. There was no difference between the groups' performance when searching for happy faces. The theory has been developed further: see Eysenck (2000) for a useful review.

Weinberger, Schwartz and Davidson (1979) highlighted a major difficulty with assessing anxiety/neuroticism using a questionnaire: what should be inferred if a person shows a low score? They found that some people who obtained low scores on a questionnaire actually showed quite marked physiological and behavioural signs of anxiety. They seemed to experience anxiety, but denied that they had these emotions when completing the questionnaire. Derakshan and Eysenck (1999) show that these individuals seem to be genuinely out of touch with their emotions (rather than consciously trying to mislead the experimenters) and a common approach has been to scrutinize the social desirability scores of those who produce low scores on an a questionnaire measure of anxiety or neuroticism. Those with high social desirability scores are thought to be emotional repressors. So only those with low scores on both measures are regarded as genuinely experiencing low anxiety.

Reinforcement sensitivity theory (RST)

Reinforcement sensitivity theory (RST) is a modern, biologically based theory of personality that stems from the work of Jeffrey Gray in the 1960s. You will recall that Eysenck initially proposed that Extraversion and Neuroticism were independent (uncorrelated) and so they were often represented as shown in Figure 7.2 (a).

Gray proposed that instead of placing the axes as suggested by Eysenck, they could be spun round slightly as shown in Figure 7.2 (b) to give two main personality factors: one indicating sensitivity to reward, the other sensitivity to punishment. Why? Gray's background was in animal psychology and by positioning the axes as shown, they better described how animals (rats) behave: Gray's theory of personality is an animal model that has been extrapolated to people. As the axes are just rotated (rather than introducing other dimensions of personality), it is important to appreciate that it is easy to transform scores from Eysenck's questionnaire measures of extraver-

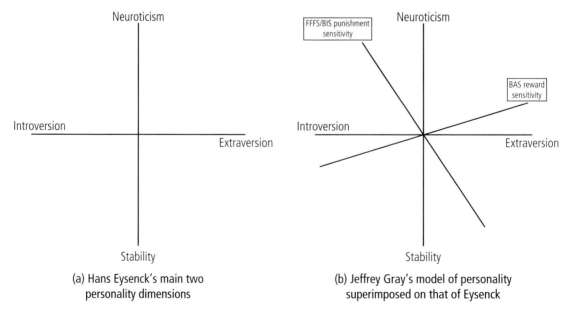

(a) Hans Eysenck's main two personality dimensions

(b) Jeffrey Gray's model of personality superimposed on that of Eysenck

Figure 7.2 Eysenck's and Gray's models of personality.

sion and neuroticism into scores on Gray's two dimensions, using a little elementary trigonometry, although this does not seem to be done in practice. (See the section on factor rotation in Chapter 17 if these ideas seem a little strange.)

Eysenck's biological model sought to relate scores on personality tests directly to physiological measures (e.g. those reflecting autonomic nervous system activity or cortical arousal). Gray's theory instead suggests that individual differences in the physiology of the nervous system, together with the individual's reinforcement history and their level of arousal, may determine the way in which the components of the 'conceptual nervous system' the cns operate. (*CNS* in capitals is the abbreviation for the central nervous system, as usual.) According to Gray (1982) the cns consists of various neurological systems that lead to rather universal sets of behaviours shown by many animals and by humans: for example, running away from or cautiously approaching a novel object or 'freezing' when encountering it. These sets of behaviours have been studied using three main means. The first examines how animals (typically rats) react when they encounter novel objects. What patterns of behaviour do they display and what features of the environment determine which action they show? The second method examines the effects of drugs on animal behaviour. For example, some drugs will stop animals from showing any interest in food and inhibit the normal 'cautious approach' behaviour when an animal encounters a novel object. Some drugs alter the behaviour of rats after they have been given an electric shock: they do not avoid the area/object in which the shock was delivered, neither do they run away as vigorously following shock. Anthropomorphically, one might speculate that they feel less fear. Other drugs others cause animals to 'freeze', apparently unable to make decisions about what to do. Finally, physiological psychologists have also studied those areas and systems of the brain that seem to be important for these types of behaviour, typically by observing differences in how they react when certain parts of the brain of living animals are removed or destroyed or (in humans) by noting which areas of the brain are activated when encountering pleasant or potentially dangerous objects. McNaughton and Corr (2008) offer a comprehensive account of this area.

Self-assessment question 7.5

What are the two main differences between Eysenck's and Gray's personality theories?

The key point is that the various components (Gray calls them 'systems') of the cns each produce their own distinctive behaviours and (perhaps) subjective feelings, such as pleasure or anxiety or fear. These are states – they come and go in response to environmental events – but the important thing about RST is that the various physiological systems that influence our responses to interesting or potentially dangerous objects are thought to 'kick in' in different ways for different people. Thus some people are more likely than others to show the state anxiety response. Such a person will therefore show a high score on a test measuring trait anxiety, as they experience anxiety much of the time, in response to life events that would leave some others unaffected. Thus the habitual sensitivity of the various parts of the cns should effectively determine a person's personality. However, in order to describe how an individual will behave in a particular situation, it is also possible to consider the effects of particular stimuli on the various cns systems: the same systems can explain both personality (how the person generally behaves) and mood/emotion (resulting from the sensitivity of the components of the individual's cns and the particular stimuli being evaluated).

Gray's theory has evolved considerably since it was first proposed. The initial ideas appeared in Gray (1970), were developed more fully in Gray (1982), revised by Gray and McNaughton (2000) and then modified again by McNaughton and Corr (2004). The differences are sometimes quite subtle but sometimes quite far reaching. (One colleague who will probably want to remain anonymous has commented, somewhat waspishly, that it is difficult to evaluate the theory because every time it seems not to work it just metamorphoses into something else.) But to avoid confusion this book will deal with only the most recent version of the theory.

In the latest versions of the theory, and for humans, it is thought that unexpected non-reward is equivalent to punishment and that unexpected non-punishment is equivalent to reward. For example, if you are used to being given a birthday present by a relative, if s/he does not give you a gift one year you will experience this in much the same way as you would a punishment. Likewise, if you expect negative consequences from an action and these do not happen, you will experience this in much the same way as reward. For example, if every time you play a video game your character is killed at the same spot, you will feel a surge of pleasure on an occasion when your character survives. These issues may sound obvious, but strict behaviourists would make a distinction between non-reward and punishment: the rest of us (and Gray) would be happy to talk in cognitive terms about people's (and perhaps animals') expectations.

Systems of the conceptual nervous system

The basic principle of Gray's theory is very simple. How an animal or person reacts to some entity (e.g. dish of food, snake, person, statistics textbook) depends on (a) whether the entity is perceived positively or negatively, (b) its proximity and (c) whether it is possible to physically get away from it. Gray suggested that there are three main elements of the conceptual nervous system that are directly related to personality traits.

Behavioural approach system (BAS)

'Appetitive stimuli' is the term used by behaviourists to describe things that animals and people approach or will work to achieve: food, potential mates, electrical stimulation of the hypothalamus, etc. Some stimuli are also conditioned to these stimuli (using operative or classical conditioning techniques) and these conditioned reinforcers (also known as secondary reinforcers) also act as appetitive stimuli. For example, our cat loves ham. For her, ham is an appetitive stimulus: if you put some on the floor, she will run towards it and devour it. Ham comes in a plastic wrapper that makes a distinctive sound when touched and because the rattle of the wrapper occurs before she is given ham, the sound has been classically conditioned and now serves as a conditioned reinforcer. Pip will therefore run towards anyone who rattles plastic. I have deliberately specified this in very 'dry' language so as not to annoy strict behaviourists (if there are any left in the world): more colloquially, we could just say that the BAS reflects the tendency to approach things that are anticipated with pleasure, either because they are intrinsically pleasant (e.g. food) or have previously been associated with pleasant things (e.g. money, going shopping).

Pickering, Smillie and Corr (2008) discuss this system in some detail. They make the point that the BAS motivates people to seek out potential sources of reward and also focuses attention on signs of reward, making it more likely that new stimuli will become conditioned onto the rewarding stimulus. If our cat has an unusually active BAS, she will focus on finding 'fun' things to do (e.g. searching out leaves to play with, food to eat rather than sitting or sleeping) and will also learn which things are associated with rewards (e.g. the rattling ham wrapper, a word that means that she will be fed) more readily than other cats.

At a gross level, the physiological basis of the BAS seems to be linked to the level of the neurotransmitter dopamine in the brain. The review by Schultz (1998) makes it clear that drugs that reduce the amount of dopamine available to brain cells (e.g. leva-dopa) lead to reduced motivation, reduced feelings of pleasure and weaker learning and additional evidence to support this view comes from studies such as one showing that dopamine levels are apparently reduced when one eats a substantial meal after fasting (important, because eating will bring about lower motivation towards food; Small, Jones-Gotman and Dagher 2003). Drugs that increase dopamine levels in the brain (e.g. haloperidol, Ritalin) have the opposite effect (see Volkow et al. 2002 for a comprehensive review): they lead to greater levels of motivation.

As far as personality is concerned, someone with a highly reactive BAS may be impulsive (doing things because they think there is a chance that this may lead to a reward) optimistic (forever looking out for signs of reward) and may be more susceptible to rewarding events (e.g. the effect of recreational drugs, which may lead to an increased chance of addiction). Thus the theory leads to clearly testable hypotheses. It should be possible to relate some aspects of behaviour and personality directly to the ways in which some parts of the brain function.

Several personality questionnaires have been developed to try to measure which characteristics are typical of someone with a highly sensitive BAS. Most people use the Carver and White (1994) BAS scale. This consists of items measuring drive, fun seeking and reward responsiveness, although other scales have been developed (Torrubia, Avila and Caseras 2008). However, many of these scales have problems. Unlike (for example) Eysenck's EPQ questionnaire, which forms factors precisely as it should (Eysenck, Eysenck and Barrett, 1985), the Carver and White BAS items generally form two factors, reward sensitivity and impulsivity suggesting that BAS is not a unitary concept as far as personality is concerned. Advocates of RST claim that the BAS should be able to explain why activity in some dopamine systems may be linked to various aspects of behaviour – even though (unlike some other theories, such as Eysenck's) the identification and measurement of personality traits has been the last step in the process, rather than the first.

But which of the many dopamine systems in the brain are linked to the BAS? Neurophysiological evidence suggests that the ventral striatum is involved. This is a small area deep down underneath the cortex at the front of the brain, tucked cosily against the basal ganglia. In one study (Pessiglione et al. 2006), some human participants were given drugs to reduce dopamine levels, some were given drugs to increase dopamine levels and some were given a placebo. They then took part in a task where they could choose one of two stimuli on a computer screen, only one of which was a fairly strong predictor of a monetary reward ($p = 0.8$). Dopamine levels affected performance at this task exactly according to expectations: those with increased dopamine levels won more money because they were more sensitive to the sign of reward. But the important thing about this task is that fMRI analysis showed that activity in the ventral striatum and their afferents were related to task performance; it seems probable that the BAS is essentially located here. Pickering et al. (2008) review other evidence that leads to much the same conclusion.

In summary, then, animal models suggest that a set of behaviours (sensitivity to signs of reward) corresponding to the BAS tend to occur together. This should hardly be a surprise: after all, the whole notion of the BAS stemmed from animal work in this area. In humans, people with a highly reactive BAS should, in theory, react positively to novel objects/people/events and be more likely to approach them, should spend more time seeking out possible sources of reward **109** and should learn which events predict reward more easily than other individuals. The Carver and White BAS scale seems to form two factors rather than one, which is a definite problem for the theory. However, this scale was (apparently arbitrarily) built of items measuring fun seeking, responsiveness to signs of reward and drive: it is not clear why it contains nothing on impulsivity, for example. The brain areas that are linked to the BAS are now starting to be understood, and it does seem likely that in humans, 'approach behaviour' mediated by the BAS has its origins in the dopamine system and that the ventral striatum is likely to be involved.

Behavioural inhibition system (BIS) and the flight-fright-freeze system (FFFS)

Imagine that you were to encounter a dangerous wild animal when walking in a remote part of the countryside. What would you do? There seem to be three obvious options open to you: escaping (e.g. running away or climbing a tree – but can it outrun you or climb?), staying very still (in case it mistakes you for an inanimate object or believes that you are dead) or moving towards it, attacking it and trying to scare it away. Or should you perhaps take no special action at all – for example, if it is so far away that it poses no threat to you. These are the sorts of encounter experienced by many animals every day and so it seems probable that humans too may have evolved/inherited systems that are broadly similar in order to deal with them. If so, it is possible that there may be individual differences in the ease with which these systems are activated, their reactivity, which may lead to individual differences in personality.

> These systems may also link in directly to the experience of emotion. What emotion would you feel when you saw the savage animal? What emotion would you feel as you decide whether to run, freeze or confront the animal?

One might perhaps expect there to be one system to explain escape behaviour, another for freezing behaviour and a third (perhaps connected to the BAS) to explain approach/fighting behaviour. (It is possible that the systems that deal with responses to threat may also connect to the BAS, given that the third option involves approaching and attacking the threatening object.) However, matters are a little more complicated than that and based on behaviour and physiological evidence just two systems have been proposed: the behavioural inhibition system (BIS) and the fight-flight-freeze system (FFFS). In humans, at least, the BIS corresponds to anxiety and the FFFS to fear. These two systems interact to influence sensitivity to punishment, as shown in Figure 7.1.

The purpose of the FFFS is to keep the animal alive by escaping from the situation, confronting the threat (but only if the threat is at, or close to, the defensive distance) or staying still (freezing). Fear and anxiety are two separate emotions that may be felt during this process – anxiety being thought to occur as the animal approaches the source of potential threat and fear being experienced as the animal leaves the area of danger.

The BIS typically deals with conflict between competing goals. When there is a clear course of action (for example, if the animal is offered food without any obvious risk or when a predator appears at a particular defensive distance) then the BAS or FFFS will determine what the animal will do. However very often, there are costs and benefits to be weighed. What if the potential 'food' is alive and has teeth? Is it better to approach the prey to satisfy hunger, but risk injury, or to avoid it completely? When activated in this example, the BIS involves the animal evaluating the signs of danger and possible benefits of approaching the object, perhaps gathering more information (e.g. studying its behaviour or thinking about previous encounters) until eventually a decision is taken whether to approach the object or flee. The precise mechanisms involved in this are uncertain, although the BIS is thought to raise levels of arousal. Corr (2008a: 11) suggests that the BIS inhibits both the FFFS and the BAS (so that the animal neither flees from nor approaches the threat). The BIS also sets in train risk assessment and inputs to the FFFS which provides the negative emotional fuel to the BIS. If the level of threat is deemed high, then the FFFS-mediated escape/avoidance kicks in, otherwise the level of threat is lowered and behaviour reverts to BAS-mediated approach. The important point about defensive distance is that it activates selective neural modules and therefore specific defensive behaviours. Fear and anxiety reducing drugs do not affect all behaviours, but can be understood only by reference to changes in perceived defensive distance and its effects on selective modules/behaviours. Subjectively, Corr suggests that the operation of the BIS may feel like worry – 'what to do'.

As far as personality is concerned, Corr (2008a: 11) suggests that if the BIS is not easily activated, the animal will approach threat when it probably should not. In people, this may translate into someone who cannot see danger when it exists and indulges in risky behaviours ('sensation seeking', impulsivity, etc.). By the same token, someone whose BIS activates too easily may worry excessively as a result of seeing potential threats and spend far too much time weighing up various possible courses of action.

The BIS does more than determine whether to approach or flee from a potential threat (weighing up the demands of the BAS and FFFS). There may be conflicts between several FFFS outputs or between several BAS outputs. For example, a few minutes ago your BIS may have made you agonize about whether you should read this book (which may have positive outcomes in terms of helping you to pass your exams, making you appear knowledgeable to your tutor etc.) or instead go out with your friends and enjoy a night's chat and relaxation. That is an example of how the BIS may be used to choose between two different 'approach' possibilities identified by the BAS.

But does the animal decide whether to attack, run or freeze? 'Defensive distance' is a term used to describe the perceived strength of the threat to which the animal is exposed. This will affect the behavioural response that is made. Suppose that an animal normally runs away if a certain predator approaches closer than 10 metres. If the animal encounters a more dangerous predator, the flight response will occur at a greater distance. Thus the behaviour of the animal should depend on its cognitive evaluation of the severity of the threat and the physical proximity of the threat. If animals behaved consistently like this, it might be possible to estimate the animal's perception of the threat offered by various predators. It is proposed that defensive distance is related to both behaviour and emotion. A threat encountered very close (e.g. a rat ambling across your desk: a small defensive distance) would lead to 'explosive attack' (Corr 2008a: 15), you might perhaps throw this book at it and feel panic. If the rat appeared on the other side of the room, you are perhaps likely to run out of the door and feel fear: if the rat is between you and the door, you might well just freeze and stay as still as possible. And if you see the rat at a very great distance (e.g. outside) you are unlikely to react at all. Thus the 'defensive distance' is thought to determine whether the FFFS leads to a 'fight' response, a 'flight' response, or no response.

The biological basis of this work comes from Blanchard, Blanchard, McNaughton and Andrews **111**

(1990) who studied the responses of rodents at various distances from predators. When they encountered a predator very close up, the rodents attacked it violently. If the predator was a little further away, the rodent made threatening sounds and signs towards it. If the predator was still little further away, the rodent ran away if there was an escape route or froze if not.

What happens if animals are given either drugs which reduce anxiety in humans? One would expect the former to reduce the perceived defensive distance: the rat can approach a human more closely before the escape response is triggered. McNaughton and Corr (2008) summarize the considerable literature showing that anxiety-reducing drugs influence a number of brain structures, such as the amygdala and cingulate cortex (areas that are also implicated in Eysenck's biological theory). One interesting (and perhaps counterintuitive) result to come from this work is the suggestion that fear and anxiety are very different, with fear being associated with escape from threat (FFFS) and anxiety being associated with cautious approach towards something that may or may not turn out to be dangerous.

Summary

This chapter has examined theories that view personality as either a social or a biological phenomenon and it should be clear by this stage that neither of the views is exclusively correct. Chapter 11 will reveal that the main personality factors have a substantial genetic component, which suggests that purely social explanations of behaviour are unlikely to be adequate. However, when we delve into the psychophysiological literature, it is equally clear that relatively few experiments provide unequivocal evidence in support of Eysenck's model of extraversion. Stimulus intensity has an annoying habit of confusing results. However, the fact that several of the studies do show significant correlations seems to suggest that there may be some underlying truth in the premise that extraversion is related to the degree of arousal in the cortex, although two studies that correlate personality with resting metabolic rate in the cortex do not support the theory.

Perhaps this is to be expected. The biological theory of extraversion essentially assumes that the *only* determinant of whether a person is lively, sociable, optimistic and impulsive is the amount of electrical activity in their ARAS and it really does seem fairly likely that myriad other social, cultural, motivational, cognitive and time-of-day variables that are difficult to assess will also affect people's behaviour. These uncontrolled variables will, of course, all tend to reduce the strength of the correlation between psychophysiological measures and extraversion, so the finding that some measures (such as cortical blood flow) can explain up to about one-seventh of the variability in people's levels of extraversion is, perhaps, about as good as could reasonably be expected.

Gray's theory is growing in popularity, although it is not always easy to grasp the nuances of the interactions between the various cns systems and how these may relate to behaviour and/or brain functioning. The basic question is whether one should relate personality directly to neural functioning (Eysenck) or instead identify various systems of behaviour (which form the cns) and develop models of how these relate to both personality and neural functioning. There are certainly plenty of problems with RST, as shown by Matthews and Corr (2008). From a psychometric viewpoint, it is embarrassing for the theory that factor analysis of responses to personality questionnaires consistently finds factors of E and N, rather than sensitivity to reward and punishment. Neither do the Carver and White BIS/BAS scales form clean factors and the distinction between fear and anxiety, which is a strong feature of the theory, is not supported by the literature on mood structure (Chapter 12). And there is the nagging question about whether humans are so different from other animals (in terms of knowledge representation, language, ability to predict events and so on) that attempts to develop a model that does not involve cognition is perhaps brave.

Suggested additional reading

There is no shortage of good texts and papers on the biological basis of personality. The main problem is that some of them are very technical, while others go into such detail that it is difficult to keep sight of the broad picture. Barrett (1997), Bates and Wachs (1994), Eysenck (1994, 1997), Gale and Eysenck (1992) and the special issue of Volume 58 of the *Journal of Personality* (1990) are fairly approachable and Gale (1983) makes some still relevant points about the conceptual problems of brain research. Zuckerman (1991) is excellent, although very detailed. Matthews and Gilliland (1999) offer an excellent summary of Eysenck's theory and the empirical literature.

As far as Gray's theory is concerned, Corr (2008b) is by far the best available source: it contains many of the papers cited in this chapter and is commendably up to date. Care should be taken to ensure that anything else that you read cites McNaughton and Corr (2004). It may otherwise be based on an older version of the theory.

Answers to self-assessment questions

SAQ 7.1

There is generally no control group (or sophisticated statistical analysis) to guard against the possibility that the child *might* have developed in much the same way had it been brought up in a completely different family environment – the child may show certain patterns of personality because of its genetic similarity to its parents. The genes may influence the parents to bring up the child in a certain way and also influence the child's personality and there may be no causal link between parental behaviour and personality at all. One way round this would be to perform such studies using only adopted children.

SAQ 7.2

Several objections to reductionism can be entertained. First, it may be unwise to point to brain structures as explanations for behaviour unless one knows why, precisely, these brain structures developed in the way that they did. For it is possible that life events (e.g. childrearing practices) can influence the brain structures. In this case, a 'biological' theory of personality could be explained by social processes! There is a tendency to assume that the biology of the nervous system is fixed, immutable and thus somehow more fundamental than social theories, although the evidence for this is not always clear. Second, the theories clearly fail to take into account the importance of interactions between personality types and certain environments. It seems quite likely that certain life events will have a profound impact on those who are biologically disposed to react in a certain way. If this is so, then any attempt to explain personality by purely biological (or purely social) processes will clearly be unsatisfactory. Contrariwise, it may be sensible to explore how adequately simple (e.g. purely social or purely biological) models can predict personality before beginning the much more complex task of developing models that are based on interactionism.

SAQ 7.3

There are several possible approaches. The most obvious would be to measure the levels of male hormones, etc., in a sample of 'normal' male volunteers and to correlate the levels of such chemicals with their scores on the P scale of the EPQ(R) (or else use a statistical technique called 'multiple regression' to determine how much of the variation in the P scale can be predicted by individual differences in the levels of several such chemicals). Consideration could be given to the feasibility (and ethicality) of an intervention study in which some individuals' levels of such hormones are increased, while a control group would receive a placebo. A one-between and one-within analysis of variance could then establish whether P scale scores increase more in the experimental group. However, this design is probably not feasible (even if it were ethical) because it would presumably need to be carried out over a period of days or weeks. Another approach might be to compare the P scale scores and hormonal levels of normal controls and violent criminals, in the expectation that the group with higher P score would also have higher levels of hormone. However, this approach does not show the size of the relationship between hormones and the P score in the general population and for this reason the first design is probably the better.

SAQ 7.4

We have not had space to discuss this in much detail, but many of the reasons should be fairly clear. First, it allows us to answer two criticisms that are levelled at personality theory by social psychologists, namely that personality theories are 'circular' (inferring personality from behaviour and then trying to *explain* the behaviour by invoking a personality trait) and that they are not genuine properties of the individual, but rather the results of stereotyping, attributional biases, etc. If it can be shown that the main personality traits are linked to behaviour in quite different domains (e.g. patterns of electrical activity in the cortex), then it will be clear that the personality questionnaires are measuring some rather broad property of the organism. Neither can they merely reflect attributional biases, etc. The second reason for studying processes is, of course, scientific curiosity – a desire to understand how and why certain individuals come to display characteristic patterns of personality. Finally, such work may have some important applications. For example, if a 'negative' adult personality trait such as neuroticism or psychoticism could be shown to be crucially dependent on some kind of experience during infancy, society might well want to ensure that all children receive special attention at this stage.

SAQ 7.5

a. Eysenck studied the personality dimensions of extraversion–intraversion and neuroticism–stability, whereas Gray studied personality factors that are mixtures of the two, as shown in Figure 7.2.

b. Eysenck sought to relate personality directly to brain physiology (e.g. correlating extraversion with electrical activity in the cortex). Gray suggested that the various structures of the conceptual nervous system (cns) mediate this relationship. The cns reflects ways in which animals behave – e.g. approach or avoidance of novel objects.

References

Barrett, P. T. (1997). Process models in individual differences research. In C. Cooper and V. Varma (eds), *Processes in Individual Differences*. London: Routledge.

Bates, J. E. and Wachs, T. D. (1994). *Temperament: Individual Differences at the Interface of Biology and Behavior*. Washington, DC: American Psychological Association.

Blanchard, R. J., Blanchard, D. C., McNaughton, N. and Andrews, G. (1990). An ethoexperimental analysis of defense, fear, and anxiety. In *Anxiety*. Dunedin New Zealand: University of Otago Press.

Byrne, A. and Eysenck, M. W. (1995). Trait anxiety, anxious mood, and threat detection. *Cognition & Emotion 9*(6), 549–62.

Carver, C. S. and White, T. L. (1994). Behavioral inhibition, behavioral activation, and affective responses to impending reward and punishment: the BIS/BAS scales. *Journal of Personality and Social Psychology 67*(2), 319–33.

Claridge, G. S., Donald, J. R. and Birchall, P. M. (1981). Drug tolerance and personality: some implications for Eysenck's theory. *Personality and Individual Differences 222*, 153–66.

Coopersmith, S. (1967). *The Antecedents of Self-Esteem*. San Francisco: Freeman.

Corr, P. J. (2008a). Reinforcement sensitivity theory (RST): introduction. In *The Reinforcement Sensitivity Theory of Personality*. New York: Cambridge University Press.

Corr, P. J. (2008b). *The Reinforcement Sensitivity Theory of Personality*. New York: Cambridge University Press.

Deckersbach, T., Miller, K. K., Klibanski, A., Fischman, A., Dougherty, D. D., Blais, M. A. et al. (2006). Regional cerebral brain metabolism correlates of neuroticism and extraversion. *Depression and Anxiety 23*(3), 133–8.

Derakshan, N. and Eysenck, M. W. (1999). Are repressors self-deceivers or other-deceivers? *Cognition & Emotion 13*(1), 1–17.

Eysenck, H. J. (1967). *The Biological Basis of Personality*. Springfield, IL: Charles C. Thomas.

Eysenck, H. J. (ed.) (1973). *Handbook of Abnormal Psychology*. London: Pitman.

Eysenck, H. J. (1994). Personality: biological foundations. In P. A. Vernon (ed.), *The Neuropsychology of Individual Differences*. San Diego, CA: Academic Press.

Eysenck, H. J. (1997). Can the study of personality ever be objective? In C. Cooper and V. Varma (eds), *Processes in Individual Differences*. London: Routledge.

Eysenck, H. J. and Eysenck, M. W. (1985). *Personality and Individual Differences*. New York: Plenum.

Eysenck, M. W. (2000). A cognitive approach to trait anxiety. *European Journal of Personality 14*(5), 463–76.

Eysenck, M. W. and Byrne, A. (1992). Anxiety and susceptibility to distraction. *Personality and Individual Differences 13*(7), 793–8.

Eysenck, S. B. G., Eysenck, H. J. and Barrett, P. (1985). A revised version of the Psychoticism scale. *Personality and Individual Differences 6*(1), 21–9.

Fahrenberg, J., Schneider, H. J. and Safian, P. (1987). Psychophysiological assessments in a repeated-measurement design extending over a one-year interval – trends and stability. *Biological Psychology 24*(1), 49–66.

Gale, A. (1983). Electroencephalagraphic studies of extraversion-intraversion: a case study in the psychophysiology of individual differences. *Personality and Individual Differences 4*(4), 371–80.

Gale, A. and Eysenck, M. W. (eds) (1992). *Handbook of Individual Differences: Biological Perspectives*. New York: Wiley.

Gray, J. A. (1970). Psychophysiological basis of intraversion-extraversion. *Behaviour Research and Therapy 8*(3), 249–66.

Gray, J. A. (1982). *The Neuropsychology of Anxiety*. Oxford: Clarendon.

Gray, J. A. and McNaughton, N. (2000). *The Neuropsychology of Anxiety: An Enquiry into the Functions of the Septo-hippocampal System* (2nd edn). Oxford: Oxford University Press.

Hagemann, D., Hewig, J., Walter, C., Schankin, A., Danner, D. and Naumann, E. (2009). Positive evidence for Eysenck's arousal hypothesis: a combined EEG and MRI study with multiple measurement occasions. *Personality and Individual Differences 47*(7), 717–21.

Haier, R. J., Sokolski, K., Katz, M. and Buchsbaum, M. S. (1987). The study of personality with positron emission tomography. In J. Strelau and H. J. Eysenck (eds), *Personality Dimensions and Arousal*. New York: Plenum.

Honess, T. (1979). Children's implicit theories of their peers: a developmental analysis. *British Journal of Psychology 70*, 417–24.

Johnson, D. L., Wiebe, J. S., Gold, S. M., Andreasen, N. C., Hichwa, R. D., Watkins, G. L. et al. (1999). Cerebral blood flow and personality: a positron emission tomography study. *American Journal of Psychiatry 156*(2), 252–7.

Kim, S. H., Hwang, J. H., Park, H. S. and Kim, S. E. (2008). Resting brain metabolic correlates of neuroticism and extraversion in young men. *NeuroReport: For Rapid Communication of Neuroscience Research 19*(8), 883–6.

Kline, P. (1981). *Fact and Fantasy in Freudian theory*. London: Methuen.

Kline, P. (1993). *The Handbook of Psychological Testing*. London: Routledge.

Lacey, J. I. and Lacey, B. C. (1970). *Physiological Correlates of Emotion*. New York: Academic Press.

Mathew, R. J., Weinman, M. L. and Barr, D. L. (1984). Personality and regional cerebral blood flow. *British Journal of Psychiatry 144*, 529–32.

Matthews, G. and Corr, P. J. (2008). Reinforcement sensitivity theory: a critique from cognitive science. In P. J. Corr (ed.), *The Reinforcement Sensitivity Theory of Personality*. New York: Cambridge University Press.

Matthews, G. and Gilliland, K. (1999). The personality theories of H. J. Eysenck and J. A. Gray: a comparative review. *Personality and Individual Differences 26*(4), 583–626.

McNaughton, N. and Corr, P. J. (2004). A two-dimensional neuropsychology of defense: fear/anxiety and defensive distance. *Neuroscience and Biobehavioral Reviews 28*(3), 285–305.

McNaughton, N. and Corr, P. J. (2008). The neuropsychology of fear and anxiety: a foundation for reinforcement sensitivity theory. In P. J. Corr (ed.), *The Reinforcement Sensitivity Theory of Personality*. New York: Cambridge University Press.

Minnix, J. A. and Kline, J. P. (2004). Neuroticism predicts resting frontal EEG asymmetry variability. *Personality and Individual Differences 36*(4), 823–32.

Pennebaker, J. W. (1982). *The Psychology of Physical Symptoms*. New York: Springer.

Pessiglione, M., Seymour, B., Flandin, G., Dolan, R. J. and Frith, C. D. (2006). Dopamine-dependent prediction errors underpin reward-seeking behaviour in humans. *Nature 442*(7106), 1042–5.

Pickering, A. D., Smillie, L. D. and Corr, P. J. (2008). The behavioural activation system: challenges and opportunities. In P. J. Corr (ed.), *The Reinforcement Sensitivity Theory of Personality*. New York: Cambridge University Press.

Pineles, S. L., Vogt, D. S. and Orr, S. P. (2009). Personality and fear responses during conditioning: Beyond extraversion. *Personality and Individual Differences 46*(1), 48–53.

Robinson, D. L. (1996). *Brain, Mind, and Behavior: A New Perspective on Human Nature.* Westport, CT: Praeger /Greenwood Publishing Group.

Schultz, W. (1998). Predictive reward signal of dopamine neurons. *Journal of Neurophysiology 80*(6), 1–27.

Small, D. M., Jones-Gotman, M. and Dagher, A. (2003). Feeding-induced dopamine release in dorsal striatum correlates with meal pleasantness ratings in healthy human volunteers. *Neuroimage 19*(4), 1709–15.

Torrubia, R., Avila, C., and Caseras, X. (2008). Reinforcement sensitivity scales. In P. J. Corr (ed), *The Reinforcement Sensitivity Theory of Personality.* New York: Cambridge University Press.

Tran, Y., Craig, A. and McIsaac, P. (2001). Extraversion-intraversion and 8-13 Hz waves in frontal cortical regions. *Personality and Individual Difference, 30*(2), 205–15.

Volkow, N. D., Wang, G. J., Fowler, J. S., Logan, J., Jayne, M., Franceschi, D. et al. (2002). 'Nonhedonic' food motivation in humans involves dopamine in the dorsal striatum and methylphenidate amplifies this effect. *Synapse 44*(3), 175–80.

Weinberger, D. A., Schwartz, G. E. and Davidson, J. R. (1979). Low-anxious, high-anxious and repressive coping styles: psychometric patterns and behavioral and physiological responses to stress. *Journal of Abnormal Psychology 88*, 369–80.

Zuckerman, M. (1991). *Psychobiology of Personality.* Cambridge: Cambridge University Press.

8 Structure and measurement of abilities

Background

The study of individual differences in ability is one of the very oldest areas of psychology and is certainly one of the most applicable. Tests assessing individual differences in mental ability have been of great practical value in occupational, industrial and educational psychology. The psychology of ability is one of the four main branches of individual differences (the others being personality, mood and motivation) and the present chapter outlines what is now known (and generally accepted) about the nature and structure of human abilities.

Recommended prior reading

Chapters 14, 16 and 17.

Introduction

Howard Wainer (1987) reminds us that ability testing has a long and illustrious history, stretching back 4000 years to when the Chinese used a form of ability testing to select for their civil service. He also notes a biblical reference to forensic assessment of ability (Judges 12: 4–6). This is hardly surprising, for few areas of psychology have proved of such practical usefulness as the capacity to measure human abilities. The accurate identification of which individuals will best be able to benefit from an advanced course of education or which job applicants are likely to perform best if selected (rather than selecting randomly or on the basis of time-consuming and potentially unreliable procedures, such as interviews), brings important financial and personal benefits. Tests of ability are also useful for identifying other forms of potential and problems, e.g. to identify outstanding musical talent or to help in the diagnosis of dyslexia and some types of brain disease.

It is probably sensible to begin by attempting to define some terms. The word 'mental ability' is used to describe a person's performance on some task that has a substantial information-processing component (i.e. that requires thinking, sound judgement or skill) when that person is trying to perform that task as well as possible. For example, writing a sonnet, adding the numbers 143 and 228, designing a building, reading a map, structuring an essay, inventing a joke and diagnosing a fault in a computer are all examples of mental abilities if (and only if) they are assessed when individuals are really trying to do their best. Some other abilities (e.g. pruning a rosebush, running a race) do not require vast amounts of cognitive skill for their successful completion and so are not usually regarded as mental abilities.

Neither are tests of attainment, which (as discussed in Chapter 14) are designed to assess how well individuals have absorbed knowledge or skills *that have been specifically taught*. For example, an attainment test in geography might take a sample of facts and skills that pupils should have learned, e.g. by sampling items from the syllabus. Tests of ability, by way of contrast, involve *thinking* rather than remembering and use test items that the individual will not have encountered previously. Or at least the individual will not know that they are to be tested on them. Thus mental abilities should be measured by assessing a well-motivated person who is asked to do their best in performing some task with a substantial cognitive component, the exact nature of which is unfamiliar to them, but for which they have the necessary cognitive skills.

Mental abilities, then, are traits that reflect how well individuals can process various types of information. They reflect cognitive processes and skills and since one of the functions of the education system is to develop some of these (e.g. numeracy, literacy), it is difficult to define what is meant by an ability without taking individuals' educational backgrounds and interests into consideration. Individual differences in the speed of solving differential equations might be regarded as an important ability for physics students or engineers, but not for many others. Thus it is not really possible to define ability independently of cultural and educational background.

For this reason, it seems to be conventional to consider only those mental abilities that everyone can be assumed to have acquired as part of a basic education or which are not formally taught at all. Thus performance in solving cryptic crossword puzzles, evading income tax, thinking up novel uses for objects, assembling jigsaws or performing simple arithmetic would be regarded as mental abilities. Those abilities that reflect specialized knowledge or training or that are non-cognitive in nature would be excluded from the list. Hence being able to breathe life into a dull party, identify fungi, sprint, play the sitar, grow championship onions, recite the capitals of the states of the USA or call a touch of Belfast Surprise Major (a *very* esoteric mental skill involving church bells!) would not generally be regarded as mental abilities within the general population.

But how many abilities *are* there? After all, the number of 'tasks with a substantial cognitive component, the exact nature of which is unfamiliar' (our putative definition of a mental ability) is potentially enormous. In fact, it is almost infinite, meaning that it would be impossible in practice ever to understand fully a person's abilities simply by measuring all of them.

The alternative is to examine the correlations between mental abilities using factor analysis. This might show that there is some overlap between all these tasks measuring mental abilities and with luck this might reduce the number of distinct abilities to a manageable level. So, just as with the psychology of personality, psychometric studies of mental ability attempt to achieve two objectives:

- to establish the basic structure of abilities

- once there is some consensus about the number and nature of the main abilities, to try to understand the nature of the underlying social, biological, cognitive and other processes that *cause* these individual differences to emerge.

This chapter deals with the basic structure of abilities, and Chapters 9 and 11 address some of the underlying processes.

Structure of human mental abilities

You will already be familiar with most of the research techniques that are used in the study of mental abilities, as most authorities agree that factor analysis of the correlations between ability test items can reveal the underlying structure of abilities. Therefore, precisely the same techniques **119** that showed up personality characteristics such as extraversion and neuroticism should also be able to reveal the structure of abilities. If we measure individuals' performance on a very wide range of tasks that seem to require thought for their correct solution, correlate their scores on the items (or tests) together and factor analyse this table of correlations, the factors that emerge should represent the main dimensions of ability.

> **Self-assessment question 8.1**
>
> Think creatively for a few minutes about how you might draw up a list of as many abilities as possible.

Which abilities should we analyse?

When studying personality, Cattell used the 'personality sphere' concept in an attempt to ensure that all possible descriptions of behaviour were included in factor analyses that were designed to reveal all of the main personality traits. No similar approach has been followed for abilities, presumably because it is recognized that the dictionary may not contain very accurate descriptions of ability. For example, I can think of no commonly used word that describes ability to solve anagrams, sing in tune or show prodigious powers of memory. (Phrases are not really helpful, since they will not be turned up by a search through the dictionary.)

This can present problems, since the personality sphere at least offered a starting point for psychologists wishing to map out the whole area of personality. Without any such guidance, it is difficult to ensure that all possible abilities have been considered when trying to develop tests to cover the whole gamut of mental abilities. This can mean that certain mental ability factors will simply not be discovered. For example, if no tests of mathematical performance are given to a group of people, it is clearly impossible for any sort of mathematical ability factor to emerge when individuals' responses are intercorrelated and factor analysed.

Cattell's Ability Dimension Action Chart (ADAC)

Cattell (1971) therefore attempted to develop a taxonomy of abilities, by means of a chart showing what types of ability could logically exist. A simplified version of this Ability Dimension Action Chart (ADAC) is shown in Table 8.1. It views abilities as consisting of three main components.

The action domain specifies which aspect of the task is 'hard' for the individual. This might be at the *input* level – that is, the task may require someone to make a fine perceptual discrimination. For example, in a test individuals may be asked to match various extremely similar colours or attend to speech presented to one ear while ignoring speech presented to the other ear. The vast majority of conventional tests of ability instead rely on *internal processing and storage* – or thinking – to make the items hard. This is the second possible aspect of the action domain. Some tasks primarily require skilled performance (e.g. singing a note in tune, tracking a moving object on a computer screen using a joystick) and so these would fall into the *output* category. The other two domains are content (the type of material given to the individual, e.g. a mental arithmetic problem or an anagram) and process (which defines which mental processes the individual is supposed to perform in order to solve the problem).

The *content* of the test items can vary considerably, from verbal, mathematical and mechanical problems to social and moral issues, to pitch perception. The processes involved in performing

Action – involvement of
- input
- internal processing and storage
- output

Content – various areas such as
- verbal
- social
- mechanical
- knowledge
- sensory modality

Process – including
- complexity of relations
- complexity of processing
- amount of remembering required
- amount of knowledge required
- amount of retrieval from memory required
- flexibility/creativity vs. convergence
- speed
- fine use of muscle

Table 8.1 A short form of Cattell's Ability Dimension Action Chart (ADAC)

the task can also take a huge number of values. Since it is highly unlikely that many tasks will involve a single process, it is necessary to categorize the degree to which each of them requires the use of memory, the degree of background knowledge needed, speed, the detection of relationships between objects (e.g. 'cat is to kitten as dog is to ???') and the amount of information that needs to be processed (e.g. drawing a circle as opposed to drawing a mural). There could be a vast number of these processes, but a list could perhaps be drawn up on the basis of the main findings of cognitive psychology.

The problem is, of course, that the categorization of tests according to this model will not generally be straightforward. How can one specify (without performing myriad experiments) how great the memory requirement of a task is relative to its speed?

Self-assessment question 8.2

Try to classify each of the following tasks in terms of the ADAC chart in Table 8.1:

a. singing the same note as that played on a piano

b. identifying a piece of music

c. learning a part in a play

d. solving a riddle

e. inventing a pun

f. solving this SAQ.

This chart can be useful in that it reminds us that most of the abilities identified so far require an action of 'internal processing' – we know rather less about those in the input and output domains. However, the problems arise because it has no clear theoretical rationale (e.g. not drawing the list of processes from cognitive psychology) and it is almost impossible to be sure just by looking at a task which processes are involved in its solution. Thus it is probably safest to conclude that there is no single obvious, automatic technique for discovering all of the behaviours that may be influenced by ability.

Factor analysis of ability

There is an important difference in the way in which factor analysis is generally used in the study of personality and ability. Surprisingly, this is one which does not seem to have been explicitly recognized in the literature. It relates to what precisely goes into the factor analysis. You will remember that in the case of personality psychology, the responses to individual test items are usually fed straight into the factor analysis. Thus, if one factor analyses the correlations between the items in a particular personality questionnaire, the main personality factors that correspond to the scales of the questionnaire should emerge.

It is extremely rare to find a study in the area of human abilities that calculates and factor analyses the correlations between individual test items. Almost all studies instead factor analyse the correlations between *subscales* consisting of several items – for example, individuals' scores on subscales (each consisting of 20 or so items) measuring verbal comprehension, non-literal comprehension of proverbs and 'odd word out' (some examples taken from Thurstone 1938). Most ability tests factor analyse the *correlations between groups of items*, rather than between the items themselves. How these items are grouped together in the first place has important consequences for the results that are obtained.

Suppose that a researcher wants to examine the structure of ability, which will include some arithmetical problems. He or she will have to decide whether it is better to include several different, separately timed and separately scored *subscales* measuring arithmetical ability (e.g. one for addition, one for subtraction, one for multiplication, one for division, one for geometry, one for algebra, one for long multiplication, one for long division, another for set theory, etc.) or whether to make the *assumption* that these skills all go together and so calculate a total score from a mixture of these items, hoping that it will be a reliable measure of a single ability. (Most psychometricians now accept that a high level of reliability of a scale is no guarantee that its items all measure a single factor. They could instead measure two or more correlated factors.)

In the former case, the researcher determine empirically that these various types of problem will group together to form an ability factor, whereas the latter simply assumed that they did.

Thus the *factor* that is obtained when the correlations between the subscales are analysed is often essentially the same as the score on the *scale* that is obtained when all of the items are simply put into the same test. If we factor analyse the correlations between a number of subtests, calculate individuals' scores on this factor and correlate these factor scores with the sum of their scores on the subtests, the correlation would be very high (probably well above 0.9), showing that the factor is almost identical to the simple sum of scores.

The point to note is that by factoring *subscales* one might well end up with factors that are different from those that are obtained by factoring correlations between *scales*. We shall return to

122   this distinction when we examine the work of Spearman and Thurstone.

Empirical results

Having decided (rather arbitrarily) whether to factor the correlations between scales or sub-scales, determining the basic structure of ability is rather straightforward and is fully described in Chapters 16 and 17. All that is necessary is to:

1. administer the test(s) to a large, representative sample of the population

2. add up individuals' scores on the various scales or subscales

3. correlate these scores together

4. factor analyse these correlations

5. identify the factor(s) by looking at the variables that have appreciable loadings on them

6. validate the factor(s), e.g. by establishing their predictive and construct validity

7. examine the correlations between the factors – if any are appreciable, repeat steps 4 to 7 to produce 'second-order' factors, 'third-order' factors, etc., repeating the process until either the factors are essentially uncorrelated, or just one factor remains.

Spearman and Thurstone: one ability or 12?

Charles Spearman (1904) was one of the first to perform an empirical study of the structure of abilities – indeed, he invented the technique of factor analysis for this very purpose. He constructed some rather primitive tests that, he thought, would probably assess children's thinking ability, and administered these to a sample of Hampshire schoolchildren. He gave them tests of vocabulary, mathematical ability, ability to follow complex instructions, visualization, matching colours and matching musical pitch.

With hindsight, it seems likely that some of the tests (vocabulary, mathematics and, perhaps, ability to follow complex instructions) would be influenced by formal education and were thus tests of attainment rather than of aptitude; however, the remaining three tests did not measure skills that were explicitly taught in school. He then added up children's scores on these six scales, correlated their scores together and factor analysed these correlations. Note that Spearman factored the scores between quite different scales, *not* different *subscales*.

He found just one factor, which he called *g* (for *general ability*). This result implied that, if a child performed above average on one of the tests, it was more likely than not that she would perform at an above average level on all the other tests as well. It is as if there is some basic 'thinking ability' that determines performance in all areas – some children seemed to excel at everything, some performed poorly at everything, but relatively few excelled in one area and performed poorly in another.

Self-assessment question 8.3

On the basis of this analysis, is it legitimate to say that general ability causes someone to perform at similar levels on all tests?

Thurstone (who was based in the USA) soon formed a different opinion, but this is largely because he analysed subscales rather than scales. He administered a much larger selection of tests (60 subscales in all) to a sample of just over 200 university students (Thurstone 1938). When the intercorrelations between these 60 test scores were factor analysed by hand, 12 distinct ability factors were extracted and rotated orthogonally. Thurstone termed these factors 'primary mental abilities' and most of them made good psychological sense. For example, one factor had large loadings from all subscales that involved spatial visualization, one had large loadings from all the subscales involving the use of language, while yet another subsumed all the subscales requiring numerical skills and so on.

Thurstone's primary mental abilities (PMAs) are listed in Table 8.2. Variants of the tests that Thurstone used to measure these abilities (the Test of Primary Mental Abilities) are still in print and are sometimes used to this day. Thus while Spearman found just one factor, namely general ability, Thurstone seems to have identified a dozen quite independent ability factors. How many ability factors *are* there?

I ought to mention another difficulty with Thurstone's experiment that more or less guaranteed that he obtained results different from Spearman's. The problem in using students is that they have most probably been selected on the basis of high levels of general ability. It is unlikely that many would have below average ability. Thus the range of ability in Thurstone's sample was almost certainly much less than that in the general population. We now know that one of the effects of this will be to reduce the correlations between the subscales, which will reduce the likelihood of finding a single, all-pervasive factor of general ability.

The debate that resulted from Thurstone's work was hot and furious and many psychologists were convinced that factor analysis was useless because it seemed to produce such inconsistent results. However, you should be able to understand precisely why the results were so different. The difference arises because Thurstone analysed correlations between subscales, while Spear-

Code	Factor	Brief description
S	Spatial ability	Visualizing shapes, mental rotation
V	Verbal relations	Words in context: comprehension, analogies, etc.
P	Perceptual speed	Searching
N	Numerical facility	Addition, subtraction, etc., algebra
W	Word fluency	Tasks dealing with isolated words, e.g. anagrams, spelling
M	Memory	Paired-associate learning and recognition
I	Induction	Finding rules given exemplars, e.g. number series
R	Restriction	Mechanical knowledge, spatial and verbal skills
D	Deduction	Deductive reasoning: applying a rule

. . . plus three factors that could not be easily interpreted

124 Table 8.2 Thurstone's primary mental abilities (Thurstone 1938)

man analysed correlations between scales. Indeed, some of the ability factors that were extracted from Thurstone's factor analysis (numerical ability, verbal ability and deductive reasoning/following instructions) look remarkably similar to the scales that Spearman put into his analysis. Thurstone's analysis was just performed at a lower, more detailed, level than that of Spearman.

The obvious next step is to examine the correlations between Thurstone's factors, since, if they correspond to Spearman's scales, they may correlate together to give *g*.

The problem is, of course, that Thurstone forced his factors to be at right angles to each other ('orthogonal rotation') for ease of computation. Since all correlations between these factors are zero, it is not possible to factor analyse these correlations between the primary abilities. There is another problem, too. Even Thurstone's work, involving 60 subtests, appeared to miss out some areas of ability. For example, there was nothing that measured how quickly people could come up with ideas, nothing that measured what Sternberg (1985) called 'social intelligence' (e.g. 'what's the "smart" thing to do if your potential father-in-law forbids you to marry his daughter?'), nothing that measured musical skill, judgement, coordination or a whole host of other abilities that may prove to be important.

Hierarchical models of ability

Later evidence shows that Thurstone's analyses were flawed in one important respect. Whereas he believed that the primary abilities were essentially uncorrelated, most subsequent research has revealed that these factors are correlated together to varying extents. It is therefore possible to factor analyse the correlations between the primary abilities.

In addition, several investigators extended the range of subscales that were entered into factor analyses and so discovered more and more primary mental abilities. Cattell's (1971) contribution is still useful here. His review of the literature identifies some 17 first-order factors that recur in several independent studies and that seem to be acceptably broad in scope. Hakstian and Cattell (1976) later published a test designed to assess 20 primary abilities – the 'Comprehensive Ability Battery'. The 'Kit of Factor-Referenced Cognitive Tests' (Ekstrom, French and Harman 1976) is very similar and there is good reason to believe that these two tests measure many of the most important primary mental abilities. These include abilities as diverse as originality (thinking of creative uses for objects), mechanical knowledge and reasoning, verbal ability, numerical ability, fluency of ideas (being able to produce many ideas quickly), perceptual speed (speed in assessing whether two strings of characters are the same or different), spelling and aesthetic judgement (for works of art). Thus Cattell's analyses confirm and extend Thurstone's results.

When the correlations between these primary ability factors ('primaries') are themselves factor analysed, a number of 'second-order' ability factors ('secondaries') emerge, rather as shown in Figure 8.1. The lines in this diagram show 'significant' factor loadings (those above 0.4, say). The raw data on which the analysis is performed are the scores on a number of subtests, represented by squares at the bottom of the figure. The lozenges at the next level show the factors that emerge when the correlations between these subtests are factor analysed – these are the primary mental abilities. The next level up shows what happens when the correlations between the primary mental abilities are analysed. In this example, verbal ability (V), numerical ability (N) and mechanical knowledge ability (Mk) all have substantial loadings on a second-order factor called Gc, the meaning of which will be discussed shortly. Note that none of the other primary ability factors shown in the figure has a substantial loading on Gc. It might even be possible to **125**

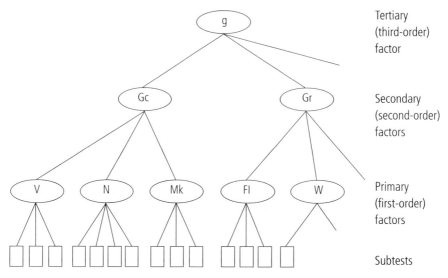

Figure 8.1 Part of a hierarchical model of ability, showing one third-order factor (general ability (g)), which influences two second-order factors (crystallized ability (Gc) and retrieval (Gr)), which, in turn, influence primary abilities such as verbal ability (V), numerical ability (N), mechanical ability (Mk), ideational fluency (Fl) and word fluency (W). At the bottom of the pyramid, the squares represent various subtests, e.g. those measuring comprehension, knowledge of proverbs and vocabulary, ability to solve simultaneous equations.

factor analyse any correlations between the second-order factors in order to obtain one or more third-order factors. As we move towards the top of the figure, we can see that each factor has an increasingly broad influence. For example, V (the verbal ability primary) affects performance on just three subscales, while Gc affects performance on ten subscales.

While there is generally good agreement about the nature of the main primary ability factors, opinions do differ somewhat about the number and nature of the second- and higher order abilities. Vernon (1950) proposed that there were two main secondaries – one essentially corresponding to verbal/educational ability ('v:ed') and the other representing practical/mechanical abilities ('k:m'). Both of these were thought to correlate together, giving general ability (Spearman's *g*) at the third level. Vernon's v:ed factor had significant loadings from primaries such as verbal ability and numerical ability and k:m loads primaries dealing with visualization and spatial abilities. This theory influenced the construction of the Wechsler tests of individual ability (the Wechsler Adult Intelligence Scale and the Wechsler Intelligence Scale for Children), which are widely used by educational psychologists and other professionals for individual assessment and guidance. These tests are still scored in order to assess verbal IQ and performance IQ (corresponding to the Vernon factors) ability, although factor analyses of the subtests tell quite a different story (Cooper 1995).

Horn and Cattell (1966) and Hakstian and Cattell (1978) identified not two but six second-order factors, a finding essentially replicated by Kline and Cooper (1984) and Undheim (1981), among others. The two most important factors in this model are known as *fluid intelligence* (Gf) and *crystallized intelligence* (Gc). Fluid intelligence is the raw reasoning ability that should develop independently of schooling, covering areas such as memory, spatial ability and inductive reasoning, while crystallized intelligence requires knowledge as well and influences primaries

126

such as verbal comprehension and mechanical knowledge. The other four second-order factors are retrieval (Gr), which is concerned with the speed with which creative ideas are produced, visualization (Gv), which had been identified as a primary by Thurstone, speed (Gps – a 'perceptual speed' factor that measures the speed with which individuals can compare two strings of letters or figures) and memory (Gm). Once again, these factors seem to make good sense.

Further support for this hierarchical model of abilities comes from Carroll (1993) who conducted a massive reanalysis of all published sets of data in the area of cognitive abilities using modern statistical techniques in order to draw up a comprehensive list of ability factors. The 'three stratum model', which he identified as best describing the data, is extremely similar to those discussed, though with the addition of more primary abilities and some more second-order abilities.

Self-assessment question 8.4

With which of Horn's second-order factors would you expect the following measures to correlate?

a. Locating one's whereabouts by map reading when lost in the country.

b. Speed of thinking what can be cooked from two eggs, an onion and a slice of bread.

c. A child's school examination marks.

d. Proofreading a complicated equation in a nuclear physics journal (i.e. checking whether the printed version is the same as the author's original typescript).

The main reason for the differing numbers of second-order factors probably lies in the nature of the abilities being measured, although differences in the factoring procedure may also have some effect. If a test battery contains less than two subtests measuring creativity or memory skills, then of course no primary or secondaries such as Gv or Gm can emerge, since the creativity or memory tasks would not show a substantial correlation with any other tasks. The other main point to remember is that fluid intelligence (Gf) bears a very striking resemblance to Spearman's g and so it is encouraging to see that when a third-order factor analysis was performed (by factoring the correlations between the secondaries), a third-order factor affected all three secondaries (Gf, Gc and Gv) that emerged when a sample of primary abilities was factored (Gustafsson 1981). Interestingly, Gustafsson's analysis showed that there was a very large correlation (approx 0.9) between g and Gf and there is an interesting debate about whether these two factors are identical (see Blair 2006 and the responses to this target article).

Where does this leave us? It seems that it is possible to conceptualize ability in several ways. First, and working our way down the hierarchy, the positive correlation between all of the primary abilities and between all the secondaries suggests that Spearman's factor of general ability (or something very like it) is a pervasive influence on cognitive performance. Some theorists have suggested that general ability may even be linked to the speed and/or efficiency with which the nervous system operates and some evidence for this claim will be scrutinized in Chapter 9. Thus it is perfectly legitimate to view all tasks as being affected by general ability. That said, there are also some 'clusters' of abilities that tend to rise and fall together – these are identified by the half-dozen or so main second-order ability factors. It is perhaps unsurprising to find that one of these factors (Gc) is related to school-based knowledge and skills. However, the rest seem to reflect pure thought processes. Then there are the individual primary mental abilities, over 20 of which have been discovered. These are thought to be the most basic mental skills, although as outlined earlier, I have some reservations about the procedures used to identify some of them from the factor analysis of subtests, the factor structure of which is not always well known.

So what should one measure? Whether one should assess *g* (using a test such as Raven's Matrices or Cattell's Culture Fair scales), second-order abilities (using something like the Wechsler scales or the General Aptitude Test Battery, or deriving scores from factoring tests of primary abilities) or simply assess primary abilities (using the Ekstrom Kit or the Comprehensive Ability Battery) depends very much on the purpose of the investigation. The measurement of 20 primary abilities takes at least 3 hours and this would be an extravagance if one just wanted to screen out low-ability applicants as part of an occupational selection process for a clerical post. Here a quick group-administered test of general ability, or perhaps perceptual speed, would be the obvious choice (depending on the nature and variety of tasks to be performed by the appointee). When assessing language ability in children in order to detect possible difficulties with language attainment, it is clearly vital to focus on just those factors that are relevant to language use. Therefore one basically selects a test at whatever level of generality seems appropriate, given some understanding of the skills and performances that one wishes to assess.

Guilford's model

It is necessary to mention Guilford's 'Structure of Intellect' model briefly, since it is still sometimes cited, despite being supported by little empirical evidence. Guilford (1967) rejected factor analysis as a tool for discovering the structure of abilities and built a model that ignored the best known finding from half a century of research – that abilities tend to be correlated positively together. Instead, he built up a taxonomy of abilities that he felt *should* exist on theoretical grounds assuming that abilities were independent of one another. He suggested that any ability has three main qualities, the first of which he called 'content'. There were four types of content – figural, symbolic, semantic and behavioural – which defined the type of material to be presented. Tasks with a behavioural content might be based on video clips showing people's actions, those with a semantic content on words, etc.

His next quality, 'operations', defined the basic mental operations that were primarily involved in problem solving – in other words, what made the task difficult. These were cognition, memory, divergent production, convergent production and evaluation. You may be surprised by some of these – 'cognition' would (these days) be regarded as a rather large and heterogeneous group of mental operations. Divergent production refers to the rapid and/or creative production of ideas, while convergent production requires someone to produce the 'best' solution to a problem. Guilford called the final quality 'products'. This defined the outcome of the problem solving (implications, transformations, systems, relations, classes or units). For example 'unit' means that the problem requires the individual to produce a single answer, 'classes' to identify what things have in common, 'implications' to see the consequences of (for example) misremembering your bank card PIN and so on. Guilford thus postulated that there were 120 (4 contents × 5 operations × 6 products) distinct abilities and devoted much energy to developing tests for these.

Figure 8.2 shows this model diagrammatically. One axis represents test content, another the cognitive operations that are performed on the test content and the third the outcome. You can imagine that each cube inside the cuboid represents one of the 120 different types of ability that

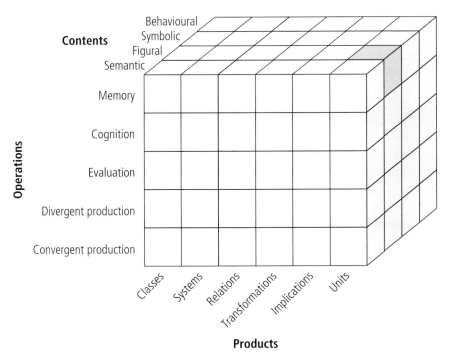

Figure 8.2 Guilford SOI cube.

Guilford proposed. The one highlighted in Figure 8.2 involves applying memory to numbers and producing a single answer.

However, the obvious problem with this model is that it is arbitrary. Whatever the faults of factor analysis, it at least explores the structure of the data and describes what is really there. Guilford's model has no obvious theoretical or empirical rationale and seems to have been invented 'off the top of his head'. In his scholarly review of theories of ability, Carroll (1993) uses phrases such as 'eccentric aberration' and 'fundamentally defective' when speaking of the theory (pp. 59–60) – sentiments with which it is difficult to disagree. The one good thing to come out of this work was Guilford's mention of 'divergent production' – the process of producing fast and/or imaginative ideas. These skills, which were thought to be related to 'creativity' (a matter of some concern to educators in the USA in the 1960s), had previously been overlooked by test designers. When such tests were incorporated into batteries such as the Comprehensive Ability Battery and Ekstrom Kit, they yielded a new secondary, Gv, discussed earlier.

Gardner's theory of multiple intelligences

Howard Gardner had doubts about the adequacy of factor analysis as a method for revealing ability traits and so he performed an extensive literature search in order to try to find groups of behaviours that varied together regularly. For example, he looked for behaviours that:

- tended to develop at similar ages
- were similarly effected by drugs or damage to a particular part of the brain

129

- appeared (or disappeared) together in geniuses and people with learning disabilities
- interfered with each other when people are asked to perform two tasks at the same time
- use common sets of symbols (e.g. music, mathematical notation)
- transfer, so that training on one task leads to good performance on a second.

Gardner (1993) identified seven 'intelligences' that met most of these criteria. These were linguistic intelligence, musical intelligence, logical/mathematical intelligence, spatial intelligence, bodily/kinaestheic intelligence, intrapersonal intelligence (self-knowledge) and interpersonal intelligence (quality of interactions with others). 'Naturalistic intelligence' has more recently been added to the list. These often seem to correspond closely to some of the most important ability traits identified by Cattell, Gustaffson and others; where there is not good agreement (e.g. bodily/kinaestheic intelligence, intrapersonal and interpersonal intelligence) it may be because these are not generally regarded as important *cognitive* abilities under the hierarchical model. However, there are two difficulties with this approach. First, Gardner *assumed* that these 'intelligences' would be uncorrelated with each other: '[T]here exists a multitude of intelligences, quite independent of each other (Gardner 1993: xxiii). Amazingly, Gardner had no evidence for making this claim, which flies in the face of a century's research on the structure of abilities. Second, it is unlikely that the list is exhaustive. Several sexual behaviours have their own symbolic language, appear (and decline) together, are all affected by drugs, brain damage etc. – so why is there no factor of sexual intelligence? It seems to me that this theory does little more than back up what is already known about the structure of abilities, but it has been marketed as something new and radical, which in my view it is not.

There is also the question of how one should best assess Gardner's intelligences to test his claim that the intelligences are independent of each other and unrelated to *g*. Several tests have been published that claim to measure Gardner's intelligences.

Think how you might assess one of Gardner's intelligences – e.g. musical intelligence or interpersonal intelligence.

In the exercise, you may well have suggested measuring musical intelligence by perhaps measuring how well someone can remember a tune or rhythm, perhaps test their musical knowledge, ask them to sing in tune, write a tune, identify which of two notes is of higher pitch, analyse a piece of music (e.g. to identify the various components of sonata form) and so on. To measure interpersonal intelligence you could perhaps ask others to rate how easy a person is to talk to, assess how clearly they can express a viewpoint at a meeting, test how well they can see things from another person's perspective and so on. If so, you are thinking like a psychologist (which is meant to be a compliment).

Unfortunately, tests to measure Gardner's multiple intelligences are not nearly so sophisticated. According to the author's website, the Teele Inventory for Multiple Intelligences 'is used in 8,000 school districts throughout the nation and in twenty-five other countries': one would expect it to be state of the art. This measure simply shows children or adults pictures of several activities, supposedly representing the seven intelligences proposed by Gardner (e.g. skateboarding for bodily/

kinaesthetic intelligence, listening to music for musical intelligence) and asks them to choose the one that they would prefer to do. There is no evidence whatsoever that the participants are any good at the activities that they claim to prefer. The *Multiple Intelligences Development Assessment Scales* developed by C. B. Shearer appears to have been privately published and so no reference can be given. However, according to the author's website it 'has been translated into Spanish, Chinese, Arabic and Korean and has been completed by over 25,000 people world-wide. It is being used in schools from Cambridge, Massachusetts to Portland, Oregon and from Vancouver, British Columbia to Jakarta, Indonesia and beyond' and so it too must be regarded as an established measure of multiple intelligences. It too never assesses level of performance objectively, but simply asks people to rate their liking for various activities (and sometimes to self-assess their level of performance): sample items are given on Shearer's website.

It is unsurprising that scores on tests such as these show small correlations with conventional intelligence tests, but that can hardly be taken as good evidence for Gardner's theoretical model. One experiment has been performed to test Gardner's theory using more sensible measures of ability. Visser, Ashton and Vernon (2006a) chose two fairly conventional ability tests to assess each of Gardner's intelligences: Gardner himself (2006) thought that these authors made 'a reasonable effort to choose tasks that are central to the domains under examination', although he complained that the tests that were used were too logical/scientific, a point rebutted by Visser et al. (2006b). Visser et al. (2006a) found that many of Gardner's supposedly independent 'intelligences' correlated substantially together, and that a clear *g* factor was found when these tests were factor analysed, although musical and kinaesthetic intelligences did not load on this. However, these data, the first to test Gardner's claim that there are eight quite independent domains of intelligence, seem to show that the whole theory is ill founded in fact.

This raises the question of why Gardner's theory is so popular with educationalists, despite not being based on any firm evidence. A consequence of Gardner's theory is that no child is disadvantaged. If a particular child is found to have lower than average levels of (say) verbal ability, because Gardner assumes that the various intelligences are uncorrelated it is thought to be quite likely that they will be above average on one of the others. Educators should accordingly identify and develop each child's strengths. Contrariwise, *g* theory suggests that if a child is well below average in one area, he is unlikely to excel in any other. The question is really whether educationalists' enthusiasm is justified, given the empirical basis of Gardner's theory.

Sternberg's triarchic theory of ability

The final theory to be considered here is that of Sternberg (1985). Sternberg argued that conventional ability tests were rather narrow in scope when compared to laypersons' views of what constituted 'smart' or 'intelligent' behaviour. In Sternberg's eyes, there seems to be relatively little difference between being 'intelligent' and 'being successful in life in twentieth-century America'. He suggests that any definition of intelligence should take into account the following three factors:

1. The context in which 'intelligent' behaviour takes place – the result of neglecting this variable is that the only behaviours seen to be relevant to 'intelligence' as measured by psychometric tests are those that are important (and can be easily measured) in a classroom testing situation. This is known as the contextual subtheory.

131

2. The experiential subtheory explicitly considers the role of novelty, experience and automaticity in solving the task. (Automaticity is the smooth performance of cognitively complex operations as a result of considerable experience, e.g. driving a car or reading.)

3. The componential subtheory considers the underlying *mechanisms* (processes) of intelligent behaviour, which include 'metacomponents' (planning of actions and cognitive strategies for solving tasks) and knowledge acquisition. The more cognitive part of this subtheory will be introduced in Chapter 13.

Sternberg's triarchic theory is an attempt to explain intelligent behaviour in terms of these three subtheories.

A real-life example may help here. My neighbour had a large, savage Rottweiler that lived in his garden, lunged against the hedge and barked at (and thoroughly terrified) anyone in our garden. As far as the contextual subtheory is concerned, 'intelligent' responses to this situation might include changing the environment (moving house), modifying the environment (persuading the neighbour to take the dog into the house or letting the dog loose in the hope that it will run away) or adapting to it (wearing earplugs when working, becoming friends with the dog or not using the garden so that the dog will not pose a problem).

The experiential subtheory seeks to understand the novel demands of the situation – both the nature of the situation itself and the possible solutions. The former may include a lack of experience of fierce dogs and less-than-considerate neighbours. The latter may include a lack of experience of confrontational situations. If I had substantial previous experience in any of these areas, my responses would be more automatic (e.g. knowing precisely how to obtain the desired result when approaching the neighbours), so my overall behaviour would appear more polished and more intelligent and would probably be more successful.

Kline (1991) raises some serious problems concerning this theory, but I am worried by a more fundamental point. By defining intelligence so broadly, it seems that Sternberg is stepping deep into the realm of personality and performance. *Style* of behaviour (which presumably includes problem solving) was, after all, how we initially defined personality. Thus it comes as no surprise that Sternberg's focus has recently turned to understanding the relationship between (his theory of) intelligence and personality (Sternberg 1994), which all seems rather circular. Whether I murder or release the dog, shout at or reason with my neighbour, abandon or defend my right to use the garden, plan my response to the Rottweiler problem or rush straight to a solution, these different approaches certainly sound like personality traits.

The experiential subtheory essentially broadens the scope of 'intelligence' to cover individual differences in the whole of human performance (individual differences in performance of highly automatized skills, e.g. typing, driving, walking, etc.). At the start of this chapter we suggested that the concept of intelligence should be kept narrow in that it should consider relatively novel problems for which one has the necessary cognitive skills. That is, tasks should be designed so as to reduce the role of individual differences in familiarity or automaticity. It remains to be seen whether Sternberg's efforts to broaden the concept of intelligence eventually prove useful.

Notion of IQ

In the early years of ability testing, it was necessary to devise a scale of mental ability that could be easily understood by parents and teachers and so the concept of 'intelligence quotient'

(IQ) was adopted. Confusingly, this term has two quite distinct meanings. Since most psychological testing was originally performed on schoolchildren, it was initially thought sensible to determine how a child's performance compared with the average performance of children of other ages. For example, Table 8.3 shows the average scores obtained on an early intelligence test by children of six age ranges. Suppose that a particular child is aged 74 months (this is their 'chronological age' or CA) and they score 30 on the test. Part (a) of Table 8.3 shows that a score of 30 is generally obtained by children aged 77 months, so the child's mental age is 77 months.

The old definition of IQ (sometimes known as the ratio IQ) is:

$$IQ = \frac{\text{mental age}}{\text{chronological age}} \times 100$$

In this example, the child's IQ is:

$$\frac{77}{74} \times 100, \text{ or } 104.$$

An IQ of 100 shows that a child is performing at an average level for their age, an IQ greater than 100 shows that they are performing better than average and an IQ less than 100 shows that they are performing below average.

There are several problems with this definition of IQ, which led to its decline. The most obvious drawback is related to the fact that performance on ability tests ceases to increase with age after the late teens. So suppose that someone aged 18 years scored 70 on the test. Since none of the higher age groups has an average score of 70, it is not possible to calculate this person's mental age or IQ using Table 8.3(b).

The ratio IQ was therefore abandoned 40 years ago. It should never be used, although alarmingly this is the only definition of IQ given in one recent dictionary of psychology. Instead, a new term called the 'deviation IQ' was introduced. By definition, deviation IQs have a mean of 100 for any particular age group and a standard deviation that is almost always 16 (although two test constructors adopt standard deviations of 15 and 18, respectively). Deviation IQs also (by definition) follow a normal (bell-shaped) distribution and the manuals of many ability tests contain a table showing which scores on the test correspond to which level of IQ.

Since deviation IQs follow a normal distribution, it is relatively straightforward to work out how extreme a particular IQ score is. One simply converts the IQ to a z score by subtracting the mean IQ and dividing by the standard deviation – these figures are 100 and 16, respectively, by

(a) Test scores of children aged 72 to 80 months

Age (months)	72	73	74	75	76	77	78	79	80
Ave. score	23	24	25	27	28	30	31	33	35

(b) Test scores of adults aged 15 to 60 years

Age (years)	15	16	17	18	25	30	40	50	60
Ave. score	62	64	65	66	65	66	65	64	64

Table 8.3 Hypothetical scores on an ability test at various ages

definition. One then consults the table of areas under the standard normal distribution which can be found in any statistics text. For example, an IQ of 131 corresponds to a z score of

$$\frac{(131 - 100)}{16} = 1.94$$

and the table of the standard normal integral shows that only 2.5% of the population will have scores above this level. An IQ of 110 corresponds to a z score of 0.625; 26% of the population will have scores above this level.

It is only necessary (indeed, it is only statistically *legitimate*) to convert scores on ability tests into IQs for the purpose of understanding the meaning of an individual's score on a test. Most of us will simply calculate *t*-tests, correlations, etc. based on the raw scores from ability tests.

Self-assessment question 8.5

a. What is the difference between ratio IQ and deviation IQ?

b. How would you respond if a member of the government berated schoolteachers because, despite a supposedly huge increase in schools' resources, a recent study showed that 50% of children still have IQs below 100 (the same figure as 10 years ago)?

Suggested additional reading

This chapter has concentrated on conveying a basic grasp of hierarchical models of ability, since these are of considerable theoretical and practical importance. Thus there has been little scope to explore Sternberg's work in any detail, but his 1985 book will repay careful study. Neither has there been much space to discuss which tests can best assess abilities. Buros is the obvious source, but texts such as those by Cronbach (1994) Anastasi (1961) and Kline (1991, 1993) also give some examples of test items. Journals such as *Educational and Psychological Measurement* and specialist journals on educational and occupational psychology can show how tests of mental abilities can predict performance in real-life settings, as can the books cited in the text. Cronbach, Anastasi and the early chapters of Anderson (1992) can be recommended as a general expansion of some of the issues discussed here. Herrnstein and Murray (1994) contains some extremely controversial interpretations of the correlates of general ability – readers may like to evaluate critically both this work and also the many counterviews that have appeared on the internet. There are now some excellent textbooks available. Brody (1992) is my favourite for scholarship, balance and readability, although its content is now quite dated. Mackintosh (1998) and Deary (2000) can also be strongly recommended. Jensen (1998) is well worth reading, although it may have an agenda. Cooper's *Intelligence and Abilities* (1999) offers a basic introduction to the topic – as does Cooper (2003), which includes a fairly typical intelligence test in an appendix.

Answers to self-assessment questions

SAQ 8.1

There are no right or wrong answers to this question, the purpose of which was to encourage thought. Some possibilities are discussed in the next section. Others might include analysing what actions requiring intelligence seem to be performed by a wide range of people, e.g. by following students, plasterers, unemployed people, pensioners, drivers, doctors, etc. during their working lives and noting either what problems they need to solve or asking them to 'think aloud'. Alternatively, one can perform a massive literature search, as Carroll (1993) has done, in an attempt to identify and classify all the distinct abilities that have ever been reported in the literature. Another approach would be to start from cognitive psychology and to try to assess individual differences in the types of thing that cognitive psychologists assess, e.g. speed of mental rotation, mental scanning, semantic priming, etc.

SAQ 8.2

I cannot guarantee that these answers are correct – they merely represent my view concerning the type of skills that might be most important in each of the tasks:

a. action – output; content – aural; process – fine use of muscle

b. input, memory and knowledge

c. internal processing, verbal and remembering

d. internal processing, verbal and complexity of relations

e. internal processing, verbal, complexity of relations and creativity

f. internal processing, knowledge, convergence and remembering.

SAQ 8.3

It is probably not sensible to conclude causality because, although the examples at the start of the chapter on factor analysis suggested that factors can *sometimes* be causal, it is not possible to extrapolate this and argue that any factor *must* be causal. For it is quite possible that things other than 'general ability' (possibly quality of education, inability to understand English, anxiety) may cause the observed results. However, if g can be shown to reflect some basic feature of the individual (e.g. the speed with which their nerves work) that cannot easily be assessed by any other means, then it may be permissible to argue causality.

SAQ 8.4

a. Gv; b. Gr; c. Gc; d. Gps.

SAQ 8.5

a.
$$\text{Ratio IQ} = \frac{\text{mental age}}{\text{chronological age}} \times 100.$$

Deviation IQ defines IQ as a normal distribution with a mean of 100 and a standard deviation of (usually) 16.

b. Because of the definition of deviation IQ given earlier (a normally distributed variable), 50% of the children will *always* be defined as having IQs below 100, even if the underlying raw scores on the test all increase dramatically over the 10-year period.

References

Anastasi, A. (1961). *Psychological Testing*. New York: Macmillan.

Anderson, M. (1992). *Intelligence and Development*. Oxford: Blackwell.

Blair, C. (2006). How similar are fluid cognition and general intelligence? A developmental neuroscience perspective on fluid cognition as an aspect of human cognitive ability. *Behavioral and Brain Sciences 29*(2), 109–60.

Brody, N. (1992). *Intelligence*. San Diego, CA: Academic Press.

Carroll, J. B. (1993). *Human Cognitive Abilities: A Survey of Factor-analytic Studies*. Cambridge: Cambridge University Press.

Cattell, R. B. (1971). *Abilities, Their Structure Growth and Action*. New York: Houghton-Mifflin.

Cooper, C. (1995). Inside the WISC-III(UK). *Educational Psychology in Practice 10*(4), 215–9.

Cooper, C. (1999). *Intelligence and Abilities*. London: Routledge.

Cooper, C. (2003). *Test the Nation: The IQ book*. London: BBC.

Cronbach, L. J. (1994). *Essentials of Psychological Testing* (5th edn). New York: HarperCollins.

Deary, I. J. (2000). *Looking Down on Human Intelligence: From Psychometrics to the Brain*. Oxford: Oxford University Press.

Ekstrom, R. B., French, J. W. and Harman, H. H. (1976). *Manual for the Kit of Factor-Referenced Cognitive Tests*. Princeton, NJ: Educational Testing Service.

Gardner, H. (1993). *Frames of Mind* (2nd edn). London: HarperCollins.

Gardner, H. (2006). On failing to grasp the core of MI theory: a response to Visser et al. *Intelligence 34*(5), 503–5.

Guilford, J. P. (1967). *The Nature of Human Intelligence*. New York: McGraw-Hill.

Gustafsson, J.-E. (1981). A unifying model for the structure of intellectual abilities. *Intelligence 8*, 179–203.

Hakstian, R. N. and Cattell, R. B. (1976). *Manual for the Comprehensive Ability Battery*. Champaign, IL: Institute for Personality and Ability Testing (IPAT).

Hakstian, R. N. and Cattell, R. B. (1978). Higher stratum ability structure on a basis of 20 primary abilities. *Journal of Educational Psychology 70*, 657–9.

Herrnstein, R. J. and Murray, C. (1994). *The Bell Curve: Intelligence and Class Structure in American Life*. New York: Free Press.

Horn, J. L. and Cattell, R. B. (1966). Refinement and test of the theory of fluid and crystallised intelligence. *Journal of Educational Psychology 57*, 253–70.

Jensen, A. R. (1998). *The g Factor*. New York: Praeger.

Kline, P. (1991). *Intelligence: The Psychometric View*. London: Routledge.

Kline, P. (1993). *The Handbook of Psychological Testing*. London: Routledge.

Kline, P. and Cooper, C. (1984). The factor structure of the comprehensive ability battery. *British Journal of Educational Psychology 54*(1), 106–10.

Mackintosh, N. J. (1998). *IQ and Human Intelligence*. Oxford: Oxford University Press.

Spearman, C. (1904). General intelligence objectively determined and measured. *American Journal of Psychology 15*, 201–93.

Sternberg, R. J. (1985). *Beyond IQ*. Cambridge: Cambridge University Press.

Sternberg, R. J. (1994). Thinking styles. In R. J. Sternberg and P. Ruzgis (eds), *Personality and Intelligence*. Cambridge: Cambridge University Press.

Thurstone, L. L. (1938). *Primary Mental Abilities*. Chicago: University of Chicago Press.

Undheim, J. O. (1981). On intelligence I: broad ability factors in 15 year old children and Cattell's theory of fluid and crystallised intelligence. *Scandinavian Journal of Psychology 22*, 171–9.

Vernon, P. E. (1950). *Structure of Human Abilities*. London: Methuen.

Visser, B. A., Ashton, M. C. and Vernon, P. A. (2006a). Beyond *g*: putting multiple intelligences theory to the test. *Intelligence 34*(5), 487–502.

Visser, B. A., Ashton, M. C. and Vernon, P. A. (2006b). *g* and the measurement of multiple intelligences: a response to Gardner. *Intelligence 34*(5), 507–10.

Wainer, H. (1987). *The First Four Millennia of Mental Testing: From Ancient China to the Computer Age* (Research Report No. RR-87-34). Princeton, NJ: Educational and Testing Service.

Ability processes

Background

This chapter considers some experiments designed to determine whether individual differences in ability have clear links to the physiology of the nervous system and to the speed with which certain cognitive operations can be performed. If such links can be found, it may be appropriate to use general ability to 'explain' behaviour, since general ability may reflect individual differences in the biological processing power of the brain and nervous system – a notion that dates back to Galton (1883) and Hebb (1949).

Recommended prior reading

Chapter 8.

Introduction

Chapter 8 made some rather important points. It indicated that almost all human abilities are positively correlated together and that it is possible to describe these correlations either by a single factor of general ability (as suggested by Spearman), by a set of 20 or more 'primary mental abilities' (as suggested by Thurstone), by a few 'group factors' (as suggested by Burt and Vernon) or, most generally, by a hierarchical model that incorporates all of these features (as suggested by Carroll, Cattell and Gustafsson). This really is quite interesting. It would logically be quite possible for human abilities to be independent of each other – after all, why *should* abilities as diverse as musical talent, mathematical skill, vocabulary, memory or ability to visualize shapes be interrelated? It is not as if there are any obvious processes (e.g. pieces of knowledge or skills taught through education) that are common to all of them and that could, therefore, account for their interrelationships.

However, knowing the structure of abilities does not mean that we understand what these abilities are. For this we need to develop 'process models' that describe intelligent behaviour in terms of lower level biological, cognitive or neural processes. Only when we have a good understanding of precisely why some people show different patterns of ability, personality and so on, can we profess to understand why people show different levels of abilities. Thirty years ago the structure of personality and ability was not particularly well understood and journals were full of articles attempting to establish the basic dimensions of ability. As there is now some consensus of opinion about the basic structure of abilities, almost all of the older theories being accommodated neatly by a hierarchical model, the focus of research has shifted. The main aim now is to identify the processes that cause individual differences in ability to appear.

Since abilities reflect the processing of information by the nervous system, the logical place to start looking for process models of individual differences is in the biology of the nervous system and in cognitive psychology. Both of these areas can sensibly be regarded as lower level, more fundamental causes of intelligent behaviour – it seems more likely that the way neurones work will affect general ability than vice versa. When one starts looking into the influence of social processes, personality, etc., the picture becomes much more complex, because it is difficult to be sure which variables are causes and which are effects. For example, suppose that it is found that children who perform poorly at mathematics hate the subject vehemently, whereas those who perform well have much more positive attitudes towards it. Perhaps we can argue that children's attitudes to a subject are an important indicator of their ability in that field – that is, that attitude influences ability. Thus any process model of ability ought to consider attitudes as important predictors.

However, this approach has several drawbacks. It is quite possible that the children's attitudes towards mathematics will *result from* their performance rather than vice versa. Achieving plenty of A grades on mathematics tests, receiving approving comments from teachers, etc., might *cause* children to enjoy the subject. Failing tests, being laughed at by one's peers and having to take extra tuition might well engender a negative attitude towards the subject. Thus it is just as likely that attitudes result from ability as that attitudes cause ability. There is a third possibility, too – that attitude and performance may both be influenced by some other factor(s), quality of teaching being one obvious variable.

These problems are not (quite) insurmountable, given excellent experimental design and statistics, such as confirmatory factor analysis. However, it makes sense to explore the simplest routes (biology and cognition) first – it is possible that individual differences in these areas may be able to explain a very sizeable proportion of the individual differences in ability. If so, there is no need to consider the (methodologically more messy) social and attitudinal approaches. However, if biological and cognitive approaches are unable to explain individual differences in ability, then these other avenues should be explored.

Neural processing and general ability

In the 1980s several theorists suggested that a person's general ability may, in part, be influenced by the way in which individual neurones in his or her nervous system process information. One theory suggests that high general ability may be a consequence of having nerve cells in the brain that conduct impulses rapidly (Reed 1984). Another theory suggests that general ability may be related to the *accuracy* with which information is transmitted from neurone to neurone (Eysenck 1982, 1986; Hendrickson 1972). The second point probably needs some explanation. Imagine that you are listening to a radio tuned to a distant station. It will be much more difficult to hear what is being said than when it is tuned to a nearby station, because the background hisses and crackles interfere with your ability to detect what is being said – they mask the signal. It may be the same with neurones. Perhaps some people's neurones switch from a very low to a very high rate of firing when stimulated by another neurone. Other people's neurones may fire quite frequently even when unstimulated or may fire only moderately frequently when stimulated. In such cases, information will not be transmitted very efficiently from one neurone to others. Some upstream neurones will 'think' that a neurone has fired when it has not or they may fail to detect a modest increase in firing rate that corresponds to a real psychological event.

These theories lead to similar predictions. They suggest that people whose neurones conduct information quickly along the axon and/or which transmit information efficiently and accurately **139** across the synapses are likely to be more efficient at processing information than those whose nerves transmit information slowly or have a low signal-to-noise ratio.

How can one measure speed/efficiency of neural conduction? Several techniques have been developed for this, including direct measurement, inspection time, reaction time and evoked potential studies. These will be considered in the following.

Direct measurement of neural conduction velocity

In principle, such direct measurement is easy. One merely has to apply two electrodes (as far apart as possible) to a single neurone. An electric current is applied to one electrode, to stimulate the neurone to fire. The second electrode is used to time how quickly the impulse travels down the axon of the nerve. If the distance between the two electrodes is measured with a rule, it is a simple matter to calculate the nerve conduction velocity. If this experiment is performed with a large sample of people whose scores on a test of general ability are also known, then theory would predict that there should be a substantial positive correlation between general ability and nerve conduction velocity (NCV).

Vernon and Mori (1992) and Wickett and Vernon (1994) performed such experiments using nerves in the arm and wrist and found that there was a significant correlation (of the order of 0.42–0.48) between general ability and NCV. Thus it does appear from these studies that intelligent people have nerves that simply transmit information more quickly than those of individuals of lower general ability. However, other workers have failed to replicate this finding (e.g. Reed and Jensen 1991; Rijsdijk, Boonsma and Vernon 1995), although Reed, Vernon and Johnson (2004) have managed to find a small relationship, along with a sex difference (males being faster). However, these tasks do not involve any synaptic transmission and so, if the individual differences arise at the synapses, the Vernon and Mori task could not be expected to work. At Belfast, Margaret McRorie and I have run some experiments to determine whether higher ability individuals show faster reflex responses than lower ability ones (latency of knee-jerk reflex and speed of withdrawal from a painful electric shock). These tasks do involve synaptic transmission (although no conscious thought at all) and there is a link between speed of withdrawal and IQ (McRorie and Cooper 2001, 2004) supporting the Reed/Eysenck/Jensen theory.

Indirect measurement of neural conduction velocity

Inspection time

Several techniques have been developed to measure NCV using indirect methods. The simplest to understand is a technique known as inspection time (Vickers, Nettelbeck and Willson 1972). This simply measures how long a simple stimulus has to be presented in order to be perceived correctly. For example, suppose that either shape (a) or shape (b) in Figure 9.1 is flashed on to a screen for a few thousandths of a second and a volunteer is then asked whether the longer line was on the left or the right. Shape (c) is presented immediately after (a) or (b) to act as a mask (if you

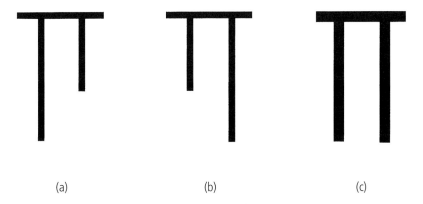

(a)   (b)   (c)

Figure 9.1 Stimulation for an inspection time task.

are not familiar with the principles of masking you can safely ignore this detail). It is important to realize that inspection time is a measure of how long it takes to see a stimulus and *not* of how quickly a person can respond to it – in the inspection time task an individual can take as long as they want to make their decision.

The aim of inspection time studies is to determine how long it takes an individual to perceive such stimuli. Since the retina is essentially an outgrowth of the brain, one might expect people with accurate and/or rapid neurones to be able to make this simple discrimination more rapidly than others. Thus it is possible that highly intelligent individuals will be able to see the stimulus correctly after a shorter time than those of lower general ability – that is, there will be a negative correlation between general ability and inspection time.

The amount of time a person needs to see the figures can be estimated by repeating the experiment several times (e.g. 50–100 times) for each of several exposure periods. The percentage of correct answers can be noted and plotted on a graph such as that shown in Figure 9.2. You can see

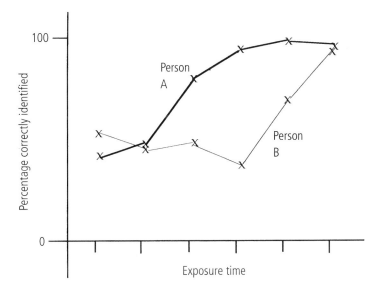

Figure 9.2 Percentage of stimuli correctly identified at several exposure durations during an inspection time task.

that at the fastest exposure time both Person A and Person B perform at chance level. However, as the presentation time increases, it is clear that Person A can see which line is longer rather more quickly than Person B – her percentage of stimuli correctly identified rises quite rapidly. It is possible to calculate a statistic for each individual to reflect these differences – for example, the exposure time at which there is an 80% chance that they will be able to solve the problem correctly. Such statistics can be correlated with measures of general ability in order to determine whether inspection time (and hence, indirectly, speed and/or efficiency of neural processing) is related to general ability.

Tens of studies show that it is. Most find that the correlations between measures of general ability and inspection time are of the order of −0.3 to −0.5. Several alternative methods of assessing inspection time have also been devised and they yield broadly similar results. However, the interpretation of such data is a little more controversial. Without going into details, it has been suggested that the correlations between inspection time and general ability may be influenced by attention span or by the use of cognitive strategies, such as flicker detection, which will reveal whether the shorter leg of the masked stimulus were presented to the left or the right (Mackenzie and Bingham 1985). Yet even when these are taken into account, there is still an appreciable correlation between the measures (Egan and Deary 1992). Thus it seems that there is a very substantial link between inspection time and general ability. More recent studies have tried to develop more effective masks that do not allow people to develop strategies for solving the task (e.g. Stough, Bates, Mangan and Colrain 2001) and alternative paradigms, such as ability to detect the apparent direction of a tone briefly presented through earphones (McCrory and Cooper 2005; Parker, Crawford and Stephen 1999). Acton and Schroeder (2001) revisit links between g and sensory discrimination in general, while Grudnik and Kranzler (2001) report a meta-analysis of inspection time studies and conclude that the size of the underlying correlation is approximately −0.51 after correcting for reliability and restriction of range.

Self-assessment question 9.1

Why would it be serious if inspection time were shown to be influenced by cognitive strategies, such as flicker detection?

Reaction time

Inspection time estimates the time for which a stimulus has to be presented in order to be correctly recognized, but it is also possible to assess how long it takes an individual to *respond* to a stimulus. This, too, might be related to general ability – if highly intelligent individuals have neurones that transmit information particularly quickly or accurately, these individuals should be able to respond more rapidly to a signal than people of lower general ability. This idea was first proposed by Galton (1883), who attempted to test it and eventually concluded that no such relationship existed. However, the accurate measurement of reaction times was problematic a century ago and Jensen and Munroe (1974) were the first to re-examine this issue in the English-language journals. They measured reaction time using the apparatus shown diagrammatically in Figure 9.3.

The apparatus consists of eight green lights (here depicted by squares) arranged in a semicircle on a metal panel. Beside each light is a button (denoted by a black circle) with an additional

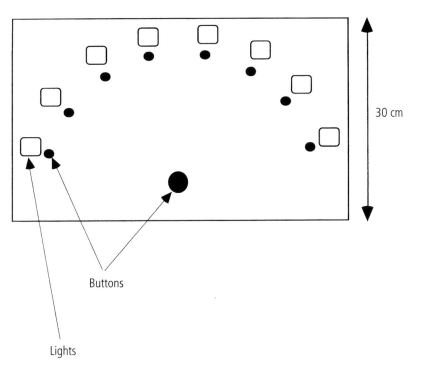

Figure 9.3 Jensen and Munroe's (1974) choice reaction time apparatus.

'home button' centred 15cm away from all of the other buttons. The lights and buttons are connected to a computer that controls the experiment. The task is straightforward and participants are asked to react as quickly as possible. The index finger of the preferred hand is placed on the home button. After a (random) period of a few seconds, one of the lights is illuminated – the 'target light'. The participant lifts their finger from the home button and presses the button beside this light. Two time intervals are recorded:

- the interval between the 'target' light being illuminated and the finger leaving the home button, known as the reaction time (RT)

- the interval between the finger leaving the home button and pressing the target button, known as the movement time (MT).

This is repeated several times (usually at least 30). Measurements are also obtained for different numbers of lights (varying from one to eight), the unused lights and buttons being masked off by metal plates.

When the mean reaction times are plotted as a function of the number of lights (do not worry about why the numbers on the x axis are not equally spaced), a graph similar to that shown in Figure 9.4 is obtained for each individual. Straight lines may be fitted to the RT and MT graphs as shown and the equations of these straight lines can be obtained by simple algebra. The height of these lines (the 'intercept') shows how quickly the participant reacted overall. The slope of the lines shows how much their RT (or MT) changes as the number of potential targets increases. RT typically increases as the number of potential targets increases (a phenomenon known as 'Hick's law'), whereas MT stays almost constant. We thus have four measures for each participant, cor-

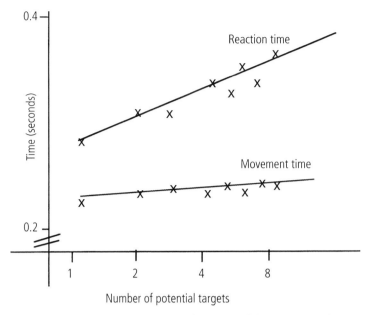

Figure 9.4 Reaction time and movement time as a function of the number of potential targets.

responding to the slope and the intercept of the two lines. These measures are correlated with general ability.

The intercept of the RT graph generally shows a significant negative correlation with general ability – in the order of –0.3 (Jensen 1987). That is, highly intelligent people respond more quickly overall and their RT does not increase much as the number of potential target lights increases (Barrett, Eysenck and Lucking 1986; Jensen 1982). MT shows no correlation with general ability, although the *variability* in MT often does (Barrett et al. 1986; Jensen 1982). The correlation between the slope of the line and general ability is much less well documented (Barrett et al. 1986; Beauducel and Brocke 1993). More recently, rather more complex models have been developed of how the brain may make the decision to respond to a stimulus (e.g. Ratcliff, Van Zandt and McKoon 1999) and Paul Wilson and I hope that such diffusion models may help to clarify the relationship between *g* and cognition. However, these models are mathematically rather complex and so will not be considered here.

Not everyone would agree that this implies that intelligence is related to speed of processing. Longstreth (1984) suggests that the more intelligent participants may be able to devise efficient cognitive strategies for responding quickly (Sternberg's 'metacomponents'). The correlations between RT and general ability may thus reflect the use of such strategies rather than anything more fundamental. However, experiments performed in order to test such hypotheses show that these strategies cannot explain the underlying correlation between RT and general ability (Matthews and Dorn 1989; Neubauer 1991). Reaction time does seem to show a negative correlation with general ability, as expected.

The problem with these experiments is that the correlation between reaction time and general ability is stronger when the task becomes more complex. For example, a reaction time task with eight alternatives (such as that shown in Figure 9.3) produces a much higher correlation with general ability than does a two-choice or a four-choice task. Indeed, the literature suggests that simple reaction time (measured by pressing a button as quickly as possible in response to a single light or sound) shows a really rather modest correlation with general ability, of the order of –0.1 to –0.25 (Jensen 1980). If a high level of general ability *just* reflects individual differences in the speed of processing information, then the correlations should really be higher than this.

One alternative explanation for the low correlation could be that either general ability or simple reaction time was measured with low reliability. Reaction times can have their reliability assessed in just the same way as questionnaire items, and it is unfortunate that most reaction time studies do not estimate reliability. However, May, Cooper and Kline (1986) showed that highly reliable estimates of simple reaction time can be made from a relatively modest number of trials and so low levels of reliability are unlikely to be the cause of the low correlations observed. It is much more probable that more complex kinds of decision making or strategy use are at work.

Self-assessment question 9.2

a. What is the difference between inspection time and reaction time?

b. Name three measures derived from the Jensen task that have been found to correlate substantially with general ability.

Evoked potentials

A fourth way of exploring the link between neural activity and general ability relies on recording the electrical activity from brain cells. If one sticks (quite literally!) a few electrodes on the surface of the scalp and attaches these to sensitive amplifiers, it is possible to measure electrical activity in the brain – not in individual neurones, but in whole areas of the brain. Average auditory evoked potential recordings are, as their name suggests, measures of brain voltages (potentials) that are evoked by a sound. They show how the brain processes a simple sound.

In the simplest experimental design, the participant is seated in a comfortable chair, electrodes are attached to their scalp and a pair of headphones is placed over their head. They are simply told to remain sitting, with eyes closed, and do nothing. They are informed that they will hear clicks or tones through the headphones from time to time, but that these should be ignored. A hundred or so clicks are presented over a period of about 10 minutes. What could be simpler, from a participant's point of view?

The brain's electrical activity is recorded for a couple of seconds following each click. In practice, the voltages are typically measured every thousandth of a second following the onset of the click and at the end of the experiment each of these 1000 voltages is averaged across the 100 replications (hence it is known as the *average* auditory evoked potential). The 1000 averaged voltages may then be plotted as a graph, rather as shown in Figure 9.5, which is based on the pioneering work of Ertl and Schafer (1969). This shows time on the *x* axis and voltage on the *y* axis (a positive voltage being downwards, by convention). This process therefore produces a different graph for each participant. Several features of these graphs have been linked to IQ.

Hendrickson and Hendrickson (1980) suggested that high IQ participants appear to have longer, more spiky waveforms and this could be assessed simply by measuring the length of the graph over a particular period of time (such as 0.25 seconds). They called this the 'string measure' (since it was originally measured by putting a piece of string over graphs such as those shown in Figure 9.5 and then straightening it out and measuring its length). Using this technique, they **145**

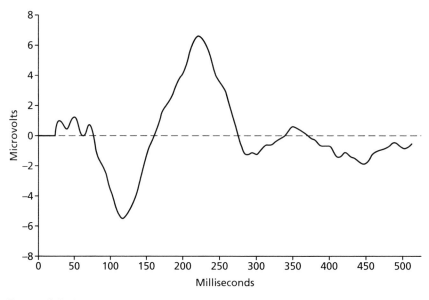

Figure 9.5 Average auditory evokes potential recording.

found a correlation of 0.7 between string length and IQ in Ertl and Schafer's data. They subsequently recorded correlations of the order of 0.7 within another sample of over 200 schoolchildren (A. E. Hendrickson 1982; D. E. Hendrickson 1982) – a highly significant result, but one that has proved difficult to replicate. Some (e.g. Gilbert, Johnson, Gilbert and McColloch 1991; Stough, Nettelbeck and Cooper 1990) observed an effect as expected, while others (e.g. Bates and Eysenck 1993; Shagass, Roemer and Straumanis 1981) did not. A technically sophisticated study by Barrett and Eysenck (1992) could find no evidence whatsoever for a positive correlation between general ability and the string measure. If anything, the data show that the correlation should be negative. Given the scale and methodological sophistication of this study, this failure to replicate the previous findings is worrying. There are theoretical problems with the string measure, too. A spiky average trace can only arise if (a) each individual trace contains a lot of high-frequency components and (b) the time course of these components is consistent from trial to trial; if this is not the case the peaks and troughs will tend to average out to produce a straight line. So a flat trace could arise for two very different reasons – a lack of high-frequency activity or inconsistent time courses. It would surely make sense to analyse each of these variables separately.

The measurement of evoked potentials is a highly technical business and pushed technology to its limits in the 1960s and 1970s. There is concern that some methodological problem may have influenced the results, particularly as Hendrickson's (1982) study involved testing at more than one site, with the subsample of high-ability subjects all being tested at the same location. It has also emerged that attention interacts with general ability in determining string length, even in a small sample of undergraduates (Bates, Stough, Mangan and Pellett 1995). When participants are asked to pay attention to the tones, this affects the string length of higher ability individuals. The results of these evoked potential studies are inconsistent, which may well reflect subtle but important differences in experimental procedures and instructions. But overall there are enough strong correlations reported in the literature to suggest that there is most probably *some* underlying relationship between string length and general ability.

Many other more conventional analyses of such waveforms (e.g. measuring their amplitude and the delay between the stimulus and each peak and trough) have been performed and Deary and Carryl (1993) have provided an excellent and thoughtful summary of the older literature. Once again, the results are somewhat variable, although they generally support a link between general ability and electrical activity in the brain. However, a detailed description of these studies is beyond the scope of this chapter.

General ability and cognitive tasks

It would be amazing if the kinds of ability described in Chapter 8 were completely unrelated to the types of process studied by cognitive psychologists and so in this section and the next we shall consider some areas of overlap between the two. Carroll (1980) suggested that some of the tasks traditionally studied by cognitive psychologists, such as the Sternberg memory-scanning paradigm or the Watson and Clarke sentence verification task, should be related to mental abilities. The great advantage of such tasks is that they are thought to measure single cognitive processes – the experiments were designed to measure the time taken to perform a single elementary cognitive operation (ECO). For example, the Sternberg memory scanning paradigm (1969) presents a list of numbers or characters for several seconds, followed by a 'target character'. The participant is asked to push one button if the target character was in the preceding list and another if it was not. The reaction time is found to be related to the length of the list. After a little statistical juggling (involving regression lines), it is possible to estimate how long it takes an individual to 'take in' the meaning of the target and how long it takes that individual to compare the target with one of the stored representations of a character.

Two main approaches have been adopted in order to test such theories. One is fairly crude and involves correlating the durations of various elementary cognitive operations with ability. The other attempts to model solution times to complex tasks.

The first and cruder approach simply involves estimating how long it takes each individual person in a sample to perform some of these elementary cognitive operations, using experiments such as the Sternberg memory scanning paradigm. The second stage is to check whether the people who perform these basic cognitive operations fastest also perform well on certain ability tests that may require the (repeated) use of some of these ECOs, among other things. The time taken for each subject to perform each ECO can thus be correlated with his or her scores on various psychometric ability tests. (Statistically sophisticated readers may appreciate that multiple regression techniques may be used to determine the relative importance of each ECO to each ability trait. The beta weights may show the relative number of times each ECO is performed during the course of each ability test. However, readers unfamiliar with regression techniques can skip this detail.)

Several studies have examined the relationship between abilities and the time it takes to perform some of these ECOs. For example, Hunt (1978) suggested that verbal ability is closely related to individual differences in ability to retrieve lexical information (i.e. the meaning of letters) from long-term memory. His participants performed two experiments. In the first, they were asked to decide (as quickly as possible) whether pairs of letters were the same (e.g. AA, aa, BB or bb) or physically different (e.g. AB, aA, bA, ab). In the second experiment, they were asked to decide whether the two characters referred to the same letter of the alphabet (e.g. Aa, AA, aA, Bb) or not (e.g. AB, bA, ab, aB). The average time taken to make each decision (correctly) was calculated for each experiment. The average time taken to decide whether the two characters were physically **147** identical was then subtracted from the average time taken to decide whether the two characters referred to the same letter of the alphabet. This was thought to be related to the amount of time taken to access the meaning of each character in long-term memory. It was consistently found that the correlation between this statistic and verbal ability was of the order of −0.3 – statistically significant, but once again not large enough to support the claim that verbal ability is *just* speed of lexical access. So perhaps we need to perform some more complex experiments in order to try to *model* the processes that are used when solving a more complex task.

Self-assessment question 9.3

Is it possible that some cognitive strategies could affect performance on either of these experiments?

Plenty of other attempts have been made to explore the links between cognition and mental ability in other areas, too (see, for example, Mulhern 1997; Stankov, Boyle and Cattell 1995).

The second approach involves a careful analysis of the steps involved in performing some really quite complex cognitive tasks. Robert Sternberg (1977) (no relation of S. Sternberg) performed some remarkably elegant experiments in this area. He argued that if the sequence of cognitive operations required to perform a fairly complex task were known, and if it was possible to estimate (through experiments such as those described earlier) how long it takes each individual to perform each of these basic cognitive operations, it might be possible to predict quite accurately how long it would take an individual to solve the problem. In other words, one first identifies all the ECOs that are thought to be involved in a particular task and draws up a flowchart to show how these are organized. The next step is to assess how long it takes *each individual* to perform each of these mental operations, using carefully designed experiments. Having done this, it should be possible to 'plug in' the amount of time that it takes an individual to perform each ECO in order to predict how long it should take a person to solve a particular problem.

Moreover, since most mental tasks may involve the same basic ECOs, albeit strung together according to different flowcharts, it might be possible to measure how long it takes a person to perform each ECO and on the basis of this to predict how long they will take to solve other mental tasks. Essentially, ECO durations would replace ability traits as the unit of analysis.

Much of Sternberg's work focused on nonverbal analogy problems – for example, analogy items based on the 'people-piece' cartoon characters. These characters differed from each other in the following four basic ways:

- gender – male/female
- height – tall/short
- girth – fat/thin
- colour – shaded/unshaded.

A typical analogy task using these characters would be like that shown in Figure 9.6. You have probably already encountered verbal analogies – for example, 'cat is to kitten as dog is to bitch' [sic]. Participants would have to decide whether each of these items were true or false. Sternberg moved away from such verbal analogies because he felt that the use of language may complicate the process of solving these problems. Instead, he argued that 'people-piece' characters can be

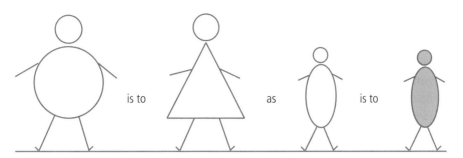

Figure 9.6 Example of a schematic analogy task, reading 'Tall fat unshaded man is to tall fat unshaded woman as short thin unshaded man is to short thin shaded man' – an incorrect analogy. If correct, the fourth character would be a short, thin unshaded woman.

used in the same way. In Figure 9.6 the only thing that differs between the first pair of characters is their sex. Their shading, height and girth are the same. Applying the same rule to the second pair, the fourth character *should* clearly be a short, thin, unshaded female. However, is not, so the analogy is false.

Sternberg argued that six main cognitive processes underpinned performance on these tasks, namely encoding (the recognition of each feature of the cartoon characters), inference (noting which features changed between the first pair of characters, thus inferring the rule to be applied to the second pair of characters), mapping the relationship between the first and third characters, applying the rule to the third character, comparing the fourth character to what it should be and responding appropriately. He drew up several plausible flowchart models for solving these problems on the basis of these elementary cognitive operations. Through the use of some ingenious experiments involving pre-cueing (sometimes showing some of the characters before the others, thereby allowing some of the ECOs to be performed prior to the measurement of the reaction times), he was able to assess the duration of each of these components independently for each person (Sternberg 1977).

The problem is that, even with a relatively simple task such as this, the number of plausible models for solving the analogies becomes quite large. For example, it is possible to suggest that some cognitive operations may be performed in parallel, rather than sequentially. Cognitive strategies for solving the problems can also complicate the picture enormously. For example, if three of the characters are shaded but one is not or if one figure is a different height from the other three, then the analogy *must* be incorrect. Some (but not all) of the individuals performing this task seem to check for such possibilities before analysing the problem in detail. One attempt to replicate this work (May, Kline and Cooper 1987) found that the model really did not fit the data very well. Neither did the estimated durations of Sternberg's six basic cognitive processes correlate very strongly with other cognitive measures.

Working memory and the neuropsychology of intelligence

There is currently much interest in the relationship between working memory and intelligence. Working memory, as studied by cognitive psychologists, is known to be closely related to general **149** intelligence (Colom, Abad, Quiroga, Shih and Flores-Mendoza 2008). Working memory tasks require a person to keep information in short-term storage while performing some other cognitive operation. For example, it may involve showing someone a story consisting of several sentences, one sentence at a time but where a word is missing from each sentence whose nature can be guessed from the context. For example, 'John took his umbrella because the forecast predicted _____' could be one of the sentences. Participants are asked to find the missing word in each sentence – and remember them all, in sequence. Or they may be asked to listen to a string of numbers – e.g. 1, 4, 9, 2, 7 – and asked to repeat them backwards, so that is necessary to remember the original list and also process it in reverse.

This is, perhaps, hardly surprising. The 'digit backwards' task appears in several intelligence tests (e.g. the WISC-IV) and so the question arises about whether cognitive psychologists are just discovering *g*. This is a particular concern since there is a burgeoning literature on the link between working memory and other outcomes, such as reading performance (e.g. Gathercole, Alloway, Willis and Adams 2006). Some rather detailed models are now being developed that use fMRI scans to determine which areas of the brain are active when solving intelligence test-type problems, which are involved with working memory, others related to attention and so on – however some of this literature is quite technical. Haier (2009) provides an accessible, brief summary of some of the main issues. Interestingly, it seems that spatial abilities seem to be much more consistently localized (in terms of brain functioning) than other abilities. Luders, Narr, Thompson and Toga (2009) provide an excellent (and readable) account of the links between intelligence and brain activity, as revealed by MRI and fMRI scans. Findings of note are that:

1. Brain size (volume) correlates quite substantially with intelligence (between 0.26 and 0.56), with some suggestion that grey matter volume is more important that white matter volume.

2. The amount of grey matter in the lateral and medial frontal cortex and the anterior cingulate seems to be particularly related to *g*.

3. There is evidence that the thickness of some areas of the cortex is related to *g*.

4. There does not seem to be much evidence for an overall relationship between the amount of convolution (folding) in the cortex and intelligence.

5. The size of the corpus callosum *is* related to intelligence.

There are thus clear links between psychometric *g* and brain structure and function, but one of the more interesting findings is that *g* involves multiple areas of the cortex (Colom et al. 2009).

Summary

In this chapter we have looked at some biological and cognitive processes that are associated with mental abilities. The picture is still somewhat tantalizing in that there are a number of variables (e.g. inspection time, RT slope, lexical access time) that show statistically significant correlations with mental abilities, although the correlations are not large enough to suggest that these variables can completely *explain* the abilities. Furthermore, more complex modelling of cognitive processes (as with Sternberg's model) soon runs into problems, since the number of potential flowcharts becomes very large, as individuals may use different cognitive strategies when solving the tasks.

So far, we have assumed that intelligence and abilities are real characteristics of individuals, perhaps related to the way in which neurones operate or to the way in which individuals process information. That is, we have assumed that abilities exist and that they influence behaviour. Not everyone shares this view. For example, Howe (1988a) argues that these abilities are a convenient way of *describing* how people behave, but are essentially 'constructions' of the observer, rather than any real property of the individual. According to this view, it would be quite wrong to use general ability as an explanation – for example, to say that a child performs well at school because he or she is intelligent would imply that general ability is some basic property of the individual, rather than just a convenient way of describing their behaviour.

The experiments described in the present chapter all attempt to relate performance on ability tests to some more basic biological or cognitive processes. They are important because they can show whether it is legitimate to regard abilities as the behavioural manifestations of more fundamental properties of the brain and cognitive systems. If this is so, it may be legitimate to argue that abilities can truly explain behaviour.

Howe's argument collapses if experiments show that abilities are closely linked to some fundamental properties of individuals' nervous systems or speed of cognition or if there is evidence for a substantial genetic influence on general ability (evidence for which will be scrutinized in a later chapter). In a rejoinder to Howe's paper, Sternberg (1988: 745) suggests that many of Howe's points are based on a somewhat selective reading of the literature and that several important empirical studies undermine his conclusion. You will find it very useful to consult these papers by Howe and Sternberg and draw your own conclusions.

Some of the earlier studies described in this chapter are really rather crude. Psychometrically, most have focused on general ability rather than a broader range of ability factors. Experimentally, none of the studies of brain activity has considered that general ability may be related to the localization of brain activity. Some evidence suggests that processing is more highly localized in high-ability individuals.

Several studies have been performed using undergraduates, who will all (presumably!) have above average general ability, while others (such as work on working memory) have used samples of very low IQ. Using a sample with a small range of individual differences in mental ability will underestimate the true, underlying correlations between general ability and other variables.

We are starting to see the development of testable models such as the Jung-Haier parieto-frontal integration theory (Jung and Haier 2007), showing how intelligence results from cortical activity and its relationship to attentional, memory and other cognitive processes and this must surely be the way forward.

Suggested additional reading

The theoretical rationale for looking behind pencil-and-paper tests of *g* is to determine whether or not psychometric tests that assess general ability also reflect some rather basic biological or cognitive properties of the nervous system, e.g. the speed with which it can process information. If so, some theorists would argue, it is reasonable to use the term 'general ability' to explain why some individuals perform better than others on a very wide range of mental tasks. Two papers by Howe (1988b) and Sternberg (1988) bear directly on this issue and make interesting reading.

More detailed accounts of the link between general ability, inspection time and reaction time are given in Ian Deary's reviews (2000; Deary and Carryl 1993; Deary and Stough 1996; Jensen 1998) and a general survey of the whole field is offered by Deary (2000: Ch. 7) and Jensen (1997).

The literature on neural imaging and *g* can be rather technical, and may obscure the simplicity of the basic aims of this work: to discover which areas of the brain are active when people solve intelligence tests and to determine whether individual differences in *g* are linked to brain functioning. Papers such as Jung and Haier (2007) or Colom et al. (2009) are, however, fairly easy to understand.

Answers to self-assessment questions

SAQ 9.1

The whole rationale for correlating inspection time with *g* is that inspection time is thought to measure a rather simple and basic physiological process, namely the speed and/or accuracy with which information can be transmitted from neurone to neurone. If it is found that performance on the inspection time task is influenced by 'higher order' mental processes (such as strategy use or concentration), then it is clear that inspection time cannot be a pure measure of this physiological phenomenon and so will be less useful for testing the theory that intelligence is essentially a measure of how fast and/or accurately nervous systems can transmit information.

SAQ 9.2

a. In an inspection time task the experimenter controls the duration of the stimuli and ascertains the exposure duration at which each individual has a certain probability (e.g. 75% or 90%) of correctly identifying the stimulus. The participant can take as long as they like to make their response. A reaction time task, by way of contrast, requires participants to respond as quickly as possible to a stimulus. In the inspection time task, perceiving the stimulus is the important part of the experiment, whereas in the reaction time task it is responding quickly that is crucial.

b. The following three measures have been found to correlate substantially with general ability:

- The slope of the line obtained when response time is plotted as shown in Figure 9.4 shows a negative correlation with *g*.

- The intercept (height) of the line obtained when response time is plotted as shown in Figure 9.4 shows a negative correlation with *g*.

- The variability in the movement time (e.g. the standard deviation of individuals' movement times for a particular experimental condition) shows a negative correlation with *g*.

SAQ 9.3

It does seem possible that cognitive strategies might influence performance on both the Hunt and the Sternberg tasks. Most obviously, the standard instruction to 'respond as quickly as possible while trying not to make *any* errors' may well be interpreted rather differently by various individuals, some of whom will respond slowly in order to avoid making any errors, while others may be content to sacrifice accuracy for speed. There are other possibilities, too. For example, when scanning a list of 'target letters' in the Sternberg task, does one continue to scan to the end of the list after detecting the target or does one stop immediately? Is it possible to scan several elements of the list in parallel, rather than serially? The evidence shows that the responses to this task are influenced by such variables. Likewise, Hunt's task can involve strategies, e.g. scanning for a straight line sticking up, which necessarily indicates a 'b' rather than an 'A', an 'a' or a 'B'.

References

Acton, G. S. and Schroeder, D. H. (2001). Sensory discrimination as related to general intelligence. *Intelligence 29*(3), 263–71.

Barrett, P. T. and Eysenck, H. J. (1992). Brain evoked potentials and intelligence: the Hendrickson paradigm. *Intelligence 16*, 361–81.

Barrett, P. T., Eysenck, H. J. and Lucking, S. (1986). Reaction time and intelligence – a replicated study. *Intelligence 10*(1), 9–40.

Bates, T. and Eysenck, H. J. (1993). String length, attention and intelligence: focused attention reverses the string length/IQ relationship. *Personality and Individual Differences 15*, 363–71.

Bates, T., Stough, C., Mangan, G. and Pellett, O. (1995). Intelligence and the complexity of the averaged evoked potential: an attentional theory. *Intelligence 20*, 27–39.

Beauducel, A. and Brocke, B. (1993). Intelligence and speed of information-processing – further results and questions on Hick paradigm and beyond. *Personality and Individual Differences 15*(6), 627–36.

Carroll, J. B. (1980). *Individual Difference Relations in Psychometric and Experimental Cognitive Tasks* (No. 163). Chapel Hill, NC: L. L. Thurstone Psychometric Laboratory.

Colom, R., Abad, F. J., Quiroga, M. Ã. N., Shih, P. C. and Flores-Mendoza, C. (2008). Working memory and intelligence are highly related constructs, but why? *Intelligence 36*(6), 584–606.

Colom, R., Haier, R. J., Head, K., Alvarez-Linera, J., Quiroga, M. A., Shih, P. C. et al. (2009). Gray matter correlates of fluid, crystallized, and spatial intelligence: testing the P-FIT model. *Intelligence 37*(2), 124–35.

Deary, I. J. (2000). *Looking Down on Human Intelligence: From Psychometrics to the Brain*. Oxford: Oxford University Press.

Deary, I. J. and Carryl, P. G. (1993). Intelligence, EEG and evoked potentials. In P. A. Vernon (ed.), *Biological Approaches to the Study of Human Intelligence*. Norwood, NJ: Ablex.

Deary, I. J. and Stough, C. (1996). Intelligence and inspection time: achievements, prospects and problems. *American Psychologist 51*, 599–608.

Egan, V. and Deary, I. J. (1992). Are specific inspection time strategies prevented by concurrent tasks? *Intelligence 16*, 151–68.

Ertl, J. P. and Schafer, E. W. P. (1969). Brain response correlates of psychometric intelligence. *Nature 223*, 421–2.

Eysenck, H. J. (1982). Introduction. In H. J. Eysenck (ed.), *A Model for Intelligence*. Berlin: Springer-Verlag.

Eysenck, H. J. (1986). The theory of intelligence and the neurophysiology of cognition. In R. J. Sternberg (ed.), *Advances in the Psychology of Human Intelligence* (Vol. 3). Hillsdale, NJ: Erlbaum.

Galton, F. (1883). *Inquiries into Human Faculty and its Development*. London: Macmillan.

Gathercole, S. E., Alloway, T. P., Willis, C. and Adams, A. M. (2006). Working memory in children with reading disabilities. *Journal of Experimental Child Psychology 93*(3), 265–81.

Gilbert, D. G., Johnson, S., Gilbert, B. O. and McColloch, M. A. (1991). Event-related potential correlates of IQ. *Personality and Individual Differences 12*, 1183–4.

Grudnik, J. L. and Kranzler, J. H. (2001). Meta-analysis of the relationship between intelligence and inspection time. *Intelligence 29*(6), 523–35.

Haier, R. J. (2009). Neuro-intelligence, neuro-metrics and the next phase of brain imaging studies. *Intelligence 37*(2), 121–3.

Hebb, D. O. (1949). *The Organisation of Behavior*. New York: Wiley.

Hendrickson, A. E. (1982). The biological basis of intelligence. Part 1: theory. In H. J. Eysenck (ed.), *A Model for Intelligence*. Berlin: Springer-Verlag.

Hendrickson, D. E. (1972). An integrated molar/molecular model of the brain. *Psychological Reports 30*, 343–68.

Hendrickson, D. E. (1982). The biological basis of intelligence. Part II: measurement. In H. J. Eysenck (ed.), *A Model for Intelligence*. Berlin: Springer-Verlag.

Hendrickson, D. E. and Hendrickson, A. E. (1980). The biological basis of individual differences in intelligence. *Personality and Individual Differences 1*, 3–33.

Howe, M. J. A. (1988a). The hazard of using correlational evidence as a means of identifying the causes of individual ability differences: a rejoinder to Sternberg and a reply to Miles. *British Journal of Psychology 79*, 539–45.

Howe, M. J. A. (1988b). Intelligence as explanation. *British Journal of Psychology 79*, 349–60.

Hunt, E. B. (1978). The mechanics of verbal ability. *Psychological Review 85*, 109–30.

Jensen, A. R. (1980). *Bias in Mental Testing*. New York: Free Press.

Jensen, A. R. (1982). Reaction time and psychometric g. In H. J. Eysenck (ed.), *A Model for Intelligence*. Berlin: Springer-Verlag.

Jensen, A. R. (1987). Individual differences in the Hick paradigm. In P. A. Vernon (ed.), *Speed of Information-processing and Intelligence*. Norwood, NJ: Ablex.

Jensen, A. R. (1997). The psychophysiology of g. In C. Cooper and V. Varma (eds), *Processes in Individual Differences*. London: Routledge.

Jensen, A. R. (1998). *The g Factor*. New York: Praeger.

Jensen, A. R. and Munroe, E. (1974). Reaction time, movement time and intelligence. *Intelligence 3*, 121–6.

Jung, R. E. and Haier, R. J. (2007). The parieto-frontal integration theory (P-FIT) of intelligence: converging neuroimaging evidence. *Behavioral and Brain Sciences 30*(2), 135–54.

Longstreth, L. E. (1984). Jensen's reaction time investigations: a critique. *Intelligence 8*, 139–60.

Luders, E., Narr, K. L., Thompson, P. M. and Toga, A. W. (2009). Neuroanatomical correlates of intelligence. *Intelligence 37*(2), 156–63.

Mackenzie, B. and Bingham, E. (1985). IQ, inspection time and response strategies in a university population. *Australian Journal of Psychology 37*(3), 257–68.

Matthews, G. and Dorn, L. (1989). IQ and choice reaction time: an information processing analysis. *Intelligence 13*, 299–317.

May, J., Cooper, C. and Kline, P. (1986). The reliability of reaction times in some elementary cognitive tasks: a brief research note. *Personality and Individual Differences 7*(6), 893–5.

May, J., Kline, P. and Cooper, C. (1987). A brief computerized form of a schematic analogy task. *British Journal of Psychology 78*(1), 29–36.

McCrory, C. and Cooper, C. (2005). The relationship between three auditory inspection time tasks and general intelligence. *Personality and Individual Differences 38*(8), 1835–45.

McRorie, M. and Cooper, C. (2001). Neural transmission and general mental ability. *Learning and Individual Differences 13*(4), 335–8.

McRorie, M. and Cooper, C. (2004). Synaptic transmission correlates of general mental ability. *Intelligence 32*(3), 263–75.

Mulhern, G. A. (1997). Intelligence and cognitive processing. In C. Cooper and V. Varma (eds), *Processes in Individual Differences*. London: Routledge.

Neubauer, A. C. (1991). Intelligence and RT: a modified Hick paradigm and a new RT paradigm. *Intelligence 15*, 175–92.

Parker, D. M., Crawford, J. R. and Stephen, E. (1999). Auditory inspection time and intelligence: a new spatial localization task. *Intelligence 27*(2), 131–9.

Ratcliff, R., Van Zandt, T. and McKoon, G. (1999). Connectionist and diffusion models of reaction time. *Psychological Review 106*(2), 261–300.

Reed, T. E. (1984). Mechanism for heritability of intelligence. *Nature 311*(5985), 417.

Reed, T. E. and Jensen, A. R. (1991). Arm nerve conduction velocity (NCV), brain NCV, reaction time and intelligence. *Intelligence 15*, 33–47.

Reed, T. E., Vernon, P. A. and Johnson, A. M. (2004). Confirmation of correlation between brain nerve conduction velocity and intelligence level in normal adults. *Intelligence 32*(6), 563–72.

Rijsdijk, F. V., Boonsma, F. V. and Vernon, P. A. (1995). Genetic analysis of peripheral nerve conduction velocity in twins. *Behavior Genetics 25*(4), 341–8.

Shagass, C., Roemer, R. A. and Straumanis, J. J. (1981). Intelligence as a factor in evoked potential studies of psychopathology II: correlations between treatment-associate changes in IQ and evoked potentials. *Biological Psychiatry 16*, 1031–40.

Stankov, L., Boyle, G. J. and Cattell, R. B. (1995). Models and paradigms in personality and intelligence research. In D. H. Saklofske and M. Zeidner (eds), *International Handbook of Personality and Intelligence*. New York: Plenum.

Sternberg, R. J. (1977). *Intelligence, Information Processing and Analogical Reasoning: the Componential Analysis of Human Abilities*. Hillsdale, NJ: Erlbaum.

Sternberg, R. J. (1988). Explaining away intelligence: a reply to Howe. *British Journal of Psychology 79*(4), 527–34.

Sternberg, S. (1969). High-speed scanning in human memory. *Science 153*, 652–4.

Stough, C., Bates, T. C., Mangan, G. L. and Colrain, I. (2001). Inspection time and intelligence: further attempts to eliminate the apparent movement strategy. *Intelligence 29*(3), 219–30.

Stough, C. K. K., Nettelbeck, T. and Cooper, C. J. (1990). Evoked brain potentials, string length and intelligence. *Personality and Individual Differences 11*, 401–6.

Vernon, P. A. and Mori, M. (1992). Intelligence, reaction times and peripheral nerve conduction velocity. *Intelligence 16*, 273–88.

Vickers, D., Nettelbeck, T. and Willson, R. J. (1972). Perceptual indices of performance: the measurement of 'inspection time' and 'noise' in the visual system. *Perception 1*, 263–95.

Wickett, J. C. and Vernon, P. A. (1994). Peripheral nerve conduction velocity, reaction time, and intelligence: an attempt to replicate Vernon and Mori (1992). *Intelligence 18*(127–31).

10 Personality and ability over the lifespan

Background

We have shown that the empirical evidence suggests that it is reasonable to view personality and intelligence in terms of a small number of traits. The term 'trait' implies stability over situations and time. We have shown that there is substantial evidence that situations cannot fully explain behaviour, but have not yet explored the stability of traits over the lifespan.

Recommended prior reading

Chapters 4, 7, 8, 9 and 15.

Introduction

The issue of change in personality and cognitive abilities is one of the more muddled areas of individual differences, for 'change' means different things to different psychologists and there is often confusion about what, precisely, is meant by the term. It seems that there are four quite different issues running through the literature:

1. Do levels of personality and/or ability vary in same-aged individuals over time? For example, are today's 20 year olds any more or less neurotic than the 20 year olds in our grandparents' generation?

2. Do personality and cognitive abilities typically vary much over the lifespan? For example, does neuroticism generally rise or fall at certain ages? Are 40 year olds generally any more or less sociable than 60 year olds, regardless of their year of birth?

3. Are personality and ability stable over time? Is someone who is highly extraverted (relative to their peers) at age 20 also highly extraverted relative to their peers at age 70? This question differs from (2) because the correlation coefficient that is used to investigate this issue ignores any shift in the mean level of the trait over time.

4. How much do specific life events (e.g. psychotherapy, an enhanced early educational environment, experience of war) alter personality and/or abilities?

To further complicate things, experiments need to be designed carefully to avoid confusing genuine changes in scores within individuals with differences in scores between generations or administering an unreliable test on two or more occasions and incorrectly inferring that personality/ability changes over time.

Self-assessment question 10.1

What sorts of experiment might you design to determine whether a trait changes in the four ways just listed?

There is also the question of whether a chance in a test score necessarily implies that the underlying trait has changed. For example, suppose that a group of children were coached intensively on the sorts of problem used in ability tests – putting sequences of pictures in the correct order, practising defining words for hours and generally honing the specific skills required to perform well on some ability tests. They are then found to perform better than a control group when given an ability test. Does this imply that they are more intelligent? It probably does not, as the ability test is only a valid measure if IQ when used with naive participants. The enhanced performance is likely to be specific to the sorts of items on which they have been trained and may not generalize even to other IQ tests, let alone to real-world performance (e.g. it may not indicate that the individual will be well suited for a demanding college course or will perform well in a job requiring the exercise of general intelligence).

Similar issues may affect personality tests. Society's values change over time, so the proportion of people agreeing that they believe in marriage (for example) would probably be less than it was a generation ago – making people appear more unconventional. In addition, some words used in personality tests (e.g. 'wicked') may have changed their meaning substantially. So it is possible that people will *appear* to be more unconventional, extraverted or whatever than their parents just because of this.

Changes in lifestyles may also affect performance on ability tests. As a result of computer games, games consoles etc. children now have far more opportunity to hone their spatial skills and their hand–eye coordination than they did a generation ago. Might this accidental training artificially inflate their scores on some IQ tests? It seems possible, but I do not think that anyone really knows for sure. In order to tell, one would really need to perform a regression analysis against some stable criterion in order to see whether the improved test performance is reflected in better performance in the real world. But there are few criterion measures that stay stable. For example, one cannot test whether changes in spatial and psychomotor performance are genuine by determining whether people now find it easier to fly an aircraft as aircraft design has changed and this could account for any observed differences. Thus it is remarkably difficult to establish whether any changes in scores on ability tests are real or artefactual. Most authors simply assume that they are real and we shall follow their example for the rest of this chapter.

The reason why these issues can be controversial centres on the nature–nurture argument outlined in Chapter 11. It is sometimes asserted that because a personality or ability trait has a strong genetic component, this makes it somehow immutable. Thus interventions (such as enriching the environment or improving thinking skills of disadvantaged children) will be unlikely to be effective. This argument is misguided for three reasons. First, I know of no personality or ability trait that has a near total genetic component: in every case, environmental influences, either within or from outside the childhood family, will have some influence on levels of the trait. Second, genes cannot express themselves as behaviours unless they are given a particular environment: for example, the gene which causes the illness phenylketonuria cannot express itself (lead to the disease) unless patients eat or drink a source of phenylanaline. A child whose genetic makeup means that they have an above average predisposition to excel at music is unlikely to do so if

157

reared in an environment where this talent is neither recognized nor developed. Third, it is easy to forget that estimates of heritabilities refer to the population being studied, not to an individual. Just because a trait has a heritability of 0.5 and the common (family) environment has no influence at all on its level in adulthood (e.g. general intelligence) it does not follow that if one takes a particular child and raises it in an enriched (or an impoverished) environment then this will not affect the child's ultimate level of cognitive ability. It most probably will: the genetic estimates can only speak about the likelihood of what will happen to children given the sorts of environment typically experienced within a particular culture.

Ability change

Do abilities change from generation to generation?

There is excellent evidence that performance on ability tests has improved from generation to generation. This is often known as the Flynn effect, after one James Flynn, a New Zealand sociologist who reported the phenomenon in 1987, although Deary (2000: 226–7) gives some references to the earlier literature, which shows that the phenomenon had been recognized in the 1940s. How can such a change in abilities be determined? Some large organizations (such as the military) routinely test the mental abilities of their recruits and tend to use the same test for many years. Thus it is a simple matter to discover whether the average scores obtained in each year tends to rise or fall over time. This approach requires two major assumptions to be made. First, it must be assumed that any change is not due to later generations being more familiar with the nature of the tests and test items than were earlier generations (for example, as a result of hearing older relatives discussing the test items). Second, it must be assumed that the proportion of each ability level in the population who enter the armed forces should stay the same. For example, in a volunteer army, it may be the case that fewer high-ability people apply in some years than in others, perhaps because of the availability of alternative employment, the political Zeitgeist or ongoing military action. But in societies where virtually all adults are required to perform military service, the armed forces' ability tests will provide useful information about the stability of abilities from year to year.

Every time a new version of an ability test such as the Wechsler Intelligence Scale for Children is produced, it has to be renormed (that is, administered to a large sample of people, carefully chosen to represent the population in terms of age, sex, ethnic background, area of residence etc.). This expensive exercise is necessary because when new items are added to the subtests (or old ones are removed) the mean and standard deviation of each of the subtests will change by an unknown amount. Thus it is necessary to discover the new mean and standard deviation for each of the subtests by renorming. Sometimes, people take both the old and the new version of a test at the same time. In such cases, it is almost invariably the case that they score better on the old version than on the new. For example, an 8 year old might have an IQ of 100 when assessed using the version of a test that was normed in 1978, but an IQ of 94 on a near identical test that was normed in 1998. As both tests are given at the same time, this cannot reflect any developmental change in the children. Instead, it probably means that people have become more intelligent over the 20-year period and this is reflected in the scores of the normative group. So a level of performance that was average by 1978 standards will be below average by the standards of 1998.

Figure 10.1 is taken from Flynn (1999) and shows the effect graphically. It seems that scores

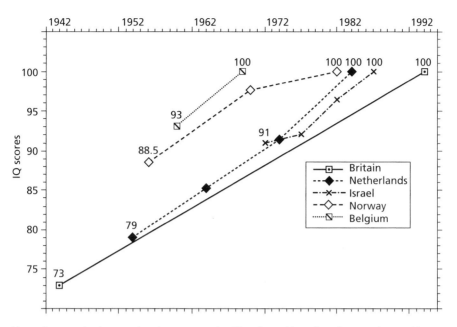

Note. Every nation is named on its own samples. Therefore, although nations can be roughly compared in terms of different rates of IQ gain, they cannot be compared in terms of IQ scores. That is, the fact that the mean IQ of one nation appears higher than another at a given time is purely an artifact. Sources for these data are Flynn (1987b, pp 172–174), Flynn (1998d), Raven, Raven, and Court (1998, Graph G2).

Figure 10.1 Intelligence test scores in five countries as a function of year of birth. (From Flynn (1999).)

on ability tests rise by about a standard deviation every 50 years or three IQ points per decade. Interestingly, the effects seem to be most pronounced on tests that require reasoning – 'culture fair' tests, such as Raven's Matrices, rather than tests of knowledge. Indeed, a study of Piagetian conservation tasks shows that performance here has fallen by half a standard deviation in a generation (Shayer and Ginsburg 2009).

The finding that the Flynn effect is associated with abstract reasoning, Gf rather than Gc, suggests that it is not a simple consequence of better education or access to knowledge (e.g. through cheap paperback books, radio, television and the internet); it is found in both prosperous and less prosperous countries, too, which also argues against this explanation (Brouwers, Van de Vijver and Van Hemert 2009). The finding that he phenomenon appears worldwide (Flynn 1984, 1987) also argues against the possibility that change in teaching methods within one culture enhances student thinking and learning.

Can it really be the case that intelligence is increasing at such a rate? There are other possible explanations, such as increased familiarity with solving the types of problem used in the ability tests, together with various theories as to why people's intelligence may have improved, such as improved nutrition (Lynn 1990) or better education (but why does Gc then not increase?). Flynn's current suggestion (2007) is that individuals with a genetic advantage are now better able to take advantage of this, through greater access to knowledge, intellectually demanding activities and clever people – a point originally made by Plomin, Loehlin and DeFries (1985). But these are **159** really just plausible post-hoc rationalizations of the observed facts, rather than proper theories that can be disconfirmed.

The Flynn effect raises particular problems for the theory of *eugenics*. Proponents of this approach argue that human intelligence is in danger of declining, since people with lower IQ tend to have more children than those with higher IQ. Given the appreciable heritability of intelligence, one might therefore expect that the genes that produce high intelligence will gradually become rarer within the population. The Flynn effect appears to show that the opposite is happening, for reasons that are not well understood.

It has been found that the rate of increase in IQ over time may be levelling off. Teasdale and Owen (2000) report data from the Danish military. Virtually all Danish men serve in the armed forces from age 18 and so scores on the ability tests administered to these recruits closely resemble those of the male population. The scores appear to show a three- or four-point per decade rise during the 1960s and 1970s, but only a one-point rise during the 1990s. The obvious possibility that substantial numbers may now score 100% on the tests so guaranteeing that the scores cannot show any further improvement, does not seem to be supported by the data. While this work needs to be replicated in other countries, it certainly shows that in Denmark at least, the rise in IQ over time may not be inexorable.

Cognitive abilities over the lifespan

Scores on all ability tests improve with age up until the late teens, when scores stabilize and remain fairly stable until the age of about 60. For example, Figure 10.2 shows the average score on the Kaufman Adolescent and Adult Intelligence Test (a test of general ability) obtained by adults of

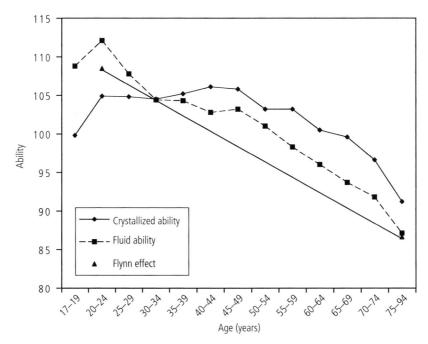

Figure 10.2 Fluid ability and crystallized ability scores as a function of age. (Drawn from data in Kaufman and Horn (1996).)

various ages. Fluid ability reflects abstract thinking ability and crystallized ability the knowledge that is acquired when one exercises one's fluid ability in the world. It can be seen that fluid ability peaks in the early 20s and then declines inexorably with age, whereas crystallized ability is reasonably well preserved until at least the late 50s. What we lose in quickness of thought, we may be able to make up with knowledge.

That is the accepted view of the topic. However, there may also be some merit in scrutinizing how far these data depart from the 'Flynn effect' line, also shown in Figure 10.2. This shows the baseline level of intelligence: the average IQ for each age group. From this perspective, it is true that the oldest participants seem to have lower fluid ability than the younger ones – but they probably always did! So when the Flynn correction is applied it seems likely that an *individual's* fluid and cognitive abilities may well not decline. Of course younger people will be smarter, but this may reflect the generational increase in IQ rather than an age-related drop in individuals' cognitive capabilities. However, this view is not prevalent in the literature, most of which takes the view that cognitive abilities decline over time (e.g. Ryan, Sattler and Lopez 2000).

Stability of ability over time

This essentially corresponds to the test–retest reliability of ability tests: the correlation that is obtained when people sit the same test (or two parallel ones) months or years apart. Being based on a correlation, it ignores any shifts in scores over time as a result of aging or the Flynn effect. It determines whether people's position relative to their peers alters substantially.

Perhaps the most compelling evidence for the stability of general intelligence is a study conducted by Ian Deary and his colleagues at Edinburgh and Aberdeen (Deary et al. 2000). They discovered the scores from mental tests administered to all 11 year olds who attended school in Scotland on 1 June 1932 and tracked down 101 of these individuals. They sat the same test 66 years (to the day) later and performed rather better than they did when they were 11 (an increase of one standard deviation). The correlation between scores on the two occasions was 0.63. However, this underestimated the true correlation, as (a) the older sample showed a lower range of ability scores than the original and (b) the test was not perfectly reliable. After correcting statistically for these two influences, it seems likely that the true correlation is at least 0.8. This is a remarkable result, indicating that a person's intelligence (measured by a simple group test at age 11) is a powerful predictor of their performance on the same test several generations later. And this study is in no ways unique. Using highly reliable tests such as the Wechsler Adult Intelligence Scales researchers typically find correlations in the order of 0.9 over a 10-year period (e.g. Mortensen and Kleven 1993).

The correlations between measures of childhood cognitive ability and adult intelligence are generally rather smaller than those obtained solely in adulthood. In a typical example, Kangas and Bradway (1971) found a correlation of 0.41 between general ability measured at 4 and 42 years of age. There are several reasons for this. Children may develop at slightly different rates, unrelated to their ultimate levels of intelligence. Testing young children can be problematical because of their short attention span. And the content of some tests used to assess the ability of very young children are really very different from that of adult ability tests: they include assessments of whether a child can pay attention to a novel stimulus (such as a bell) or name things, rather than anything more cognitive. Reznick and Corley (1999) give a useful précis of this literature.

It certainly seems that general ability is a stable phenomenon and intelligence measured in middle childhood is a good predictor of intelligence in later life. Although even if the correlation **161** were 1.0 it would be logically possible for some environmental influence to boost the ability of children who received it. Just because the trait shows high stability in children or adults living in the 'normal' world, it does not follow that it will be immutable in the face of an intervention.

Interventions to change general ability

Many attempts have been made to change (improve) children's levels of cognitive ability, over and above the methods used in schools. For example, the HeadStart programme was a government-funded project to try to improve the academic performance of children from disadvantaged backgrounds. It is typically found that children from poor areas perform poorly at school (and on ability tests) and it is possible that this is caused by an unstimulating environment during their early years that fails to equip them for school. These children may be less able to learn because they lack the background skills (particularly language skills) developed by children reared in middle-class homes.

A huge number of environment-enrichment programmes have been developed, implemented and evaluated, mostly in the United States. They include the Milwaukee Project (Garber, Begab and American Association on Mental Retardation 1988), which assigned 40 children randomly to an experimental group or a control group. Those in the experimental group received an enriched, social environment specifically designed to improve the children's cognitive skills from 3 months to 5 or 6 years. And it seems to have worked. The children in the experimental group showed IQs in the order of 120 for the first 6 years of the project: the control group showed IQs below 100 during this period. However, after the project finished, the gains shown by the experimental group rapidly diminished and flattened out at an IQ of 105 from age 6–13. This is still substantially higher than the IQ of the control group, which hovered between 80 and 90.

The big issue here is whether the intervention improved IQ or just test-taking skills. Jensen (1989) observed that the substantial differences between the experimental and control groups did not seem to be reflected in the academic performance of the children, which was quite similar (e.g. 11th percentile vs. 9th percentile on a fourth-grade mathematics achievement test; 19th and 9th percentile on the Metropolitan Test of Achievement in the fourth grade). This seems to be a fair comment.

The Carolina Abecedarian project (Ramey, Yeates and Short 1984) is similar. It randomly assigned 85 children who were identified as 'at risk' on the basis of their mother's measured intelligence and social deprivation to an experimental or a control group. The children in the experimental group experienced an enriched environment from the age of 3 months until they started school. The intervention was for 8 hours a weekday, 50 weeks a year for over 4 years: no one could reasonably argue that these studies are too small scale to be effective!

The cognitive abilities of the children in the experimental and control groups were measured every 6 months, and there were significant differences between groups (in the expected direction) at all ages between 18 and 48 months. But what happened then? Figure 10.3 shows the growth curve from Campbell et al. (2001). This indicates that children in the experimental group showed a marked decline in their cognitive performance after starting school (age 4.5), whereas those in the control group did not. Thereafter, both groups showed a gradual decline in their cognitive scores.

So once again, marked differences were found in the early years (18 IQ points at 18 months; 16 points at 3 years) but by age 21 the difference has narrowed considerably (IQs of 89.7 vs. 85.2: $t(102) = 2.39$, $p < 0.01$).

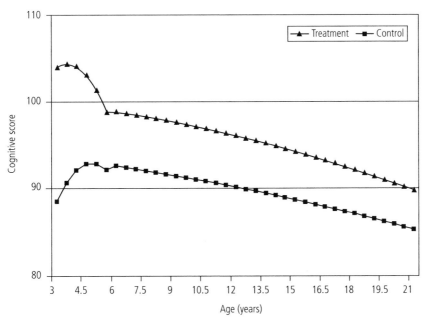

Figure 10.3 Cognitive growth curves as a function of preschool treatment. (From Campbell et al. (2001).)

Perhaps the most obvious thing about the growth curve is that the experimental group performs much better than the control group even at the very youngest ages. This finding can be interpreted in three ways:

1. The most crucial period for boosting IQ was in the first few weeks and months of the project: the enhancements obtained in the very early weeks of the project caused the sizable differences between the groups that were seen at 6 months and 18 months (Ramey and Campbell 1987, cited by Spitz 1997).

2. The children in the experimental group were more intelligent than those in the control group at the outset and this explains why they remain so in later life: the intervention probably had no effect at all (Spitz 1997, 1999) given that the differences observed in the school-aged children and adults were no larger than they had been at 6 months of age.

3. The tests used to assess IQ in the very young children are not particularly reliable and so it may not matter too much that the experimental group appeared to outperform the control group at the early age – the two groups really were equivalent at the outset. However the unreliability of the tests will, of course, be reflected in the significance tests.

Just looking at Figure 10.3, it does not appear that the two groups started from the same point at age 3. The 16-point difference there is enormously significant (($t(96) = 5.9$, $p < 0.01$ from the data in Campbell et al. 2001) so one either has to suppose that the key influences happened in the first 30 months or that the groups were not well matched at the outset.

I have described these two studies in some detail as they appear to be the best designed attempts to evaluate intensive early interventions and are also the ones which appear to produce the best results. Others (generally with much less intense stimulation) are summarized by the Consor- **163** tium for Longitudinal Studies (1983). Quite what is to be made of these results is still uncertain. Although both the Milwaukee and Abecedarian projects seem to show that intensive intervention can improve the IQs of 'at risk' children, there is some dispute about whether the IQ gains in the Milwaukee project were caused by training children to take the tests: they did not seem to be reflected in educational performance. This was not a problem for the Abecedarian project, where children and adults in the experimental group outperformed those in the control group on mathematics and verbal performance tests (Campbell et al. 2001). But were the children in the experimental group brighter at the outset than those in the control group? The consistently better performance of the experimental group in even the earliest months of the project certainly make this a possibility.

As well as educational interventions, there has been a flurry of studies investigating the link between nutrition and intelligence. This work is important because Lynn (1990) suggests that improvements in nutrition may explain why the Flynn effect is found, rather than the expected dysgenic fall in IQ over time. Benton and Roberts (1988) gave 30 Welsh schoolchildren a vitamin and mineral supplement every day for 8 months. Despite the small sample size it was found that the experimental group gained about ten points in nonverbal IQ, the control groups showing much smaller increases. There are two difficulties with this work. First, it is an example of 'blunderbuss psychology' – firing a huge range of vitamins and minerals into participants without any clear theoretical expectation of which one(s) are important. If the intervention is successful then one still has to tease out precisely what is causing the increase in IQ and why. Second, the finding has proved hard to replicate. Schoenthaler et al. (1991) gave 13-year- old Californian delinquents similar supplements for 13 weeks and again found a statistically significant increase in IQ of about 0.3 of a standard deviation, but failures to replicate include Crombie et al. (1990). Benton (2001) gives a useful review of the literature that makes some telling points. The studies cited all seem to show that at the end of the trial, members of the experimental (supplement) groups have higher nonverbal IQs than the control groups and nine out of the 17 were significantly so. The effect only seems to appear for nonverbal scores: verbal scores fail to show any increase following vitamin supplementation. This is thought to be because the nonverbal scores reflect the more biological aspects of general ability. Finally, he discusses the effects of some specific supplements and considers the dietary needs of the children: supplements only seem to be effective when the children have below average levels of the nutrients – although it seems that plenty of children do have diets that lack certain minerals and vitamins. Supplementation may well be of value for many children.

Self-assessment question 10.2

a. Why do you think that vitamins may only affect nonverbal ability scores?

b. What is missing from these studies?

Personality change
Does personality change from generation to generation?

The Flynn effect has revealed the gradual increase in performance on ability tests from generation to generation: do personality traits vary in the same way? Unfortunately, I have been unable to find any literature that can help answer this question. There are several reasons for this. First, there has really only been any consensus about the structure of personality since the 1960s while intelligence tests have been used for an extra 60 years. Thus there are few useful personality data available from those born much before 1930. Second, because personality questionnaires are generally much less useful to occupational psychologists than are ability tests, they are less often administered to large samples of people (e.g. military recruits) year after year. This makes it difficult to identify trends. Third, few (if any) personality tests appear to be renormed as carefully as ability tests. Tests such as the Wechsler Intelligence Scales are administered to large samples of people, painstakingly chosen so as to represent the population in terms of gender, age, ethnicity, area of residence, etc., as this is necessary to estimate the distribution of scores in the population in order to use the test diagnostically. This is a phenomenally expensive operation, but it is essential as these tests help make life-changing decisions about people's future capabilities and educational needs. Because personality scales are not used in this fashion, tables of norms are far more haphazard – if, indeed, they exist at all. Thus it is impossible to detect changes in personality over time by scrutinizing people's scores when renorming.

The obvious difference between ability tests and personality tests is that to perform well on ability tests, one actually has to *demonstrate* a high level of ability, through solving difficult problems. To obtain a score indicating a high level of extraversion (or any other trait), it is only necessary to *claim* to do certain things (e.g. feel more optimistic than most; to enjoy parties). So even if we could detect shifts in scores on personality tests, there would always be the niggling doubt that these may not reflect real shifts in personality. Instead, it may just be that certain behaviours have become more socially acceptable and so people are more likely to claim to show them. Thus even if excellent normative data were available for personality tests, it would be far harder to draw inferences about generational change than for abilities.

Personality over the lifespan

There is a substantial literature outlining how scores on personality tests vary over the lifespan. These changes seem to be quite marked before the age of 30, quite trivial after that age, and surprisingly consistent across cultures. McCrae et al. (1999) report a series of cross-sectional studies from Germany, Italy, Portugal, Croatia and Korea, analysing the personality scores for several age groups. Sample sizes ranger from 2205 (Germany) to 462 (Croatia). The quality of the data varied widely from country to country, some samples (e.g. the Portuguese) being admirably random, while others (e.g. the Italian) were recruited by undergraduates.

Eysenck (1979) had reported only small age-related trends in neuroticism within a British sample and the neuroticism scale of the NEO-PI(R) was the only one that did not show significant age differences in all countries. Neuroticism scores were generally higher in the youngest adults (18–21) in the German, Portuguese and Korean samples (planned comparisons being statistically significant) and there was not much variation between the neuroticism scores in the three other age bands (22–29, 30–49, 50+). Extraversion scores showed a steady decline with age in all cultures. The effect was quite substantial, being at least half a standard deviation. Planned comparisons again showed that the youngest age group scored higher than all the others combined. Openness scores also declined with age, although here the appeared to be a substantial drop between the 30–49 and the 50+ age groups. Agreeableness increased substantially with age in all cultures, as did conscientiousness.

These data are reasonably consistent with those gathered in the United States. Here Costa et al. (1987) found rather trivial age-related trends in a huge population sample aged 35–84, while students under 30 are known to score about half a standard deviation higher on neuroticism, extraversion and openness and lower on agreeableness and conscientiousness (Costa and McCrae 1994).

The mechanisms underlying these changes do, however, need to be clarified. Given the moderate heritabilities of most personality traits (see Chapter 11) it is possible that these changes reflect genes switching on or off at various ages. Or it could be that common life experiences (e.g. obtaining a job, establishing a relationship) may account for some of the differences between the youngest groups and the others. Loehlin and Martin (2001) shed some light on this by examining age trends in heritabilities of extraversion, neuroticism and psychoticism in Australian twins (5400 pairs). The age-related trends reported by these authors correspond closely to those discussed earlier. The heritability estimates are also broadly in line with the previous literature (heritabilities of 0.28, 0.47, and 0.40 for P, E and N; common family environmental influences close to zero) and these heritabilities showed rather little variation between sexes or between age groups, although Jang, Livesley and Vernon (1996) provide data suggesting that genetic components are more important later in life.

Stability of ability over time

Because there seem to be few long-term longitudinal studies of personality on a par with that conducted by Deary et al. (2000) for general ability (neither is there any evidence for or against a 'Flynn effect' for personality) the evidence here is not so clearcut as for the stability of cognitive abilities. Test–retest studies are numerous and are summarized in a meta-analysis by Roberts and DelVecchio (2000). Test–retest correlations (estimated over a time span of 6.7 years) increase with age, from 0.3 in childhood to 0.7 between ages 50 and 70 and Conley's classic (1984) paper likewise estimated year-on-year stability of personality at about 0.96 per year, implying a test–retest reliability of about 0.75 over 7 years.

> **Self-assessment question 10.3**
>
> What is the difference between this type of change and that discussed in the previous section?

Interventions to change personality

Can personality be changed? This seemingly simple question leads in several directions. For example, there is an extensive literature on personality change following head injury and the administration of a wide range of drugs (e.g. benzodiazepines, alcohol). There is also a substantial literature on the treatability of patients diagnosed with personality disorders, but none of these studies addresses the malleability of *normal* personality traits with which this chapter is concerned. The reason why no such studies seem to have been performed is simple. While general ability appears to be a highly valued characteristic in our society (not least because it predicts desirable properties, such as income and longevity) there is no pressure to ensure that a child (for example) maximizes his extraverted potential. Society seems to function quite well with a mixture of extraverts and intraverts, tough and tender-minded individuals, worriers and the irritatingly calm. The only times when attempts are made to try to alter personality is when the individual is at one extreme of a scale, such as when they suffer debilitating anxiety or shyness.

The clinical evidence shows that personality traits such as extraversion or neuroticism/anxiety an sometimes be modified by clinical procedures. For example, Ost and Breitholtz (2000) found that both relaxation and cognitive therapy significantly reduced the anxiety experienced by adult patients, while behaviour therapy may also be useful in treating social phobia (possibly an extreme form of intraversion: Turner et al. 1996). However, there appear to be no interventions that are designed to modify 'normal' levels of personality, so no firm conclusions can be drawn about the sensitivity of personality to interventions.

Summary

This chapter has argued that when discussing the variation in a trait, four distinct research questions need to be addressed:

- the change in the trait from generation to generation
- changes that occur as a function of ageing
- whether the ordering of people on a trait is similar at different points in time
- the effects of behavioural interventions on traits.

Quite a lot is known about these issues in the case of cognitive abilities. The Flynn effect shows that abilities seem to be rising from generation to generation for reasons that are poorly understood, but which may have something to do with improvements in nutrition. The rise in cognitive abilities through childhood is well established; so too is their decline after age 50. When people are retested on ability tests their scores are strikingly similar, even several decades later. And although attempts to improve cognitive abilities by 'hothousing' children from disadvantaged backgrounds during their early years have frequently been interpreted as showing that intelligence can be boosted, both of the two main studies have a number of problems that make this conclusion dangerous.

Far less is known about how these questions relate to personality. Nothing is known about how personality shifts from generation to generation. Developmental changes in personality are well established (agreeableness increasing and openness to experience and extraversion decreasing in old age and anxiety falling as one passes through the 20s. The test–retest reliability of personality traits is high, although few long-term longitudinal studies have been performed to test this across the entire lifespan. And finally, no deliberate attempts seem to have been made to modify 'normal' personality traits, although the clinical literature provides hints that these may be more susceptible than abilities to change.

Suggested additional reading

Spitz (1997, 1999) gives a highly sceptical look at the HeadStart projects: in the interests of balance, it would also be sensible to read some publications from the authors of such interventions, such as Campbell et al. (2001). Deary et al. (2000) provide a fascinating evidence for the stability of individual differences in mental ability from childhood to old age, while Flynn's (2007) book gives a detailed account of how intelligence levels seem to have changed from generation to generation. Although the review of the empirical literature is now out of date, Chapter 6 of Brody (1992) gives an excellent discussion of environmental determinants of intelligence, while Costa and McCrae (1994) discuss personality change over the lifespan.

Answers to self-assessment questions

SAQ 10.1

a. Locate test scores from an old experiment. Match individuals to members of the old sample with respect to age, sex, etc. Administer the test to these individuals. If sample sizes allow, factor analyse the items from the original and new samples (separately) to ensure that all the items work properly. If any items fail to perform well in both samples, drop them. Then compute the total scores on the remaining items and compare the two groups' scores using a t-test or similar.

b. Perform a longitudinal study and perform an ANOVA comparing scores at various ages. Consider using year of birth as a covariate to compensate for any gradual increase or decrease in scores associated with year of birth.

c. Measure the same sample on two occasions. Correlate scores on the two occasions.

d. Design an intervention study with proper control groups. Assess the trait regularly during the intervention and for as long a follow-up period as possible. Analyse using analysis of variance (between-subjects factor of occasion, between-subjects factor of group).

SAQ 10.2

a. Cattell's distinction between fluid and crystallized intelligence viewed fluid intelligence as abstract thinking power, whereas crystallized ability resulted from choosing to apply these skills to gain knowledge in some area. If fluid ability is indeed largely biological, then it would probably be easier to detect any enhancements in fluid ability. Also there may be a time lag between boosting fluid ability and the acquisition of crystallized knowledge: it would be interesting to retest the children.

b. Long-term follow-up, to see whether the effects are permanent (cf. the HeadStart programmes).

SAQ 10.3

As it is based on a correlation, test–retest analysis ignores any differences in level (or variability) in a trait over time. For example, if some people scored 10, 11, 12, and 14 on a test on one occasion and 30, 32, 34 and 38 on a second, the correlation between these two scores would be 1.0 even though the mean has changed as has the range of scores.

References

Benton, D. (2001). Micro-nutrient supplementation and the intelligence of children. *Neuroscience and Biobehavioural Reviews 25*, 297–309.

Benton, D. and Roberts, G. (1988). Effect of vitamin and mineral supplement on the intelligence of a sample of school children. *The Lancet, 23 January*, 140–4.

Brody, N. (1992). *Intelligence*. San Diego, CA: Academic Press.

Brouwers, S. A., Van de Vijver, F. J. R. and Van Hemert, D. A. (2009). Variation in Raven's Progressive Matrices scores across time and place. *Learning and Individual Differences 19*(3), 330–8.

Campbell, F. A., Pungello, E., Miller-Johnson, S., Burchinal, M. and Ramey, C. T. (2001). The development of cognitive and academic abilities: growth curves from an early childhood educational experiment. *Developmental Psychology 37*(2), 231–42.

Conley, J. J. (1984). The hierarchy of consistency: a review and model of longitudinal findings on adult individual differences in intelligence, personality and self-opinion. *Personality and Individual Differences 5*, 11–25.

Consortium for Longitudinal Studies. (1983). *As the Twig is Bent: Lasting Effects of Preschool Programs*. Hillsdale, NJ: Erlbaum.

Costa, P. T. and McCrae, R. R. (1994). Stability and change in personality from adolescence to adulthood. In C. F. Halverson, G. A. Kohnstamm and R. P. Martin (eds), *The Seveloping Structure of Temperament and Personality from Infancy to Adulthood*. Hillsdale NJ: Erlbaum.

Costa, P. T., Zonderman, A. B., McCrae, R. R., Cornonihuntley, J., Locke, B. Z. and Barbano, H. E. (1987). Longitudinal analyses of psychological well-being in a national sample – stability of mean levels. *Journals of Gerontology 42*(1), 50–55.

Crombie, I. K., Todman, J., McNeill, G., Florey, C. D., Menzies, I. and Kennedy, R. A. (1990). Effect of vitamin and mineral supplementation on verbal and nonverbal reasoning of school-children. *Lancet 335*(8692), 744–7.

Deary, I. J. (2000). *Looking Down on Human Intelligence: From Psychometrics to the Brain*. Oxford: Oxford University Press.

Deary, I. J., Whalley, L. J., Lemmon, H., Crawford, J. R. and Starr, J. M. (2000). The stability of individual differences in mental ability from childhood to old age: follow-up of the 1932 Scottish mental survey. *Intelligence 28*(1), 49–55.

Eysenck, H. J. (1979). Personality factors in a random sample of the population. *Psychological Reports 44*, 1023–7.

Flynn, J. R. (1984). The mean IQ of Americans – massive gains 1932 to 1978. *Psychological Bulletin 95*(1), 29–51.

Flynn, J. R. (1987). Massive IQ gains in 14 nations: what IQ tests really measure. *Psychological Bulletin 101*, 171–91.

Flynn, J. R. (1999). Searching for justice – the discovery of IQ gains over time. *American Psychologist 54*(1), 5–20.

Flynn, J. R. (2007). *What is Intelligence? Beyond the Flynn Effect*. New York: Cambridge University Press.

Garber, H. L., Begab, M. J. and American Association on Mental Retardation (1988). *The Milwaukee Project: Preventing Mental Retardation in Children at Risk*. Washington, DC: American Association on Mental Retardation.

Jang, K. L., Livesley, W. J. and Vernon, P. A. (1996). The genetic basis of personality at different ages: a cross-sectional twin study. *Personality and Individual Differences 21*(2), 299–301.

Jensen, A. R. (1989). The Milwaukee project – preventing mental retardation in children at risk – Garber, H. *Developmental Review 9*(3), 234–58.

Kangas, J. and Bradway, K. (1971). Intelligence at middle age: a thirty-eight year follow-up. *Developmental Psychology 5*, 333–7.

Kaufman, A. S. and Horn, J. L. (1996). Age changes on tests of fluid and crystallized ability for women and men on the Kaufman Adolescent and Adult Intelligence Test (KAIT) at ages 17–94 years. *Archives of Clinical Neuropsychology 11*, 97–121.

Loehlin, J. C. and Martin, N. G. (2001). Age changes in personality traits and their heritabilities during the adult years: evidence from Australian Twin Registry samples. *Personality and Individual Differences 30*(7), 1147–60.

Lynn, R. (1990). The role of nutrition in secular increases in intelligence. *Personality and Individual Differences 11*(3), 273–85.

McCrae, R. R., Costa, P. T., de Lima, M. P., Simoes, A., Ostendorf, F., Angleitner, A. et al. (1999). Age differences in personality across the adult life span: parallels in five cultures. *Developmental Psychology 35*(2), 466–77.

Mortensen, E. L. and Kleven, M. (1993). A Wais longitudinal study of cognitive development during the life-span from ages 50 to 70. *Developmental Neuropsychology 9*(2), 115–30.

Ost, L. G. and Breitholtz, E. (2000). Applied relaxation vs. cognitive therapy in the treatment of generalized anxiety disorder. *Behaviour Research and Therapy 38*(8), 777–90.

Plomin, R., Loehlin, J. C. and DeFries, J. C. (1985). Genetic and environmental components of 'environmental' influences. *Developmental Psychology 21*, 391–402.

Ramey, C. T., Yeates, K. O. and Short, E. J. (1984). The plasticity of intellectual development – insights from preventive intervention. *Child Development 55*(5), 1913–25.

Reznick, J. S. and Corley, R. (1999). What twins tell us about the development of intelligence – a case study. In M. Anderson (ed.), *The Development of Intelligence*. Hove: Psychology Press.

Roberts, B. W. and DelVecchio, W. F. (2000). The rank-order consistency of personality traits from childhood to old age: a quantitative review of longitudinal studies. *Psychological Bulletin 126*(1), 3–25.

Ryan, J. J., Sattler, J. M. and Lopez, S. J. (2000). Age affects on Wechsler Adult Intelligence Scale–III subtests. *Archives of Clinical Neuropsychology 15*, 311–7.

Schoenthaler, S. J., Amos, S. P., Eysenck, H. J., Peritz, E. and Yudkin, J. (1991). Controlled trial of vitamin–mineral supplementation – effects on intelligence and performance. *Personality and Individual Differences 12*(4), 351–62.

Shayer, M. and Ginsburg, D. (2009). Thirty years on – a large anti-Flynn effect? (II): 13–and 14-year-olds. Piagetian tests of formal operations norms 1976–2006/7. *British Journal of Educational Psychology 79*(3), 409–18.

Spitz, H. H. (1997). Some questions about the results of the abecedarian early intervention project cited by the APA task force on intelligence. *American Psychologist 52*(1), 72.

Spitz, H. H. (1999). Attempts to raise intelligence. In M. Anderson (ed.), *The Development of Intelligence*. Hove: Psychology Press.

Teasdale, T. W and Owen, D. R. (2000). Forty-year secular trends in cognitive abilities. *Intelligence 28*, 115–20.

Turner, S. M., Beidel, D. C., Wolff, P. L., Spaulding, S. and Jacob, R. G. (1996). Clinical features affecting treatment outcome in social phobia. *Behaviour Research and Therapy 34*(10), 795–804.

Environmental and genetic determinants of personality and ability

Background

Empirical studies of the extent to which personality and ability can be inherited provide valuable evidence as to the relative importance of biological and social factors in development. They can also show whether individual differences are 'real' characteristics of organisms (as trait/biological theorists would argue), or whether personality is best viewed as a 'social construction' – an inference drawn by others that need have no basis in the biology of the individual.

Recommended prior reading

Chapters 4 and 8.

Introduction

The question of whether personality and ability are socially determined or whether they are substantially influenced by our genes is generally seen as being one of the most important issues in psychology. It is certainly one of the best researched, with studies of varying quality dating back to the early years of the twentieth century. So why is it so important to understand whether personality and intelligence are influenced by genes? The answer is quite simple. You will have gathered by now that there are two schools of individual difference theorists. The first, rooted in social psychology and sociology, claims that the *environment* is of paramount importance in determining how individuals behave. An extreme form of this view stresses that personality is not 'something inside' the individual at all. Instead, personality is inferred by other people, who may choose to 'see' constancies in behaviour that really do not exist. For these theorists, the only interesting issue in personality study is to examine the social process by which personality traits and abilities are attributed to others. On what *grounds* may I decide that John is mean? What evidence would it take to make me change my mind? You can see now that Howe (1988) took essentially this point with regard to intelligence.

Other researchers claim that personality and intelligence appear to have some clear links with the biology of the nervous system. They point to evidence that is consistent with the idea that personality and intelligence are behavioural consequences of biological structures that really are 'inside' the individual. If this is so, it seems reasonable to ask whether these behaviours may be influenced by individuals' genetic makeup. If it can be shown that a trait is substantially influenced by genetics, this means that the characteristic is as much a property of the individual as their eye colour or weight and that sociological or social psychological theories will be unable completely to explain behaviour. To do this it is necessary to look at individual differences in the biology of the nervous system.

When I refer to genes in the following sections, I mean those genes that vary between people. Most of our genetic material determines that we have the characteristics of humans, rather than chimpanzees or mushrooms: all humans of the same sex will have exactly the same sequences of these genes. These are of no interest to us. The crucial genes from the point of individual differences are those which vary. Some of these code for physical features (e.g. eye colour, hair colour, height) but the function of most of them is unknown. They may each affect several behaviours; a gene that determines eye colour might also influence personality, which explains why several theorists scrutinize correlations between physical characteristics and individual differences (e.g. Deary and Carryl 1993). Thus when I refer to the similarity of people, I mean their similarity with respect to the 1% or so of the genes that vary in normal people – and not the 99% that define the characteristics of our species.

It is important to understand the distinction between variations in a characteristic within families and variation that occurs between families. If the family environment influences the level of a trait then this will result in all the children showing similar levels of the trait. For example, if relaxed, accepting parenting styles lead to children developing low levels of neuroticism, all the children in the family should show low neuroticism, since each will have experienced the same parenting style. Children within a family differ somewhat with respect to their genetic makeup; they share only about 50% of their genes, as each child inherits a random 50% of the genetic material from each parent. Thus you would not expect them to be entirely similar. If genes rather than parenting styles influence neuroticism, children within the same family will *differ* somewhat in their level of neuroticism because they each result from a different throw of the genetic die. So it is common to compare the amount of variation in a trait within families to the amount of variation between different families to determine whether a trait has a genetic basis.

Pairs of randomly selected strangers should show no similarity on a trait, because they have shared neither a common environment nor any genes (other than the ones that make us all human). Brothers and sisters brought up in the same family will tend to be highly similar to each other if the family environment shapes behaviour and only moderately similar to each other if genes are important (because they will share just half of their genes, on average).

Before we start to examine the data, it may be useful to look at the political implications of both an extreme environmental and an extreme hereditarian position. This may sound odd in a psychology text. However, the whole issue of heredity vs. environment has become heavily politicized and, thus, it generates strong emotions.

Politics of individual differences

Suppose that personality and abilities are completely shaped by the environment – the settings in which adults live and children develop, their interactions with other people, schools, parental attitudes to education and so on. This is the view often taken by the political left, since it suggests that improved social conditions can allow everyone to develop to their full potential. Without such interventions, the outlook for a child being brought up in a poor environment is grim indeed –

the accident of birth will mean that he or she is unlikely to develop a high IQ, for example. Since IQ is generally found to correlate with income, it means that the whole dreary cycle of poverty, low opportunity and low achievement is likely to continue from one generation to the next. By way of contrast, children of the upper middle classes, who enjoy a good education and have plenty of books, computers and encouragement will all (presumably) turn into geniuses, since there is nothing in their environment or their biological makeup to stop them from doing so. Similar arguments can be put forward for personality traits. A child who suffers a traumatic childhood will inevitably become depressed, anxious and neurotic. About the only good thing about this vision is that improvements to the disadvantaged underclass would be expected to lead to a dramatic improvement in their personality and ability.

Would the situation be any better if our traits were entirely genetically determined? Social background would not now affect IQ, since high ability would show itself no matter what happened to individuals as they grew up. A child born and reared under the most appalling social conditions might still turn out to be another Einstein. The expensive educations enjoyed by the middle classes would give them no advantage in terms of IQ and personality and so in a meritocracy (a system in which people rise to positions of power and influence on the basis of individual merit) one would expect the power to devolve to high-ability people from both backgrounds – who will then sometimes marry each other. The children of such marriages are also likely to be of above average ability (as we assume that ability is genetically determined) – the same is true for low IQ individuals. So this too results in a split society, only this time based on ability rather than on the accident of being born into wealth.

Since schooling will predominantly affect a child's *knowledge* (and not their genetically determined *ability*), it probably will not matter too much if schools and universities are underfunded and crowded. What if there are clear racial or other group differences in IQ or personality traits? If members of each community tend to select partners from within that community (as seems likely in practice), these differences are unlikely to decrease over time – members of some ethnic groups will always end up being appointed to the top jobs. *Worse is to follow.* Since we suppose that IQ is determined purely by genetic factors, it is not difficult to increase the average IQ in the country. Indeed, this may be thought desirable since it may lead to greater economic competitiveness. For it to be achieved, it is merely necessary to ensure that high IQ individuals produce more children (preferably with other high IQ individuals) than do low IQ individuals – an extremely controversial principle known as 'eugenics', which has been discussed by psychologists such as Lynn (2001).

The last view has, of course, been associated with the political right. Even if we ignore the implications of race differences and eugenics, both scenarios sound profoundly depressing to me. However, I mention these political fantasies (and no doubt reveal my ignorance of sociological principles!) in order to encourage you to understand some of the moral issues that can emerge from the simple question of whether individual differences arise because of nature or because of nurture – that is, because of genetic or environmental influences.

The unfortunate problem is that some psychologists and other social scientists seem to decide what the answer to the nature/nurture question *should* be, rather than looking at the evidence dispassionately. Many even argue that it is unethical to examine these issues, even if the methods used to do so are capable of yielding accurate results – an attitude that seems to smack of scientific Luddism. It is terribly tempting to forget that similarities in behaviour may arise because two people are related and not just because they have lived together.

In the sections that follow I have tried to survey the literature as objectively as possible, but you **173** will quite probably hear rather different interpretations given by others, particularly sociologists and social psychologists, who are understandably keen to emphasize the importance of the *environment* in determining behaviour. Because of the importance of this issue, it is vital that you read the primary sources and critically evaluate the merits of any interpretation of the data – including, of course, my own.

Methods for studying the nature/nurture issue

You will probably remember that, during the process of conception, there is a 50–50 chance that each of the genes in the fertilized egg will be derived from the father or the mother – something rather like a vast game of musical chairs takes place, with several versions of a gene (one from the father, and one from the mother) trying to sit on one site at each position on the chromosome. This means that we would expect *about* 50% of an individual's genetic material to come from their father and the other 50% from their mother. A large number of the parents' genes will be identical (since it is the genes, after all, that determine whether the DNA produces a human hair, a frog's leg or an oak leaf), but some of the parents' genes will be different, i.e. the parents will show some *genetic variability*. This chapter considers whether individual differences in these genes do, in any way, relate to individual differences in personality or ability. This discipline is known as *behaviour genetics.*

The consequences of parents' genetic variability are rather well known so far as physical characteristics are concerned. Eye colour, hair colour, blood group, inability to taste the chemical phenylthiocarbamide and colour blindness are among the physical characteristics that can be inherited and it can be shown that just a few genes determine each of these outcomes. That is, if the genetic makeup of the parents is known, it is possible to predict rather accurately the probability of (say) a particular hair colour.

Personality traits and abilities are rather different from these characteristics, in that they are *continuous* traits rather than taking just a few possible values. Thus geneticists suspect that most traits are influenced by a large number of genes, each of which makes a small influence in enhancing (or reducing) a person's level of a trait. Animal breeders have long known that it is possible to breed selectively individuals with certain physical characteristics. Cows that produce copious amounts of high-fat milk are repeatedly mated with bulls whose mother and sisters also produce large amounts of good-quality milk in the hope that, in some cases, the resulting calf will receive one set of 'high milk yielding' genes from each parent and so will produce even more prodigious amounts of excellent quality milk than either parent.

Animal breeders can also breed for psychological characteristics ('traits') and so it is unsurprising that psychologists have also considered whether genetic factors underpin human abilities and personality. My neighbour's Rottweiler tries to attack me whenever I move towards her territory, whereas a golden retriever comes bounding up wagging her tail whenever I go through *her* garden gate. More formally, Tryon (1940) managed to breed selectively two strains of rat, some of which quickly learned how to run through a maze in search of food (described as 'maze bright') and others that were slow in learning to do this (referred to as 'maze dull'). The methods of behaviour genetics can be used to estimate the extent to which individuals' scores on psychological traits are influenced by their genes.

It follows that if a trait (such as general intelligence, extraversion, etc.) is influenced by our genetic makeup, we would expect individuals who have a similar genetic makeup to show similar scores on the trait, provided that they are brought up in conditions which allow the gene to express itself. If genes have no influence on our intelligence (that is, if it is our environments alone that determine intelligence), we would not expect people who are genetically similar to have similar scores on the psychometric test unless they have also been brought up in similar environments.

All this sounds very straightforward, but there is, of course, one huge problem. People tend to be brought up within families. This means that genetically similar individuals (parents and their offspring) are often found to be living in the same place, sharing the benefits (or hardships) of a particular income level and perhaps bringing to bear the same attitudes to education and learning that their parents gave to *them*. So although members of a family are to some extent genetically similar, it is *not* possible simply to conclude that any similarity between their scores on some psychological test implies that this trait has a genetic component. It is just as likely that social factors (income, attitudes, etc.) could cause their scores to be similar.

'Assortive mating' creates difficulties, too. This is the tendency of 'like to attract like' – couples may come together because they see in each other characteristics (environmentally or genetically determined) that they both share. High intelligence is a good example. It is fairly unusual for partners to show a massive discrepancy in their IQ. So can *this* explain any similarity in their offspring's intelligence? How can we tell the extent to which environmental or genetic factors influence personality or intelligence? The answer is to look at genetic similarity within families (as well as between families), although this method is rather beyond the scope of the present chapter.

Several different experimental designs have been used to examine the extent to which personality and ability traits are influenced by genetics and the environment.

Twin studies

Identical twins have identical genes; non-identical twins on average share only half the genes that vary in humans. Suppose that a trait is measured in many pairs of identical twins and in pairs of non-identical twins, each pair of twins being brought up together in a normal family. If pairs of identical twins are found to have scores that are more similar than the scores of pairs of non-identical twins, this suggests that the trait has a genetic component – that is, that their greater genetic similarity *causes* them to have scores that are more similar than are those of pairs of non-identical twins. If pairs of identical twins are no more alike than pairs of non-identical twins, this suggests that the trait has no genetic component.

Very occasionally identical twins are separated at birth and reared in quite different environments. Studying *their* personality and abilities later in life can also yield valuable information about the genetics of personality and ability, since any similarity in trait scores can (arguably) be ascribed only to their identical genetic makeup.

> **Self-assessment question 11.1**
>
> What would you conclude if identical twins' scores on IQ tests were found to be no more similar than the scores of non-identical twins (who share only half their genes, on average)?

Family studies

Each parent shares half their genes with each of their children and this implies that the children will also, on average, share half their genes with each other. Figure 11.1 shows some other linkages. If a trait is influenced by genetic factors, one would expect children who are very similar genetically **175**

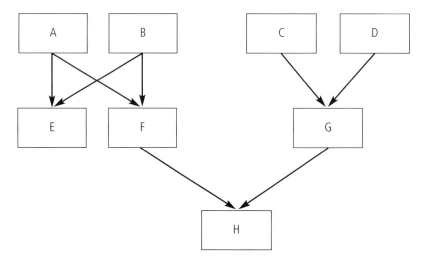

Figure 11.1 A single family tree showing genetic linkages. Lines indicate which offspring receive about half of their genetic material from which other individuals. A, B, C and D are unrelated individuals. E and F are the children of A and B, while G is the child of C and D. H is the child of F and G. Siblings will share about half of their genes with each other, and with their parents, so E and F, E and A, F and A, E and B, G and C and G and D will each share about half of their genes. H will share about a quarter of her genes with her grandparents (A, B, C and D) and aunt or uncle (E).

to show similar scores on the trait and children who are less genetically similar to differ more. If the individual's environment determines the level of the trait, all children reared in the same environment (regardless of their genetic background) should show similar levels of the trait. Family units in which a grandchild of an older daughter may be brought up alongside uncles and aunts of a similar age may be useful here, although for some reason such studies are rarely reported.

Adoption studies

These are valuable since they allow one to see the extent to which the environment can influence scores on a trait. An adopted child shares no variable genes with the other children in his or her adoptive family. If a study shows that adopted children generally have similar levels of a trait to other members of their adoptive family, this suggests that the trait is strongly influenced by the family environment, rather than by genetics.

Genetic influences over the lifespan

One has to be careful about the age of individuals in genetic studies. As Pedersen and Lichtenstein (1997) have observed, the relative importance of genetic and environmental effects is quite likely to vary with age for several reasons. First, some genes are known to influence behaviour only at specific times – the genes that control the production of certain hormones (and thus bring about puberty) are one example. Thus, even if a certain group of genes can potentially influence an individual's personality and intelligence, they need not all be active at all ages. Hence the extent to which our intelligence or personality is influenced by our genes is likely to vary over our lifespan simply because not all genes are influential all the time. Second, it might be that genetic influences on personality or ability are important only early in life. It seems quite possible that, as one gets older, the accumulation of experience and the variety of life events may become far more influential than our genetic makeup in determining how we think or behave, so perhaps genetic influences on personality and ability decline with age. Third, one can argue entirely the opposite case. It might be that the environment will tend to *magnify* any early genetically influenced individual differences in personality or behaviour. For example, a child who is identified as being of higher than average intelligence might be encouraged to take plenty of examinations, stretch his or her abilities to the limit by taking demanding university courses and so on. The studies have been performed and they indicate that our genetic background certainly continues to affect our personality and general intelligence into middle age and beyond (Loehlin 1992; Pedersen and Lichtenstein 1997; Pedersen, Plomin, McClearn and Friberg 1988). In the case of general intelligence, it seems that the influence of genetic factors is actually far more pronounced during middle age than during childhood or adolescence (McGue, Bouchard, Iacono and Lykken 1993). Thus it is emphatically *not* the case that our genetic background influences our behaviour only in childhood or adolescence. Rather, it seems to set us up for life.

Methods of quantitative genetics

Let us consider what influences the personality or ability of children in a family. In the previous section, I referred rather vaguely to 'environmental effects' as a blanket term for everything that is not genetic. However, geneticists distinguish between two types of environment. The first is the *shared environment* (sometimes also known as the *common environment* and hence denoted by 'C'), which basically represents the living conditions and the ethos experienced by all members of a family. It covers every influence that may make members of the same family show similar traits, including parental income, quality of housing, parental attitudes to education and discipline, nutrition and any other environmental events that would be expected to influence the development of all members of the family in much the same direction.

Not every environmental influence on a child will be shared by other children in the family. Friendships outside the family (e.g. with classmates) that are not shared with other family members, a good (or bad) relationship with a particular teacher, the effects of illnesses, disability or bullying and every other experience that is not shared by other family members together form the individual's *unique environment* (generally referred to as 'E'). The shared environment is composed of influences that will make family members similar to one another, whereas the unique environment describes environmental influences that tend to make family members different from one another. In addition to these environmental influences, it is possible that genetic similarities between family members will also influence their levels of certain traits. We represent the influence of these genetic factors by 'A'.

We assume that individuals' scores on a particular test can be completely explained by these three sources of variance (shared environment, unique environment and genetic similarity), each of which can be expressed as a number between 0 and 1. Thus we may write:

$$\text{total variation} = 1 = A + C + E$$

The basic aim of these genetic analyses is to establish the values for A, C and E in the equation – that is, to establish the relative importance of genetics, the shared environment and the unique environment in determining a particular behaviour. **177**

Note that the values for A, C and E (a) describe what happens in the population, and not to an individual, and (b) depends on the culture tested. So if it is found that general ability has a heritability of 0.5, this implies that about half the variation within the population can be attributed to the effects of genes. It does not mean that about half of a particular individual's intelligence is due to their genes. Furthermore, most of the children in countries where these studies are performed have had a reasonable standard of living: few live in extreme poverty, all have gone to school and so on. If studies were performed in cultures where there was far greater environmental variation between families than in western society, it is highly probable that larger values for A and smaller values for C would be found.

It should be intuitively obvious that the only factor that could cause a 'family' of unrelated children (e.g. adopted or fostered children) to show similar scores on a test would be the common environment. The only factor that could cause identical twins reared in the same family to show different scores on a test would be the influence of the unique environment (as their genetic makeup and the shared environment are identical). The only factor that could cause identical twins who are separated after birth and reared in different environments to have similar levels of a trait would be their genetic similarity (since their common and shared environments are very different). So it is only necessary to administer a test to these children and to calculate the correlation between the test scores of members of these groups, in order to be able to draw some rather powerful conclusions about the heritability of whatever trait is measured by the test. It is also possible to perform a few fancy calculations based on the relative similarity of the test scores of identical (monozygotic) and non-identical (dizygotic) pairs of twins.

The following self-assessment question is vital for a proper understanding of the methods of behaviour genetics. It is well worth trying to work it out for yourself.

Self-assessment question 11.2

Since dizygotic twins share half their genes and the common environment, we may write $r_{dz} = 0.5A + C$, while for monozygotic twins $r_{mz} = A + C$. We can test samples of twins and estimate values for r_{dz} and r_{mz}. So we need to solve these two simultaneous equations for A and C, to estimate how important genes and the family environment are for determining the level of this trait. Spend a few minutes now trying to do this.

Suppose that many pairs of dizygotic twins were given the same ability test, and the scores of these twin-pairs were correlated together, giving $r = 0.4$. Suppose the experiment was repeated with monozygotic (identical) twins, giving $r = 0.6$. What would you conclude about the relative importance of the genetic makeup, shared environment and the unshared environment? (*Hint*: to determine the contribution of the unshared environment, look back at our earlier equation.)

There are two main problems with the study outlined in self-assessment question 11.2. First, it must assume that the monozygotic twins are not more similar than non-identical twins for environmental (rather than genetic) reasons, e.g. being dressed similarly. The second problem is that measurement error (e.g. that brought about by using an unreliable test or thinking that twins are identical when they are not) can also be confused with variation due to the non-shared environment. Suppose that the correlations were found to be exactly zero for monozygotic and dizygotic twins because the test was completely riddled with measurement error. You should verify for yourself (using the equations given in the answer to self-assessment question 11.2) that the genetic effects and the shared environment would seem to have no influence on the trait, but that all of the variation would appear to arise from the unique environment. In a typical experiment (in which there is *some* measurement error), we may therefore expect the effect of the unique environment to be rather overestimated. Statisticians have developed ways of 'tweaking' the formulae to allow for this, but this is rather too detailed an issue for us to consider here.

You should be able to appreciate that it is possible to draw up systems of equations for other family members of known genetic similarity (e.g. cousins reared in the same environment) and so to estimate the relative importance of A, C and E by several different methods.

Multivariate genetics

The technique of multivariate genetics sounds complex, but is not. This technique seeks to answer a simple question. Suppose that two variables (verbal ability and numerical ability, for example) are found to be correlated. Suppose too that behaviour genetic studies show that both verbal ability and numerical ability have a genetic component. It might be the case that one set of genes influence verbal ability and another, quite different, set of genes affect numerical ability; the reason why verbal and numerical ability are correlated might be due to quality of schooling or something similar. Or it might be that the same genes influence performance on both verbal and numerical ability. Genes that influence performance on several traits are known as *generalist genes*.

Multivariate genetics is a fairly simple extension of the behaviour genetic methods described earlier that allows one to determine the extent to which a correlation between two variables occurs because certain genes influence both of them. It typically involves giving one member of each pair of identical twins a test of verbal ability and the other twin a test of numerical ability. The same is then done for pairs of non-identical twins and, after some mathematical wizardry, it is possible to determine the extent to which the correlation between verbal and numerical ability (in this example) is caused by generalist genes. The interesting point is that generalist genes abound – e.g. Davis, Haworth and Plomin (2009). This has some quite interesting implications for conditions such as dyslexia, for example. For should this be viewed as a specific, genetically influenced neurological problem which makes some individuals quite different from the rest of the population, and for which special interventions may be required or just an extreme form of low reading ability that is not qualitatively different from 'normal' reading? However, these issues are way beyond the scope of this book.

Molecular genetics

Now that the human genome is completely mapped, the hunt is on to find what various genes actually do – and especially to discover which ones code for intelligence. Robert Plomin and his co-workers at the Institute of Psychiatry have been taking a mixture of DNA from within various groups that are homogeneous with respect to intelligence (e.g. a group of very intelligent children; a control group of children with IQs close to the mean). They then look for differences in the DNA of these two groups of children. Differences are just starting to be found – replicated results are reported by Chorney et al. (1998) and Fisher et al. (1999), for example, but the whole field is rather technical and not particularly accessible to the non-specialist. However, the early optimism of researchers has faltered as it seems likely that intelligence is influenced by *many* genes, each having a rather small influence. This makes them hard to detect. Plomin, Kennedy and **179**

Craig (2006) give an excellent and highly readable summary of the issues. The search is also on for genes influencing personality, but there seem to be fewer replicable results in this area.

Genetics of ability

Few issues in psychology have received as much attention as the origins of intelligence, perhaps reflecting the importance that we attach to this concept. Bouchard and McGue (1981) reviewed over 140 studies of the relative importance of genetic factors, shared environment and the unique environment for determining general intelligence. Their conclusion (and one that is entirely consistent with later evidence) is that approximately 50% of the variation in adult and child intelligence is attributable to our genes. This finding used to be highly controversial, with environmentalists such as Kamin (1974) bitterly disputing the evidence. However, most social scientists now accept that genetic factors can influence general intelligence (Snyderman and Rothman 1987). The effects can be discerned very early in life, although the measurement of cognitive ability in young children is a notoriously difficult and unreliable process and some studies must be discounted because they used inadequate tests.

Plomin (1988) has summarized a vast amount of data from twin, family and adoption studies. These reveal the following findings:

- Identical twins reared apart have IQs that correlate 0.74, suggesting that genetic factors account for about three-quarters of the variation in children reared within this culture.

- Identical twins reared together have IQs that correlate 0.87, while fraternal (non-identical) twins reared together have IQs that correlate 0.53. Substituting these values into the formulae derived in the answer to self-assessment question 11.2, this suggests that IQ has a heritability of $2(0.87 - 0.53) = 0.68$, the shared environment accounts for $2(0.53 - 0.87) = 0.19$ of the variation in IQ and the unique environment explains the remaining 13% of the variability.

- Pairs of unrelated children living together and adoptive parents and adoptive children show correlations in IQ of 0.23 and 0.20, suggesting that the shared environment explains about 20–25% of the variation in IQ.

The really interesting findings concern the relative influence of the shared environment on IQ as children get older. Theorists such as Skinner seemed to believe that the childhood environment and childhood experiences should play an important part in children's eventual cognitive development. So, too, do parents who pay to send their children to expensive schools in order to develop their potential to the full. However, does the shared environment of childhood really influence adult IQ?

The answer seems to be a firm *no*. Studies of pairs of unrelated children brought up in the same family show that the correlations between their IQs fall to zero by adulthood – the shared environment has *no* influence on children's eventual cognitive ability. (Note that this applies to *all* children, not just those who are adopted. The purpose of considering adopted children is to eliminate genetic influences.) Family influences have no impact whatsoever on adult intelligence, which is certainly a good thing for those children reared under difficult circumstances.

A great many studies have examined the general intelligence of identical and non-identical twins who are brought up in a normal family environment. These studies are based on rather large samples – the Louisville Twin Study alone considers some 500 sets of twins. Wilson (1983) reports the correlations between the cognitive functioning of pairs of twins during early life. Between the ages of 3 and 18 months, identical twins and non-identical twins show rather similar correlations (of the order of 0.55 to 0.7) indicating that the family environment influences their scores on the tests. However, at 18 months of age the correlation is 0.82 for identical twins but 0.65 for fraternal twins, the values at 24, 30 and 36 months being broadly similar. This suggests (as you should verify using the formulae derived in your answer to self-assessment question 11.2) that genetic factors seem to account for about a quarter to one-third of the variation in the cognitive abilities of even these young infants. Later analyses suggest that the heritability increases from about 0.4 at 1 year of age to 0.57 at 4 years and 0.7 at 7 years (Cherny, Fulker and Hewitt 1996).

What happens as children get older? It used to be supposed that their environments (learning experiences, schooling, etc.) become more varied and so the effects of genetic makeup on ability would decrease. In fact, quite the opposite is found. Thompson (1993: 112) cites evidence from the Western Reserve Twin Project based on 148 sets of identical twins and 135 sets of fraternal twins aged 6–12 years, which suggests that general cognitive ability has a heritability of 0.5 at this age level. That is, genetic factors account for 50% of the variation in the children's scores on the test. The shared environment accounts for an additional 42% of the variance, with the unique environment having relatively little effect. In other words, the genes and the 'family ethos' are of almost equal importance as influences on the child's intelligence at this age.

After this age, the influence of the shared environment almost disappears. When the same experiment is repeated with adolescents, the genetic influence is much the same, but the shared environment has a negligible effect on the mental abilities of young teenagers (LaBuda, DeFries and Fulker 1987). This is a surprising finding. It seems that, at this age, it simply does not matter what family background, facilities, encouragement or difficulties the children enjoy – their intellectual ability appears to be influenced in equal measure by their genetic background and their non-shared environments. The influence of the family seems to have virtually no effect on the child's intellectual ability after the early teenage years.

This raises some interesting issues concerning the effectiveness of educational interventions. It shows that it is wrong to regard children's minds as identical blank slates and consequently that even the most favourable environmental stimulation is unlikely to have the potential to change any child into a genius, as genetic factors will also influence the child's ultimate intellectual performance. This is consistent with the finding discussed in Chapter 10 that the effects of an enriched environment at some critical stage of development are not as massive as had been expected.

This is not necessarily a bad thing, of course. It means that even the most ghastly environment will not be able to 'pull down' all children's IQs. It also seems that factors outside the family are much more potent influences on the adolescent's IQ than any family influences, although family influences can be important for younger children. The most consistent finding to emerge from these hundreds of studies is that some children do appear to have a definite advantage in life when it comes to IQ and that these genetic influences do not decline with age. About 50% of the variability in IQ can be explained by a knowledge of individuals' genetic backgrounds and this applies to adults at least as much as it does to children.

This is not to say that educational interventions should not be attempted. After all:

- The interventions are designed to improve educational performance rather than IQ, and since the studies never really sought to boost IQ, it may be unreasonable to conclude that because they cannot do so, no intervention is likely to prove effective in increasing intelligence.

- They may be able to motivate children to work hard and motivational/attitudinal influences may have a profound influence on educational performance (although not necessarily on IQ).

- Genetic factors account for only about 50 to 70% of the variability, implying that environmental improvements can have a marked influence on IQ.

However, the evidence does show very clearly that theories that seek to 'explain' intelligence purely in terms of social processes will, at best, be able to explain 50% of the variation in IQ. Although many of us would wish that it were not so, the literature indicates that an individual's genetic makeup is as important as *all* of their environmental influences in determining their ultimate level of intelligence. Children are simply not born with equal intellectual potential.

Genetics of personality

The issue of the genetics of personality is much less controversial than the genetic basis of ability, simply because society does not really care too much whether an individual has an extreme personality type. Individuals who are three standard deviations above the mean on extraversion are, on the whole, treated in much the same way as individuals who are three standard deviations *below* the mean. They are not (some of us intraverts would add 'thankfully') encouraged to develop their extraversion to its maximum extent. Rates of pay will not be influenced by levels of extraversion. Thus the social consequences of having a particular type of personality are much less marked than those of ability.

Several studies have examined the extent to which the main personality traits are determined by genetic makeup, using the methodologies described earlier – for once again we make the assumption that an individual's position along a particular personality trait is influenced by the additive effects of a large number of genes. For example, Loehlin (1992) used twin and adoption data to determine the extent to which each of the 'big five' personality factors of Costa and McCrae (1992) is influenced by genetic makeup. The heritability values for these scales range from about 0.3 to 0.5 (the best agreed factors of extraversion and neuroticism having the highest levels of heritability). Zuckerman (1991) provides useful summaries of the older literature, again showing that:

- heritabilities are substantial

- the influence of genetic effects does not disappear by adulthood

- the shared (family) environment really plays a rather minor part in determining personality at any age, the non-shared environment being a much more potent influence on all personality traits.

For example, Table 11.1 shows the correlations between the personality test scores of identical twins and fraternal twins for three broad types of personality factor (these are grouped, since not all investigators used the same scales), namely extraversion/sociability, neuroticism/emotionality and psychoticism/impulsivity/unsocialized sensation seeking. The figures in each column vary somewhat, since the studies used different tests (that varied in reliability and validity). You will see that some of these studies are based on *enormous* samples of identical and fraternal twins, and that there is a considerable degree of consistency in the results. If genetic makeup had no influence on personality, one would expect sets of identical twins to have personality traits that

Study	Age	Number of sets		Personality trait					
				E-Sy		N-Emo		P-Imp	
		I	F	I	F	I	F	I	F
Loehlin and Nichols (1976)	18	490	317	0.61	0.25	0.54	0.22	0.54	0.32
Tellegen et al. (1988)	21	217	114	0.54	0.06	0.54	0.41	0.58	0.25
Rose (1988)	14–34	228	182	0.60	0.42	0.41	0.22	0.70	0.41
Floderus-Myrhed et al. (1980)	17–49	2279	3670	0.47	0.20	0.46	0.21	—	—
Rose et al. (1988)	17–49	2720	4143	0.54	0.21	0.54	0.25	—	—
Rose et al. (1988)	24–49	1027	2304	0.46	0.15	0.33	0.12	—	—
Rose et al. (1988)	24–49	1293	2520	0.49	0.14	0.43	0.18	—	—
Eaves and Young (1981)	31	303	172	0.55	0.19	0.47	0.07	0.47	0.28
Pedersen et al. (1988)	59	151	204	0.54	0.06	0.41	0.24	—	—

Table 11.1 Correlations between test scores of sets of identical twins (I) and fraternal twins (F) (reared together) on personality scales assessing the three major dimensions of personality, namely extraversion (E-Sy), neuroticism (N-Emo) and psychoticism/impulsivity (P-Imp) (adapted from Table 3.2 of Zuckerman (1991))

were about as similar as sets of fraternal twins – that is, the correlations in the 'I' columns in Table 11.1 should be about the same size as the correlations in the 'F' columns for the same trait. You do not need any fancy statistical analyses to see that this simply is not so. Pairs of identical twins have really quite similar levels of extraversion (r values of between 0.46 and 0.61), whereas pairs of non-identical twins tend to be considerably less alike in their degree of extraversion (r values ranging from 0.06 to 0.42). Similar trends can be seen for the other two main personality traits. This strongly suggests that these three main personality traits have a substantial genetic component. When the correlations from the Floderus-Myrhed studies (chosen because they involve the largest samples of twins) are entered into the formula shown in the answer to self-assessment question 11.2, the estimated heritability of extraversion can be seen to be of the order of 0.54 to 0.66. Similarly, the influence of the shared environment is essentially zero.

Like the finding that the shared environment is of little importance in determining adult intelligence, the last mentioned result is, I feel, one of the most remarkable discoveries in the whole of psychology. Given all that has been written about the importance of the family in childhood, it is truly amazing to discover that some aspects of personality seem to be almost entirely uninfluenced by the type of family in which one is brought up. Given the range of family environments typically found in our culture, it does not generally matter a jot which of these a child experiences – any influences on the child's later personality must be understood in terms of the genes that are inherited from their parents and *not* in terms of their childhood experiences per se. The correlation between genetically dissimilar children who are brought up (adopted) in the same family is typically almost zero (Zuckerman mentions an r value of 0.07).

As Brody and Crowley (1995) have observed: '[I]f shared environmental influences are close to zero, most of the variables that have typically been studied by developmental psychologists have little or no influence on personality [and] it is usually a mistake to study environmental influences on personality and intelligence without a consideration of possible genetic effects'. Given that virtually *all* the studies point to the same conclusion, it is difficult to argue with this analysis. It certainly appears that all the ingenious environmentally based developmental theories of Rogers, Freud, Skinner, Bandura, etc., are simply incorrect (at least in that the family environment spectacularly fails to influence the two major personality traits, namely extraversion and neuroticism). This kind of result is not at all popular with social psychologists or sociologists.

The evidence suggests that personality is determined by a mixture of genetic factors and the non-shared environments of children – the influence of particular teachers on a child, the 'special' relationship between a child and other members of his or her family or the influence of friends from outside the family. However, it is necessary to qualify this assertion somewhat. *Some* personality traits (or behaviours) *have* been found to be substantially influenced by the common environment. For example, Stevenson's (1997) twin study examined the extent to which prosocial behaviour (empathy, helping behaviour and altruism), antisocial behaviour (aggression or destructive behaviour) and sociability were genetically determined. Antisocial behaviour was found to have a comparatively small genetic component (0.24, as opposed to 0.54 and 0.67, respectively) and was the only behaviour for which the influence of the shared environment was substantial (0.54, as opposed to 0.2 and 0, respectively). Thus it is clear that some behaviours, at least, can be moulded by the family – it just so happens that the main personality traits are not shaped in this way.

The study by Pedersen et al. involved 59-year-old males, while participants in the studies by Loehlin and Nichols (1976) and Tellegen et al. (1988) were aged 18 and 21 years, respectively. The influence of genetic factors on personality does not seem to decline with age. If it did, Pedersen's identical twins and fraternal twins would show similar correlations. If anything, the data suggest that genetic influences become relatively *more* important as one gets older.

Summary

We now know a great deal about the relative importance of environmental and genetic influences on personality or intelligence. The problem is that social psychologists, sociologists and the like are unhappy with the idea that one's genetic makeup can moderate (and arguably dominate) the effects of the environment, while eugenicists are reluctant to acknowledge the very potent influence of the unshared environment. There are certainly many facts that the simple models described in this chapter cannot explain, e.g. the 'Flynn effect', discussed in Chapter 10.

Plomin et al. (1995) suggested that the child's unique environment may itself be influenced by genetic factors, which at first glance seems a bizarre proposition. However, suppose that intelligence/personality *is* substantially influenced by genetic factors. It seems quite likely that the intelligent child will actively seek out intellectually stimulating environments – playing chess, asking parents for educational games, joining several clubs at school, reading educational magazines and perhaps making friends who are also of above average ability. Thus the child's unique environment may be determined, at least in part, by his or her genetic makeup (i.e. intelligence). The lifestyle of the extravert (their unshared environment) may also be created so as to allow the free expression of extraverted behaviour, while that of the neurotic may be designed to be as safe, predictable and unthreatening as possible. Thus the types of unshared environment experienced by individuals may, at least in part, be influenced by their genetic makeup. This is an interesting idea that is beginning to be explored.

Much current research involves examining the effects of individual genes on behaviour and on scores on tests of personality and ability. One of the most promising findings here is that a gene was identified many years ago that was related to levels of anxiety (Lesch et al. 1996); several others have now been found (e.g. Gunthert et al. 2007).

Given the exciting nature of the findings discussed in this chapter, it is necessary to remind ourselves of one basic point before moving on to the next chapter. You will recall that there is some opposition to the very notion of traits. Intelligence is seen not as a real property of people, but as a convenient social abstraction (Howe 1988), while personality traits have received the same treatment at the hands of some social psychologists (Hampson 1988). The finding that intelligence and personality traits all have a very substantial genetic component seems to suggest that neither of these views can be entirely correct and that the individual differences that we measure by means of psychological tests are, to a considerable extent, the behavioural consequences of individual differences in certain biological structures.

Suggested additional reading

There are several excellent texts and journal papers that introduce basic genetic concepts (such as those described here) before going on to describe more complex issues, such as multivariate models. These include (in no particular order) Bouchard (1993), Krueger, Tackett, Robins and Fraley (2007), Stevenson (1997), Bouchard (1995), Pedersen and Lichtenstein (1997), Plomin et al. (1995), Krueger, Johnson, Kling, Mroczek and Little (2006), Brody and Crowley (1995); there **185** are plenty of others. I make no apology for the age of some of these references: the basic facts about the heritability of traits were established some time ago and the subsequent literature has become rather technical.

Answers to self-assessment questions

SAQ 11.1

Each child will inherit half its genetic makeup from its mother and so you would conclude either that the trait has a genetic component or that it is influenced by the environment and the identical twins are treated more similarly than non-identical twins. I have not considered the latter possibility in much detail in the text, since studies suggest that the different ways in which identical twins are treated more similarly than fraternal twins (e.g. being dressed similarly) are unlikely to have much effect on their personality or intelligence.

SAQ 11.2

Subtracting the two equations gives:

$$r_{mz} - r_{dz} = 0.5A + 0$$

Multiplying both sides by two gives $A = 2(r_{mz} - r_{dz})$.

Multiplying both sides of the first equation by two and subtracting the second equation gives:

$$2r_{dz} - r_{mz} = 0 + C$$

So substituting in the values for the correlations:

$$A = 2(0.6 - 0.4) = 0.4$$
$$C = 2 \times 0.4 - 0.6 = 0.2$$

Hence:

$$E = 1 - A - C = 1 - 0.4 - 0.2 = 0.4$$

showing that, in this hypothetical case, genetic influences and the unique environment are of equal importance and each is about twice as important as the shared environment in determining scores on that trait.

These important results were included as a self-assessment question since it might be easier (and safer) to derive the formulae from first principles during an examination, rather than trying to memorize them.

References

Bouchard, T. J. J. (1993). The genetic architecture of human intelligence. In P. A. Vernon (ed.), *Biological Approaches to the Study of Human Intelligence*. New York: Ablex.

Bouchard, T. J. J. (1995). Longitudinal studies of personality and intelligence: a behavior genetic and evolutionary psychology perspective. In D. H. Saklofske and M. Zeidner (eds), *International Handbook of Personality and Intelligence*. New York: Plenum.

Bouchard, T. J. J. and McGue, M. (1981). Familial studies of intelligence: a review. *Science 212*, 1055–8.

Brody, N. and Crowley, M. J. (1995). Environmental (and genetic) influences on personality and intelligence. In D. H. Saklofske and M. Zeidner (eds), *International Handbook of Personality and Intelligence*. New York: Plenum.

Cherny, S. S., Fulker, D. W. and Hewitt, J. K. (1996). Cognitive development from infancy to middle childhood. In R. J. Sternberg and E. Grigoranko (eds), *Intelligence: Heredity and Environment*. Cambridge: Cambridge University Press.

Chorney, M. J., Chorney, K., Seese, N., Owen, M. J., Daniels, J., McGuffin, P. et al. (1998). A quantitative trait locus associated with cognitive ability in children. *Psychological Science 9*(3), 159–66.

Costa, P. T. and McCrae, R. R. (1992). *NEO-PI(R) Professional Manual*. Odessa, FL: Psychological Assessment Resources.

Davis, O. S. P., Haworth, C. M. A. and Plomin, R. (2009). Learning abilities and disabilities: generalist genes in early adolescence. *Cognitive Neuropsychiatry 14*(4), 312–31.

Deary, I. J. and Carryl, P. G. (1993). Intelligence, EEG and evoked potentials. In P. A. Vernon (ed.), *Biological Approaches to the Study of Human Intelligence*. Norwood, NJ: Ablex.

Fisher, P. J., Turic, D., Williams, N. M., McGuffin, P., Asherson, P., Ball, D. et al. (1999). DNA pooling identifies QTLs on chromosome 4 for general cognitive ability in children. *Human Molecular Genetics 8*(5), 915–22.

Gunthert, K. C., Conner, T. S., Armeli, S., Tennen, H., Covault, J. and Kranzler, H. R. (2007). Serotonin transporter gene polymorphism (5-HTTLPR) and anxiety reactivity in daily life: a daily process approach to gene–environment interaction. *Psychosomatic Medicine 69*(8), 762–8.

Hampson, S. E. (1988). *The Construction of Personality: An Introduction* (2nd edn). London and New York: Routledge.

Howe, M. J. A. (1988). Intelligence as explanation. *British Journal of Psychology 79*, 349–60.

Kamin, L. J. (1974). *The Science and Politics of IQ*. Harmondsworth: Penguin.

Krueger, R. F., Johnson, W., Kling, K. C., Mroczek, D. K. and Little, T. D. (2006). Behavior genetics and personality development. In *Handbook of Personality Development*. Mahwah, NJ: Erlbaum.

Krueger, R. F., Tackett, J. L., Robins, R. W. and Fraley, R. C. (2007). Behavior genetic designs. In *Handbook of Research Methods in Personality Psychology*. New York: Guilford Press.

LaBuda, M. C., DeFries, J. C. and Fulker, D. W. (1987). Genetic and environmental covariance structures among WISC-R subtests: a twin study. *Intelligence 11*, 233–44.

Lesch, K. P., Bengel, D., Heils, A., Zhang Sabol, S., Greenburg, B. D., Petri, S. et al. (1996). Association of anxiety-related traits with a polymorphism in the serotinin transporter gene regulatory region. *Science 274*, 1527–30.

Loehlin, J. C. (1992). *Genes and Environment in Personality Development*. Newbury Park, CA: Sage.

Loehlin, J. C. and Nichols, R. C. (1976). *Heredity, Environment and Personality*. Austin: University of Texas Press.

Lynn, R. (2001). *Eugenics: A Reassessment*. Westport, CT: Praeger.

McGue, M., Bouchard, T. J., Jr., Iacono, W. G. and Lykken, D. T. (1993). Behavioral genetics of cognitive ability: a life-span perspective. In R. Plomin and G. E. McClearn (eds), *Nature, Nurture and Psychology*. Washington, DC: American Psychological Association.

Pedersen, N. L. and Lichtenstein, P. (1997). Biometric analyses of human abilities. In C. Cooper and V. Varma (eds), *Processes in Individual Differences*. London: Routledge.

Pedersen, N. L., Plomin, R., McClearn, G. E. and Friberg, L. (1988). Neuroticism, extraversion and related traits in adult twins reared apart and reared together. *Journal of Personality and Social Psychology 55*, 950–7.

Plomin, R. (1988). The nature and nurture of cognitive abilities. In R. J. Sternberg (ed.), *Advances in the Psychology of Human Intelligence* (Vol. 4). Hillsdale, NJ: Erlbaum.

Plomin, R., Kennedy, J. K. J. and Craig, I. W. (2006). Editorial: the quest for quantitative trait loci associated with intelligence. *Intelligence 34*(6), 513–26.

Plomin, R., McClearn, G. E., Skuder, P., Vignetti, S., Chorney, M. J., Kasarda, S. et al. (1995). Allelic associations between 100 DNA markers and high versus low IQ. *Intelligence 21*(1), 31–48.

Snyderman, M. and Rothman, S. (1987). Survey of expert opinion on intelligence and aptitude testing. *American Psychologist 42*, 137–44.

Stevenson, J. (1997). The genetic basis of personality. In C. Cooper and V. Varma (eds.), *Processes in Individual Differences*. London: Routledge.

Tellegen, A., Lykken, D. T., Bouchard, T. J., Wilcox, K., Segal, N. and Rich, A. (1988). Personality similarity in twins reared together and apart. *Journal of Personality and Social Psychology 54*, 1031–9.

Thompson, L. A. (1993). Genetic contributions to intellectual development in infancy and childhood. In P. A. Vernon (ed.), *Biological Approaches to the Study of Human Intelligence*. Norwood, NJ: Ablex.

Tryon, R. C. (1940). Genetic differences in maze-learning ability in rats. *Yearbook of the National Society of Student Education 39*, 111–9.

Wilson, R. C. (1983). The Louisville Twin Study: developmental synchronies in behavior. *Child Development 54*, 298–316.

Zuckerman, M. (1991). *Psychobiology of Personality*. Cambridge: Cambridge University Press.

12 Psychology of mood and motivation

Background

While Chapters 4, 5, 6, and 8 have focused on the nature and assessment of stable traits (such as general ability or extraversion), so far there has been no mention of the assessment of states – moods and motivation.

Recommended prior reading

Chapters 1, 4, 14, 15, 16 and 17.

Introduction

This chapter is all about the measurement of *states*. Unlike traits, states are not stable, constant features of individuals as are (for example) extraversion and verbal ability. Instead, states are highly volatile, changing from hour to hour or from minute to minute, often (although not necessarily) in response to life events. Two broad classes of state have been identified, namely *mood states* and *motivational states*. Moods are the familiar surges of emotions that we feel on the morning of an examination, on seeing a beautiful sunset, on viewing a moving performance on stage or screen or after seeing our team win an important match. Some theorists draw distinctions between moods and emotions, but I have suggested elsewhere that this is a dangerous practice (Cooper 1997). Motivational states are internal feelings that drive us to eat when hungry, to spend hours assuaging our social conscience through voluntary work, to spend time and money finding a partner and so on.

Scales that measure states, just like those that assess traits, must be shown to be reliable and valid. How can the reliability of a mood scale be assessed? One property that it most certainly must *not* show is high temporal stability (test–retest reliability). Because moods change over time while traits do not, if individuals are found to have similar scores on two occasions this strongly suggests that the scale is measuring a trait of some kind, rather than a state. However, it is possible to calculate the internal consistency reliability of a mood scale and it should be clear from Chapter 15 that this is, in any case, the more theoretically useful measure of reliability.

Assessing the *validity* of scales that measure states is rather more problematical, for as states (by definition) last only for a short time and are susceptible to environmental influences, it is necessary to measure the mood (or motivation) and to assess the criterion behaviour(s) at almost the same time. There would be little point in measuring mood (once) on Monday and then correlating these scores with some criterion data on Friday, as the level of mood/motivation will almost certainly have changed.

The construct validity of mood scales could, perhaps, be assessed by correlating scores on once measured moods or motivation with scores on other criterion measures, such as sexual behaviour, anxiety (as rated by an observer) and so on. However, there is a problem with this approach, **189** since it may confuse the mood (or motivation) with personality. For example, suppose the sample contains some individuals who are *always* anxious (i.e. high on the trait of anxiety or neuroticism). Any significant correlations between self-reported anxiety (in a mood questionnaire) and rated anxiety might simply show that the items in the questionnaire measure trait anxiety. For this reason, it is much better to perform longitudinal studies and to see how mood or motivational state varies relative to each individual's own baseline.

It is also possible to establish the content validity of mood scales, since many intense moods have clinical overtones – anxiety, depression, etc. For example, it would be difficult to argue that a mood scale that asked about all the symptoms of depression in DSM-IV was not valid. However, this is rather more difficult for motivational states.

Worse still, a huge number of cognitive variables may affect states. The emotions that you experience when a stranger pours a drink over you will vary enormously depending on whether or not you believe it was an accident. We can also evaluate whether or not we are experiencing negative moods ('stress') and explore our options for reducing such feelings (e.g. dropping out of university, improving our time management skills, blaming lecturers' unrealistic expectations rather than ourselves or heading for the bar).

It is also necessary to consider which *aspects* of states we should assess. When measuring traits there is only one sensible thing to measure, namely the person's level of the trait, which is assumed to be a stable feature of that individual. However, many more options are available when measuring mood or motivational states. For example, one could choose to measure:

- a person's level of the state(s) at one particular instant, e.g. their level of anxiety prior to an examination

- the extent to which a person's state score changes between two situations, e.g. their level of anxiety before an examination minus their level of anxiety when sitting relaxing on a beach

- a person's *average* level of the state(s), e.g. the average strength of a person's sex drive over a period of weeks or months

- the variability of a person's state(s) from hour to hour, day to day or week to week

- periodic fluctuations in states, e.g. the extent to which a person's level of state(s) can be predicted by some regular daily, weekly, monthly or annual cycles

- the speed with which a person's score on a state changes following some intervention.

While with traits it was only necessary to try to understand which variables affected the *level* of the trait (e.g. the biological basis of intelligence), it is clear that any comprehensive study of moods and motivational states will need to consider all of these variables, at least. This makes it difficult to construct and test any comprehensive theories of mood and motivation and ensures that the field is far too broad to be covered in any depth in this chapter!

Mood

Nature of mood

Much research into moods has been driven by clinical interest, e.g. the development of tests to assess patients' levels of anxiety and depression. Thus many inventories have been designed to measure depression, anxiety, hopelessness and the like, with rather few attempting to assess the more pleasant moods, such as elation, sociability or *joie de vivre*. There are two problems with this approach. First, it means that different clinicians may have devised scales that measure the same construct, but may have labelled these constructs differently. One person's 'anxiety' scale may measure precisely the same thing as another theorist's scale of 'state neuroticism', 'tense arousal' or 'negative affect' and this can create enormous confusion until the scale items are jointly factored to reveal the extent of their overlap. The second problem is that this ad hoc approach to the construction of mood scales may leave certain important aspects of mood unmeasured. Apart from the work of Storm and Storm (1987), which did not use factor analysis, and a little early work by Cattell (1973) there has been little attempt to ensure that mood scales – even supposedly comprehensive ones – actually measure the full range of possible moods. Different mood theorists tend to use different samples of items and so discover different numbers of factors.

A glance at the mental measurement yearbooks will reveal that a quite bewildering range of tests has been developed to assess mood, in particular. Some of these have been designed to assess single moods (e.g. the State–Trait Anxiety Inventory and the Depression Adjective Checklist), while questionnaires such as the Profile of Mood States (POMS) (Lorr and McNair 1988), the Howarth Mood Adjective Checklist (HMACL-4) (Howarth 1988), the Eight State Questionnaire (8SQ) (Curran and Cattell 1976), the Differential Emotions Scale (DES-III) (Izard, Dougherty, Bloxom and Kotsch 1982), the Nowlis Mood Adjective Checklist (Nowlis and Nowlis 1956), the UWIST Mood-Adjective Checklist (Matthews, Jones and Chamberlain 1990) and the Clyde Mood Scale (Clyde 1963) all claim to measure a number of distinct mood states. There is good evidence that all of these multi-scale tests measure two broad dimensions of mood known as positive affect and negative affect (Lorr and Wunderlich 1988; McConville and Cooper 1992b; Watson, Clark and Tellegen 1988; Watson and Tellegen 1985; Zevon and Tellegen 1982). These scales are very widely used, POMS in particular having attracted widespread interest in the area of sports psychology.

Four problems in measuring mood

Most of the scales just mentioned were constructed by administering samples of adjectives to groups of volunteers and asking them to rate how accurately each of the adjectives described how they felt or behaved *at that instant*, rather than how they usually felt or acted. Supporters of this approach to mood scale construction believe that this is sufficient to guarantee that the scale measures a state rather than a personality trait.

However, there are problems with almost all of the scales mentioned. First, it is generally not at all obvious how or why each scale selected those particular items for inclusion. There is no guarantee that the items are a random sample of potentially mood-describing adjectives. Second, no attempt is made to eliminate synonyms – many of the scales may be highly reliable simply because all the adjectives contained within them mean precisely the same thing. The finding that a group of items *unexpectedly* vary together is what allows us to infer the presence of some 'source trait'. We should not (sensibly) infer the operation of some source trait where the items *have* to form a factor because they are just synonyms, but this does not stop most theorists from doing so. The third problem is more obvious. This method of constructing mood scales (factoring correlations between items following a single administration of the test to a large group of people) is precisely the same technique as that used to find personality traits. So how can we ever be sure that these scales measure mood *states* at all? Different techniques must be developed. Finally, moods are supposedly exquisitely sensitive to environmental conditions, so the setting in which people complete the questionnaires is likely to influence the scores that are obtained, and this will itself influence the number and nature of the mood factors that are derived. Asking undergraduates to complete mood questionnaires in a large group thus seems to be rather short-sighted – it is difficult to imagine how *anyone* could feel fearful, exuberant, zestful or excited (for example) when sitting in a lecture theatre ploughing through a questionnaire containing hundreds of items for the sake of course credit.

Discovering the main dimensions of mood is thus a tricky problem and there is little firm evidence that we have arrived anywhere near a solution. Most attempts to solve the problem have fallen foul of one of the four problems just mentioned and anomalies often arise when the scales are examined in detail. For example, Curran and Cattell's (1976) Eight State Questionnaire supposedly measures eight quite distinct moods, yet the correlation between some of the scales is of the order of 0.7 to 0.8, once their reliability is taken into account (Matthews 1983). Much the same is true of Howarth's scale (Howarth 1988). This suggests that the convergent validity of some of the scales is dubious. There is no space here to examine the psychometric properties of all of these scales in detail, but a hardnosed reading of the test manuals and published literature often fails to reveal much convincing evidence for their validity. However, in the next section we shall consider a method of scale construction guaranteeing that a scale will measure a mood state, rather than a trait, so eliminating one of the major problems outlined earlier.

Identifying moods using factor analysis

The key feature that distinguishes mood from personality traits is that moods vary over time, whereas personality traits remain more or less constant. This basic distinction can be used to construct scales that can be shown to measure mood rather than personality. Consider, for example, the five-item questionnaire shown in Table 12.1.

Suppose that just one person were asked to answer the questions shown in Table 12.1 at the same time of day on 20 consecutive days. It would be possible to show how the responses vary from day to day by drawing graphs rather like those shown in Figure 12.1. (I arbitrarily decided to

		Strongly agree	Agree	Neutral	Disagree	Strongly disagree
(a)	At the moment I feel quite cheerful	5	4	3	2	1
(b)	It is easy for me to concentrate	5	4	3	2	1
(c)	My heart is pounding	5	4	3	2	1
(d)	I am worrying more than usual	5	4	3	2	1
(e)	I generally prefer my own company to that of other people	5	4	3	2	1

Table 12.1 Five items from a hypothetical questionnaire

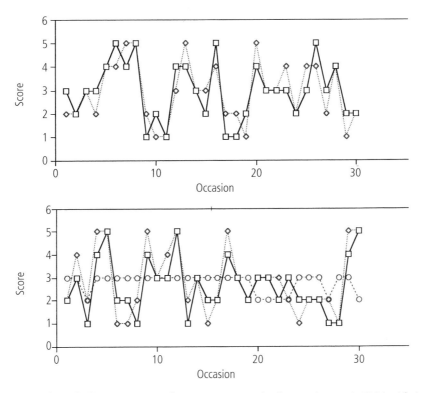

Figure 12.1 Daily responses of one person to the items shown in Table 12.1.

plot the daily responses to items (a) and (b) on the first graph and the daily responses to items (c), (d) and (e) on the second graph, since plotting all five items on the same graph appeared confusing.) It is possible to learn rather a lot about the structure of moods from graphs.

For example, it is clear that items (a) and (b) tend to move up and down together – when one of them is high, so is the other. The same is true for items (c) and (d). Item (e) is quite interesting, since responses to this item vary relatively little from day to day, which is hardly surprising since the item appears to measure a personality trait rather than a state. (It asks the person how they *generally* feel, rather than how they feel *at this moment*.) Thus just by looking at this graph it is clear that the five items measure two distinct states plus one trait.

However, plotting graphs such as this is a time-consuming business and interpreting the results is not particularly 'objective' – neither is it easy to see what is going on when the number of items becomes large. Fortunately, you already know how to analyse these data.

Suppose we correlated together the person's scores on the five items in the questionnaire. This may seem rather odd – we have previously calculated correlations only for many people tested on one occasion, rather than for one person tested on many occasions. One simply enters the data obtained on 30 occasions as if they had been obtained from 30 individuals and uses the same statistical package as usual.

Factor analysis is the obvious tool to explore the structure of these correlations, and Table 12.2 shows the factor matrix that results from a principal components/VARIMAX analysis of the correlation matrix, rotating two factors. This analysis can tell us how many groups of items tend **193**

Rotated factor matrix

Variable	Factor 1	Factor 2
V1	−0.33391	−0.85188
V2	−0.32985	−0.87516
V3	−0.94627	−0.08151
V4	−0.94616	−0.15725
V5	−0.16903	−0.34585

Table 12.2 Factor analysis of one person's responses to the five-item questionnaire administered on 30 occasions

to rise and fall together from day to day in a single individual. Items that do not vary much (or which do vary, but in a different way from any other items in the questionnaire) will not load on any of the factors, as you can see by looking at item (e) in Table 12.2. Thus this technique of factor analysis is able to distinguish traits from states, which is precisely what is required when developing a mood questionnaire.

This form of factor analysis, in which correlations between items are calculated after administering the items to one individual on many occasions, is known as P-technique, to distinguish it from the more usual method of factor analysis (R- or regular technique).

Suppose that ten people each completed the mood questionnaire on 30 occasions. Much the same technique can be used to analyse these data: the experimenter can either perform ten separate analyses using P-technique (each based on 30 occasions) or else the ten tables of data can be stacked one on top of each other, so that the computer program 'thinks' it is analysing the data from one individual on 300 occasions. This is sometimes known as 'Chain-P' technique. It is prudent to standardize the scores on the items for each person (i.e. to transform the scores so that each person has a mean of 0 and a standard deviation of 1: z scores) before stacking the data and performing the P-factor analysis. This will guard against any contamination by traits, as you may care to verify using some made-up data.

It is also possible to administer questionnaires to large groups of people on two occasions, to calculate the difference between individuals' scores on each of the items on the two occasions and factor analyse these difference scores. This technique, too, will reveal any states that run through the questionnaire quite independently of any traits that might be present and is sometimes known as dR (for 'differential-R') technique, since it is based on difference scores.

Self-assessment question 12.1

a. Why are P-, Chain-P and dR techniques used when constructing mood scales?

b. How might you discover the number and nature of the main dimensions of mood using P-technique?

Structure of mood

Reanalysis of the correlations between mood scales (Watson and Tellegen 1985) and hierarchical factor analyses of mood items drawn from the major mood scales (McConville and Cooper 1992b) reveals five primary mood factors: depression, hostility, fatigue, anxiety and energy/extraversion (also known as 'positive affect'). Since the first four of these are very substantially intercorrelated, it is possible to group these four scales together and call them 'negative affect'. Thus one can conclude that there are either five main dimensions (the five primary factors) or two main dimensions ('positive affect' and 'negative affect') of mood.

It is a great pity that the terms 'positive affect' and 'negative affect' were used to describe the two main dimensions of mood, since there is much confusion in the literature about what these scales mean. Positive and negative affect are *not* opposite ends of the same dimension of mood. Instead, they represent two completely different dimensions of mood. Negative affect is the proverbial 'bad mood' (feelings of depression, anxiety, anger, etc.). Positive affect refers to feelings of energy, enthusiasm and high activity level: in other words, arousal.

The approach to developing mood scales by using P-technique, Chain-P technique or dR technique has been advocated by Cattell and was used to develop the Eight State Questionnaire (Curran and Cattell 1976). Unfortunately, however, when the correlations between the items in the test are factor analysed, they simply fail to form the eight scales that Cattell predicted (Barton, Cattell and Connor 1972). There would seem to be plenty of scope for repeating this research, using P-technique, Chain-P technique or dR technique to discover the main mood factors that run through a carefully sampled set of items from which synonyms have been removed.

The experimental designs discussed already also have clear implications for determining the validity of mood scales. For example, in dR technique, ratings of behaviour (e.g. trembling, if we are interested in assessing anxiety) could be obtained at the same time that the questionnaires are completed – the difference between individuals' rated behaviour on the two occasions could be correlated with their responses to items or factors. In P-technique, the individual's score on each of the factors on each occasion can be correlated with their levels of behaviour.

Changes in mood

It is surprisingly easy to alter levels of mood experimentally, using the 'Velten technique' (Martin 1990; Velten 1968) and its derivatives. In the original version of this technique, subjects read a standard series of statements and were asked to try to experience the mood implied by them. The first statements are fairly innocuous (e.g. 'I'm feeling a little "down" today'), but they soon plumb the depths of despair (e.g. 'I feel so wretched that I just want to die') and after working their way through the series of cards, individuals really do seem to feel the depression. This is reflected in their scores on questionnaires and also in other 'objective tests' of depression (such as longer decision times). Thus this does seem to be a genuine effect, rather than some kind of demand characteristic (in which the participant sees the purpose of the experiment and resolves to give the experimenter the sort of results that they want). Other interventions (such as viewing videoclips and listening to extracts of music) have also been used.

Life events, both positive and negative, also affect mood, with minor hassles (such as rainy weather, missing a train or losing an umbrella) having a surprisingly strong influence on mood (e.g. Gruen, Folkman and Lazarus 1988). Likewise, apparently trivial positive events (such as finding some small change left in a public telephone) can induce pleasant moods (Isen and Levin 1972). **195**

Models of mood and mood change

Life soon becomes complicated when we turn to the physiological causes of mood, as a bewildering variety of chemicals can influence moods – yet it is not nearly so clear whether levels of mood are normally associated with elevated (or lowered) levels of certain neurotransmitters, such as the catecholamines. As Schnurr (1989) observes, the evidence now seems to suggest that moods such as depression are not simple functions of the levels of these chemicals and not all depressed individuals show similar (low) levels of these chemicals.

One state that has been well researched is anxiety, one of the primary mood factors mentioned at the start of this chapter. Several questionnaires have been designed to measure this state, most of them containing rather unsubtle items such as 'how anxious do you feel right now?'. Of these, Spielberger's State–Trait Anxiety Inventor' (STAI) (Spielberger, Gorsuch and Lushene 1970) is a well-known, reliable and valid measure of both the state of anxiety and its corresponding trait (habitual level of anxiety). Scores on the trait version of the STAI correlate substantially with scores on Eysenck's neuroticism scale, suggesting that anxiety is an important component of neuroticism (Eysenck 1992).

The cyclical nature of mood

The time course of moods has also been extensively studied, although one immediately encounters a formidable methodological problem. It is extremely difficult to separate the effects of time from the effects of life events. For example, suppose it was found that individuals showed a dip in certain moods each evening. Would this indicate that these moods were under the control of some 'biological clock' that causes the levels of mood to rise and fall with a particular frequency (e.g. every 24 hours)? The answer is, of course, that it would not. Moods may dip at a particular time of day because of fatigue, the physiological after-effects of eating dinner or a whole host of other factors that just happen to occur at the same time each day because we tend to live fairly regular lifestyles.

Some studies have circumvented this problem by monitoring the mood of individuals who are kept in a laboratory in which there are no windows and the length of the 'day' is artificially changed (generally increased) from its 24-hour norm. If the daily frequency of moods changes, this will indicate that the moods are a by-product of life events. If the moods remain locked to their 24-hour cycle, this would suggest that they are under the direct control of a biological clock, possibly mediated by chemicals such as cortisol. One such study found that individuals' levels of happiness were influenced both by their life events and by the 24-hour cycle (Boivin et al. 1997), suggesting that this mood is, to some extent, under physiological control.

Several studies also suggest that a 7-day cycle influences mood levels (e.g. Larsen and Kasimatis 1990). However, it is not altogether clear whether the 7-day cycle is biological in origin or whether it reflects social habits that happen to be tied to a 7-day week (perhaps socializing at weekends and feeling gloomy when returning to work on Monday).

Mood variability

Mood variability is a particularly interesting issue, since there are remarkably large individual differences in the extent to which people's moods change over time. Chris McConville (McConville and Cooper 1992a) asked people to complete a mood scale each day for about 30 days. Figure 12.2 shows the daily mood scores of two participants in this study. It can be seen that one participant shows considerable variability from day to day, while the other person's moods vary relatively little.

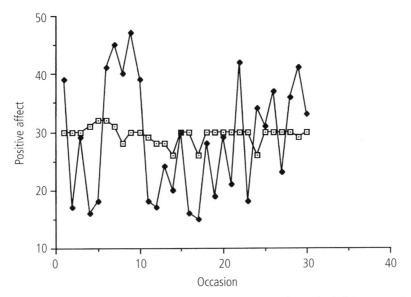

Figure 12.2 Mood levels of two volunteers on 30 days, showing individual differences in variability of mood. (From McConville and Cooper (1992a and 1992b).)

It is a well-established finding that *all* of a person's moods vary to a similar and characteristic extent (Wessman and Ricks 1966). This implies that we can regard mood variability as a kind of trait and postulate some type of 'regulating mechanism' that controls the extent to which individuals' moods swing either side of their habitual level. When mood variability is correlated with personality, however, there is an almost complete lack of agreement between studies. Some have found that extraversion affects mood variability, while others have not, and some have found that neuroticism has a powerful effect, while others have not. Moreover, some have found that psychoticism has an effect, while others have not (McConville and Cooper 1992a). We simply do not know why individual differences in mood variability are found or whether any underlying regulatory mechanism has a physiological basis.

However, mood variability does seem to show a very substantial correlation with levels of depressed mood among normal people (Larsen and Kasimatis 1990; McConville and Cooper 1996). Depressed individuals seem to have remarkably variable moods, in strange contrast to the *Diagnostic and Statistical Manual* (DSM) definitions, which would appear to suggest that flattening of affect (i.e. low variability) is associated with depression. Similar results have been reported for clinically depressed patients (Hall, Sing and Romanowski 1991).

Motivation

Measurement of motivation looks deceptively easy. It might appear that motivation is exactly the same as strength of interest or strength of attitudes and so to tap motivation all that is necessary is to put together a few well-chosen test items (e.g. 'on a scale of 1 to 5 how important are (a) sex, (b) food (c) security ...?'), push them through some item analyses and factor analyses and publish a motivation scale. This is, in fact, exactly what has been done. Several tests have been designed to measure specific aspects of motivation, e.g. 'achievement motivation' (McClelland 1961), which **197** supposedly measures why some individuals 'drive themselves hard' while others take a more relaxed approach to life. However, when this scale is factor analysed with personality scales, it is found that it is a measure of personality, rather than of motivation, which is, after all, fairly obvious from the nature of the concept – it is not obvious how achievement motivation will rise and fall over time (which, as we saw earlier, is the hallmark of a motivational state). Exactly the same has been found for tests that were designed to measure the 'drives' postulated by McDougall (1932) and Murray (1938). (See Kline 1999 for further details.)

The main criticisms levelled against mood questionnaires apply with equal force to questionnaires that claim to measure motivation. Many (perhaps all) questionnaires that supposedly assess motivation actually seem to show rather substantial correlations with the main personality factors – that is, they fail to measure mood states at all. Likewise, there is no guarantee either that the items in these scales are randomly sampled (e.g. from words in the dictionary that could possibly describe motivation) or that synonyms have been removed. The conditions under which the questionnaires are administered are as likely to influence motivation as they are to affect mood. Even if an individual entered the room with (for example) strong lustful feelings for the person sitting next to them (a high degree of sex drive), it seems likely that spending an hour answering a tedious motivation questionnaire would cause these feelings to decline.

Instinct theories were popular in the early part of the century. These suggested that people are aggressive because they have an 'instinct' for aggression. However, the theories are circular as the instinct 'aggression' is invoked to explain why people display aggressive behaviour, but the only evidence for this instinct of aggression is the aggressive behaviour itself. Moreover, there is potentially no limit to the number of instincts that can be identified. Thus a better way of assessing motivation is needed.

Cattell's theory of motivation

Once again, Cattell offers some sound theoretical direction (Cattell & Child 1975; Cattell, Horn and Sweney 1970; Cattell and Kline 1977) and argues that two basic issues need to be addressed:

- Our interests in objects or activities can shed light on what motivates us. It is possible that our degree of interest in an object or activity may manifest itself in many ways (e.g. by slips of the tongue, behaving irrationally, misperceptions such as misreading signs so as to 'see' the name of an object or person of interest or mistaking a stranger for someone who is known to us) and so questionnaires may not be able to tap all aspects of interest strength.

- Each of these areas of interest can fulfil several basic needs. For example, playing football might provide an individual with company, an opportunity to behave aggressively (pugnaciously), as well as the intrinsic (physiological) pleasure afforded by the exercise.

First, it is necessary to be able to identify (and measure) precisely what we mean by 'interest strength' and then to look at the specific goals that are achieved and emotions that are experienced, through following these interests. Cattell is particularly critical of the narrow view of attitudes taken by social psychologists – with good reason, in my view. First, there is empirical evidence (mentioned earlier) that suggests that most 'motivation' questionnaires actually tap stable personality traits and so tell us absolutely nothing about motivational states. Second, he argues that people may simply be unaware of their true feelings and behaviour, which will make self-reports of dubious value.

Cattell and Child (1975), reprinted in Cattell and Kline (1977) describe 68 'objective' ways of assessing strength of interest. These include preferences (e.g. expressed preference for praying over a number of other specified activities), reading preference (proportion of religious books), inability to see faults (e.g. being unable to list many disadvantages of the chosen form of religion), various physiological changes (e.g. increase in heart rate when shown a relevant religious symbol), proportion of time and money spent in religion-related activity, knowledge of religious facts (which is, of course, also likely to be influenced by intelligence), better memory for religion-related than for non-religious material in a laboratory-based test of memory, a belief that religion-related activities are in some way better than other activities (e.g. 'it is better to spend a spare 10 minutes praying rather than talking to one's partner') and so on.

Suppose that we ask a large group of individuals to identify some issues or activities in which people are likely to have varying degrees of interest (e.g. their job, football playing, their religion, abortion, socialism and gastronomy) and we assess the strength of interest in each of these using some or all of Cattell's 68 techniques – the *interest measures*. Do these all rise and fall together for each activity or are there several distinct ways in which 'interest' can manifest itself? Cattell (1957) reported just such a study. He found that, when the correlations between these various interest measures were factor analysed, not one but seven factors emerged. This is important, for it suggests that measuring strength of interest by one method alone (e.g. by questionnaire) is likely to be inadequate, since strength of interest itself has several quite distinct aspects.

Alpha is the term Cattell gave to the component that reflects conscious wishes, including those that are illogical. Buying a dress despite the fact that you know that you cannot afford it is a good example of the alpha component of your interest in clothes. *Beta* reflects conscious, rational preferences, of the type that will be expressed when responding to questionnaires that ask how much one likes or dislikes certain objects or activities. Buying a computer because you know that it is useful for your studies is an example of beta-type motivation. The third factor, *gamma*, is a form of motivation that arises because the individual feels that he or she *ought* to take an interest in something. Someone might feel pressured into listening to a particular piece of music or experimenting with drugs because they feel that this is the kind of behaviour that is expected of their peer group. *Delta* is a purely physiological response to certain stimuli that (interestingly) appears to be quite distinct from the other aspects of interest – it seems that certain sights and sounds can lead directly to changes in activity of the autonomic nervous system. The nature of the remaining three factors is not well understood.

Self-assessment question 12.2

a. (i) A man's pulse races when he sees his next door neighbour. (ii) When walking down the street he misreads a shop sign, thinking it shows the neighbour's name. When asked about the neighbour, he (iii) describes them as 'just a neighbour' and (iv) says that he feels that it would be wrong to feel any emotional attraction. Try to categorize this man as having low or high scores on components alpha to delta.

b. Cattell claims that there is more than one factor of attitude strength, although this finding needs to be replicated. If it were to be replicated successfully, what would its implications be for social psychology?

The second part of Cattell's theory tries to discover where these interests lead – that is, what the 'payoffs' of these interests actually are. For example, if a person is found to have a strong alpha, beta, gamma and delta interest in vintage cars (thus indicating that cars are probably really rather important to them at a number of levels) it seems reasonable to ask what needs are met by this interest. Perhaps the local vintage car club provides company. The person may possibly like to bask in the interest awakened in onlookers when he or she drives around in it. The car may be seen as a financial investment, or perhaps the *real* reason is the pleasure inherent in fixing it when it breaks down – having to manufacture parts from scratch. If psychologists can discover the ultimate reasons underlying such interests, they may claim to have understood motivation.

If someone is asked to give as many answers as possible to describe why they are performing a particular activity (e.g. 'why are you reading this book?') they will presumably answer 'to pass my exams', 'so that I don't look a fool in next week's tutorial', 'because it interests me' or something similar. The process can then be repeated (*why* is it important to pass one's examinations or not to appear stupid in class?) time and time again until, eventually, the explanation cannot be taken any further. Eventually, something just *is* rewarding.

These ultimate goals are known as *ergs* and *sentiments* in Cattell's model and some of them are shown in Table 12.3. Ergs are thought to be direct biological drives whose fulfilment is intrinsically pleasurable (e.g. having sex, eating when hungry, protecting one's life, socializing, exploring, etc.). Sentiments are socially determined and are likely to vary in strength from person to person and from culture to culture. If a person does not have parents/an interest in sport/a partner/a religious interest, then these clearly will not motivate that individual, and acquiring money *for its own sake* (rather than for what it can buy or do) may not be an important goal in some societies.

Cattell has developed adult and children's versions of a test, known as the Motivation Analysis Test, which claims to measure the strength of the main ergs and sentiments (Cattell et al. 1970). Unfortunately, however, the adult version simply does not seem to form the factors that Cattell

Ergs	Sentiments
Hunger	Profession
Sex	Parents
Fear	Husband/wife/partner
Gregariousness	Superego (conscience)
Exploration	Religion
Self-assertion	Sport and fitness
Narcissism	Scientific interests
Pugnacity	Money
Acquisitiveness	Aesthetic interests

Table 12.3 Some ergs and sentiments from Cattell's theory of motivation (from Cattell and Child (1975)

claims (Cooper and Kline 1982), although Cattell disagrees with this view (1982). Nevertheless, I have discussed Cattell's theory in some depth because it does seem to be by far the most technically sophisticated approach to the measurement of motivation and it raises several important issues (such as the inadequacy of assessing interest strength by means of self-report measures alone) that clearly deserve to be explored more thoroughly.

Apter's theory of motivation

Michael Apter (e.g. 1982) set out a novel theory of human functioning some of which is relevant to the psychology of motivation. He took issue with the assumption of trait theories that people experience life consistently over time (in line with their personality traits) and argued instead that our subjective experience of a single activity can change both dramatically and quickly. For example, the act of cooking dinner can begin as a mundane chore but turn onto something much more exciting as one struggles to produce something creative from the contents of the larder: the task may be objectively the same (an observer would just notice us preparing dinner) but our experience of it may alter radically. Some activities are intrinsically satisfying (and so may perhaps be regarded as basic drives) and are performed for this reason. Listening to music is one obvious example. Other activities are performed as a means to some other end (e.g. someone enduring an awful job because the pay allows them to indulge their hobbies). Apter, Mallows and Williams (1998) suggest that we tend to approach tasks in five ways, as shown in Table 12.4.

The five 'metamotivational states' shown in Table 12.4 are not dimensions like traits. Instead, Apter suggests that we flip from one extreme to the other: our experience of a task is either that it

	Pole 1		Pole 2	
	Name	**Description**	**Name**	**Description**
1	Telic	Serious Goal directed	Paratelic	Fun Spontaneous Intrinsically rewarding
2	Conformist	Rule based Focuses on obligations	Challenging	Exploratory Free Non-conforming
3	Autic mastery	Control of people or events Dominance	Autic sympathy	Need to be attractive, sympathized with and popular
4	Alloic mastery	Need to identify/join powerful teems or organizations	Alloic sympathy	Need to nurture and support others
5	Tranquil	Need for peace and removal of problems	Arousal seeking	Need to experience excitement

Table 12.4 Ways in which we approach tasks

is intrinsically rewarding and fun (*paratelic*) or that it is something that has to be done to satisfy some long-term objective (*telic*), that it is either to be performed according to certain rules or with creativity, that we are dominant or supportive when performing it and we focus on our own or others' needs. There are no half-measures.

Telic behaviour is associated with trying to achieve some long-term goal or fulfilling a biological need (for example, studying to pass an exam, earning money to buy food or pay one's credit card bill): if this telic behaviour were not performed it is likely to make us feel anxious or over-aroused, so when in telic mode we try to reduce our level of arousal. Paratelic behaviour is something that is performed because it is intrinsically enjoyable. In paratelic mode, we may seek out stimulation (excitement: e.g. risky sports, stimulating conversation) in an attempt to increase our levels of arousal. So, according to this theory, whether we try to increase or reduce our level of arousal depends crucially on whether we are currently operating in the telic or paratelic mode.

Questionnaires such as the Motivational Style Profile (Apter et al. 1998) and the Telic/Paratelic State Instrument (O'Connell and Calhoun 2001) have been devised to assess the proportion of time an individual spends in each of the five modes (e.g. telic vs. paratelic) and to measure whether an individual is currently in a telic or paratelic state. The latter 12-item questionnaire is probably just a bloated specific, with items such as 'feeling playful/feeling serious minded', 'feeling playful/feeling serious', 'just having fun/trying to accomplish something'. Sports psychologists have adopted this theory with enthusiasm, for example, determining whether participants in risky sports differ in their telic dominance from participants in safe sports. They do (Cogan and Brown 1999). The technique is also used to try to understand the psychology of humour, crime, sexual dysfunction and another of other important phenomena.

But is the theory correct? More fundamentally, is it possible to show that it is incorrect? Finding that bungee jumpers function in paratelic mode while people completing their tax returns operate in telic mode would probably be regarded as evidence for the theory by most researchers. But how could it be otherwise? If someone chooses to take part in an activity for no reason other than its pleasurable sensation, then how can they possibly be in telic mode? Who could possibly go through the nausea of balancing their books in paratelic mode, given that they are forced to do so on penalty of paying a fine? So I am not at all sure whether this sort of evidence tells us anything useful. Neither does the study of physiological correlates. Svebak and Murgatroyd (1985) and others have shown telic dominance to be reflected in physiological indices (muscle tension, skin conductance, depth of breathing) when people play a racing-car simulation game. However as telic dominance correlates -0.55 with extraversion (and -0.41 with neuroticism) according to Apter et al. (1998) it is not entirely clear whether the best researched aspect of Apter's theory is any more than a mixture of these two personality traits. Also, as the theory is not explicitly tied to a physiological model, this finding is just an interesting correlate – not support for any causal model leading from physiology to behaviour.

Second, the theory talks about broad classes of motivation (hence 'metamotivational states') rather than anything as specific as ergs or sentiments. For example, it argues that focusing on obligations/rules is one kind of motivational state while thinking creatively is another. But how does this translate into behaviour? What kinds of rule do people typically focus on? What kinds of creative activity do they follow? It seems to me that the theory is more a way of rationalizing what people do into some theoretical framework rather than a technique for the prediction of behaviour.

Third, are the five metamotivational states genuinely types rather than traits? Is a person either totally controlling or totally needing sympathy? There are sophisticated statistical techniques that can be used to test hypotheses such as these, but they appear not to have been applied to reversal theory.

Fourth, it is surely necessary to understand not just the average amount of time that a person spends in which state of each of the five metamotivational components, but what causes them to flip. Otherwise, the danger is that the theory can 'explain' any behaviour performed by anyone at any time. I certainly have reservations about the theory.

Summary

This chapter has explored the nature and assessment of the major 'states' – moods and motives. I have suggested that there are four major flaws in the common practice of constructing mood scales in much the same way as personality scales are developed and that Cattell's alternative methodologies are much to be preferred – even though the mood scale created by this technique does not appear to work. Finally, we have considered the topic of motivation, about which relatively little is known. I have suggested that motivation strength can be inferred by examining the benefits to the individual of performing various activities that interest them strongly, but I have pointed out that the assessment of strength of interest may require much more than the conventional attitude scales. Cattell's and Apter's theories have been described, but both are found wanting.

Suggested additional reading

Apart from Apter's work, it is difficult to recommend any texts on the psychology of motivation, as Cattell's book (Cattell and Child 1975) is both ancient and difficult to read and the measurement issues (discussed in Chapter 19) need to be firmly grasped. Paul Barrett (1997) argues that 'somewhere along the line psychometricians seem to have forgotten about motivation', a point with which I wholeheartedly agree.

However, mood is a great deal easier. Eysenck (1997) provides a lucid description of his theory about the cognitive correlates of anxiety (plus a review of several other relevant theories), Zajonc's (1980, 1984) old papers speculate about some links between mood and cognition, which will be of interest to the cognitively inclined, while Leander et al. (2009) similarly examine some of the origins of mood.

Answers to self-assessment questions
SAQ 12.1

Most of these scales were constructed in the same way as scales measuring traits, so there is no guarantee that they assess mood at all. Most of them have no clear rationale for deciding whether items should be included in the analysis. Several items that mean the same thing may be included (synonyms) and any such items are bound to form a factor, but this factor is not necessarily of any psychological interest. Administering mood questionnaires under standard conditions is likely to make all participants feel bored and listless and so prevent the research from detecting more 'positive' moods.

SAQ 12.2

a. To ensure that a scale measures a state rather than a trait.

b. Compile a questionnaire consisting of a broad range of mood items (but without synonyms). Ask a single person to complete this questionnaire on a very large number of occasions (ideally more than 100) while performing a number of different activities. Correlate the responses to the individual items and factor analyse them in order to determine whether any particular groups of items tend to rise and fall together.

SAQ 12.3

a. High delta, high alpha, low beta, low gamma.

b. It means that simply asking people about their attitudes is not sufficient, as individuals may not even be *aware* of all of their attitudes. Thus, theories (e.g. attribution theory) that are based on simple self-report measures of attitudes may have severe limitations.

References

Apter, M. J., Mallows, R. and Williams, S. (1998). The development of the motivational style profile. *Personality and Individual Differences 24*(1), 7–18.

Barrett, P. T. (1997). Process models in individual differences research. In C. Cooper and V. Varma (eds), *Processes in Individual Differences*. London: Routledge.

Barton, K., Cattell, R. B. and Connor, D. V. (1972). The identification of state factors through P-technique factor analysis. *Journal of Clinical Psychology 28*, 459–63.

Boivin, D. B., Czeisler, C. A., Dijk, D. J., Duffy, J. F., Folkard, S., Minors, D. S. et al. (1997). Complex interaction of the sleep-wake cycle and circadian phase modulates mood in healthy subjects. *Archives of General Psychiatry 54*(2), 145–52.

Cattell, R. B. (1957). *Personality and Motivation Structure and Measurement*. Yonkers, NY: New World.

Cattell, R. B. (1973). *Personality and Mood by Questionnaire*. San Francisco: Jossey-Bass.

Cattell, R. B. (1982). The psychometry of objective motivation measurement. *British Journal of Educational Psychology 52*, 234–41.

Cattell, R. B. and Child, D. (1975). *Motivation and Dynamic Structure*. London: Holt, Rinehart & Winston.

Cattell, R. B., Horn, J. L. and Sweney, A. B. (1970). *Manual for the Motivation Analysis Test*. Champaign, IL: Institute for Personality and Ability Testing.

Cattell, R. B. and Kline, P. (1977). *The Scientific Analysis of Personality and Motivation*. London: Academic Press.

Clyde, D. J. (1963). *The Clyde Mood Scale*. Coral Gables, FL: University of Miami, Biometrics Lab.

Cogan, N. and Brown, R. I. F. (1999). Metamotivational dominance, states and injuries in risk and safe sports. *Personality and Individual Differences 27*(3), 503–18.

Cooper, C. (1997). Mood processes. In C. Cooper and V. Varma (eds), *Processes in Individual Differences*. London: Routledge.

Cooper, C. and Kline, P. (1982). The internal structure of the motivation analysis test. *British Journal of Educational Psychology 52*, 228–33.

Curran, J. P. and Cattell, R. B. (1976). *Manual of the Eight State Questionnaire*. Champaign, IL: IPAT.

Eysenck, M. W. (1992). *Anxiety: The Cognitive Perspective*. Hove: Erlbaum.

Eysenck, M. W. (1997). *Anxiety and Cognition: A Unified Theory*. Hove: Psychology Press/ Erlbaum/Taylor & Francis.

Gruen, R. J., Folkman, S. and Lazarus, R. S. (1988). Centrality and individual differences in the meaning of daily hassles. *Journal of Personality* 56(4), 743–62.

Hall, D. P., Sing, H. C. and Romanowski, A. J. (1991). Identification and characterisation of greater mood variance in depression. *American Journal of Psychiatry* 148(10), 1341–5.

Howarth, E. (1988). Mood differences between the 4 Galen types. *Personality and Individual Differences* 9, 173–5.

Isen, A. M. and Levin, P. F. (1972). The effect of feeling good on helping: cookies and kindness. *Journal of Personality and Social Psychology* 34, 384–8.

Izard, C. E., Dougherty, F. E., Bloxom, B. M. and Kotsch, N. E. (1982). *The Differential Emotions Scale: A Method of Measuring the Subjective Experience of Discrete Emotions*. Nashville, TE: Vanderbilt University Department of Psychology.

Kline, P. (1999). *The Handbook of Psychological Testing* (2nd edn). London and New York: Routledge.

Larsen, R. J. and Kasimatis, M. (1990). Individual differences in entrainment of mood to the weekly calendar. *Personality and Individual Differences* 58, 164–71.

Leander, N. P., Moore, S. G., Chartrand, T. L., Moskowitz, G. B. and Grant, H. (2009). Mystery moods: their origins and consequences. In *The Psychology of Goals*. New York: Guilford Press.

Lorr, M. and McNair, D. M. (1988). *Manual, Profile of Mood States, Bipolar Form*. San Diego, CA: Educational and Industrial Testing Service.

Lorr, M. and Wunderlich, R. A. (1988). Self-esteem and negative affect. *Journal of Clinical Psychology* 44, 36–9.

Martin, M. (1990). On the induction of moods. *Clinical Psychology Review 10*, 669–97.

Matthews, G. (1983). *Personality, Arousal States and Intellectual Performance*. Cambridge: Cambridge University Press.

Matthews, G., Jones, G. and Chamberlain, A. G. (1990). Refining the measurement of mood: the UWIST mood adjective checklist. *British Journal of Psychology 81*, 17–42.

McClelland, D. C. (1961). *Achieving Society*. New York: van Nostrand.

McConville, C. and Cooper, C. (1992a). Mood variability and personality. *Personality and Individual Differences 13*(11), 1213–21.

McConville, C. and Cooper, C. (1992b). The structure of moods. *Personality and Individual Differences 13*(8), 909–19.

McConville, C. and Cooper, C. (1996). Mood variability and the intensity of depressive states. *Current Psychology 14*(4), 329–38.

McDougall, W. (1932). *The Energies of Men*. London: Methuen.

Murray, H. A. (1938). *Explorations in Personality*. New York: Oxford University Press.

Nowlis, J. and Nowlis, H. (1956). The description and analysis of mood. *Annals of the New York Academy of Science 55*, 345–55.

O'Connell, K. A. and Calhoun, J. E. (2001). The telic/paratelic state instrument (T/PSI): validating a reversal theory measure. *Personality and Individual Differences 30*(2), 193–204.

Schnurr, P. P. (1989). Endogenous factors assiciated with mood. In W. N. Morris (ed.), *Mood: The Frame of Mind*. Berlin: Springer-Verlag.

Spielberger, C. D., Gorsuch, R. L. and Lushene, R. E. (1970). *STAI Manual for the State Trait Inventory*. Palo Alto, CA: Consulting Psychologists Press.

Storm, C. and Storm, T. (1987). A taxonomic study of the vocabulary of emotions. *Journal of Personality and Social Psychology 53*, 805–16.

Svebak, S. and Murgatroyd, S. (1985). Metamotivational dominance – a multimethod validation of reversal theory constructs. *Journal of Personality and Social Psychology 48*(1), 107–16.

Velten, E. J. (1968). A laboratory task for the induction of mood states. *Behavior Research and Therapy 6*, 473–82.

Watson, D., Clark, L. A. and Tellegen, A. (1988). Development and validation of a brief measure of positive and negative affect: the PANAS scales. *Journal of Personality and Social Psychology 54*(6), 1063–70.

Watson, D. and Tellegen, A. (1985). Towards a consensual structure of mood. *Psychological Bulletin 98*, 219–35.

Wessman, A. E. and Ricks, D. F. (1966). *Mood and Personality*. New York: Holt, Rinehart & Winston.

Zajonc, R. B. (1980). Feeling and thinking: preferences need no inferences. *American Psychologist 35*, 151–75.

Zajonc, R. B. (1984). On the primacy of affect. *American Psychologist 39*, 117–23.

Zevon, M. A. and Tellegen, A. (1982). The structure of mood change: an idiographic/nomothetic analysis. *Journal of Personality and Social Psychology 43*, 111–22.

Applications of individual differences

Background

Psychological tests are of great practical use and this chapter examines just some of the practical applications of individual differences. These can be considerable. For example, the finding that g appears to be more important even than job experience when selecting applicants for a huge variety of jobs comes as a surprise to most people. However, discovering an empirical link between scores on some test and performance is generally the easy part: interpreting what the correlation means is usually much harder. For example, the discovery that there is a link between childhood intelligence and academic performance could be explained by suggesting that high g is needed to grasp the more abstract concepts or it could perhaps be due to social deprivation in childhood affecting both scores on ability tests and academic performance. Thus applied research often helps to develop important theories.

Recommended prior reading

Chapters 4, 5, 6, 8, 14 and 15.

Introduction

One of the delights of working with individual differences is its applicability. Most if not all branches of applied psychology seem to need to measure individual differences for one reason or another and so this overview is necessarily selective: covering the whole of each area in depth would require another book. The tests that are used should have been constructed as described in Chapter 18, although occasionally applied psychologists have been known to cut corners and use tests without strong evidence that they are valid for the purpose which is intended or where the reliability within the particular population is either unknown or lower than one would hope. This list is by no means comprehensive. For example, sports psychologists use mood scales extensively, particularly the Profile of Mood States (Lorr and McNair 1988), but the use of such techniques is fairly obvious and the results are pretty much as one would expect. I have instead mentioned a few areas in some depth because of their theoretical or practical importance.

Practical problems using tests

Before moving on to consider applications of individual differences in occupational psychology, health psychology etc., it will be useful to raise a few issues about the problems of using tests for real-life purposes.

Impression management

There is good evidence that people will try to give a good impression of themselves when answering the items in a personality questionnaire: more specifically, we know that if they are trying to give a good impression of themselves, people will typically try to make themselves appear more extraverted, agreeable, conscientious and open and less neurotic than they really are. (How do we know this? By asking people to fill in questionnaires under two conditions – e.g. honestly and as if they want to portray themselves in a good light – and note the difference in means.) Worryingly, it seems that such effects may be prevalent even when a test is administered for research purposes. This is particularly problematic, as one would rather hope that respondents would be honest in these circumstances, given that the questionnaire scores do not have any real-life consequences for them. Bäckström (2007) gave a Swedish translation of an IPIP (International Personality Item Pool) big five personality questionnaire to a large sample of people and used confirmatory factor analysis (see Appendix A) to determine whether there was a sixth, social desirability, factor with a negative loading on neuroticism and positive loadings on the other big five factors. There was, and scores on this factor correlated strongly with a test measuring impression management, suggesting that this sixth general factor was, indeed, measuring an aspect of impression management.

You do not have to be an expert psychometrician to appreciate that this causes problems for the practical use of tests. For example, if a personality questionnaire is used as part of the selection process for a job, it is highly likely that an applicant would realize that saying that they often felt depressed, did not take much care over their work or often argued with other people would do little for their chances of being selected.

Self-deception

It is also possible that people give inaccurate answers on questionnaires because they are genuinely misguided about how they behave and how others see them. For example, you may genuinely believe that you are open to new ideas and experiences, yet everyone else regards you as closed-minded and conventional. It is obviously harder to detect this form of bias: it can perhaps be inferred if two raters who know a participant well agree closely with each other about the participant's personality, but the participant herself produces a very different profile. Or it could just be that the participant is good at 'putting on a front' and fooling the people they know. Paulhus, Robinson, Shaver and Wrightsman (1991) discuss this, and related issues, in some depth.

Bias

As we discuss in Chapter 19, a test if biased if it systematically over- or underestimates the scores of group members. For example, if a teacher were to tell their class the correct answers to the first four questions in a nationwide test of mathematics, the pupils in their class would have higher scores than they should do, given their true levels of ability. The test would overestimate their ability. If another teacher gave their children less time to complete the test than the instructions stated, the scores of the children in their class will also show bias. In this case, the test scores would underestimate the ability of members of that class.

The problem is that there might also be genuine differences between the scores of various groups: for example, it might be the case that some classes of children perform much better than others (without being told any of the answers) – perhaps as a result of good teaching, close adherence to the syllabus or extensive use of practice test papers. Determining whether differences between groups are real or whether they are caused by biased tests is a major problem for psychologists. For example, take general intelligence. There is a massive literature showing that there a difference in scores on ability tests between black Americans and white Americans, although evidence suggest that this difference in scores is decreasing from generation to generation (e.g. Dickens and Flynn 2006) perhaps as a result of the improvement of living standards for black Americans. You can see why this is an issue. Is the difference real? Is it the case that black Americans genuinely are less intelligent (as some have controversially claimed) or because the tests that are used to assess intelligence are unfair to members of the black community? There are many possible reasons why the tests could produce biased scores (i.e. underestimate the intelligence of this minority group):

- As there is evidence that black Americans are more socially disadvantaged than whites, it could be the case that poor schooling (particularly language skills) may affect test performance.

- Tests developed in a white, middle-class culture may contain items that mean little to someone in a socially deprived inner city area and are therefore harder for them to solve. (For example, items involving currency conversion may be easier for people who have been on foreign holidays.)

- There may be attitudinal or motivational differences: for example, members of the minority group may have come to believe that they are less intelligent, perhaps because their teachers tell them so, and may therefore not value the tests or take them so seriously.

There are plenty of other possible reasons, too, and a good deal of research has been carried out to explore the reasons for these differences. However, the important issue for now is to consider the consequences of possible test bias when tests are used in real life.

The problem is that if a test does underestimate scores on some trait, then any decisions made using that test will be discriminatory. For example, if a biased IQ test were used for personnel selection purposes, too few members of the black minority group would be accepted for employment. The issue of test bias is quite a technical subject and there are many approaches for detecting it. However, one of the most straightforward involves examining the test scores of majority and minority groups and comparing these with measures of performance (e.g. educational performance, job performance). If a test is biased against members of a minority group (i.e. the test scores underestimate their true potential), these individuals should perform better than expected on the measure of performance, assuming that this is not biased. For example, it might be found that children from the majority group who score 30 on a test of general ability usually achieve a mark of 120 on a national test of mathematics. If minority group children with a score of 30 on the ability test usually score 130, this suggests that the ability test underestimated their true level of ability.

By the same token, if their score on the mathematics test is similar to the majority group, this may suggest that the groups show a real difference in ability is real, rather than an apparent difference caused by a biased test. Of course, all of this assumes that the performance measure is not itself biased in any way.

Traits as a proxy for other variables

As we shall see later, it is easy to find substantial relationships between scores on ability tests (and, on occasions, personality tests) and real-life behaviour – for example, correlations between tests **209** of general ability and performance at school or at work. Deciding whether the trait is the *cause* of the real-world behaviour is much more difficult. This is because traits are often correlated with other variables. For example, there is a substantial literature showing that general ability correlates with one's parents' social class. So, if general ability is found to be correlated with educational performance (as discussed later), it could be argued that this correlation only really comes about because socially disadvantaged children are less well nourished (or less well taught, less encouraged at home, less well motivated at school, less likely to have suitable role models, more likely to be under peer pressure to give up at school ...) and this leads to poorer educational performance. It could also be argued that performance on ability tests is determined by educational performance rather than vice versa: Ceci and Williams (1997) give examples of such suggestions. So although we simple-minded individual difference psychologists may imagine that children differ in their levels of intelligence, and having high levels of intelligence makes learning easy, this could be quite wrong. It could be that social factors bring down some children's educational attainment and their level of intelligence.

Self-assessment question 13.1

This is more of a creative exercise than SAQs usually are, but think how you might check whether schooling influences intelligence or whether intelligence influences academic performance.

If you have read Chapter 11 already, you may now start to appreciate its relevance to this debate. Social class will be a major influence on the common family environment (as it will affect all children in the family in the same way) and we saw that there is compelling evidence that this has zero effect on adult intelligence. It is also possible to gather data about both parents and their (grown up, earning) children – e.g. parental income, parental educational qualifications, child intelligence, child income, child education – and perform some analyses known as structural equation modelling (SEM) to determine which variables influence which others.

Figure 13.1 shows a number of boxes representing things that were measured from fathers (shaded boxes) and one of their children (unshaded boxes). The curves with two arrows on them

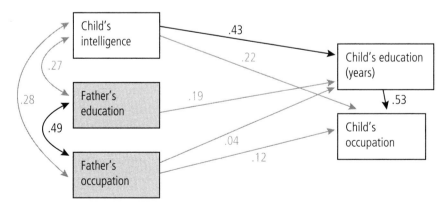

Figure 13.1 Variables affecting occupational status. (Adapted from Duncan, Featherman and Duncan (1972).)

show the size of the correlation between two variables (e.g. father's education and father's occupation). An arrow with a number of it suggests that one variable causes the other: the number on the line shows how large the relationship is. If you are familiar with regression analysis, you will recognize the numbers on these lines as being regression coefficients. For convenience the small relationships (less than 0.3) have been shown in light print. This sort of analysis is incredibly important. It can show (for example) whether there is a substantial direct link between the father's occupation (a measure of social class) and the child's occupation – as one would expect if the sociologists are correct and social background is the key determinant of occupational status. You can see that this relationship is tiny (a coefficient of 0.12). Likewise the amount of education received by the children is hardly influenced at all by the parents' occupation (0.04) or education (0.19). Neither does the children's intelligence directly predict their occupational status. But what the analysis does show is that the child's intelligence influences level of education (0.43) and this, in turn, influences future occupation (0.53).

Only by performing these kinds of analysis can we tease out whether intelligence has a direct influence on performance or whether other variables (such as the socioeconomic status of the family in which the child was brought up) are the 'real' cause of the relationship.

Occupational psychology

Psychological tests are widely used in personnel selection. Although the use of personality tests is still controversial, because of the problems caused by faking: job applicants may well be able to identify undesirable characteristics and play these down when filling in personality questionnaires. Care must be taken to ensure that the tests are not biased against members of minority groups. Furthermore, in the UK at least, equality laws require that selection tests must not show any differences between the genders or racial groups, even if these are genuine and not due to bias. So even if there *are* real differences in the test scores of males and females (as is found with Eysenck's psychoticism scale from the EPQ, where males typically score at least a third of a standard deviation higher than females; Eysenck, Eysenck and Barrett 1985) a test such as this, which shows appreciable gender differences, could not be legally used for selection purposes, even if the reason for sex differences is reasonably well understood and the problems with faking could be resolved. According to this approach, one could presumably not use a rule to measure height, as it would be discriminatory.

Tests are used in several ways within occupational psychology; for example, by knowing her own strengths and weaknesses, a senior employee may better decide what her role in the organization should be – for example, which types of activity should sensibly be delegated. However, one of the major applications of individual differences is in the area of personnel selection and so we will focus mainly on this.

Abilities and intelligence

One of the big success stories of psychology concerns the use of psychological tests for personnel selection. The basic premise is simple. One administers a set of tests, the scores on which have previously been shown to predict some aspect of job performance, the idea being that if one only selects the applicants with the higher scores on the tests, the quality of job performance should rise. There have been two main types of study used to determine the link between abilities and job performance. One can either measure the test scores of people in various occupations, to establish **211** if there is a link between intelligence (or any other ability) and the type of employment towards which people gravitate. Or one can correlate scores on tests with performance *within* a particular type of job. For example, one could determine whether level of spatial ability (as measured by a psychometric test) is higher in military pilots who perform well than in pilots who struggle to complete their flying training.

Intelligence levels of various occupational groups

The literature on the first type of study goes back a long way and some interesting information came from the assessment of recruits in the Second World War. Soldiers who were recruited into the United States' Army had their general intelligence assessed and this was related to their prior occupation as shown in the left-hand section of Table 13.1. Another way of establishing the relationship between occupation and intelligence is simply to test a sample of the population. This happens each time an IQ test is standardized and the data in the right-hand section of Table 13.1 are from Reynolds, Chastain, Kaufman and McLean (1987).

The differences between these groups are statistically highly significant: it seems that general intelligence is related to the status of one's occupation. It is, however, important to also look at the standard deviations. These tend to be lower for the 'high status' occupations (particularly in the 1945 data), suggesting that there is quite a narrow range of scores on either side of the mean, whereas the standard deviations are larger for low status jobs. Why? The answer is probably that in order to succeed as a lawyer, teacher etc., everyone has a similar degree of intelligence, whereas it is possible that some intelligent individuals did not have the opportunity to study in order to become professionals and so may have ended up in manual jobs such as mining or driving trucks, perhaps because they needed to leave school as early as possible in order to help to sup-

Occupation	Mean IQ	Standard deviation	Occupation	Mean IQ	Standard deviation
Lawyer	128	11	Professional and technical	111	13
Teacher	123	13			
Clerk	117	13	Manager, clerical, sales	104	13
Electrician	109	15	Skilled workers	99	13
Plumber	102	16			
Tractor driver	99	19	Semi-skilled workers	93	14
Cook	97	21			
Truck driver	96	20			
Farmhand	91	21	Unskilled workers	89	15
Miner	91	20			

Table 13.1 General intelligence for various occupational groups (from Harrell and Harrell (1945) as cited by Schmidt and Hunter (2004) and Reynolds, Chastain, Kaufman and McLean (1987)

port their family financially. Another meta-analysis, which produces similar conclusions about the substantial correlation between childhood intelligence and career status, may be found in Strenze (2007).

It is tempting to look at Table 13.1 and infer that in order to become a lawyer, one needs a high level of intelligence. However, this is incorrect. As we saw in Figure 13.1 (Duncan, Featherman and Duncan 1972), I demonstrated that there is a substantial link between general intelligence and educational attainment (parental occupational status did not influence this at all) and so the children who obtain the highest educational qualifications will tend to be the most intelligent, not the most affluent. And, of course, to enter training as a lawyer, teacher etc., one needs to have good academic record. So the model shown in Figure 13.1 makes good sense: although there is a substantial correlation between intelligence and the status of one's job, this only occurs because intelligence is one of the factors that affect the number of academic qualifications obtained and academic qualifications are the passport to training courses for the professions.

It is important to appreciate that just because certain professional training courses require high educational qualifications to enter them and high levels of intelligence are required to obtain these qualifications, it does not follow that high levels of intelligence are necessary to function well within the profession. For example, suppose that medical schools only selected individuals with large feet (analogous to high academic achievements). After a few years, the average foot size of doctors would be well above that of the general population (cf. Table 13.1). But it does not follow that it is necessary to have large feet to function effectively as a doctor.

Intelligence and performance with each occupational group

Given that colleges and universities tend to select individuals on the basis of their educational qualifications, we need another way of testing the relationship between intelligence and occupational performance. The obvious thing is to look at correlations *within* each job. For example, is there a correlation between general ability and effectiveness of managers? Are the most effective delivery drivers, salespersons etc. the most intelligent? Schmidt and Hunter (2004) famously performed a meta-analysis showing the correlations between general intelligence and job performance based on many thousands of studies. Meta-analyses basically summarize the results from many studies; think of them as averaging the correlations between intelligence and job performance from many studies (although these correlations are also corrected for unreliability and measurement error, effectively giving more weight to studies that used large samples of people, and correcting them for measurement error if the correlations were based on unreliable measures of job performance or *g*).

One obvious problem is knowing which studies to combine. For example, is it reasonable to bundle all types of job together? It could be that *g* matters for jobs that require intellectual effort (such as computer programming) but not for managing people or manual work. Hunter and Hunter categorized jobs as shown in Table 13.2 and found that, in all cases, a simple test of general intelligence predicted job performance rather well. They also analysed the effectiveness of other measures, such as interviews, references and academic qualifications. These were considerably less useful than ability tests and these authors demonstrate that using ability tests (rather than random selection of job applicants) saved the US government alone over $15 billion a year in improved productivity. The humble ability tests even worked better than letting someone try out the job and then deciding whether to hire them based on their performance and were more useful predictors than previous experience on the job.

213

Job	Correlation between job performance and g
Manager	0.53
Clerk	0.54
Salesperson	0.61
Protective professions worker	0.42
Service worker	0.48
Trades and crafts worker	0.46
Elementary industrial worker	0.37
Vehicle operator	0.28
Sales clerk	0.27

Table 13.2 Correlations between general ability (g) and job performance for nine classes of occupation (adapted from Table 1 of Hunter and Hunter (1984))

Schmidt and Hunter (2004) have extended this work and the correlations between g and job performance from 12 meta-analyses are shown in Table 13.3. (Several military meta-analyses are included because they used different criteria: e.g. technical proficiency or general soldiering performance.) The two columns show the correlations between g and performance on the job itself and the correlation between g and performance in training.

	In job	In training
Medium complexity	0.51	0.57
Clerical	0.52	0.71
Law enforcement	0.38	0.76
Military – enlisted	0.63	
Military – enlisted	0.65	
Military – enlisted		0.63
Military – enlisted	0.45	
Military – enlisted		0.60
First-line supervisors	0.64	
Administrative clerks	0.67	
Computer programmers	0.73	
Refinery workers	0.31	0.50

Table 13.3 Correlations between g and performance within various jobs (from Schmidt and Hunter (2004))

Self-assessment question 13.2

Why do you think the correlations between g and the various occupations shown in Table 13.1 vary?

Why do ability tests prove so successful? There is actually quite a degree of misunderstanding about this. Following my 'Test the Nation' television shows, comments on the BBC website showed clearly that the public at large believed quite firmly (and without any evidence) that because the sorts of problem that feature in tests of intelligence or other cognitive abilities do not resemble the sorts of problem that people solve in everyday life, intelligence tests can be of no use in predicting job performance. The assumption that they make is that ability tests can only work because the items in these tests form a sample of the sorts of problem that people encounter at work.

Some occupational psychologists ('organizational psychologists' in the USA and Canada) do indeed put together samples of work like this and assess how well applicants cope with it. For example, applicants for a customer services management position might be asked to deal with a (simulated) angry customer on the telephone, work out how to resolve a dispute about holiday dates and prepare a summary of sales figures and calculate bonuses. This approach, sometimes called the 'work sample' or 'work basket' approach, is totally atheoretical, requires that different tests must be devised for each position (which is expensive) and also cannot logically predict how an individual is likely to perform should the requirements of the job change or should they be promoted into another role within the organization.

This sort of thinking is shown in Figure 13.2. Here the orange boxes at the top represent variables that might be related to the outcomes shown on the right. An line with an arrow indicates a direct relationship, so according to this model, genetic makeup, nutrition and socioeconomic

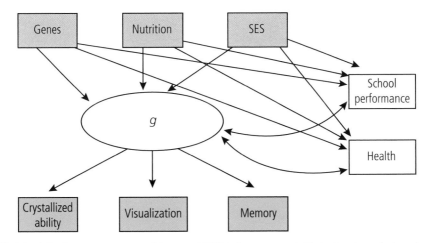

Figure 13.2 Model where genes, nutrition and SES influence real-life behaviour (school performance and health) and also general ability (g). g influences performance on ability tests (green boxes) but does not mediate the relationship between genes (etc.) and real life. (Curves with two arrows represent correlations.)

status (SES) all have a direct influence on both health and school performance. They also all influence general ability, *g*. But there is no line with an arrow showing that *g* influences either school performance or health. So, according to this model, although *g* might be correlated with educational performance, for example, it would be quite wrong to ever try to use *g* in order to explain why children differ in educational performance. It implies that *g* exists, but it is of academic interest only, and does not influence any important real-world behaviours.

The model shown in Figure 13.3 is an alternative explanation. It suggests that genes, nutrition and socio-economic status may directly influence a person's level of general intelligence, *g*, and that their level of *g* influences both their performance on other ability tests (green boxes) and various aspects of real-life behaviour (yellow boxes). Rather than there being direct links between (say) genetic makeup and educational performance as shown in Figure 13.2, this model suggests that genes influence *g* and *g* influences behaviour.

This has implications for how tests should be used to predict behaviour. If *g* has a causal influence on real-world behaviour, then to predict real-world behaviour (e.g., a child's likely level of educational attainment, or a person's job performance) then one should use any convenient, accurate test of *g*. Unlike the work-basket approach, it matters not a jot that the material in that test looks different to the performance that one is trying to predict. According to Figure 13.3, it is perfectly sensible to measure *g* using tests of abstract thinking (analogies, etc.) to predict educational performance or job performance, even though the items in that test do not look as if they are relevant. The items may well not resemble anything which is taught in school, or anything which resembles what a person will do at work, yet they should still prove potent predictors of performance. The work of Schmidt & Hunter (2004) suggests that this model is appropriate for occupational performance, at any rate.

According to the first view, to determine how good a pilot an applicant will be, they should logically be taken to a flight simulator, given some standard training and then evaluated to see how well they can perform. According to the second view, it would be sufficient to give some paper-and-pencil or more abstract tests (e.g. asking people to find their way through a life-size maze, having been shown a map beforehand).

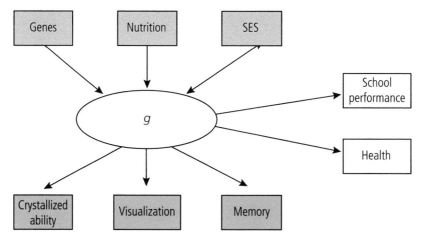

Figure 13.3 Model where genes, nutrition and SES influence intelligence (*g*) and *g* influences performance on both ability tests (visualization etc.) and real life (health, school performance etc.).

Most psychologists follow the second approach and it is usual to assess performance on a number of standard tests of cognitive ability, chosen following a job analysis. Job analysis typically involves a psychologist following staff and noting what they do: they then draw up a list of the key cognitive skills (and perhaps other skills, such as leadership or interpersonal skills) that are required to excel in that post. This guides the choice of tests, which should be validated as described in Chapter 15, before being used to select individuals using a regression-based or multiple-hurdle approach (again, as described in Chapter 15). A paper by Thorndike (1985) makes an interesting point, however.

Suppose that a test of spatial ability is a potent predictor of success in a particular job. This could be because spatial ability is a useful skill for the worker to possess. Or it could be because spatial ability correlates with general intelligence, g, and high levels of g are important for job success. Thurstone's analyses, and some later analyses by Schmidt and Hunter (2004), show that the data support the second option. These analyses show that the only reason that ability tests correlate with occupational performance is because they all measure g to some extent: this is the 'active ingredient' that runs through each and every ability test that allows them to predict performance. Schmidt and Hunter conclude that: '[W]eighted combinations of specific aptitudes (e.g. verbal, spatial or quantitative aptitude) tailored to individual jobs do not predict job performance better than GMA [General Mental Ability – g] measures alone, thus disconfirming specific aptitude theory'. This viewpoint suggests that detailed job analyses may be rather a waste of time (as far as tests of cognitive ability are concerned, anyway) and that a good test of general ability should be able to predict success at almost anything.

Leadership

Brief mention must be made of leadership ability that is not apparently measured by the standard ability tests, but which is thought to be of great importance for the world of work. The suggestion is that some individuals can inspire others to work hard and effectively, can identify the various problems that arise within the organization and develop effective and appropriate solutions (perhaps varying their style of leadership depending on the nature of the problem) and can plan effectively for the future. There have been many attempts made to measure these skills, many involving rather straightforward questionnaires, as any literature search will show.

An alternative approach was followed by Lock and Wheeler (2005) in their *Leadership Judgement Indicator* – an important development allowing individuals to demonstrate whether they can identify effective solutions to problems; it also shows the extent to which they prefer to use four leadership styles: delegation, direction, consensus, consultation.

An example will make it clearer. This is taken from the publicity material for the Leadership Judgement Indicator (LJI) with permission:

You have a meeting with a member of your team arranged for tomorrow. You have led the team for three months, a role for which this person applied. An important project has landed on your desk for which you will need her experience and support. The problem is that she now appears to have little relish for her work, a quality for which she was previously renowned. For a variety of good reasons you want her to lead the project, although you are prepared to do so yourself if you have to. Please rate each of the following options for their appropriateness using the 1–5 rating scale shown below.

a. Tell her that you understand how she must have been feeling but insist she now puts these feelings behind her and leads this project.

b. Ask her to tell you how she is feeling, listen, but reserve the right to insist that she does not dwell on the past and leads the project.

c. Ask her to describe how she is feeling, listen and then come to a joint decision about leadership.

d. Tell her what you have noticed and give her some time to reflect on who should lead and then come back to you. Go along with what she decides.

(1) Totally inappropriate (2) Inappropriate (3) Unsure (4) Appropriate (5) Highly appropriate.

The LJI consists of a number of scenarios like this, each of which has been administered to experts – chief executives of major organizations – who have been shown to generally agree about the merits of each of the possible strategies. The similarity of the candidate's responses to those of the experts is taken as a measure of how well they can identify the most promising solutions to each of these intractable problems. The problems themselves have been chosen so that a variety of different leadership strategies are appropriate. Some will require the leader to take a 'hands on' approach, while others will benefit from delegation, consultation or working in cooperation with others.

Personality

As well as standard personality factors (such as the big five), occupational psychologists have studied number of other traits which they believe to be different to the big five factors and which they claim are relevant to job success and tests such as the Occupational Personality Questionnaire have been used to try to obtain more information on personality factors.

It is an empirical fact that faking is a problem for personality inventories such as the NEO-PI(R) (e.g. Winkelspecht, Lewis and Thomas 2006). The question is whether it is possible to overcome this issue. Three main approaches have been followed in the literature:

1. Several tests of socially desirable responding have been developed in addition to the EPQ lie scale. The Marlowe-Crowne social desirability scale (Crowne and Marlowe 1960) is ancient but widely used and effective; the items are reproduced in the journal article. There are more recent alternatives, but these are commercial products. Any of these scales can be used to 'design out' social desirability when the test is being constructed. This can simply be achieved by correlating scores on each item with scores on the Marlowe-Crowne scale: items with large correlations should be removed and so should never appear in the version of the test that is published.

2. It may also be possible to detect whether a person has been faking their responses by using a so-called 'lie scale', 'dissimulation index' or a 'positive presentation management scale'. This is typically a set of items measuring very minor shortcomings (e.g. 'I have sometimes told a lie'). If someone claims to have few of these faults, they are presumed to either be deliberately trying to make themselves appear good or are out of touch with how they really behave. The items in such scales sometimes occur naturally in the test, where they are supposed to measure other personality factors. In the case of the EPQ, the lie scale is tailored for the purpose and its items are interspersed with the items measuring the three main personality factors.

Costa and McCrae (1997) argue (without much evidence) that such scales are of limited use and so the NEO-PI(R) does not include any form of dissimulation index, although Schinka

(Schinka, Kinder and Kremer 1997; Young and Schinka 2001) have developed some, based on socially desirable items in the NEO-PI(R). Reid-Seiser and Fritzsche (2001) have studied whether individuals who gave highly socially desirable scores on the NEO-PI(R) when being selected for a real job – and so who may have been trying to give a good impression of themselves – performed any worse on the job than did applicants who appeared to be more honest. Surprisingly, perhaps, they did not, although the data in this paper show that this is probably because the NEO was itself only a very weak predictor of job success, the highest correlation with either of the criteria used being 0.19.

Some tests that have been developed for occupational selection ask participants to choose between two items *from different scales* that have previously been matched for social desirability by simply showing groups of people the items when the test is being developed and asking them to rate how socially desirable each of them is. Then two items from different scales that are equal in terms of social desirability are put together as alternatives for a test item. This should mean that social desirability will not influence which one is chosen.

3. A typical item might be:

If I won the lottery, my first priority would be to:

i.   throw a big party, or

ii. visit exotic parts of the world.

I made up this item, so it has not been validated, but you can see that the first option may indicate extraversion, while the second one might measure openness to experience. To score this sort of test, one simply adds up the number of times that each scale is chosen. There are some problems with the analysis and interpretation of these tests, because the total score for each person (summed across all scales) is always equal to the number of items in the test which makes factor analysis and the calculation of coefficient alpha problematic. However, some tests constructed this way such as the Occupational Personality Questionnaire claim to have considerable success in predicting job performance (Robertson and Kinder 1993). Although the authors score the test rather differently and claim that it measures their own model of personality, it seems to measure the big five personality traits (Beaujouan 2000).

Educational psychology

The use of psychometric tests in educational psychology is somewhat controversial. Critics of such assessments have two main objections. The first is that scores on tests are not usually accurate enough to allow professionals to make the fine discriminations between children that are necessary. In other words, tests may not be reliable enough, or valid enough, to be used. The second main objection is one of stigmatizing children. If a child is assessed and found to have a low IQ, it is quite likely that teachers will lower their expectations and the child may themselves feel a failure and effectively give up trying to learn. A famous study by Rosenthal and Jacobson (1968) gives weight to this idea: children who the teachers believed were 'gifted' showed substantial gains on an IQ test, although in reality the children had been selected at random. That teacher expectations affects IQ became widely expected – despite experts such as Cronbach (1975) arguing that they 'were an artefact of crude experimental design and improper statistical analysis'.

Ability

There is a substantial correlation between childhood intelligence and educational outcomes. For example, Benson (1942) shows a substantial relationship between IQ and the age at which children left school, while Strenze (2007) provides a more recent overview of the literature in this area and concludes that the size of the correlation between intelligence and academic performance is approximately 0.56. And as can be seen from Figure 13.1, educational success appears to be determined largely by general ability, rather than by socioeconomic status. This is a very substantial relationship. However, it is of limited practical utility, given that academic selection by means of an IQ test (which used to be commonplace in the UK) has now largely disappeared.

An exception is the scholastic assessment test (SAT) in the United States. Students seeking admission to universities and colleges complete these nationwide standardized tests: colleges set minimum criteria, so that the most popular courses (and the most prestigious institutions) will only select the very best students. The SAT consists of two parts: a subject-specific section and a reasoning test, for which Frey and Detterman (2004) demonstrate a substantial correlation (in the order of 0.83) with g. Whether or not this part of the SAT is solely a measure of g is currently a matter of some debate, with a study by Coyle and Pillow (2008) suggesting that the non-g-related aspect of the SAT can also predict academic performance in college. This is a good example of the widespread use of ability testing.

Self-assessment question 13.3

Some countries use performance on national examinations rather than psychological tests to select people for college. Think of some advantages and disadvantages for each approach.

Ability tests are widely used in the assessment of dyslexia – a learning disorder that affects reading, grammar and spelling. It is necessary to distinguish between dyslexia and low general ability and educational psychologists usually do so using individually administered ability tests such as the Wechsler Intelligence Scale for Children (WISC-IV). These consist of a number of tasks, designed to measure different aspects of intelligence (although curiously the number and nature of these tasks is not related to any recognizable modern model of intelligence) of the kinds discussed in Chapter 8. Some of these involve language (e.g. vocabulary, verbal reasoning), while others do not (e.g. arranging a series of pictures so that they tell a logical story; arranging coloured blocks to form a particular pattern). If a child has language difficulties, they are likely to perform much better on the latter type of task than on the former and there are ways of assessing whether the difference between the two sets of scores are large enough to lead to a confident diagnosis of dyslexia.

Clinical/counselling psychology

The influence of Carl Rogers can hardly be underestimated and Rogerian therapy is a mainstay of clinical and counselling psychology. That said, there are still some psychoanalytically inclined psychologists around (albeit not usually in the public sector in the UK) and a very few who swear by personal construct theory. As far as personality theory is concerned, as opposed to methods of therapy, much of the relevant work of clinical psychologists involves personality disorders and affective disorders (anxiety, depression etc.) and so the 'normal' personality models discussed in Chapters 4–6 are not of enormous use.

Psychological tests have been developed using the principles outlined in Chapter 18 to measure a number of traits of clinical interest. Curiously, although anxiety and depression usually correlate substantially together in the general population (and form the trait of neuroticism), there is substantial evidence that they involve rather different physiological processes (different drugs affect them, for example) and so scales such as the State Trait Anxiety Inventory (Spielberger 1983) and the Beck Depression Inventory (Beck et al. 1961) are sometimes used for research purposes, although not normally as part of clinical assessments. However, as most clinicians accept that the main aim of any form of therapy is to treat people as individuals, the type of approach adopted by individual difference theorists – looking for ways to group people together on the basis of personality and ability traits – is of limited relevance.

Forensic psychology

Forensic psychology concerns individuals who are in contact with the legal system – for example, through the prison system, probation service or police service. Like clinical psychology, much of the work is based on individuals and is highly specialized, so the broad theories of individual differences laid out in previous chapters are of limited relevance.

One major application of ability testing concerns the assessment of fitness to plead. For example, is a person who commits a murder (a) necessarily aware that this is wrong, (b) aware of what the court process implies and what a plea of 'guilty' or 'not guilty' means and (c) able to construct a case for his/her defence and instruct lawyers? These issues are known as the Pritchard criteria and date back to 1836. Under the British legal system, if psychiatrists decide that the person is unfit to plead, he is compulsorily admitted to a secure hospital. In the USA, the procedure is rather less subjective and several psychometric tests have been developed to assess whether an individual should be tried in court. Akinkunmi (2002) summarizes several such measures and shows that one agrees quite closely with psychiatrists' views. Some legal systems (e.g. Florida, at the time of writing) formalize this sort of approach by exempting those with an IQ below 70 from the death penalty.

A second major problem concerns the assessment of people who have been convicted of extremely serious offences (typically multiple murders or sex crimes, cannibalism etc.) where we find a diagnosis of personality disorder has been made. Such people are (in the UK) normally detained in 'special hospitals' – highly secure units where psychiatric and psychological assessments and interventions are carried out with the ultimate aim of returning offenders to society when it is safe to do so.

Two types of personality disorder are related to psychopathic behaviour. *Antisocial personality disorder* symptoms include:

- a history of disregard for the rights of others
- non-conformance to society's rules (often with many arrests)
- a history of manipulation/deceit for personal gain
- impulsiveness
- failure to consider long-term consequences of behaviours
- anger and physical violence.

Narcissistic personality disorder symptoms include:

- grandiose ideas

- a feeling that the world owes them a lot

- lack of humility

- tendency to exaggerate achievements

- demanding praise and admiration despite worthy achievements

- feel that they can only be understood by other 'superior' people.

These characteristics are certainly rather different from those that we have discussed in 'normal' personality theories. How should one assess such people? One method is the Hare Psychopathy Checklist – Revised (Hare 1991), which consists of four subfactors in addition to an overall measure of psychopathy, two relating to antisocial personality disorder and two to narcissistic personality disorder. It is administered by a professional psychiatrist or psychologist and the items are answered following a structured interview and a review of case notes. This is necessary because one of the key features of psychopaths is that their tendency to lie and deceive others (and to show no remorse or even grasp that they have done wrong). Administering a simple questionnaire would, therefore, be doomed to failure as it is highly probable that the psychopathic individual would recognize that, in order to be released, it is necessary to produce a 'normal' profile and so would do their best to fake 'good'. However, given the superficial charm and often high intelligence of psychopathic individuals, there is no guarantee that a psychiatrist would not be fooled into thinking that a dangerous offender was fit for release, although the instrument does show some predictive validity in that it can predict re-offending in less serious offenders to some extent (Leistico, Salekin, DeCoster and Rogers 2008; Walters, Knight, Grann and Dahle 2008). This is hardly rocket science, however: the factor that seems to work is the antisocial lifestyle factor. People who have offended a lot in the past tend to offend again. Who would have thought otherwise?

How, though, should one proceed to assess psychopaths? This is an extremely difficult question to address and, unlike most applications of psychology, innocent people's lives may well depend on the accuracy of the assessments that are made. If objective tests of personality were more effective, this would be an ideal choice, if the individual were truly unaware of what a questionnaire or other test measured or were physically unable to alter their response (e.g. some physiological responses).

A useful (and practical) summary of some possible methods is given by O'Rourke and Hammond (2007), but overall it is clear that this is an extremely difficult area and it seems that no one has yet found a method of assessing personality in individuals who are determined to deceive.

Health psychology

Ability

Ten years ago virtually nothing was known about links between intelligence and health. This all changed when Ian Deary from Edinburgh University and Lawrence Whalley from Aberdeen came across a treasure trove of data. All Scottish children born in 1921 who were still alive in

1932 (87,498 of them) were given an intelligence test in a research programme known as the Scottish Mental Survey (SMS). It all happened again (using the same test on all children born in 1936) in 1947 and some follow-up studies were also conducted on this group: Maxwell (1961) summarizes some findings. Ledgers holding the names of the children and their test scores (together with some family background information) were found mouldering in a basement in 1997.

Why, you may ask, is this exciting? Deary and Whalley, both of whom had a background in medicine (although Ian Deary is a psychologist as well) realized that because the cohort of children was so large, many of them should still be alive and it would be possible to determine whether scores on simple test of intelligence, administered to the children in groups when they were aged 11, could predict what happened to the children 66 years later. For example, is intelligence related to length of life? Or to the likelihood of developing heart disease, dementia etc? And if so, why? These types of question are normally almost impossible to address. It is easy enough to identify groups of people who have lived to a ripe old age or who have developed heart disease but the problem is that it is impossible to tell how intelligent they were when they were younger or well. It would make little sense to test groups of old or sick people, because (a) it is quite probable that ill health would affect intelligence test scores, so one could never be sure that intelligence *caused* anything, and (b) because some people have died, one can never know whether the ones that are left in any particular age group are unusually high or low on tests of *g*, especially when using tests that have been carefully normed. The SMS thus gave rise to a new branch of psychology called *cognitive epidemiology*, which studies the effects of intelligence on health and development. The results from this work are fascinating.

First, having high intelligence makes it likely that you will live longer. For the Scottish 11 year olds tested in 1932, having an IQ that is 15 points (one standard deviation) above the average made them 21% less likely to die over the next 65 years than someone with an average score. Women were 29% less likely to die. Put another way, 70% of women with IQs in the top quartile were alive aged 76: less than half of the women with IQs in the bottom quartile were still alive at that age (Whalley and Deary 2001). It can be seen that a simple test administered at age 11 seems to be a potent predictor of this outcome, at any rate. However, the interpretation of these data might not be that simple. It is well known that measures of intelligence are correlated with social class (albeit with some fairly bitter disagreements about whether social advantage/deprivation influences intelligence or whether intelligence influences the type of work that is obtained and therefore determines social advantage/deprivation). So it is possible to speculate that the more intelligent children in the survey were also the most well to do and this caused them to live longer. It is also possible that the Second World War may have distorted the figures and one could conjecture that perhaps those with lower IQs were sent to fight rather than being given safe desk jobs, for example. (The hard data show that high IQ males had a greater chance of being killed during that conflict, however.) Such alternative explanations have been considered and are unlikely to explain the results. Full descriptions of these studies and details of the analyses are given in Deary, Whalley and Starr (2009), which cannot be recommended too highly.

Finding a relationship is, in one sense, the easy part. It is also necessary to discover why it emerges. For example, are more intelligent people more likely to heed warnings about smoking and drinking or be better able to identify and avoid dangerous activities such as driving too fast and too close? Is high intelligence one of many signs of 'biological fitness' as authors such as Prokosch, Yeo and Miller (2005) have suggested: in other words, do adverse biological factors during gestation and early development affect intelligence and also predispose one to later health problems? There are other possibilities, too, which we cannot consider in detail here.

This relationship between g and good health is not just a Scottish phenomenon or restricted to those who generally die of old age. O'Toole and Stankov (1992) followed 46,000 Australian ex-servicemen, whose mental abilities had been tested while serving with the military. They focused on those who had died other than through illness: most died in accidents such as car crashes. They found that in these middle-aged men, a lower level of intelligence was a far better predictor of mortality than any of the health-related variables they had expected to be relevant. Having an IQ of 85 as opposed to 115 made an individual approximately twice as likely to die – a huge effect.

Whalley and Deary's data can also shed light on what happens to people's mental processes as they age. The studies showed fairly unequivocally that clever children usually became clever adults (Deary et al. 2004) as the correlation between intelligence test scores at age 11 and age 77 was 0.63 (0.73 once some corrections had been applied).

Finding links between childhood IQ and mental illness proved to be difficult, because of the lack of a national database showing (for example) details of those diagnosed with schizophrenia or dementia. Whalley et al. (2000) eventually managed to unearth a sample of 50 people who were born in 1921, who were tested in Aberdeen in 1932 and who were diagnosed with late-onset dementia in Aberdeen in or after 1986. Their 11-year-old scores were compared with those of other individuals who were also born in 1921 and who had also lived in Aberdeen since 1932. Although the sample size was modest, some differences did emerge – but not until the participants were aged 72 or older. What normally happens is that the average ability at age 11 normally increases in older samples, as the people who die from year to year tend to be those with lower ability scores. This happened in the control group. However, it did not happen at all in the group containing people who developed dementia. The average aged 11 test score within this group was lower than for the control group and fell by about a sixth of a standard deviation over the period from 1986 to 1991: the aged 11 test scores of those who did not have a diagnosis of dementia went up slightly. This led to significant differences between the two groups for all ages over 71, with the control group showing higher childhood intelligence scores than the group later diagnosed with dementia.

Deary, Whalley and Starr (2009) describe a number of other analyses too – for example, showing that the a higher level of intelligence at age 11 made it less likely that one would receive psychiatric contact during one's lifetime: this book also summarizes the results from a great swathe of studies performed to try to discover precisely why these relationships exist. But one thing is clear. Simple ability tests have a surprising capability of predicting health outcomes some 60 years later.

One other area ought to be briefly mentioned: that of compliance with drugs. This is a particular problem with some drugs, where failure to take medication regularly may prove life-threatening. It has been consistently found that cognitive performance is one of the variables that influences whether patients take their drugs at the correct times (Stilley et al. 2004) and may also fail to understand the meaning of the dosage instructions on drug packets (Wolf et al. 2007). Once again, it seems that cognitive ability can have far reaching implications for wellbeing.

Personality

There have been some important links discovered between personality and illness (such as heart disease) and also between personality and health behaviour (such as exercise). Twenty years ago there was a huge focus on what became known as Type A behaviour – Type A individuals being impatient, aggressive and ambitious 'adrenalin junkies' who always felt under time pressure. This personality type was measured via a structured interview or the Jenkins Activity Survey (Jenkins, Zyzanski and Rosenman, 1971), which is a brief questionnaire. The Type B personality was effectively the opposite of this: relaxed, and non-driven. Some years later Hans Eysenck also claimed that some 'repressive' personality types, people who were reluctant to reveal their emotions, were more likely to develop cancers than other personality types. This became known as the Type C personality type and Eysenck et al. (2000) describe it alongside the Type A personality. More recently a Type D personality has come along. It can be measured by a short questionnaire (Denollet 2005) and is once again thought to be related to heart disease – although this time to how well one typically recovers after it. The Type D individual (depressed and socially inhibited) fares poorly following a heart attack (Schiffer et al. 2008).

While the evidence seems to suggest that the Type D personality may be a useful concept, Type A and Type C personalities turned out to be dead ends, with small effects and contradictory results (Myrtek 2001) and they are now rarely mentioned. These approaches are odd in two ways. First, they sought to *type* people. Thus, one is either a Type A personality or a Type B personality: there is no continuous scale, like a trait. Second, it is surprising (to put it mildly) that clinicians should be able to develop scales that are completely different from those that personality psychologists have been developing for nearly a century. One of the problems with the Type A personality is that the various components did not correlate together the way that items in a personality test should. You may have thought to yourself that the Type D personality certainly sounds like a neurotic intravert – and this is exactly correct (De Fruyt and Denollet 2002). It looks as if it is a mixture of two traits, rather than a single novel one.

Summary

This chapter has outlined some applications of individual differences research and demonstrated the practical importance of this work. General ability, *g*, turns out to be particularly useful as a predictor of real-life behaviour. Surprisingly, perhaps, the reason why ability tests predict behaviour seems to be that they are all imperfect measures of *g*: for example, tests of spatial ability seem generally to be of no intrinsic value for predicting performance on tasks that require people to visualize things: they only predict performance because they measure *g* to some extent. The other exciting development is the discovery that not only is *g* surprisingly stable across the lifespan, but it seems to be related to health behaviour, for reasons that are only just being understood. Not all the relationships are huge, but the relationship between intelligence and death is certainly large enough to be of practical interest.

By the same token, there are some areas in which conventional methods of assessing personality clearly do not work, such as the assessment of offenders.

Suggested additional reading

Deary et al. (2009) provide an excellent summary of the literature linking abilities to health outcomes: it is engrossing and remarkably easy to read. The other obvious source is the Hunter work on abilities and job performance (Hunter and Hunter 1984; Schmidt and Hunter 2004) or Thorndike's (1985) venerable paper on the central importance of *g* as a predictor of job success. However, none of the papers cited in this chapter is particularly technical.

Answers to self-assessment questions

SAQ 13.1

To test whether schooling influences education, the sensible strategy would involve measuring the intelligence of groups of children some of whom have attended school and some of whom have not. Of course, these groups should be as similar as possible. (It would make no sense testing the ability of 18 year olds, some of who left school at 18 and others who went to college, as these could well have self-selected on the basis of intelligence and so the finding that the older students are more intelligent would not imply that college has made them so.) There are, however, two types of study that may prove useful here. Some children in Holland did not attend school for 18 months during the Second World War and their IQ was then found to be five points lower than the norm, suggesting that schooling may influence intelligence (De Groot 1951). However, (a) after a few years the scores returned to their expected level and (b) these children may have suffered in other ways from the effects of warfare (malnutrition etc.). Another source of evidence considers the variation in IQ between schools of differing quality (after controlling for SES etc.). The rationale for this approach is that if schools truly influence IQ, the better schools should produce highly intelligent children and the worst schools should produce children who are less intelligent than one would expect. According to Jencks (1972), this is simply not the case.

SAQ 13.2

The most likely reason concerns the demands of the individual jobs. For example, in a job that is largely manual, such as building, it is possible that the only aspects of the job that require thought rather than strength might be planning ahead (so that equipment etc. is available when needed), scheduling the order in which tasks should be performed, troubleshooting when things go wrong, etc. By way of contrast, a managerial post may be almost entirely cognitive. So, crudely put, the proportion of time that is spent thinking might differ between jobs.

SAQ 13.3

I would argue that, for fairness, the system that should be used ought to be the one that shows the highest validity: in other words, the one with the highest correlation between test/exam performance and performance at university or college. Unfortunately, I have been unable to find many recent data on this for the UK system. However, a system such as the SAT seems to have advantages in that it:

- is consistent nationally as opposed to having several different examination boards, which might set papers differing in difficulty

- measures potential (g) as well as attainment

- may perhaps be easier and more reliable to score (as at least partly multiple choice).

  Contrariwise, some might argue that:

- the idea of a national syllabus is perhaps too restrictive

- if minority groups perform poorly on the cognitive ability section of the SAT, this part of the test merits both scrutiny for bias and a political decision about what to do about any group differences that are found after accounting for bias.

References

Akinkunmi, A. A. (2002). The MacArthur Competence Assessment Tool – fitness to plead: a preliminary evaluation of a research instrument for assessing fitness to plead in England and Wales. *Journal of the American Academy of Psychiatry and the Law 30*(4), 476–82.

Bäckström, M. (2007). Higher-order factors in a five-factor personality inventory and its relation to social desirability. *European Journal of Psychological Assessment 23*(2), 63–70.

Beaujouan, Y.-M. (2000). The convergence of the factorial structure of the OPQ (Occupational Personality Questionnaire) towards the five factor model, in seven countries. *European Review of Applied Psychology/Revue Européenne de Psychologie Appliquée 50*(4), 349–57.

Beck, A. T., Ward, C. H., Mendelson, M., Mock, J. and Erbaugh, J. (1961). An inventory for measuring depression. *Archives of General Psychiatry 4*, 561–71.

Benson, V. E. (1942). The intelligence and later scholastic success of sixth-grade pupils. *School & Society 55*, 163–7.

Ceci, S. J. and Williams, W. M. (1997). Schooling, intelligence, and income. *American Psychologist 52*(10), 1051–8.

Costa, P. T., Jr. and McCrae, R. R. (1997). Stability and change in personality assessment: the revised NEO personality inventory in the year 2000. *Journal of Personality Assessment 68*(1), 86.

Coyle, T. R. and Pillow, D. R. (2008). SAT and ACT predict college GPA after removing g. *Intelligence 36*(6), 719–29.

Cronbach, L. J. (1975). Five decades of public controversy over mental testing. *American Psychologist 30*(1), 1–14.

Crowne, D. P. and Marlowe, D. (1960). A new scale of social desirability independent of psychopathology. *Journal of Consulting Psychology 24*(4), 349–54.

De Fruyt, F. and Denollet, J. (2002). Type D personality: a five-factor model perspective. *Psychology & Health 17*(5), 671–83.

De Groot, A. D. (1951). War and the intelligence of youth. *Journal of Abnormal and Social Psychology 46*(4), 596–7.

Deary, I. J., Whalley, L. J. and Starr, J. M. (2009). *A Lifetime of Intelligence: Follow-up Studies of the Scottish Mental Surveys of 1932 and 1947* (1st edn). Washington, DC: American Psychological Association.

Deary, I. J., Whiteman, M. C., Starr, J. M., Whalley, L. J. and Fox, H. C. (2004). The impact of childhood intelligence on later life: following up the Scottish mental surveys of 1932 and 1947. *Journal of Personality and Social Psychology 86*(1), 130–47.

Denollet, J. (2005). DS14: standard assessment of negative affectivity, social inhibition, and Type D personality. *Psychosomatic Medicine 67*(1), 89–97.

Dickens, W. T. and Flynn, J. R. (2006). Black Americans reduce the racial IQ gap: evidence from standardization samples. *Psychological Science 17*(10), 913–20.

Duncan, O. D., Featherman, D. L. and Duncan, B. (1972). *Socioeconomic Background and Achievement*: Oxford: Seminar Press.

Eysenck, H. J., Kenny, D. T., Carlson, J. G., McGuigan, F. J. and Sheppard, J. L. (2000). Personality as a risk factor in cancer and coronary heart disease. In *Stress and Health: Research and Clinical Applications*. Amsterdam: Harwood Academic Publishers.

Eysenck, S. B., Eysenck, H. J. and Barrett, P. (1985). A revised version of the psychoticism scale. *Personality and Individual Differences 6*(1), 21–9.

Frey, M. C. and Detterman, D. K. (2004). Scholastic assessment or *g*? The relationship between the scholastic assessment test and general cognitive ability. *Psychological Science 15*(6), 373–8.

Hare, R. D. (1991). *The Hare Psychopathy Checklist – Revised*. North Tonawanda, NY: Multi-Health Systems.

Hunter, J. E. and Hunter, R. F. (1984). Validity and utility of alternative predictors of job performance. *Psychological Bulletin 96*, 72–98.

Jencks, C. (1972). *Inequality: A Reassessment of the Effect of Family and Schooling in America*. New York: Basic Books.

Jenkins, C. D., Zyzanski, S. J. and Rosenman, R. H. (1971). Progress toward validation of a computer-scored test for the type A coronary-prone behavior pattern. *Psychosomatic Medicine 33*(3), 193–202.

Leistico, A.-M. R., Salekin, R. T., DeCoster, J. and Rogers, R. (2008). A large-scale meta-analysis relating the Hare measures of psychopathy to antisocial conduct. *Law and Human Behavior 32*(1), 28–45.

Lock, M. and Wheeler, R. (2005). *The Leadership Judgement Indicator*. Oxford: Hogrefe.

Lorr, M. and McNair, D. M. (1988). *Manual, Profile of Mood States, Bipolar Form*. San Diego, CA: Educational and Industrial Testing Service.

Maxwell, J. (1961). *The Level and Trend of National Intelligence: The Contribution of the Scottish Mental Surveys*. London: University of London Press.

Myrtek, M. (2001). Meta-analyses of prospective studies on coronary heart disease, type A personality, and hostility. *International Journal of Cardiology 79*(2–3), 245–51.

O'Rourke, M. M. and Hammond, S. M. (2007). Risk assessment in forensic practice. *Issues in Forensic Psychology 6*, 32–9.

O'Toole, B. I. and Stankov, L. (1992). Ultimate validity of psychological tests. *Personality and Individual Differences 13*(6), 699–716.

Paulhus, D. L., Robinson, J. P., Shaver, P. R. and Wrightsman, L. S. (1991). Measurement and control of response bias. In *Measures of Personality and Social Psychological Attitudes*. San Diego, CA: Academic Press.

Prokosch, M. D., Yeo, R. A. and Miller, G. F. (2005). Intelligence tests with higher *g*-loadings show higher correlations with body symmetry: evidence for a general fitness factor mediated by developmental stability. *Intelligence 33*(2), 203–213.

Reid-Seiser, H. L. and Fritzsche, B. A. (2001). The usefulness of the NEO PI-R positive presentation management scale for detecting response distortion in employment contexts. *Personality and Individual Differences 31*(4), 639–50.

Reynolds, C. R., Chastain, R. L., Kaufman, A. S. and McLean, J. E. (1987). Demographic characteristics and IQ among adults: analysis of the WAIS-R standardization sample as a function of the stratification variables. *Journal of School Psychology 25*(4), 323–42.

Robertson, I. T. and Kinder, A. (1993). Personality and job competences – the criterion-related validity of some personality variables. *Journal of Occupational and Organizational Psychology 66*, 225–44.

Rosenthal, R. and Jacobson, L. (1968). *Pygmalion in the Classroom: Teacher Expectation and Pupils' Intellectual Development*. New York: Holt, Rinehart & Winston.

Schiffer, A. L. A., Pedersen, S. S., Broers, H., Widdershoven, J. W. and Denollet, J. (2008). Type-D personality but not depression predicts severity of anxiety in heart failure patients at 1-year follow-up. *Journal of Affective Disorders 106*(1–2), 73–81.

Schinka, J. A., Kinder, B. N. and Kremer, T. (1997). Research validity scales for the NEO-PI-R: development and initial validation. *Journal of Personality Assessment 68*(1), 127.

Schmidt, F. L. and Hunter, J. (2004). General mental ability in the world of work: occupational attainment and job performance. *Journal of Personality and Social Psychology 86*(1), 162–73.

Spielberger, C. D. (1983). *Manual for the State–Trait Anxiety Inventory (Form Y) ('Self-Evaluation Questionnaire')*. Palo Alto, CA: Consulting Psychologists Press.

Stilley, C. S., Sereika, S., Muldoon, M. F., Ryan, C. M. and Dunbar-Jacob, J. (2004). Psychological and cognitive function: predictors of adherence with cholesterol lowering treatment. *Annals of Behavioral Medicine 27*(2), 117–24.

Strenze, T. (2007). Intelligence and socioeconomic success: a meta-analytic review of longitudinal research. *Intelligence 35*(5), 401–26.

Thorndike, R. L. (1985). The central role of general ability in prediction. *Multivariate Behavioral Research 1985*(20), 241–54.

Walters, G. D., Knight, R. A., Grann, M. and Dahle, K.-P. (2008). Incremental validity of the psychopathy checklist facet scores: predicting release outcome in six samples. *Journal of Abnormal Psychology 117*(2), 396–405.

Whalley, L. J. and Deary, I. J. (2001). Longitudinal cohort study of childhood IQ and survival up to age 76. *British Medical Journal 322*, 72–90.

Whalley, L. J., Starr, J. M., Athawes, R., Hunter, D., Pattie, A. and Deary, I. J. (2000). Childhood mental ability and dementia. *Neurology 55*(10), 1455–9.

Winkelspecht, C., Lewis, P. and Thomas, A. (2006). Potential effects of faking on the NEO-PI-R: willingness and ability to fake changes who gets hired in simulated selection decisions. *Journal of Business & Psychology 21*(2), 243–59.

Wolf, M. S., Davis, T. C., Shrank, W., Rapp, D. N., Bass, P. F., Connor, U. M. et al. (2007). To err is human: patient misinterpretations of prescription drug label instructions. *Patient Education and Counseling 67*(3), 293–300.

Young, M. S. and Schinka, J. A. (2001). Research validity scales for the NEO-PI-R: additional evidence for reliability and validity. *Journal of Personality Assessment 76*(3), 412–20.

14 Measuring individual differences

Background

This chapter provides an introduction to psychometrics, the branch of psychology that deals with the measurement of individual differences. It introduces the concepts of trait and state and shows how knowledge of an individual's traits and states may be used to predict behaviour. Various types of psychological test are outlined and the interpretation of individual scores through the use of norms is discussed. Finally, some guidance is given as to how to select a test and use it ethically.

Recommended prior reading

Chapter 1.

Introduction

One of the most important distinctions between psychology and other disciplines that also claim to give insight into the 'human condition' is that of measurement. Students of literature are happy to make suggestions about the personality, motives and moods of figures such as Hamlet, Hannibal or Hagar and although these contributions may be scholarly, they are not truly scientific in that they cannot ever be shown to be wrong. This is where psychology differs radically from other methods of understanding how humans function. While great literature, religious doctrines, therapists' explanations, old wives' tales, psychoanalytical interpretations of the causes of neurosis, armchair speculation and 'common sense' *may* provide some accurate and useful insights, it is perfectly possible that some or all of these are simply incorrect.

We certainly cannot tell what is true just by our emotional reactions. A favourite trick of academics is to ask students to complete personality questionnaires that are then taken away for computerized scoring. The next week, the students are given a talk about the ethics of testing, are handed sealed envelopes each holding a computer-generated analysis of their personality and asked to rate how accurate they find it. In my experience, most students are amazed by how insightful and accurate the results are and astounded by the depth of these insights. Asking members of the class to compare their descriptions is probably the kindest way of showing that everyone in the class has received precisely the same personality assessment! The point is that one simply cannot trust one's emotional judgements to sort out fact from fiction. The fact that the results obtained from some personality test 'feel right' to an individual is not an adequate criterion. This, of course, is unsurprising – given that we are all human beings, it will be possible to make some broad descriptions about how human beings *in general* behave, which is a far cry from the scientific assessment of individual differences. Instead, we need to develop more rigorous techniques.

Psychometrics is the branch of psychology concerned with the scientific measurement of individual differences and half of this book is devoted to psychometric principles. This is because the accurate assessment of individual differences, using proper psychological tests or other techniques, is absolutely vital for a proper, scientific study of the discipline. It is important for three reasons.

First, it is only possible to test theories if individual differences can be measured accurately. For example, in the nineteenth century, Galton surmised that 'intelligent' people might be able to react faster than less intelligent people – a theory that has some value in so far as it suggests that intelligence may be linked to the speed with which our nervous systems can process information. To test this hypothesis, it is necessary to measure some individuals' reaction times *and also their intelligence* – the analysis might involve correlating these two scores together. Without effective measures of both intelligence and reaction time, the hypothesis is untestable. In the case of reaction times, it would be possible to program a computer to switch on a light at random intervals and time how long it takes the person to push a button. This operational definition of 'reaction time' will incorporate arbitrary decisions. How bright should the light be? Does its colour matter? Why not use a tone instead of a light? How much 'play' should there be in the response button? What should be done if someone often anticipates the light coming on? To measure intelligence one will probably use the scores on a particular intelligence test, chosen to be appropriate for the age and ability of the people being tested. Or one could use teachers' ratings, school-leaving qualifications or even more rough and ready approximations.

The problem is that it is often impossible to know how good one's operational definition is. So if one finds no relationship between intelligence and reaction time (and this is what Galton found) this could either be because there is, in reality, no link between intelligence and reaction time or that in reality there *is* such a link, but this cannot be detected because one or both of the concepts have inadequate operational definitions. (In reality, Galton's means of measuring reaction time was somewhat crude, as were his attempts at assessing intelligence and so he reluctantly concluded that the two were unrelated: we now know that there is a modest link between these variables, as shown in Chapter 9.) The intelligence test and/or the method of measuring reaction times may be flawed. The extent to which a test measures what it is supposed to is known as its validity and we shall return to this concept in Chapter 15. The key point is that we need highly valid psychological tests in order to provide operational definitions of abstract terms. Without such tests to provide solid operational definitions of psychological concepts, theories degenerate into mere speculations of little scientific value.

The second reason for studying psychometrics is that almost all modern models of personality, ability, mood and motivation are based on a psychometric technique called 'factor analysis'. Without understanding the basic principles of this, it is impossible to grasp how these theories have developed, their strengths and weaknesses and whether a particular theory is based on a sound methodology.

The third reason for studying psychometrics is because psychological tests are so widely used in applied psychology. Occupational psychologists and personnel managers use tests to assess the potential of job applicants. Educational psychologists may use tests to detect learning difficulties, difficulties in using language, etc. Medical psychologists may use a questionnaire to identify individuals whose 'Type A' personality puts them at risk of a heart attack. It is vitally important that test users understand how these instruments are constructed, how they should be administered, scored and interpreted and the importance of assessing measurement error, bias and other important and potentially litigious issues.

Furthermore, the types of test used are likely to become increasingly complex. Printed tests will almost certainly be replaced by computer programs that present different people with quite different sets of test items. Some participants will sit very easy tests and some will sit very difficult tests. Yet although people have taken tests that differ greatly in difficulty, the programs can estimate the relative ability of all those taking part. Once again, test users will need to grasp the basics of these methods in order to be able to interpret the results of such measures.

Self-assessment question 14.1

a. What is an operational definition?

b. Try to think what you might use as operational definitions of French-speaking ability and meanness.

Most readers of this book will use psychological tests in some shape or form, either as dependent variables for testing psychological theories or in applied psychology, and everyone will need to understand some basic principles of psychological measurement in order to grasp modern theories of ability and personality. Given the prevalence and importance of psychological tests in academic and applied psychology, it is embarrassing to admit that many are simply not worth the paper that they are printed on. Some patently useless tests are slickly marketed and widely used by the unwary and so one aim of this book is to teach you enough about the basics of psychological measurement to allow you to choose a test that is likely to provide a suitable operational definition for the concepts that you wish to assess.

Traits and states

Most psychological tests measure 'traits' of one kind or another. Traits are simply useful descriptions of how individuals generally behave. For example, 'sociability' is generally regarded as a trait, since few people are the life and soul of the party one day and a virtual recluse the next. Since individuals tend to have a characteristic level of sociability we term it a trait. There are plenty of others.

Self-assessment question 14.2

Try to decide which of the following are (probably) traits:

a. musical ability

b. hunger

c. liberality of attitudes

d. anger

e. good manners.

It is conventional to group traits into three classes, namely attainments, ability traits and personality traits. Measures of attainment are of little interest to psychologists. They measure how well an individual performs *in a certain area, following a course of instruction*. School examinations are an example of attainment tests. If children attend lessons and read and memorize the textbook, they should be able to achieve a perfect mark in a knowledge-based attainment test. Levels of attainment are specific to a particular area. If a pupil has a first-rate knowledge of British social history in the nineteenth century, it is not possible to say whether or not she knows anything about modern economic theory, seventeenth-century history or anything else. It all depends on what she has been taught. The distinction becomes a little more blurred at university level, where students are required to search out references, think about their implications and make a coherent argument when writing an essay – in this situation, abilities, personality traits and motivational factors will also play a part. Here, an essay mark will, in part, measure attainment, but will also be influenced by motivation, the student's ability to express themselves and so on.

Ability traits are concerned with a person's level of cognitive performance in some area, e.g. how well he or she can read maps, solve mental arithmetic problems, solve crossword clues, visualize shapes, understand a passage of prose or come up with creative ideas. These refer to thinking skills (rather than knowledge) either in areas that are not explicitly taught (e.g. visualization of rotated shapes) or in areas in which everyone can be presumed to have had the same training (e.g. being taught to read and comprehend prose). Abilities are related to future potential, i.e. thinking skill in a particular area, rather than to prior achievement.

Personality traits, by way of contrast, reflect a person's *style* of behaviour. Words such as 'slap-dash', 'punctual', 'shy' or 'anxious' all describe how (rather than how well) a person usually behaves. These are broad generalizations, since how we behave is obviously also influenced by situations – even the bubbliest extravert is unlikely to tell risqué jokes during a funeral service. Nevertheless, like abilities, these traits may be useful in helping us to predict how individuals will probably behave *most* of the time.

Cattell (e.g. 1957) also argues that it is necessary to consider two types of 'state'. Unlike traits, states are short-lived, lasting for minutes or hours rather than months or years. Moods (or emotions, as the distinction is not clear) refer to transient feelings such as fright following a near miss when driving or joy or despair on learning one's examination results. He also identifies 'motivational states' – forces that direct our behaviour. For example, the basic biological drives (food, sex, aggression, company, etc.) can direct our behaviour, but only for a short time. After we have eaten, our desire for food declines. So these, too, are states, not traits.

Measuring traits

How might we measure individual differences in practice? We consider the measurement of states in Chapter 12 and so this section will focus on personality and ability traits. The key point about *all* psychological tests is that the individuals taking them should have precisely the same experience, no matter who administers the test or in which country it is given. Great care has to be taken to ensure that the testing situation is standardized. Time limits must be strictly followed, the test instructions must be given precisely in accordance with directions and no variation should be made to the format of the question booklet or answer sheet lest performance be affected. The way in which the test is scored (and interpreted) also has to be precisely explained and followed rigidly.

Ability tests and personality questionnaires

Some tests are designed to be administered to just one person at a time – for instance, those involving equipment or in which there is a need to build up a good testing rapport. However, most tests are designed for administration to groups of people, either in a classroom or in a computer laboratory.

Ability tests are simply samples of problems, each of which is thought to rely on a particular mental ability. For example, a test designed to assess mathematical ability might consist of some puzzles involving addition, subtraction, multiplication, fractions, geometry, simultaneous and quadratic equations, algebra, calculus, etc. However, it is not possible merely to put together a set of items and call it a test. For example, there is absolutely no guarantee that all of these items do, in fact, measure the same underlying ability – it is possible that the ability to perform addition, subtraction, multiplication and division is quite unrelated to the other, 'higher level' mathematical skills. This can be checked using the techniques discussed in Chapter 16. Ability tests involve free responses (e.g. 'what number comes next: 1, 8, 27, ...?') or multiple-choice questions ('the next number is (a) 32, (b) 36, (c) 48, (d) 64'), although other options are available. These may include asking a child to insert the most appropriate missing word (from a list) into a space in a sentence or to make up a test item in order to show that they have understood a concept. As Gulliksen (1986) has observed, psychologists and educators are not particularly creative in the ways in which they devise test items and he offers some valuable alternative formats.

Perhaps the most obvious way of measuring personality is through self-report questionnaires. However, it is important to bear in mind two points about such tests. First, it is not possible simply to devise a few questions, decide how the responses should be scored and then administer the test. The reasons for this will be covered in some detail in Chapters 15 and 19, but the basic issue is that there is no guarantee that the questions that you ask will measure the trait that you expect. Instead, it is necessary to perform some statistical analyses to validate the test before it can be used.

The second important point is that, just because someone ticks a box in a questionnaire in a certain way, this does not imply that we can accept their response at face value. To borrow an example from Cattell (1973): suppose someone strongly agreed with an item in a questionnaire that said 'I am the smartest man in town'. One can treat this piece of information in two ways. The first would be to assume that what the person said is accurate and credit them with high intelligence, and Cattell terms this Q'-data. A response is treated as Q'-data if the psychologist chooses to believe that the person has made a true, accurate observation about himself. This is common practice in social psychology, but is regarded as rather naive by those who work in the field of individual differences.

The second approach pays no heed to the apparent meaning of the answer, but only to its pattern of relation to other things. Responses to questionnaires are regarded as 'box-ticking behaviours' for statistical analysis, rather than as true, insightful descriptions of how the individual behaves. Cattell calls this 'Q-data' and argues that lack of self-insight, deliberate attempts to distort responses and other variables considered in Chapter 19 make Q'-data of little value for a scientific model of personality. This is an important point that is often misunderstood both by psychologists and by individuals who are exposed to psychological tests. *Most psychologists do not believe that people are making true statements about themselves when they answer items in personality tests.* They do not *need* to do so when the responses are analysed statistically. For example, suppose that a firm wants to use some kind of test to identify those applicants who will develop into highly successful salesmen. They may find (by asking existing sales staff to complete a questionnaire) that successful sales staff all strongly agree that 'they are the smartest man in town', while no one else holds this belief. This is an empirical fact and need not be tied to any theory. Thus it would be reasonable just to *use* this question as part of the selection procedure. No one is interested in whether the applicants are *really* the smartest individuals (logically they could not all be!), so the response is treated as Q-data rather than as Q'-data. Techniques for developing tests along similar lines are discussed in Chapters 16, 17 and 18.

This also highlights an important difference between ability/attainment traits and all other questionnaire measures of personality, mood or motivation. People can only get the items of ability/attainment tests correct by obtaining the right answers: a high score demonstrates that they *can* identify the next number in a sequence. Items in personality, mood and motivation scales, however, do not actually measure the behaviours of interest. Instead, they ask people to introspect about how they behave. This means that the answers may not be entirely accurate for several reasons. For example, if a person is asked to rate themselves on a five-point scale as to how nervous they feel in lifts (1 = totally relaxed, 5 = terrified), they may misremember their true feelings, try to paint a favourable impression of themselves or wrongly assume that, as everybody feels totally panic stricken in a lift, their experience of only moderate terror shows they are much more relaxed than the norm and should thus get a rating of 2 rather than 4.

It is possible to detect deliberate faking. Eysenck favours the use of a 'lie scale' – a list of common but socially undesirable peccadilloes embedded in the personality questionnaire, e.g. 'Did you ever cheat at a test in school?' Someone who admits to few of these is either a saint, out of touch with how they really behave or distorting their responses. However, there has been surprisingly little research into how people go about rating themselves on self-assessment items in personality, mood and motivation questionnaires.

Ratings of behaviour

The second main form of evidence stems from ratings of behaviour. Raters can be carefully trained how to classify behaviours according to a particular checklist. If they then follow individuals around for a long period (months, rather than days) in a wide variety of situations, these ratings of how people behave in their everyday life may give useful insights into their personality or abilities. Cattell terms this 'L-data' (for 'life record'). Ratings of behaviour are often used to assess personality during interviews and other selection exercises and there are probably some important characteristics (e.g. leadership quality, social skills) that are difficult to assess by other means. However, because behaviour is observed only for a short time, and in one or two situations, it is unreasonable to expect such assessments to be highly accurate – and indeed they are not (see, for example, Cronbach 1994).

Objective tests

The third form of evidence stems from analyses of the behaviour of individuals (generally in laboratory situations) who are either unaware of which aspect of their behaviour is being measured or are physically unable to alter their response. These tests should therefore overcome the principal objection to questionnaires, which is that responses can easily be faked. For example, Cattell and Warburton (1967) suggested that highly anxious people are likely to fidget more than others. **235**

In order to measure fidgeting (and hence anxiety), they fitted a special chair with microswitches and left it in a waiting room outside the laboratory. Volunteers arriving for testing sessions sat in the chair without realizing that their behaviour was being measured – a procedure that raises some interesting ethical problems.

In another even more bizarre example, equipment was used to measure volunteers' skin resistance under three conditions – while sitting relaxed in a chair, while reading the words 'frightful horror' on a card and following the firing of a starting pistol just behind the volunteer's head. (Ethical issues were not fully appreciated in the 1960s.) Here, the unfortunate volunteer would be unable to control the reaction of their autonomic nervous system, which would result in a dramatic fall in their skin resistance. Cattell termed the data from such experiments 'T-data' (since they arose from objective tests) and argues that they should form an excellent basis for measuring personality, since they are entirely objective. In particular, since individuals do not know which aspect of their behaviour is being measured or are unable to manipulate their responses, such tests are difficult to fake. However, it is very difficult to devise and develop suitable objective tests and few have so far been found to be of any practical use, as will be shown later. However, I think the basic principle is sound and I suspect that this is one area of ancient literature that will see a resurgence of interest.

Objective tests can also be used to assess ability – here, they are often known as 'performance tests'. For example, children could be timed to see how quickly they can complete jigsaws, arrange some wooden blocks to form a certain pattern or arrange a series of cartoon pictures into the most logical order. Job applicants can be presented with a sample of the types of problem that they would be expected to deal with if they were appointed and simply told to get on with solving them – the so-called 'in-basket' approach. Their performance on these tasks can later be assessed (although this is not usually a straightforward procedure). Alternatively, some specific skills can be measured, e.g. tests of manual dexterity assess the amount of time it takes applicants to use tweezers and screwdrivers to assemble objects using small nuts and bolts.

Projective tests of personality

'Projective tests' provide a fourth source of evidence about personality. In these tests, individuals are presented with some ambiguous, unclear or completely meaningless stimuli and are assumed to reveal their personalities, experiences, wants, needs, hopes, fears, etc., when describing these. The Rorschach inkblots are probably the most famous projective test. In this test, participants are shown a series of inkblots, rather similar to that shown in Figure 14.1 and are asked to describe in their own words what they 'see' in them. (Be warned that replying 'an inkblot' is classed as distinctly pathological!) Their responses are scored according to any one of about three main scoring systems and are supposed to reveal hidden depths of personality. The really odd thing about these scoring systems is that they have few compelling links to any mainstream psychological theory. For example, they code whether the person pays attention to the whole stimulus or just part of it, whether they report movement without justifying why this is thought to be clinically interesting. Because of this and the Byzantine complexity of the scoring schemes, such tests simply do not work and are now rarely used. However, 'multiple-choice' projective tests (in which respondents choose responses from a list, rather than describing the pictures in their own words) may be of some value (e.g. Holmstrom, Karp and Silber 1993).

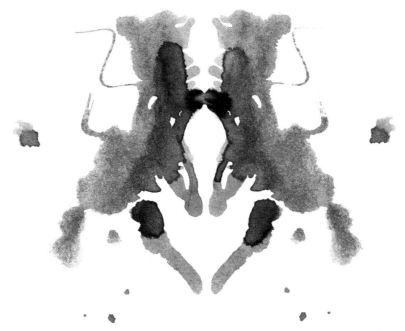

Figure 14.1 Example of an inkblot, similar to those used in Rorschach's test.

Self-assessment question 14.3

What is or are:

a. Q-data

b. L-data

c. Q'-data

d. T-data

e. projective tests?

Scoring tests

Every test must have some clearly defined technique for converting an individual's responses into some kind of score. Details of how to administer, score and interpret the test will almost always be given in the test manual. This is generally a substantial booklet that contains other information that may be useful in assessing the merit of the test, although some tests rely on journal articles to provide this information. In the vast majority of cases (projective tests being the only real exception), the score will be a number, since the test seeks to *quantify* the ability or personality trait. Multiple-choice ability tests are perhaps the easiest to score. In the vast majority of cases, **237** one point will be awarded for each correct answer. Sometimes, in an attempt to prevent guessing, one point will be deducted for each incorrect answer. Items that have not been attempted almost invariably score zero. Multiple-choice tests are generally scored either by computer (most test publishers provide a postal scoring system – at a price) or by using templates. These are usually acetate sheets that are positioned over the top of the answer sheet and which clearly indicate the correct answer for each item. The beauty of this system is that it is almost 100% accurate and requires no subjective judgements. Cattell (never one to resist a neologism) calls such scoring schemes highly 'conspective' (literally, 'looking together'), meaning that different markers will arrive at the same conclusion, as opposed to essays, for example.

Scoring free responses from ability tests can be problematic. Much depends on the quality of the test manual and the skill of the person administering the test. For example, suppose that in a comprehension test a child is asked to define the meaning of the word 'kitten' and they reply that it is 'a type of cat' – an answer that is neither completely correct nor totally wrong. Good test manuals will provide detailed instructions, with examples, to show how such answers should be scored. Where actions are timed (e.g. the amount of time to solve a jigsaw is recorded), the test manual will show how many points to award for a particular solution time.

Most personality scales do not have answers that are either right or wrong. A typical item measuring sociability might be as follows:

I enjoy big, wild parties

(a) strongly agree (b) agree (c) neutral (d) disagree (e) strongly disagree

where one of the choices (a) to (e) is marked. Since there are five possible answers that form a scale of degree of liking for parties, a response of (a) would generally be given 5 points, (b) 4 points and so on. If another item in the scale was phrased in the reverse direction, such as:

I like nothing better than a quiet night at home

(a) would receive 1 point and (e) would receive 5 points. Most personality scales urge participants to answer all of the questions and so there should be no missing items, unlike ability tests, in which time limits often mean that most individuals will fail to complete all of the items.

The scoring of most projective tests is very complex, which is why they are now rarely used. Those who wish to use these tests professionally have to serve an apprenticeship under the guidance of an experienced user of the test in order to appreciate fully the intricacies of the scoring system. Even so, the level of conspection of most projective tests is lamentably low: two different people are likely to come to vastly different conclusions when interpreting the same set of responses, a point that has been made with some force by Eysenck (1959). However, there seems to be no good reason why responses to projective tests cannot be coded objectively, using some form of content analysis – that is, specifying a large list of characteristics (e.g. 'mentions any non-human animal'), each to be coded as present or absent.

Exercise

Suppose that Jane completes a 20-item test of musical ability and gives correct responses to 15 items. What can be concluded about her musical ability?

The answer is simple – nothing. You may possibly have thought that, since there were 20 items in the test and Jane answered more than half of them correctly, this would indicate that her score was above average, but, of course, it does not, for in almost all cases, a person's score on a test depends on the level of difficulty of the test items. The items may have been so trivially easy that 99 out of 100 children might have obtained scores *above* 15 on this test, in which case Jane would be markedly *less* musical than other children of her age. To interpret the meaning of an individual's test score it is necessary to use *norms*.

Tables of test norms simply show the scores of a large, carefully selected sample of individuals. For example, the test might be given to 2035 children aged between 96 and 99 months, ensuring that the sample contains equal numbers of males and females, that they are sampled from different regions of the country (in case some regions are more musical than others) and that the proportion of children from ethnic minorities is consistent with that in the general population. A frequency distribution of these scores can be drawn up in a similar way to that shown in Table 14.1. The first column shows each possible test score, the second column shows the number of children in the sample who obtained each score, the third column shows the number of children who obtained each score *or less* and the fourth column shows this figure as a percentage – a figure known as the percentile.

Many test manuals show the percentile scores, so it is a simple matter to interpret an individual's test score – it is merely necessary to look across and discover that 62% the children scored 15 or less on the test. Sometimes, however, percentiles are not shown. If these scores follow a normal (bell-shaped) distribution whose mean and standard deviation are known, it is still straightforward to estimate the percentage of the population having a score as low as any particular test score. For example, the mean ($\overline{x}$) of the scores shown in Table 14.1 is 14.47 and the standard deviation (s) is 4.978. Suppose that we want to estimate what percentage of the population has a score of 15 or below. To do this, simply calculate:

$$z = \frac{x - \overline{x}}{s} = \frac{15 - 14.47}{4.978} = 0.106$$

A table of the standard normal distribution (found in almost any statistics book) will then show the proportion of individuals having a score lower than this value, which is 54%. This figure is similar (but not quite identical) to the one that we read directly from Table 14.1. The discrepancy arises because we assumed that the scores follow a normal distribution, whereas, in fact, they do not quite do so. However, this approach can be useful if you know the mean and standard deviation, but do not have access to the full table of norms.

Children's performance on cognitive tasks increases with age, so when evaluating a child's score on a test it is essential to compare their scores to those of other children of the same age. Norms for these tests are typically gathered for 3-month age intervals (e.g. 7 years 6 months, 7 years 9 months, etc.) to facilitate this.

Most test manuals contain several different tables of norms, e.g. those collected in different countries, separate norms for each sex and (almost invariably in the case of ability tests) at different ages. All that is necessary is to choose the table that is the most appropriate for your needs, ensuring that it is based on a large sample (a minimum of several hundred) and that care has been taken to sample individuals properly.

Self-assessment question 14.4

Why are different norms used for different ages in ability tests?

Score	Number of children with this score	Number of children with this score or lower	Percentile
0	3	3	$100 \times 3/2035 = 0.15$
1	2	3 + 2 = 5	0.25
2	6	3 + 2 + 6 = 11	0.54
3	8	19	0.93
4	8	27	1.33
5	13	40	1.97
6	17	57	2.80
7	23	80	3.93
8	25	105	5.16
9	33	138	6.78
10	57	195	9.58
11	87	282	13.86
12	133	415	20.39
13	201	616	30.27
14	293	909	44.67
15	357	1266	62.21
16	270	1536	75.48
17	198	1734	85.21
18	126	1860	91.40
19	100	1960	96.31
20	75	2035	100.00

Table 14.1 Norms for a test of musical ability, based on a (hypothetical) random sample of 2035 children aged 96 months

Finally, I ought to mention that tables of norms are only necessary for the interpretation of one individual's score on a test. Researchers will often just want to correlate scores on a test with individuals' scores on other variables (e.g. correlating intelligence with head size) or to compare the test scores of two groups (e.g. using a *t*-test to determine whether males and females are equally musical). Then it is not only unnecessary to convert the norms to percentiles, but also bad practice, for you will find that the original distribution of scores is much more bell-shaped than that of the corresponding percentiles and this is an assumption of most statistical techniques.

Using test scores to predict behaviour

The psychometric model, as defined by Cattell, proposes that if we could measure all of an individual's abilities, personality traits, motivational states and mood states, we should be able to predict their behaviour. More specifically, he suggests that the likelihood of any particular behaviour in a particular situation can be predicted by what he calls a 'specification equation'. This shows how the probability of someone acting in a particular way depends on each of the following:

- How strongly each of the traits or states predicts the behaviour of interest. This can be estimated from another sample of individuals using a statistical technique called multiple regression and these values will appear as numbers in the equation, known as 'weights'. A positive weight indicates that a high score on that trait/state increases the probability of the behaviour occurring. A near zero weight implies that the trait or state is irrelevant when predicting the behaviour. A negative weight means that the higher a person's score on a trait or state, the less likely he or she is to show the behaviour.

- The individual's score on each of the traits and states. This might be measured by psychological tests or by other techniques discussed already. Since the tests will probably have different means and different standard deviations, it is necessary to rescale the scores so that they have a mean of zero and a standard deviation of 1.0 (standardized scores or z scores) by subtracting the mean and dividing by the standard deviation.

So if the weights and an individual's scores on all traits and states are known, it should be possible to determine which of several courses of action a person is most likely to follow by plugging these numbers into the 'specification equations' for each course of action in order to determine which gives the highest value. For example, suppose that you have some prints made from a photograph and discover that the picture quality is poor. There might be three common responses to this situation:

- returning to the shop and asking for replacements

- moaning to one's friends but doing nothing

- throwing the prints in the bin.

The equation for the first action might be as follows:

$$0.7 \times \text{drive for assertion} + 0.6 \times \text{angry mood} - 0.3 \times \text{neuroticism}$$

and for the second:

$$-0.6 \times \text{drive for assertion} - 0.4 \times \text{angry mood} + 0.4 \times \text{neuroticism}$$

By inserting an individual's scores on tests of these variables into the equations, it should be possible to work out which action is the most likely. Thus knowledge of a person's traits and states may lead directly to predictions about how that individual is likely to behave.

The technique is particularly useful in applied psychology. For example, it can be used to predict how well each job applicant is likely to perform if appointed.

Obtaining and using tests

Psychological tests cannot be bought over the counter by anyone. There are two reasons for this. First, imagine what would happen if a photocopy of a commercial intelligence test reached student **241** common rooms. Groups of students would wile away some time by trying to solve the items and (given that it is a group effort with unlimited time) might well succeed in solving most items in the test. Suppose some individuals were then given the same test as part of a screening process for employment. Those who had had previous experience of the test might well be able to remember at least some of the correct answers and so would score higher than they 'should' do, reducing the effectiveness of the test in selecting the best applicants.

Second, it would be disastrous if tests were given out to people who had no training in test administration, scoring or interpretation. They may well use a test that was inappropriate for a particular application or which was manifestly useless for measuring *anything*. Even if they did choose an appropriate test they might not bother with the standard instructions, so that participants may not fully understand what they are expected to do. They may not be meticulous about time limits, which would mean that the test scores would be meaningless. They might not be able to score it, they might give the individuals who had been tested incorrect feedback and they might fail to keep the test results confidential. In other words, test users may not adhere to proper ethical standards.

In the UK, the British Psychological Society oversees a three-tier system of licensing test use in psychology. At the lowest level are test administrators, who are qualified only to administer certain group-administered tests under the direction of a more highly qualified psychologist ('test administrator's certificate'). The next level involves training in the selection, scoring and interpretation of certain ability tests ('level A qualification'). The highest level of certification involves demonstrable skill in choosing, administering and interpreting the results from personality tests ('level B'). Test publishers will only supply tests to properly qualified individuals. At the time of writing, these standards apply to occupational, educational and clinical tests. Similar systems are developing worldwide to ensure that psychological tests are not abused, although with the advent of testing over the internet, it will be far more difficult to ensure that the tests are given under ethical conditions.

The professional associations of most countries have also produced guidelines for the use of psychological tests. These provide broad principles covering the selection of appropriate tests, guidance for their administration, their scoring and the interpretation of results and some how to give feedback about test performance. One typical set of standards is shown in Appendix B and this should be studied carefully.

There are four main ways in which a suitably qualified psychologist can find out which tests are available to measure a particular aspect of personality or ability. First, one can search test publishers' catalogues – these are glossy brochures that invariably describe tests in glowing terms. Second, one can consult a book, such as Sweetland and Keyser (1991) listing brief details of tests, including the age groups for which they are suited, as well as details of publishers and prices. The problem is that neither of these sources is evaluative – they will tell you whether the test is suitable for a particular cultural or age group, but they will not help you to identify a good (valid) test. This is why it is far preferable to consult the *Mental Measurements Yearbooks*. These weighty volumes were introduced by Oscar Buros in 1938 to provide a 'consumer guide' to commercially published psychological tests. They contain indices listing tests by type, by name and by author, but the real value of these volumes lies in the critical reviews of tests, which have been written by psychometric specialists. These will often state, quite bluntly, that a particular test is so severely flawed that it should be avoided or only be considered for research purposes. It is absolutely vital to read such reviews before deciding to use any test for any purpose.

The three sources of information discussed so far cover only commercially published tests. Unfortunately, several tests are printed as appendices to journal articles rather than being commercially published. This means that they are more difficult to track down (requiring a search of the literature) and it can be even harder to find the necessary psychometric information, tables of norms and so on. The original paper containing the test should be identified using an online resource, such as the Educational Testing Service's 'test locator'. Then to find later work using this test (norms, validation studies, etc.) perform a citation search using the *Social Science Citation Index* or its computerized equivalent to find out who cites the original paper. However, when using such tests you lack the guidance of the contributors to the *Mental Measurements Yearbooks* and it is vital that you consider dispassionately whether a test is really going to suit your needs. Issues of reliability, validity and bias (discussed in Chapters 4 and 18) are of particular importance.

Summary

After having read this chapter, you should be able to describe what is meant by traits and states, describe the main types of mental test, discuss how individual test scores may be interpreted through the use of norms, outline the ethical principles associated with test use and show an understanding of how traits and states may be used to predict behaviour through the use of a specification equation.

Suggested additional reading

If you have not already done so, you should consult Appendix B of this book (or its equivalent) in order to learn about standards of testing procedure. You may find it interesting to browse through the *Mental Measurement Yearbooks* and search out some reviews, e.g. reviews of the Rorschach test, Sixteen-Personality-Factor test, Lüscher Colour Test, Adjective Checklist and/or the Wechsler Adult Intelligence Scale. You may also find it interesting to glance at any standard psychometrics or occupational psychology textbook (e.g. Cronbach 1994) to see what some typical test items look like or to practice scoring and interpreting tests (as well as satisfying your natural curiosity) by testing your own personality or ability with Eysenck (1962) or Eysenck and Wilson (1976) or searching the internet for Lew Goldberg's 'International Personality Item Pool'. This is a collection of items that assess many of the main personality traits. Unlike commercial tests, they are available at no cost.

You may also be interested in taking some online tests. Think carefully about the quality of the questions and look for evidence that the interpretation of scores that you are offered is based on a proper set of norms – rather than on some arbitrary assumption of the test constructor (e.g. that the 'average' score on a 30-item test will be 15).

Answers to self-assessment questions

SAQ 14.1

a. Any score from a psychological test or other device that is used as if it measured some theoretical concept.

b. A person's score on a test of appropriate difficulty consisting of whatever items are thought to make up the concept of 'French-speaking ability', e.g. items measuring knowledge of colloquialisms and vocabulary and ratings of quality of accent and fluency. The measurement of meanness is a much more difficult proposition. Direct self-report questions will probably not work – who would admit to this quality? Asking if any regular payments to a charity are made from bank accounts may be more useful. Ratings by friends may be a possibility, as may 'objective tests' (e.g. asking for a loan, or observing behaviour in the vicinity of a beggar). However, most of these measures could indicate 'poverty' instead of 'meanness'.

SAQ 14.2

a., c., e.

SAQ 14.3

a. Responses to questionnaire items that are analysed in ways that do not assume the truth of what the respondent is saying.

b. Ratings of behaviour.

c. Responses to questionnaires that are analysed as if the respondents are making some true comment about themselves. For example, if a person strongly agrees that they are happy, the psychologist would conclude that they are, indeed, happy.

d. Data from objective tests of personality – tests whose purpose is hidden from the test participant or in which the test participant physically cannot alter his or her response.

e. Personality tests in which an individual is asked to describe or interpret an ambiguous stimulus (e.g. a picture, an inkblot or a sound). The rationale for such tests is that the way in which the stimuli are interpreted will provide some insight into the individual's personality, needs and experience. Scoring the responses to such tests is notoriously difficult, as Eysenck has shown.

SAQ 14.4

Because abilities tend to increase with age. In order to determine whether a particular child is performing markedly better or worse than 'the average child', it is important to compare them with other children of the same age. Almost all abilities increase with age as a result of physiological maturation and education. Suppose that a test had a table of norms that covered a fairly broad range of ages (e.g. children aged 6–10). It would not be possible to use these to interpret a child's score, since an 'average' (or median) score could indicate a 6 year old who was performing much better than most 6 year olds, an 8 year old of average ability or a 10 year old whose performance was below average. The best ability tests give norms at 3-month intervals (e.g. one table for children aged 74–76 months, another table for children aged 77–79 months, etc.).

References

Cattell, R. B. (1957). *Personality and Motivation Structure and Measurement*. Yonkers, NY: New World.

Cattell, R. B. (1973). *Personality and Mood by Questionnaire*. San Francisco: Jossey-Bass.

Cattell, R. B. and Warburton, F. W. (1967). *Objective Personality and Motivation Tests: A Theoretical Foundation and Practical Compendium*. Urbana: University of Illinois Press.

244   Cronbach, L. J. (1994). *Essentials of Psychological Testing* (5th edn). New York: HarperCollins.

Eysenck, H. J. (1959). Review of the Rorschach inkblots. In O. K. Buros (ed.), *Fifth Mental Measurement Yearbook*. Highland Park, NJ: Gryphon Press.

Eysenck, H. J. (1962). *Know Your Own IQ*. Harmondsworth: Penguin.

Eysenck, H. J. and Wilson, G. D. (1976). *Know Your Own Personality*. Baltimore, MD: Penguin.

Gulliksen, H. (1986). Perspective on educational-measurement. *Applied Psychological Measurement 10*(2), 109–32.

Holmstrom, R. W., Karp, S. A. and Silber, D. E. (1993). Relationship between the Apperceptive Personality Test and verbal intelligence in a university sample. *Psychological Reports 73*(2), 75–8.

Sweetland, R. C. and Keyser, D. J. (1991). *Tests: A Comprehensive Reference for Assessments in Psychology, Education, and Business* (3rd edn). Austin, TX: Pro-Ed.

15 Reliability and validity of psychological tests

Background

Chapter 14 made the point that individuals' scores on psychological tests are often used as operational definitions of abstract psychological concepts. It is thus vitally important to be able to check that the scores on any psychological test have little random measurement error associated with them (high reliability) and that the inferences drawn from test scores are accurate (high validity).

Recommended prior reading

Chapter 14.

Introduction

This chapter covers some basic principles about measurement – both in the physical world and when assessing individual differences. In particular, we shall examine the concepts of systematic and random errors of measurement and see how these principles lead naturally to an important aspect of psychometrics known as *reliability theory*. Finally, we shall consider how we can determine whether inferences drawn about the meaning of a particular score on a particular test are correct: that is, whether the test is *valid*.

All measuring instruments share three basic principles. The first is that they should assess only one aspect of an object (person) at a time. For example, when an object is weighed, the reading shown on a set of scales is influenced only by the object's mass – not by its colour, density, shape or any other characteristic. The second is that there should be as little random error as possible associated with the measurement. For example, trying to weigh a struggling cat whose true weight is 4 kg on a set of bathroom scales which can only be read to an accuracy in the order of ±1 kg will produce a reading that is likely to be quite a lot higher or lower than the cat's true weight. It would be better to weigh the relaxed or sedated cat on a set of scales that can be read to an accuracy of 0.01 kg or so. The third basic principle is one that we usually take for granted in the physical sciences – that the instrument actually measures precisely what it claims to. We assume that a rule actually measures length, that a set of scales measure mass, that an electronic blood pressure meter actually measures blood pressure, rather than anything else. If this assumption is wrong, we will draw an incorrect inference about the meaning of what we have measured. For example, if the electronic blood pressure monitor actually measures wrist diameter, not blood pressure, then we would incorrectly infer that someone with a higher reading on this meter had higher blood pressure than did someone else.

When applied to psychological tests, the principle that a scale should measure only one trait or state is known as 'unidimensionality'. The principle that scores of test should be accurate, in the sense that they are little influenced by random errors of measurement, is known as 'reliability'. The principle that the inferences drawn about the meaning of a particular test score should be correct is known as 'validity'. Psychometrics is a branch of statistical theory that has been developed solely to produce tests that are unidimensional, reliable and valid.

It is also necessary to ensure that the numbers that we measure are suitable for the types of mathematical operation that we perform on them. For example, if you coded the colours of fruit as red = 1, green = 2 and yellow = 3, there is nothing to stop you computing a number from the sum of a lemon, a lime and a banana: you could even say that these three fruits are equal to eight red apples if you want to. But these mathematical operations make no sense at all: the numbers that you have measured are not suitable for mathematical operations such as this. You may feel that this point is obvious – but Michell (1997) has argued strongly that it is inappropriate to compute scores from questionnaires etc. – or indeed perform any mathematical operations without first demonstrating that the data are suitable for this. There is not space to go into these issues here, but they certainly merit some serious thought.

Random errors of measurement

Think back to the example of weighing a struggling cat using bathroom scales. Since the amount of error with which the scales can be read is large compared with the weight of the cat (4kg), it is clear that if we weight the cat once by this method, then the reading we get might be quite a lot higher or lower than the cat's true weight. How can we improve matters? It may be useful to break down the measurement that we obtain into two components – the thing we are trying to measure (the true weight of the cat) plus measurement error:

$$\text{reading obtained on any occasion} = \text{true weight} + \text{measurement error}$$

The reason this is useful is that it allows us to develop some statistical principles for reducing the amount of measurement error. In fact, it is possible to deduce much of this from common sense: if we believe that the scales are accurate then it seems reasonable to assume that the error that distorts our attempt to weigh the cat is random. That is, that we are (a) as likely to overestimate as underestimate the cat's weight on any occasion, and (b) the *amount* by which we underestimate its weight is likely to be similar to the amount by which we underestimate its weight on another occasion: the distribution of errors is likely to be symmetric rather than skewed. These two assumptions tell us that the mean for the error term is likely to be zero. (If the error term did *not* have a mean of zero this would imply that we awe will systematically over- or underestimate the weight of the cat – as would happen, for example, if the 'zeroing' knob at the back of the scales was wrongly adjusted.) Likewise, it seems more probable that we will over- or underestimate its weight by a small amount (e.g. 1 kg) than a large amount (e.g. 3kg). So if we plot a graph (histogram) showing how often we over- or underestimated the cat's weight by a particular amount, it will probably resemble a bell-shaped curve (normal distribution) with a mean of zero. The width of the curve (its standard deviation) reflects how much measurement error there is; the wider the curve, the more error there is in reading the scales. We would like the standard deviation of the measurement error to be as close as possible to zero, for this implies that a single measurement of the cat's weight is likely to be very close indeed to its true weight.

Those with a background in the physical sciences will know that even when measurement errors (such in reading a meter, or comparing two colours) is substantial, there is a simple method for **247** obtaining a more accurate reading. Assuming that the measurements we obtain are independent of each other, because we assume that the errors form a normal distribution, we simply need to measure the object several times and average the results. We could weigh the cat ten times knowing that when we do so, the average of the ten readings is much more likely to be close to the cat's true weight than is any one reading – the errors tend to cancel one another out. So measuring something on several occasions and averaging these measurements is a surefire way of improving the accuracy of our measurement. Can we apply this principle when measuring ability, mood, personality, etc.?

Given that repeated measurements reduce the amount of error in any assessment, it would seem logical to construct a test simply by simply repeating the same item over and over again. In the physical sciences (above the atomic level, at any rate) the act of measuring something does not appreciably influence the quantity being measured. The reading on the scales on any occasion reflects only the weight of the cat plus measurement error; it is not influenced by whether we under- or overestimated the cat's weight on the previous weighing. However, the same is not true in psychological tests. Once a person has solved a puzzle in an ability test, they are going to remember the solution if given exactly the same puzzle again. If a person is asked to rate how much they fear the dark, they will simply remember what they answered if asked the same question in on a second occasion: the second response will be influenced by the response they gave on the first occasion. The measurements are not independent if the same item is repeated several times in a test. So one reason why it is not possible to construct a test by repeating exactly the same item over and over again is because these measurements will not be independent of each other, as required by the statistical theory underlying the averaging of scores.

Systematic errors of measurement

There is also a second reason why it is inappropriate to repeat the same item over and over in a test. Single items in psychological tests are not unidimensional: they do *not* measure a single trait plus measurement error. The way we respond to an item is influenced by (a) the trait or state we with to assess, (b) random error and (c) several systematic errors. Systematic errors are simply traits or states other than the one we are trying to assess. Some of these may simply be personality factors or ability factors. For example, way in which people respond to the item 'Do you often procrastinate?: 1 yes/2 uncertain/3 no' will be influenced both the personality trait of conscientiousness and by their vocabulary, as some people may not know the meaning of the word 'procrastinate'. We return to systematic errors in Chapter 19. However, the key principle to note is that while readings on physical measuring devices (rules, scales etc.) are influenced by only a single characteristic of the thing being assessed (its mass or length), the way in which a person responds to an item in a test will be influenced by a whole bundle of different ability traits, personality traits, moods, motivational factors and response biases. Individual test items are not unidimensional.

Suppose that you asked a student the question 'do you enjoy drunken parties?' in a personality questionnaire and they then responded by marking a five-point scale ranging from 'strongly agree' to 'strongly disagree'. Try to make a list of half a dozen factors that might influence the response they mark.

Apart from those variables that are likely to show little variation within the group (such as being able to understand all of the words in the sentence), my list includes the following:

- their level of extraversion (a personality trait), which is what the item was designed to measure

- the number of parties they have recently attended (their liver may need a rest)

- their age

- their religious beliefs/ethnic background

- social desirability – some students may find it difficult to admit that they would much rather be working in the university library than partying and so would tend to overstate their true liking for parties

- the context in which the question is asked – a potential employer and a psychology student might well obtain different answers to this question

- the student's impression of what is being assessed – for example, one person may read the question, assume that it is being used to assess whether they have a drinking problem and answer it accordingly, whereas someone else may believe that it measures their level of extraversion and so answer it accordingly

- the way in which a person uses the five-point scale – some individuals use scores of 1 and 5 quite freely, while others never use the extremes of the scale

- a tendency to agree (acquiescence)

- the student's mood

- random error – if you asked the student the same question a couple of minutes later you might obtain a slightly different result.

Your list probably contains other important variables, too. A whole host of these 'nuisance factors' determines how an individual will respond to a single item in a personality test and we shall consider some of these in Chapter 19. Much the same applies to items in ability tests. Performance here might be affected by anxiety, luck in guessing the correct answer, misunderstanding of what is expected, social pressures (deliberately underperforming so as not to stand out from the group), perceived importance of obtaining a high mark and so on, as well as ability. We could make a similar case for ratings of behaviour (when aspects of the rater's personality and sensitivity would also affect the ratings made). Thus every piece of data collected when assessing individual differences is likely to be influenced by a vast number of factors, as shown in Figure 15.1.

The variables at the top of Figure 15.1 are systematic influences: one of these will reflect what the item is supposed to assess, while the others will be unwelcome systematic errors of measurement. The 'specific variance' component on the right will be discussed in Chapters 16 and 17. The measurement error term refers at the bottom of the figure refers to random errors of measurement. It is possible to conduct experiments in order to determine the extent to which each of these variables influences an individual's response to this particular question. If the question is designed to measure the trait of extraversion, it will be a 'good' item if the effects of all the other variables are small, in much the same way as a 'good' measure of length is influenced by distance and not temperature, air pressure or anything else. Unfortunately, in psychology, this is not the case. It is almost impossible to find a personality test item for which the personality trait accounts **249**

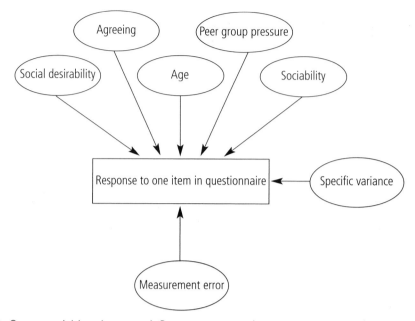

Figure 15.1 Some variables that may influence a person's response to one item on a personality inventory.

more than 20 to 30% of the variation in individuals' responses to the items. (We shall see later in this chapter how it is possible to estimate this amount by correlating scores on an item with estimates of people's true scores on a test.) Most of the variation is due to factors other than the one the item is supposed to assess.

This is rather embarrassing. It seems that it is difficult or impossible to devise items that are pure measures of a trait, since individuals' responses to a single test item are going to be influenced by a whole host of traits, states, attitudes, moods and luck. It also provides a second reason why it is nonsensical to construct a psychological test by repeatedly administering the same item over and over again. Unlike random errors, these systematic errors will *not* tend to cancel one another out when measurements are repeated. Suppose that an object is measured several times using an instrument whose reading is influenced by both the temperature and the mass of an object. Averaging several reading from the object will reduce the influence of random errors of measurement, but the average reading will still measure a mixture of temperature and mass. It will not be unidimensional.

However, there is a way round this problem. Instead of taking multiple measurements using the same instrument, it is possible to take one measurement from each of several different instruments and combine the scores. It is possible to devise several different items measuring extraversion, each of which is affected by a *different* set of 'nuisance factors'. Chapter 4 shows that Eysenck views extraverts as being sociable, optimistic, talkative and impulsive, etc., so it would be possible to phrase questions to measure these variables, too. An item such as 'do you keep quiet on social occasions?' would be influenced by a number of nuisance factors, only a few of which would be the same as for the first item. Thus if a questionnaire were constructed from a number of items, each affected by a different set of nuisance factors, the influence of the nuisance factors would tend to cancel out, while the influence of the trait would accumulate. For example, in order to stop individual differences in acquiescence (agreeing with items) from being confounded with scores on the trait of interest, it is simply necessary to ensure that about half of the items in a test are phrased so that agreeing with it implies a high score on the trait ('I enjoy drunken parties' for extraversion) while half of the items are phrased in the opposite direction ('I enjoy spending time on my own'). Thus in order to produce a more accurate measure of a trait, we need to average responses to several different items, *each of which is influenced by a different set of 'nuisance factors'*. It is important to remember this assumption, as many people write items that are so similar in content that they will be influenced by the same nuisance factors. For example:

1. Item 1. At times I think I am no good at all.

2. Item 2. All in all, I am inclined to feel that I am a failure.

3. Item 3. I feel I do not have much to be proud of.

4. Item 4. I certainly feel useless at times.

These items are taken from a real test that has over 1000 citations in social psychology, the Rosenberg inventory, which I briefly mention in Chapter 6. It is supposed to measure self-esteem, but it seems to be flawed on two counts. First, as the items are paraphrases of each other, people will remember how they answered previous items and are *bound* to answer them all similarly because they all say the same thing. Second, because they all say the same thing, each will be influenced by the same set of 'nuisance factors' (for example, 'no' seems to be the socially desirable response for all of them), so when we add together peoples scores on the items, the test score will not be unidimensional – and this is precisely what has been found.

Contrast these items with the following:

1. Item 1. I believe that insurance schemes are a good idea.

2. Item 2. I would take drugs that may have strange effects.

3. Item 3. I sometimes tease animals.

These three items (from another real test) ask genuinely different questions: people's responses to the first would not determine how they responded to the other two. The first item is scored in the opposite direction to the other two, to reduce the effects of acquiescence. And because the items vary so much in content, each is likely to be affected by a different set of 'nuisance factors' meaning that when the scores are added together these will tend to cancel out, thus leading to a test score that measures a single dimension of personality.

Reliability

Domain-sampling model

Suppose that we want to assess spelling ability. As a huge dictionary contains a list of all the words in the language, it would be possible (in theory) to ask people to spell every single word in the language. The score they obtained would be a completely accurate measure of their spelling ability, as it is based on every word in the language (the complete *domain* of items): it is known as their *true score*. Of course, administering all these words is highly impractical: it would take weeks or months to do. It makes sense to try to estimate what people's true scores on the spelling test would be through giving them tests based on samples of words taken from the dictionary. For **251** example, one could repeatedly stick a pin in the dictionary in order to produce a random sample of words which could be given to a large sample of people. If the test is effective, people's scores on the test should correlate very substantially with their true scores – the scores that they obtained when given all words in the domain.

The square of this correlation between peoples scores on a test and the scores that they obtain if they are given every possible item that could conceivably be written to measure the topic is known as the *reliability* of a test. It shows how much random measurement error is associated with people's scores on the test, a reliability of 1.0 indicating that that the test is completely free from measurement error. A term called the 'standard error of measurement' (SEM) reflects this directly. If scores on a test have a standard deviation of s and a reliability of α, the standard error of measurement is given by the formula:

$$SEM = s\sqrt{1 - \alpha}$$

So if scores on a test correlate 0.8 with the true score (implying a reliability of 0.64: see below) and the standard deviation of its scores is 10, its SEM is 6. The SEM is important since it allows us to infer how close to a person's true score their test score is: there is only a 0.05 chance that their true score will be more than 2 SEMs away from their observed score. So if a person scores 72 on a test with reliability of 0.64 and a standard deviation of 10, we can be fairly confident that their true score lies somewhere between $72 - (2 \times 6)$ and $72 + (2 \times 6)$ – that is, between about 60 and 84. (The '2' is because we know that about 95% of the scores lie plus or minus two standard deviations from the mean of a normal distribution.) Although this is the method advocated in many test handbooks it is technically not quite correct: see Nunnally (1978: 218) if you ever plan to do this in real life.

Although the idea of the domain sampling model is most obviously applicable when the number of potential items is finite (e.g. the number of words in the dictionary: the number of two-digit addition problems), the same principles apply even when the number of items that could be written is near infinite. For example, a test measuring anxiety is a sample of all the (many!) items that could conceivably have been written to measure the many aspects of anxiety. A test of mathematical ability is a sample of the near infinite number of mathematical items that could possibly have been written. The concept of reliability is useful in these cases as it is not necessary to actually compute the correlation between the true score and the scores on the test to estimate the reliability of a test. Statistics such as 'coefficient alpha' give us a good approximation of what this correlation would be.

Coefficient alpha

I earlier showed that, while an individual test item is a poor measure of a trait, a much better estimate of the value of a trait can be obtained if we add up the scores on a number of items, each of which measures some different aspect of the trait. Suppose some items are written to measure a certain trait and are then administered to about 200 people. Specialized computer programs (such as the SPSS 'reliability' procedure) can be used to calculate a statistic from these data that various authors have referred to as the 'alpha', 'coefficient alpha', 'KR20', 'Cronbach's alpha' or 'internal consistency'. It is amazingly important. For long tests, coefficient alpha is a very close approximation to the square of correlation between individuals' scores on a particular mental test and their 'true score' on a trait (Nunnally 1978). Thus a coefficient alpha of 0.7 implies a correlation of $\sqrt{.7}$ or 0.84 between scores on the test and individuals' true scores, whereas an alpha value of 0.9 implies that the correlation is as high as 0.95. Since the whole purpose of using psychological tests is to try to achieve as close an approximation as possible to a person's true score on a trait, it follows from this that tests should have a high value of alpha. The details of how alpha is calculated for a particular set of data need not concern us here, but can be found in most psychometrics texts. The key point is that it is a statistic, calculated from data, that can be used to draw some important inferences about the size of the relationship between the test score and the true score – even though we cannot measure the true score.

As you might expect from reading the previous section, coefficient alpha is influenced by two things:

- the *average size of the correlation* between the test items. Since we assumed in the previous section that different test items are affected by different 'nuisance factors', the only reason why individuals' responses to any pair of items *should* be correlated is because both of these items measure the same underlying trait. A large correlation between a pair of items thus indicates that they are both good measures of the trait; a smaller correlation suggests that responses to one or both of the items are substantially influenced by random error or by 'nuisance factors' such as social desirability, other personality or ability traits, etc.

- the *number of items* in the scale. Again, I pointed out that the whole purpose of building a scale from several test items is to try to ensure that the nuisance factors cancel out. It should hopefully be obvious that the more items there are in a scale, the more likely it is that these nuisance factors will all cancel out. The Spearman–Brown formula (given in any standard psychometrics text) is useful here. It allows one to predict how the reliability of the scale will increase or decrease if the number of items in the scale is changed.

A widely applied rule of thumb states that a test should not be used for any purpose if it has an alpha value below 0.7, and that it should not be used for important decisions about an *individual* (e.g. for assessment of the need for remedial education) unless its alpha value is above 0.9.

Unfortunately, if items are written so that they share the same 'nuisance factors' (as in the example of the self-esteem scale given earlier) the correlations between the items will be inflated and the value of alpha will be high. It is up to the person writing the items to ensure that the only possible reason why the responses to any pair of items should be correlated together is because of the underlying personality or ability trait that they are both assumed to measure and not because they are influenced by similar response biases or other traits. Unfortunately, some approaches to test construction, e.g. that advocated by Costa and McCrae (1992) virtually guarantee that many artificially high correlations will be generated and so will lead to an overestimate of alpha.

Self-assessment question 15.1

Five test items designed to measure extraversion were given to a large sample of people. The correlations between the test items were calculated, and are shown in Table 15.1.

a. What does the correlation between any pair of items show?

b. Which item seems to be the least effective measure of the trait?

c. Suppose that you calculated alpha from the correlations shown in Table 13.2 and found that it was lower than 0.7. What might you do?

	Item 1	Item 2	Item 3	Item 4	Item 5
Item 1	1.0				
Item 2	−0.02	1.0			
Item 3	0.10	0.28	1.0		
Item 4	0.15	0.31	0.24	1.0	
Item 5	0.12	0.25	0.27	0.36	1.0

Table 15.1 Correlations between five hypothetical test items, each of which has been scored such that a high score indicates the extraverted response

It is also important to ensure that the sample of individuals whose test scores are used to compute alpha is similar to the group on whom the test will be used. It is pointless to find an alpha value of 0.9 with university students and then conclude that the test will be suitable for use with the members of the general population, for university students are not a random sample of the population, as they are generally young, academically talented, middle class, literate and numerate. Again, there is no numerical way to determine whether a test that has a high alpha value in one sample will also work in another group – it is a matter of using common sense. I would certainly be wary about assuming that a personality test, developed using American college students, will work for the general population of the UK (or vice versa), but not everyone shares these misgivings. It is safest to calculate alpha whenever one uses a test, although this does presuppose that a large sample of people will be tested (Nunnally 1978 recommends a minimum of 200).

There are also other ways of estimating the reliability of a test.

Alternate-forms reliability

This involves constructing two different tests by randomly sampling items from the domain. For example, two spelling tests, Test A and Test B may each be constructed by randomly sampling 100 words from the dictionary. As these tests are the same length and are constructed in the same way, you would expect each of the test scores to show the same correlation with the true score: $r_{A,true} = r_{B,true}$: the tests will have the same reliability, which is the square of this correlation. We cannot easily measure the correlation between scores on the test and the true score. However, we can administer both versions of the test to the same group of people and work out the correlation between Test A and Test B, $r_{A,B}$. The reliability of either test can be shown to be estimated by $r_{A,B}$. So if two tests are constructed by randomly sampling items from some domain and are found to correlate 0.8 in when administered to a large sample of people, we may conclude that reliability of the test will be 0.8.

Parallel-forms reliability

This is similar to alternate-form reliability, except that it involves two tests that have been developed to have items of similar difficulty and so the distribution of scores on the two versions of the test will be the same. In order to create two parallel forms of a test, items are administered to a large sample of people and pairs of items with similar content and difficulty are identified. For example, both may involve the solution of seven-letter anagrams, the answer being a word with a similar frequency of occurrence in the language and only about 25% of the sample will be able to solve each one. One item will then be assigned to Form A of the test and the other to Form B. These two tests are marketed separately and (in theory) it should not matter which one is used for a particular application, since care is generally taken to ensure that the two versions produce similar distributions of scores (thus allowing the same tables of norms to be used for each form of the test). If both tests measure the same trait, one would expect a high positive correlation between individuals' scores on the two forms of the test, just as with alternate forms reliability. This correlation is known as the parallel-forms reliability. However, as relatively few tests *have* parallel forms, it is rarely used.

Split-half reliability

In the early days of testing, when reliability coefficients had to be calculated by hand, calculating coefficient alpha was time consuming and so a shortcut was developed to estimate alpha. Instead of adding together all of the items in a test to derive a total score, two scores were calculated – one based on the odd-numbered test items and the other on the even-numbered items. These two scores were then correlated together and after applying the Spearman–Brown formula (since the set of the odd or even items is only half as long as the full test), this yielded the *split-half reliability*. The problem is that there is no compelling reason why one should take the odd and even numbered items. Why not divide the test into three parts rather than two? Or compare the first half with the last half? There are obviously a number of different ways of dividing up the items to perform a split-half analysis and each will probably give a different result – yet there is no logical or statistical reason for preferring one method of subdividing the test to another. Split-half reliability lacks the clear statistical rationale of alpha. There seems to be no good reason to use it today.

Test–retest reliability

Test–retest reliability, sometimes known as *temporal stability*, provides us with another way of estimating the reliability of a test. As its name suggests, it checks whether trait scores stay more or less constant over time. Most tests are designed to measure traits such as extraversion, numerical ability or neuroticism and the definition of a trait stresses that it is a relatively enduring disposition. This implies that individuals should have similar scores when they are tested on two occasions provided that:

- nothing significant has happened to them in the interval between the two tests (e.g. no emotional crises, developmental changes or significant educational experiences that might affect the trait)

- the experience of sitting the test at Time 1 does not influence the scores obtained at Time 2 other than via the trait which the test assesses: for example, people cannot remember their answers to individual questions.

If a test shows that a child is a genius one month and of average intelligence the next, either the concept of intelligence is a state rather than a trait or the test is flawed.

Assessment of test–retest reliability typically involves testing the same group of people on two occasions, which are generally spaced at least a month apart (in order to minimize the likelihood of people remembering their previous answers), yet not *too* far apart (in case developmental **255** changes, learning or other life events affect individuals' positions on the trait). Test–retest reliability is simply the correlation between these two sets of scores. If it is high (implying that individuals have similar levels of the trait on both occasions) it can be argued that the trait is stable and that the test is likely to be a good measure of the trait. The problem is, of course, that the test–retest reliability is based on the total score – it says nothing about how people perform on individual items. Whereas alpha shows whether a set of items measures some single, underlying trait, a set of items that had nothing in common could still have perfect test–retest reliability. For an example of a test score that is most certainly *not* unidimensional, suppose you asked someone to add their house number, their shoe size and their year of birth on two separate occasions. This statistic would show impressive test–retest reliability, although the three items have nothing in common. Test retest reliability is therefore of little use in showing the extent to which a set of items have a common core; that is, measure the same trait.

Generalizability theory

Generalizability theory (Cronbach, Gleser, Nanda and Rajaratnam 1972) is another approach to reliability theory. A good account may be found in Cronbach (1994). This theory essentially requires investigators to be very precise about what inference is to be drawn from a set of test scores. It attempts to identify all of the sources of error that may arise in an assessment, rather as shown for individual test items in Figure 15.1. It seeks to assess each of these independently, and to correct each individual's score for the influence of these 'nuisance factors'. Suppose that some children completed a spelling test on two occasions – the same data could be analysed in many ways, e.g. to estimate the temporal stability of the spelling test, to determine how consistently children perform in spelling or to chart whether the spelling performance of the class has increased. The problem is that determining (and measuring) all of these variables is a very involved and ponderous procedure and since the variables will probably shift in importance from one sample to another (pensioners may try less hard to cheat on ability tests than students, for example), it has not been of great practical use.

Self-assessment question 15.2

a. What are the KR20 and the internal consistency of a test?

b. Why is it unwise to paraphrase the same item a number of times when designing a test?

c. What does the standard error of measurement tell you?

d. Suppose you have two tests that claim to assess anxiety. Test 1 has a reliability of 0.81, and Test 2 a reliability of 0.56. What will be the correlation between each of these tests and the true score? What is the largest correlation that you are likely to obtain if you correlate scores on Test 1 with scores on Test 2?

Validity

At the start of this chapter, we set out three criteria for adequate measurement. These are that scores should only reflect one property of the thing (person) being assessed (unidimensionality), that they should be free of measurement error (show high reliability) and that the scores on the measuring instrument should reflect the thing that the test claims to measure: a test purporting to measure anxiety should measure anxiety and not something else. The first two of these issues were dealt with in the previous section. The validity of a test addresses the third issue, that of whether scores on a test actually measure what they are supposed to.

We have seen that reliability theory can show whether or not a set of test items seem to measure some underlying trait. What it cannot do is shed any light on the *nature* of that trait, for just because an investigator *thinks* that a set of items should measure a particular trait, there is no guarantee that they actually do so. In the early 1960s a considerable literature built up concerning the 'Repression-Sensitization Scale' (R-S Scale). This scale was designed to measure the extent to which individuals used 'perceptual defence' – that is, tended to be less consciously aware of emotionally threatening phrases than neutral phrases when these were presented for very brief periods of time. The items formed a reasonably reliable scale, so everyone just assumed that this scale measured what it claimed to do – it generated a lot of research. Then Joy (1963), cited by Kline (1981), found that scores on this test showed a correlation of –0.91 with a well-established test of social desirability. The maximum correlation between two tests is limited by the size of their reliabilities, so a correlation of –0.91 actually implied that *all* of the variance in the R-S Scale could be accounted for by social desirability. It was not measuring anything new at all.

This tale conveys an important message. Even if a set of items appears to form a scale, it is not possible to tell what that scale measures just by looking at the items. Instead, it is necessary to determine this empirically by a process known as test validation.

A test is said to be valid if it does what it claims to do, either in terms of theory or in practical application. For example, a test that is marketed as a measure of anxiety for use in the general UK population should measure anxiety and not social desirability, reading skill, sociability or any other unrelated traits. A test that is used to select the job applicants who are most likely to perform best in a particular occupation really *should* be able to identify the individual(s) who will perform best. However, while the reliability of a test can be expressed as a certain number (for a particular sample of individuals), the validity of a test also depends on the purpose of testing. For example, a test that is valid for selecting computer programmers from the UK student population may not be useful for selecting sales executives. A test that is a valid measure of depression when used by a medical practitioner will probably not be valid for screening job applicants, since most individuals will realize the purpose of the test and distort their responses.

It follows that reliability is necessary for a test to be valid, since low reliability implies that the test is not measuring *any* single trait. However, high reliability itself does not guarantee validity, since as shown earlier this depends entirely on how, why and with whom the test is used.

There are four main ways of establishing whether a test is valid.

Face validity

Face validity merely checks that the test looks as if it measures what it is supposed to. The R-S Scale debacle described earlier shows that scrutinizing the content of items is no guarantee that the test will measure what it is intended to. Despite this, some widely used tests (particularly in social psychology) are constructed by writing a few items, ensuring that alpha is high (which is generally the case because the items are paraphrases of one another) and then piously assuming that the scale measures the concept that it was designed to assess. It is *vital* to ensure that a test has better credentials than this before using it. It is necessary to establish that the test has some **257** predictive power and/or that it correlates as expected with other tests before one can conclude that the test really does measure what it claims to.

Content validity

Very occasionally it is possible to construct a test that *must*, by definition, be valid. For example, suppose that one wanted to construct a spelling test. Since, by definition, the dictionary contains the whole domain of items, any procedure that produces a representative sample of words from this dictionary has to be a valid test of spelling ability. This is what is meant by content validity. To give another example, occupational psychologists sometimes use 'workbasket' approaches in selecting staff, where applicants are presented with a sample of the activities that are typically performed as part of the job and their performance on these tasks is in some way evaluated. These exercises are not psychological tests in the strict sense, but the process can be seen to have some content validity. The problem is that it is rarely possible to define the domain of potential test items this accurately. How would one determine the items that could possibly be included in a test of numerical ability, for example? Thus the technique is not often used in ability tests, although it can be useful in constructing tests of attainment, where the assessment shows how many facts a person has assimilated following a course of instruction.

Construct validity

One useful way of checking whether a test measures what it claims to assess is to perform thoughtful experiments. Suppose that a test is designed to measure anxiety in UK university students. How might its validity be checked through experiment?

The first approach (sometimes called *convergent validation*) is to check that the test scores relate to other things as expected. For example, if there are other widely used tests of anxiety on the market, a group of students could be given both tests and the two sets of scores correlated together. A large positive correlation would suggest that the new scale is valid. Alternatively, the test could be administered to a group of students who claim to have a phobia about spiders, before and after showing them a tarantula. If their scores increase, then the test might indeed measure anxiety. The basic aim of these convergent validations is to determine whether the test scores vary as would be expected on theoretical grounds. Unfortunately, a failure to find the expected relationships might be due to some problem, either with the test or with the other measures. For example, the *other* test of anxiety may not be valid or some of the individuals who say that they are phobic about spiders may not be. However, if scores on a test do appear to vary in accordance with theory, it seems reasonable to conclude that the test is valid.

Studies of *divergent validity* check that the test does not seem to measure any traits with which it should, in theory, be unrelated. For example, the literature claims that anxiety is unrelated to intelligence, socioeconomic status, social desirability and so on. Thus if a test that purportedly measured anxiety actually showed a massive correlation with any of these variables, doubt would be raised as to whether it really measured anxiety at all.

Predictive validity

Psychological tests are very often used to predict behaviour and their success in doing so is known as their predictive validity. For example, a test might be given to adolescents in an attempt to predict who would suffer from schizophrenia later in life or a psychological test might be used to select the most promising candidate for a post as a salesperson – the test would have predictive validity if it could be shown that the people with the highest scores on the test made the most sales. This process sounds remarkably straightforward, but in practice tends not to be.

The first problem is the nature of the criterion against which the test is to be evaluated. For although noting a diagnosis of schizophrenia or the volume of sales achieved is quite straightforward, many occupations lack a single criterion. A university lecturer's job is a case in point. Mine involves teaching, administration and research, committee work, the supervision of postgraduate students, providing informal help with statistics and programming, supporting and encouraging undergraduates and so on – the list is a long one and it is not obvious how most of these activities can be evaluated or their relative importance determined. In other cases (e.g. where employees are rated by their line manager), different assessors may apply quite different standards and so a higher score need not necessarily indicate better performance.

A second problem is known as 'restriction of range'. Selection systems generally operate through several stages, e.g. initial psychometric testing to reduce the number of applicants to manageable proportions, followed by interviews and more detailed psychological assessments of individuals who get through the first stage. Applicants who are eventually appointed will all have similar (high) scores on the screening tests, otherwise they would have been rejected before the interview stage. Thus the range of scores in the group of individuals who are selected will be much smaller than that in the general population. This will create problems for any attempt to validate the screening test, since this restricted range of abilities will tend to reduce the correlation between the test and any criterion. There are ways around this (Dobson 1988), but these two examples show how difficult it can be to establish the predictive validity of a test.

There are several designs that can be used to establish the predictive validity of tests. Most obviously, the tests may be administered and criterion data gathered later, such as when ability tests are used to predict aptitude in piloting an aircraft. Or the criterion data may be gathered retrospectively: for example, a test may be administered to measure adults' social adjustment and the criteria data (of the quality of interaction with peers when they were at school) may be gathered through interviewing parents, teachers, etc. This is sometimes known as 'postdiction'. Sometimes the criterion data may be gathered at the same time as the test is administered, such as when a firm is considering using a new selection test and decides to see whether it can predict the effectiveness of workers who are already in the organization. Here the test and performance measures (e.g. supervisors' ratings, sales figures) may be obtained at the same time that the test is administered, a design that is sometimes referred to as 'concurrent validity'.

Predicting performance from several sets of data

One common problem in applied psychology is knowing how to combine several different types of datum in order to predict performance. For example, an organization may have ratings of candidates' performance from an interview, plus the scores from six different psychometric tests. How should all of this information be used to predict performance? Two approaches are commonly followed. Both depend on first gathering some test data and criterion data from a large sample of people – at least 100. Then a 'minimum acceptable score' can be defined for each test that shows a significant correlation with the criterion. How this is chosen is fairly arbitrary: it might, for example, be set to the mean score obtained by the sample. Candidates are then selected if they score above the minimum acceptable level on all the tests. This is sometimes called the 'multiple-hurdle' **259** approach, as candidates are only appointed if they clear each of the barriers – that is, score above the minimum acceptable standard on every test. Although quite commonly used, this approach has several obvious problems. There is no good rationale for deciding what the minimum acceptable standard for a test is. If this is set too high, then very few applicants will fail to clear all hurdles, so virtually no one will be selected. Some soul searching is required to decide what to do if and when people only fail a hurdle by the smallest margin. And the technique does not allow marginally weak performance in one area to be balanced by superlative performance in others.

Instead, techniques such as multiple regression (or logistic regression when the criterion has only two values, such as passing or failing a driving test) are often used to predict performance. Unlike the multiple-hurdle approach, this allows good performance on one scale to compensate for poor performance on another; it shows the relative importance of the variables for predicting the criterion, as well as a statistic called the 'multiple correlation coefficient', R, which indicates how well the *optimally combined* test scores together predict the criterion. It has a sound statistical rationale and shows how the scores on the various scales should be weighted and added together to predict the criterion. For example, it may tell us that the best possible estimate of a salesperson's annual turnover is give by $100,000 + 500 \times$ extraversion score $- 130 \times$ neuroticism score. Once a regression equation like this is set up, it is possible to study the extent to which adding another variable to the selection battery improves the accuracy of the prediction. If adding a new variable (for example, including a test general intelligence as well as extraversion and neuroticism) leads to a significant increase in predictive power (a significant increase in R) then the new variable is said to have *incremental validity*.

Self-assessment question 15.3

a. Must a reliable test be valid?

b. Must a valid test be reliable?

c. What is meant by the construct, content and predictive validity of a test?

d. What are 'convergent validity' and 'divergent validity'?

Overview of validity

Establishing whether a test is valid is time consuming, difficult – and absolutely vital. The problem is that here is no short answer to questions such as 'what is the best test for assessing verbal ability'. It all depends on the age and ability of the people to be tested, their background (a test developed for white middle-class samples may well not be valid for minority group members, an issue known as 'test bias') the degree of accuracy required, the time available for testing and whether the test is to be given to individuals or groups. Some tests may make fine discriminations between people at the bottom end of the spectrum (useful for detecting dyslexia) but be unable to make fine distinctions between the most able pupils. Some may measure speed of response as well as level of response, for example, determining how many synonyms a person can identify within 5 minutes, while others may give the child as long as they want to do the test. Some tests will require participants to make an open-ended response (for example defining the meaning of a word) while others will be multiple choice. So much depends on the purpose of testing that it is rarely possible to recommend a single test for all situations.

Summary

The reliability of a test is important because it shows how closely the test score resembles a person's true score on the trait being measured. Hence, it shows whether it is reasonable to treat the score on a particular test as if it measured the underlying trait. Unfortunately, it is easy to overestimate the reliability coefficient alpha by including items in a test that are virtual paraphrases of one another – an obvious problem that is not well recognized in the literature. To avoid this, test designers need to check all pairs of test items to ensure that the assumption of local independence seems reasonable.

It is vitally important to establish the content validity, construct validity and/or predictive validity of a test before using it for any purpose whatsoever. A test with low reliability cannot be a valid measure of a trait. However, high reliability does not guarantee high *validity*.

Suggested additional reading

All psychometrics textbooks and many statistics books give accounts of reliability theory. Among the best are Cronbach (1994 and other editions), Rust and Golombok (2009), Kaplan and Saccuzzo (2001) or Murphy and Davidshofer (1994). The book that psychometricians usually recommend is still Nunnally (1978) and this derives many of the formulae mentioned earlier – for example, showing how reliability is related to the true score and how close the estimate of reliability (calculated from one sample of individuals) is to its true value (Nunnally 1978: 208; beware the misprint in equation 6.13 on p. 207). Messick (1989) offers a first-rate treatment of test validity.

Answers to self-assessment questions

SAQ 15.1

a. Assuming that each pair of items is influenced by a different set of nuisance factors, the correlation will show the extent to which the pair of items assesses the trait being measured – extraversion in this case.

b. Since Item 1 shows low correlations with all of the other items, it would appear to be a poor measure of extraversion.

c. The obvious thing would be to write more test items, give the old and new items out to a new sample of individuals (at least 200 of them) and recompute the correlations and alpha. Since coefficient alpha depends in part on the number of items in the test, increasing the number of items will increase alpha. There is also another possibility. We saw in the answer to (b) that Item 1 really is not very good – it shows low correlations with all of the other test items. Removing this item from the test will both increase the average correlation between the remaining items (from 0.206 based on ten correlations to 0.285 based on six correlations) and reduce the length of the test. The first factor will tend to increase alpha and the second will tend to decrease it. Thus it is possible – although not certain – that removing Item 1 may also increase alpha. We shall return to this in Chapter 18.

SAQ 15.2

a. Alternative names for the internal consistency or reliability of a test, which I have termed alpha throughout this book.

b. Doing so is bound to produce a very high reliability, as the items share specific variance as well as measuring the same trait.

c. The SEM shows how accurate an assessment of an individual's score is likely to be. For example, if one test suggested that a person's IQ was 100 with an SEM of 3, we would be more confident that the child's IQ really *was* 100 than if the test had an SEM of 5.

d. $\sqrt{0.81} = 0.9$ and $\sqrt{0.56} = 0.75$. Suppose that Test 2 was completely reliable. The correlation between Test 1 and Test 2 would then be the same as the correlation between Test 1 and the true score, i.e. 0.9. However, as Test 2 is *not* perfectly reliable, the correlation will be lower. It can be shown that the largest correlation that one can expect between two tests is the product of the square roots of their reliabilities. In this case, one would not expect the tests to correlate together by more than 0.9×0.75 or 0.675. This is how I was earlier able to claim that *all* of the variability in the R-S Scale could be explained by social desirability, although the correlation between the two scales was only –0.91, not –1.0.

SAQ 15.3

a. Most certainly not. High reliability tells you that the test measures some trait or state, not what this trait or state is.

b. Yes. Although beware if the reliability of a short scale appears to be too high (e.g. ten-item scales with a reliability of 0.9). This may suggest that the same item has been paraphrased several times.

c. See text.

d. In construct validation, convergent validity is a measure of whether a test correlates with the characteristics with which it *should* correlate if it is valid – for example, whether an IQ test correlates with teachers' ratings of children's academic performance. Divergent validity checks that a test shows insubstantial correlations with characteristics to which it should theoretically be unrelated. For example, scores on the IQ test could be correlated with tests measuring social desirability, various aspects of personality, etc., the expectation being that these correlations will be close to zero.

References

Costa, P. T. and McCrae, R. R. (1992). *NEO-PI(R) Professional Manual*. Odessa, FL: Psychological Assessment Resources.

Cronbach, L. J. (1994). *Essentials of Psychological Testing* (5th edn). New York: HarperCollins.

Cronbach, L. J., Gleser, G. C., Nanda, H. and Rajaratnam, N. (1972). *The Dependability of Behavioral Measurements*. New York: Wiley.

Dobson, P. (1988). The correction of correlation coefficients for restriction of range when restriction results from the truncation of a normally distributed variable. *British Journal of Mathematical and Statistical Psychology 41*, 227–34.

Joy, V. L. (1963). *Repression-Sensitization Personality and Interpersonal Behavior*. Unpublished PhD thesis, University of Texas.

Kaplan, R. M. and Saccuzzo, D. P. (2001). *Psychological Testing: Principles, Applications, and Issues* (5th edn). Belmont, CA: Wadsworth/Thomson Learning.

Kline, P. (1981). *Fact and Fantasy in Freudian Theory*. London: Methuen.

Messick, S. (1989). Validity. In R. L. Linn (ed.), *Educational Measurement* (3rd edn). Washington, DC: American Council on Education.

Michell, J. (1997). Quantitative science and the definition of measurement in psychology. *British Journal of Psychology 88*, 355–83.

Murphy, K. R. and Davidshofer, C. O. (1994). *Psychological Testing: Principles and Applications*. Englewood Cliffs, NJ: Prentice-Hall.

Nunnally, J. C. (1978). *Psychometric Theory* (2nd edn). New York: McGraw-Hill.

Rust, J. and Golombok, S. (2009). *Modern Psychometrics: The Science of Psychological Assessment* (3rd edn). New York: Routledge/Taylor & Francis.

16 Factor analysis

Background

Factor analysis is a statistical tool that lies at the very heart of individual differences research. Its many uses include constructing tests, discovering the basic dimensions of personality and ability and showing how many distinct psychological dimensions (e.g. traits) are measured by a set of tests or test items. This chapter introduces the broad concepts of factor analysis. Details of how to perform and interpret factor analyses are covered in Chapter 17.

Recommended prior reading

Chapters 1, 14 and 15.

Introduction

We should start by mentioning that the term 'factor analysis' can refer to two rather different statistical techniques. *Exploratory factor analysis* is the older (and simpler) technique and forms the basis of this chapter and the first section of Chapter 17. *Confirmatory factor analysis* and its extensions (sometimes known as 'path analysis', 'latent variable analysis' or 'Lisrel models') are useful in many areas other than individual differences and are particularly popular in social psychology. A brief outline of *this* technique is given at the end of Chapter 17. Authors do not always make it clear whether exploratory or confirmatory factor analysis has been used. If you see the term 'factor analysis' in a journal, you should assume that it refers to an exploratory factor analysis.

Chapters 14 and 15 showed why it is important that the items in a scale all measure one (and only one) psychological variable and introduced coefficient alpha as a measure of the reliability of a scale. This technique *assumed* that all the items in a test formed one scale and the reliability coefficient essentially tests whether this assumption is reasonable.

An alternative approach might involve examining a sample of test items and *discovering* how many distinct scales they contain and which items belong to which scale(s). Suppose that a psychologist administered some vocabulary items, some comprehension items and some anagram problems to a group of volunteers. It would be most useful to know whether the vocabulary items formed one scale, the comprehension items a second scale and the anagram-solving items a third scale or whether (for example) the vocabulary and comprehension items formed one scale while the anagram problems formed another. However, let us first consider a simpler example. Suppose that, in the interests of science, you were to collect the following pieces of data from a random sample of (say) 200 fellow students in the bar of your university or college:

- V1, body weight (kg)

- V2, degree of slurring of speech (rated on a scale from 1 to 5)

- V3, length of leg (cm)

- V4, volubility of talking (rated on a scale from 1 to 5)
- V5, length of arm (cm)
- V6, degree of staggering when attempting to walk in a straight line (rated on a scale from 1 to 5).

It seems likely that V1, V3 and V5 will all vary together, since large people will tend to have long arms and legs and be heavier. These three items all measure some fundamental property of the individuals in your sample, namely their size. Similarly, it is likely that V2, V4 and V6 will all vary together – the amount of alcohol consumed is likely to be related to slurring of speech and talkativeness and to difficulty in walking in a straight line. Thus although we have collected six pieces of data, these questions measure only two 'constructs', namely size and drunkenness. If you wanted to describe a person to a friend, you could just say that they were 'small and sober' rather than having to describe them on each of the six different characteristics listed: factor analysis shows that it is legitimate to summarize the data like this without losing much information. In factor analysis, the word 'factor' is usually used instead of the word 'construct' and we shall follow this convention from now on.

Exploratory factor analysis essentially does two things:

- It shows how many distinct psychological constructs (factors) are measured by a set of variables. In the last example, there are two factors (size and drunkenness).

- It shows which variables measure which constructs. In our example, it might well show that V1, V3 and V5 measure one factor and that V2, V4 and V6 measure another, quite different factor.

Scores on entire tests (rather than test items) can also be factor analysed. The imprecision of language and different theoretical background of researchers means that the same psychological construct may be given several different names by different researchers. Do six different tests that are marketed as assessing anxiety, neuroticism, negative affect, ego strength, emotional instability and low self-actualization measure six different aspects of personality or do they overlap? Factor analysis can show whether or not a set of tests assess the same thing. An *enormous* number of words can be used to describe personality, mood, emotions and abilities; Allport and Odbert (1936) found over 4500 words in the dictionary that could be used to describe personality alone. Without factor analysis there is no way of telling whether or not any of these refer to the same basic psychological phenomenon.

The technique is not restricted to test items or test scores. It would be possible to factor analyse reaction times from various types of cognitive test in order to determine which (if any) of these tasks were related. Alternatively, suppose that one took a group of schoolchildren who had no specific training or practice in sport and assessed their performance in 30 sports by any mixture of coaches' ratings, timings, mean length of throw, percentage of maiden overs obtained, goals scored or whatever performance measure is most appropriate for each sport. The only proviso is that each child must compete in each sport. Factor analysis would reveal whether individuals who were good at one ball game tended to be good at all of them, whether short-distance and long-distance track events formed two distinct groupings (and which events belonged to which group) and so on. Thus, instead of having to talk in terms of performance in 30 distinct areas, it would be possible to summarize this information by talking in terms of half a dozen basic sporting abilities (or however many abilities the factor analysis revealed).

Exploratory factor analysis by inspection

The top section of Table 16.1 shows a six-item questionnaire. Six students were asked to answer each question, using a five-point rating scale as shown in the table and their responses are shown towards the bottom of the table. These indicate the extent to which each individual agrees with each statement – a 'Likert scale'.

Look at the students' responses in the bottom section of Table 16.1. Try to decide on the basis of these figures whether there is any overlap between any of the six items – and if so, which.

Q1	I enjoy socializing	1	2	3	4	5
Q2	I often act on impulse	1	2	3	4	5
Q3	I am a cheerful sort of person	1	2	3	4	5
Q4	I often feel depressed	1	2	3	4	5
Q5	It is difficult for me to get to sleep at night	1	2	3	4	5
Q6	Large crowds make me feel anxious	1	2	3	4	5

For each question please circle ONE NUMBER that describes your reaction to each statement.

Circle '5'	if you strongly agree that a statement describes you well
Circle '4'	if it describes you fairly well
Circle '3'	if you are neutral or unsure
Circle '2'	if you feel that the statement does not really describe you well
Circle '1'	if you feel strongly that the statement does not describe you well

	Q1	**Q2**	**Q3**	**Q4**	**Q5**	**Q6**
Stephen	5	5	4	1	1	2
Ann	1	2	1	1	1	2
Paul	3	4	3	4	5	4
Janette	4	4	3	1	2	1
Michael	3	3	4	1	2	2
Christine	3	3	3	5	4	5

Table 16.1 Six-item personality questionnaire and responses of six students

In Chapter 14 it was explained that questionnaires are generally scored by adding up individuals' scores on all constituent items. It is tempting to do the same to the data in Table 16.1 and calculate that Stephen has a score of 18 on the questionnaire, etc. If you have attempted this, you should read through Chapter 15 again before continuing. Remember that it is sensible to add together individuals' scores only if the items all measure the same psychological concept – and we have no idea whether the six items in this questionnaire measure one, two, three, four, five or six quite distinct concepts. The whole point of the present analysis is to answer this question, so this is not an appropriate strategy to adopt.

Eagle-eyed readers may have noticed some trends in these data. You may have observed that individuals' responses to questions 1, 2 and 3 tend to be similar. Stephen tends to agree with all three, Ann tends to disagree with them, while the others feel more or less neutral about them. These are rough approximations, of course, but you can see that no one who rates him- or herself as '1' or '2' on one of these three questions gives him- or herself a '4' or '5' on one of the others. This may suggest that enjoying socializing, acting on impulse and having a cheerful disposition tend to go together and so these three items might be expected to form a scale. Much the same applies to items 4 to 6. Again, people such as Stephen or Ann who give themselves a low rating on one of these three questions also give themselves a low rating on the other two questions, while Christine gives herself high ratings on all three questions.

Thus there seem to be two clusters of questions in this questionnaire. The first group consists of questions 1, 2 and 3 and the second group consists of questions 4, 5 and 6. However, spotting these relationships is very difficult. Had the order of the columns in Table 16.1 been rearranged, these relationships would have been difficult or impossible to identify by eye.

Fortunately, however, a statistic called the *correlation coefficient* makes it possible to determine whether individuals who have low scores on one variable tend to have low (or high) scores on other variables. A brief summary of correlational methods is given in Appendix A, which should be consulted now, if necessary.

Table 16.2 shows the correlations calculated from the data in Table 16.1. (The detailed calculation of these correlations is not shown, as statistics books such as Howell (1992) explain this in detail.) These correlations confirm our suspicions about the relationships between the students' responses to questions 1 to 3 and questions 4 to 6. Questions 1 to 3 correlate strongly together (0.933, 0.824 and 0.696, respectively) but hardly at all with questions 4 to 6 (−0.096, etc.). Simi-

	Q1	Q2	Q3	Q4	Q5	Q6
Q1	1.000					
Q2	0.933	1.000				
Q3	0.824	0.696	1.000			
Q4	−0.096	−0.052	0.000	1.000		
Q5	−0.005	0.058	0.111	0.896	1.000	
Q6	−0.167	−0.127	0.000	0.965	0.808	1.000

Table 16.2 Correlations between the six items in Table 16.1

larly, questions 4 to 6 correlate highly together (0.896, 0.965 and 0.808, respectively), but hardly at all with questions 1 to 3. Thus it is possible to see from the table of correlations that questions 1 to 3 form one natural group and questions 4 to 6 form another – that is, the questionnaire actually measures two constructs or 'factors', one consisting of the first three questions and the other consisting of the final three questions.

While it is easy to see this from the correlations in Table 16.2, it should be remembered that the correlations shown there are hardly typical:

- The data were constructed so that the correlations between the variables were either very large or very small. In real life, correlations between variables would rarely be larger than 0.5, with many in the range 0.2–0.3. This makes it difficult to identify patterns by eye.

- The questions were ordered so that the large correlations fell next to each other in Table 16.2. If the questions had been presented in a different order, it would not be so easy to identify clusters of large correlations.

- Only six questions were used, so there are only 15 correlations to consider. With 40 questions there would be $\frac{40 \times 39}{2} = 780$ correlations to consider, making it much more difficult to identify groups of intercorrelated items.

There are several other problems associated with performing factor analysis 'by eye', not least of which is that different people might well reach different conclusions about the number and nature of the factors – the whole process is rather unscientific.

Fortunately, however, well-known mathematical methods can be used to identify factors from groups of variables that tend to correlate together and even the very largest factor analyses can now be performed on a desktop computer. Several statistics packages can be used to perform factor analysis, including R, SPSS, SYSTAT and SAS or the excellent and free factor analysis program by Lorenzo-Seva and Ferrando (2006). To understand how computers can perform this task, it is helpful to visualize the problem in a slightly different way and adopt a *geometrical* approach.

A geometric approach to factor analysis

It is possible to represent correlation matrices geometrically. Variables are represented by straight lines are of equal length, which all start at the same point. These lines are positioned such that the correlation between the variables is represented by the cosine of the angle between them. The cosine of an angle is a trigonometric function that can either be looked up in tables or computed directly by all but the simplest pocket calculators – you do not need to know what cosines mean, just where to find them. Table 16.3 shows a few cosines to give you a general idea of the concept. Remember that when the angle between two lines is small, the cosine is large and positive. When two lines are at right angles, the correlation (cosine) is zero. When the two lines are pointing in opposite directions, the correlation (cosine) is negative.

It is but a small step to represent entire correlation matrices geometrically. A line is drawn anywhere on the page representing one of the variables – it does not matter which one. The other variables are represented by other lines of equal length, all of which fan out from one end of the first line. The angles between the variables are, by convention, measured in a clockwise direction. Variables which have large positive correlations between them will fall close to each other, as Table

16.3 shows that large correlations (or cosines) result in small angles between the lines. Highly correlated variables literally point in the same direction, variables with large negative correlations between them point in opposite directions and uncorrelated variables point in completely different directions. Figure 16.1 shows a simple example based on three variables. The correlation

Angle (in degrees)	Cosine of angle
0	1.000
15	0.966
30	0.867
45	0.707
60	0.500
75	0.259
90	0.000
120	–0.500
150	–0.867
180	–1.000
210	–0.867
240	–0.500
270	0.000
300	0.500
330	0.867

Table 16.3 Table of cosines for graphical representation of correlations between variables

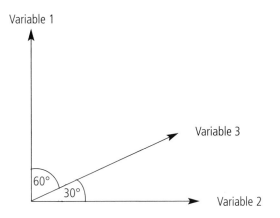

Figure 16.1 Correlations between three variables and their geometric representation.

between V1 and V2 is 0.0; the correlation between V1 and V3 is 0.5 and the correlation between V2 and V3 is 0.867. The correlation between V1 and V2 is represented by a pair of lines of equal length joined at one end; as the correlation between these variables is 0.0 the angle between them corresponds to a cosine of 0.0; that is, 90° (Table 16.3). The correlation between V1 and V3 is 0.5 corresponding to an angle of 60° and that between V2 and V3 is 0.867 (30°), so V2 and V3 are positioned as shown.

Self-assessment question 16.1

Figure 16.2 shows the geometric representation of the correlations between five variables. Use Table 16.3 to try to answer the following questions:

a. Which two variables have the highest positive correlation?

b. Which variable has a correlation of zero with V3?

c. Which variable has a large negative correlation with V3?

Without looking ahead, try to sketch out roughly how the correlations between the six test items shown in Table 16.2 would look if they were represented geometrically.

It may have occurred to you that it is not always possible to represent correlations in two dimensions (i.e. on a flat sheet of paper). For example, if any of the correlations in Figure 16.1 had been altered to a different value, one of the lines would have to project outward from the page

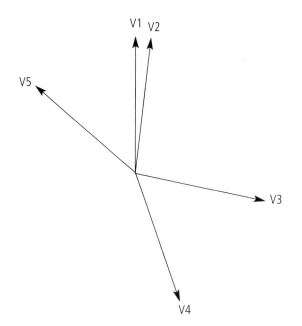

270   Figure 16.2 Geometrical representation of correlations between five variables.

to some degree. This is no problem for the underlying mathematics of factor analysis, but it does mean that it is not possible to use this geometric technique to perform real-life factor analyses.

Figure 16.3 is a fairly good approximation of the data shown in Table 16.2. Ignoring lines F1 and F2, you can see that the correlations between variables 1, 2 and 3 shown in this figure are all very large and positive (that is, the angles between these lines are small). Similarly, the correlations between variables 4 to 6 are also large and positive. As variables 1 to 3 have near zero correlations with variables 4 to 6, variables 1, 2 and 3 are at 90° to variables 4, 5 and 6. Computer programs for factor analysis essentially try to 'explain' the correlations between the variables in terms of a smaller number of factors. It is good practice to talk about 'common factors' rather than just 'factors' – later on we will encounter 'unique factors' and it is safest to avoid confusion. In this example, it is clear that there are two clusters of correlations, so the information in Table 16.2 can be approximated by two common factors, each of which passes through a group of large correlations. The common factors are indicated by long lines labelled F1 and F2 in Figure 16.3.

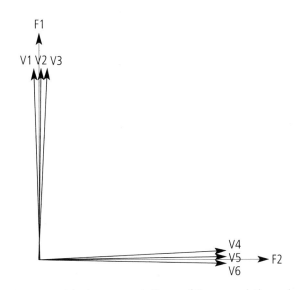

Figure 16.3 Approximate geometrical representations of the correlations shown in Table 16.2.

It should be clear that, from measuring the angle between each common factor and each variable, it is also possible to calculate the *correlations* between each variable and each common factor. Variables 1, 2 and 3 will all have very large correlations with factor 1 (in fact variable 2 will have a correlation of nearly 1.0 with factor 1, as factor 1 lies virtually on top of it). Variables 1, 2 and 3 will have correlations of about zero with factor 2, as they are virtually at right angles to it. Similarly, factor 2 is highly correlated with variables 4 to 6 and is virtually uncorrelated with variables 1 to 3 (because of the 90° angle between these variables and this factor). Do not worry for now where these factors come from or how they are positioned relative to the variables, as this will be covered in Chapter 17.

In the example just examined, the two clusters of variables (and hence the common factors) are at right angles to each other – what is known technically as an 'orthogonal solution', a term that you should note. However, this need not always be the case. Consider the correlations shown diagram- **271** matically in Figure 16.4. Here it is clear that there are two distinct clusters of variables, but it is equally clear that there is no way in which two orthogonal (i.e. uncorrelated) common factors, represented here by lines F1 and F2, can be placed through the centre of each cluster. It would clearly make sense to allow the factors to become correlated and to place one common factor through the middle of each cluster of variables. Factor analyses where the factors are themselves correlated (i.e. not at right angles) are known as 'oblique solutions'. The correlations between factors form what is called a 'factor pattern correlation matrix'. Try to remember this term – it will be helpful when you come to interpret printed output from factor analyses. When an orthogonal solution is performed, all the correlations between the various factors are zero. (A correlation of zero implies an angle of 90° between each pair of factors, which is another way of saying that the factors are independent.)

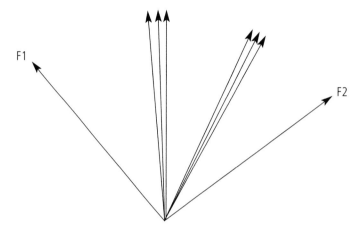

Figure 16.4 Correlations between six variables showing two factors at right angles.

It is possible to show all the correlations between every item and every common factor in a table, called the 'factor matrix' or sometimes the 'factor structure matrix'. The correlations between items and common factors are usually known as 'factor loadings'. By convention, the common factors are shown as the columns of this table and the variables as the rows. The values in Table 16.4 were obtained by looking at the angles between each common factor and each variable in Figure 16.3 and translating these (roughly) into correlations using Table 16.3.

Variable	Factor 1	Factor 2
V1	0.90	0.10
V2	0.98	0.00
V3	0.90	−0.10
V4	0.10	0.85
V5	0.00	0.98
V6	−0.10	0.85

Table 16.4 Approximate factor matrix from Figure 16.3

The factor matrix

The factor matrix is extremely important, as it shows three things.

Which variables make up each common factor

This can be seen by noting which variables have loadings that are more extreme than some arbitrary cutoff. By convention, the cutoff value is 0.4 or 0.3, which implies an angle of 60° to 75° between the variable and the common factor. The easiest way to see the variables that 'belong' to a factor is thus to underline those that have loadings higher than 0.4 or less than −0.4. Thus in Table 16.4, one would deduce that factor 1 is a mixture of V1, V2 and V3 (but not V4, V5 or V6, as their loadings lie between −0.4 and 0.4). Likewise, factor 2 is a mixture of V4, V5 and V6. Thus the factor matrix can be used to give a tentative label to the common factor. For example, suppose that 100 ability items were factored and it was found that the variables that had substantial loadings on the first common factor were concerned with spelling, vocabulary, knowledge of proverbs and verbal comprehension, while none of the other items (mathematical problems, puzzles requiring objects to be visualized, memory tests, etc.) showed large loadings on the factor. Because all of the high-loading items involve the use of language, it seems reasonable to call the common factor 'verbal ability', 'language ability' or similar.

Be warned, however, that there is no guarantee that labels given like this are necessarily correct. It is necessary to validate the factor exactly as described in Chapter 15 in order to ensure that this label is accurate. However, if the items that define a common factor form a reliable scale that predicts teachers' ratings of language ability correlates nicely with other well-trusted tests of verbal ability and does not correlate at all strongly with other measures of personality or ability, it seems likely that the factor was correctly identified.

You will remember that the square of the correlation coefficient (i.e. the correlation coefficient multiplied by itself) shows how much 'variance' is shared by two variables – or in simpler language, how much they overlap. Two variables with a correlation of 0.8 overlap to the extent of 0.8^2 or 0.64. (Consult Appendix A if this is unfamiliar ground.) As factor loadings are merely correlations between common factors and items, it follows that the square of each factor loading shows the amount of overlap between each variable and the common factor. This simple finding forms the basis of two other main uses of the factor matrix.

Amount of overlap between each variable and all of the common factors

If the common factors are at right angles (an 'orthogonal' solution), it is simple to calculate how much of the variance of each variable is measured by the factors, by merely summing the squared factor loadings across factors. (When the common factors are not at right angles, life becomes more complicated.) It can be seen from Table 16.4 that $0.90^2 + 0.10^2 (= 0.82)$ of the variance of Test 1 is 'explained' by the two factors. This amount is called the *communality* of that variable.

A variable with a large communality has a large degree of overlap with one or more common factors. A low communality implies that all of the correlations between that variable and the common factors are small – that is, none of the common factors overlaps much with that variable. This might mean that the variable measures something that is conceptually quite different from the other variables in the analysis. For example, one personality item in among 100 ability test items would have a communality close to zero. It might also mean that a particular item is heavily influenced by measurement error or extreme difficulty, e.g. an item that is so easy that everyone obtained the correct answer or was ambiguously phrased so that no one could understand the question. Whatever the reason, a low communality implies that an item does not overlap with the common factors, either because it measures a different concept, because of excessive measurement error, or because there are few individual differences in the way in which people respond to the item.

Relative importance of the common factors

It is possible to calculate how much of the variance each common factor accounts for. A common factor that accounts for 40% of the overlap between the variables in the original correlation matrix is clearly more important than another that explains only 20% of the variance. Once again it is necessary to assume that the common factors are orthogonal (at right angles to each other). The first step is to calculate what is known as an *eigenvalue* for each factor by squaring the factor loadings and summing down the columns. Using the data shown in Table 16.4, it can be seen that the eigenvalue of factor 1 is $0.90^2 + 0.98^2 + 0.90^2 + 0.10^2 + 0.0^2 + (-0.10)^2$ or 2.60. If the eigenvalue is divided by the number of variables (six in this instance), it shows what proportion of variance is explained by this common factor. Here factor 1 explains 0.43 or 43% of the information in the original correlation matrix.

> ### Self-assessment question 16.3
>
> Try to define the terms eigenvalue and communality. Then look back at Table 16.4 and:
>
> a. calculate the communalities of variables 2, 3, 4, 5 and 6
>
> b. calculate the eigenvalue of factor 2
>
> c. work out what proportion of the variance is accounted for by factor 2
>
> d. work out, by addition, the proportion of variance accounted for by factors 1 and 2 combined.

Before we leave the factor matrix, it is worth clarifying one point that can cause confusion. Suppose that one of the factors in the analysis has a number of loadings that are both large and *negative* (e.g. –0.6, –0.8), some that are close to zero (e.g. –0.1, +0.2), but no large positive loadings. Suppose that the items with large negative loadings are from items such as 'are you a nervous sort of person?' and 'do you worry a lot?', where agreement is coded as '1' and disagreement with the statements as '0'. The large negative correlations imply that the factor measures the *opposite* of nerviness and tendency to worry, so it may be tentatively identified as 'emotional stability' or something similar. While it is perfectly acceptable to interpret factors in this way, it may sometimes be more convenient to reverse *all* the signs of *all* the variables' loadings on that factor. Thus the loadings mentioned would change from –0.6, –0.8, –0.1 and +0.2 to +0.6, +0.8, +0.1 and –0.2. It is purely a matter of convenience whether one does this, as SAQ 16.4 will reveal. However, if you do alter the signs of all factor loadings you should also:

- change the sign of the correlation between the 'reversed' factor and all the other factors in the factor pattern correlation matrix

- change the sign of all the 'factor scores' (discussed later) calculated from the factor in question.

Self-assessment question 16.4

a. Use Table 16.3 to represent graphically the sets of correlations between one factor (F1) and two variables (V1 and V2) shown in Table 16.5.

b. Next, change the sign of the correlation between the variables and F1 and replot the diagram.

c. From this, try to explain how reversing the sign of all of a factor's loadings alters the position of a factor.

	F1	V1	V2
F1	1.000		
V1	–0.867	1.000	
V2	–0.867	0.500	1.000

Table 16.5 Correlations between two variables and one factor

Factor analysis and component analysis

When you completed SAQ 16.3 (d), you will have noticed something rather odd. The two common factors combined only account for 83.4% of the variance in the original correlation matrix. Similarly, all the communalities are less than 1.0. What happened to the 'lost' 17% of the variance?

Factor analysis is essentially a technique for summarizing information – for making broad generalizations from detailed sets of data. Here, we have taken the correlations between six variables, observed that they fall into two distinct clusters and so decided that it is more parsimonious to talk in terms of two factors rather than the original six variables. In other words, the number of constructs needed to describe the data has fallen from six (the number of variables) to two (the number of common factors). Like any approximation, this one is useful but not perfect. Some of the information in the original correlation matrix has been sacrificed in making this broad generalization. Indeed, the only circumstance under which no information would have been lost **275** would have been if V1, V2 and V3 had shown an intercorrelation of 1.0 (likewise for V4, V5 and V6) and if all the correlations between these two groups of variables had been precisely zero. Then (and only then!) we would have lost no information as a result of referring to two factors rather than six variables.

This, then, is the first part of the explanation of the missing variance. It is a necessary consequence of reducing the number of constructs from six to two. Suppose, however, that instead of extracting just two factors from the correlations between the six variables, one extracted six factors (all at right angles to each other and hence impossible to visualize). Since there are as many factors as there are variables, there should be no loss of information. You might expect that the six factors would explain *all* the information in the original correlation matrix.

Whether or not this is the case depends on how the factor analysis is performed. There are two basic approaches to factor analysis. The simplest, called 'principal components analysis', assumes that six factors can indeed fully explain the information in the correlation matrix. Thus when six factors are extracted, each variable will have a communality of precisely 1.0 and the factors will between them account for 100% of the variation between the variables.

Principal components analysis

More formally, the principal components model states that, for any variable being analysed:

$$\text{total variance} = \text{common factor variance} + \text{measurement error}$$

Suppose we construct a test in which ten items inquire about worries and negative moods: 'my moods vary a lot', 'I feel agitated in confined spaces', 'I get embarrassed easily', etc. with each item being answered on a five-point scale ranging from 'describes me well' to 'describes me badly'. Suppose that we know that all these items form a single factor of 'neuroticism'. The principal components model therefore states that the way a person answers an item depends only on their level of the trait that is measured by all the items (here there is only one trait: neuroticism) plus some measurement error. Measurement error in this context might reflect that some people's mind may wander, that they may make a mistake when using the rating scale or anything else implying that their response to the item is not completely accurate. It implies that when as many factors are extracted as there are variables, these common factors can explain all of the information in the correlation matrix.

Factor analysis

The assumption that anything that is not measured by common factors must just be measurement error is rather a strong one. Each test item may have some morsel of 'unique variance' that is unique to that item, but which cannot be shared with other items. The extent to which people fear enclosed spaces may not be 100% determined by their level of neuroticism: people may vary in the extent to which they show a specific fear of being shut in, perhaps as a result of childhood experiences. So to predict how a person would respond to the item, you would need to consider their level of neuroticism, their level of this specific fear of being enclosed and random measurement error. The extent to which the item measures the specific fear, unrelated to the personality factor(s) that run through all the items, is reflected in the size of its *specific factor variance*. (You will recall that we introduced the term specific variance in Figure 16.1 but left its definition until now.)

The *factor analysis* model thus assumes that for any variable or item being factor analysed:

total variance = common factor variance + specific factor variance + measurement error

The amount of specific factor variance in an item is reflected in its communality. The more variance an item shares with the other items in the test, the higher are its correlations with both them and the common factors. Therefore the higher its communality will be. (Remind yourself how communality is calculated in order to check this.) An item with a substantial amount of specific factor variance will therefore never have a communality as high as 1.0, even if the factor analysis extracts as many factors as there are variables. This is because each item has some 'specific factor variance' associated with it: some people are just more (or less) afraid of enclosed spaces than you would expect from knowing their level of neuroticism.

Self-assessment question 16.5

Suppose children are given a 20-item attainment test to assess their knowledge of the geography of Austria, following a course of instruction. Each question has two possible answers, with a point being awarded for each correct answer and a point deducted for each incorrect answer. What would you expect to influence a child's performance on this test, assuming

a. the principal components model, and

b. the factor model?

The test includes some items that involve naming Austrian towns, lakes and rivers. Which of the following behaviours would lead to random errors of measurement, and which might contribute to specific factor variance?

c. guessing when one does not know the answer

d. having previously gone on holiday to Austria

e. having a keen interest in fishing

f. getting confused by the answer sheet and marking an answer in the wrong box.

g. being absent from some of the classes on which the test is based

h. Suppose that incorrect answers were not penalised. In that case, would guessing (rather than leaving some answers blank) affect specific factor variance, or error variance?

It follows that factor analysis is a more complicated process than component analysis. Whereas component analysis merely has to determine the number of factors to be extracted and how each variable should correlate with each factor, factor analysis also has to estimate (somehow) what the communality of each variable would be if as many factors as variables were extracted. In other words, it must also work out how much of an item's variance is 'common factor' variance and how much is unique to that particular variable and cannot be shared with any other item. The good news is that, in practice, it does not seem to matter too much whether one performs a component analysis or a factor analysis, as both techniques generally lead to similar results. In fact, the authorities on factor analysis can be divided into three groups. Some believe that factor analysis should never be used. According to Stamm (1995), Leyland Wilkinson fought to keep factor **277** analysis options out of his SYSTAT statistics package. Commercial pressures eventually won. Contrariwise, some maintain that a form of factor analysis is the *only* justifiable technique (e.g. Carroll 1993); and, finally, some pragmatists argue that, as both techniques generally produce highly similar solutions, it does not really matter which of them one uses (Tabachnick and Fidell 2001).

One slightly worrying problem is that the loadings obtained from component analyses are always larger than those that result from factor analyses, as the former assume that each variable has a communality of 1.0, whereas the latter computes a value for the communality that is generally less than 1.0. Thus the results obtained from a component analysis always look more impressive (i.e. have larger common factor loadings) than the results of a factor analysis. This has clear implications for many rules of thumb, such as regarding factor loadings above 0.4 (or less than −0.4) as being 'salient' and disregarding those between −0.39 and +0.39, but these have not really been addressed in the literature. It is also vitally important that authors of papers should state clearly whether they have followed the factor -analysis or component analysis model. Few do this and some authors mention 'factor analysis' in the text even though they have performed principal components analysis.

Uses of factor analysis

Factor analysis has three main uses in psychology.

Test construction

First, it may be used to construct tests. For example, 50 items might be written more or less at random; we do not have to assume that they all measure the same trait or state. The items would then be administered to a representative sample of several hundred individuals and scored (in the case of ability tests) so that a correct answer is coded as 1 and an incorrect answer as 0. Responses that are made using rating scales (as with most personality and attitude questionnaires) are simply entered in their raw form – one point if box (a) is endorsed, two if (b) is chosen, etc. The responses to these 50 items are then correlated together and factor analysed. The items that have high loadings on each factor measure the same underlying psychological construct and so form a scale. Thus it is possible to determine how to score the questionnaire in future simply by looking at the factor matrix: if items 1, 2, 10 and 12 are the only items that have substantial loadings on one factor, then one scale of the test should be the sum of these four items and no others. It is likely that some items will fail to load substantially on any of the factors (i.e. show low communalities). This could happen for a number of reasons: in the case of ability tests, the items could be so easy (or hard) that there is little or no variation in people's scores. Personality items may refer to uncommon actions or feelings where there is again little variation – e.g. 'there are occasions in my life when I have felt afraid', an item with which *everyone* is likely to agree. Or items may fail because they are severely influenced by measurement error or because they measure something different from any of the others that were administered. Test constructors do not usually worry about why, precisely, items fail to work as expected. Items that fail to load a factor are simply discarded without further ado. Thus factor analysis can show at a stroke:

- how many distinct scales run through the test

- which items belong to which scales (so indicating how the test should be scored)

278 ● which items in a test should be discarded.

Each of the scales then needs to be validated, e.g. by calculating scores for each person on each factor and examining the construct validity and/or predictive validity of these scales. For example, scores on the factors may be correlated with scores on other questionnaires, used to predict educational success, etc.

Data reduction

The second main use of factor is in data reduction, or 'conceptual spring cleaning'. Huge numbers of tests have been developed to measure personality from different theoretical perspectives and it is not at all obvious whether these overlap. If we take six scales that measure personality traits, it is useful to know how much overlap there is between them. Do they really each assess quite different aspects of personality? At the other extreme, might they perhaps all measure the same trait under different names? Or is the truth somewhere in the middle? To find out it is simply necessary to administer the test items to a large sample, then factor the correlations between the items. This will show precisely what the underlying structure truly is. For example, two factors may be found. The first factor may have large loadings from all the items in tests 1, 5 and 6. All the substantial loadings on the second factor may come from items in tests 2, 3 and 4. Hence it is clear that tests 1, 5 and 6 measure precisely the same thing, as do tests 2, 3 and 4. Any high-flown theoretical distinctions about subtle differences between the scales can be shown to have no basis in fact and any rational psychologists seeing the results of such an analysis should be forced to think in terms of two (rather than six) theoretical constructs – a considerable simplification. (It is also possible to factor analyse the scores on the tests rather than responses to individual items when performing this sort of analysis. However, this makes the assumption that the tests were properly constructed in the first place, which may not be the case.)

Refining questionnaires

The third main use of factor analysis is for checking the psychometric properties of questionnaires, particularly when they are to be used in new cultures or populations. For example, suppose that the manual of an Australian personality test suggests that it should be scored by adding together the scores on all the odd-numbered items to form one scale, while all the even-numbered items form another. When the test is given to a sample of people in the UK and the correlations between the items are calculated and factor analysed, two factors should be found, with all the odd-numbered items having substantial loadings on one factor and all the even-numbered items loading substantially on the other. If this structure is *not* found it shows that there are problems with the questionnaire, which should not be scored or used in its conventional form.

Summary

It is easy to see why factor analysis is so important in individual differences and psychometrics. The same statistical technique can be used to construct tests, resolve theoretical disputes about the number and nature of factors measured by tests and questionnaires and check whether tests work as they should or whether it is legitimate to use a particular test within a different population or a different culture. You may even have wondered whether the size of the eigenvalue obtained when factoring a test that has just one factor running through it has any link to the test's reliability.

This chapter has provided a basic introduction to the principles of factor analysis. It has left many questions unanswered, including the following ones:

- How does one decide how many factors should be extracted?

- How can computer programs actually perform factor analysis?

- What types of datum can usefully be factor analysed?

- How should the results obtained from factor analytical studies be interpreted and reported?

These and other issues will be explored in Chapter 17.

Suggested additional reading

Eysenck's ancient paper on the logical basis of factor analysis (Eysenck 1953) is still well worth reading, while Child (2006) offers a 'student-friendly' basic introduction, and there is currently an excellent introduction on the 'statsoft' website.

Answers to self-assessment questions

SAQ 16.1

a. The smallest angle between any pair of variables in Figure 16.2 is that between V1 and V2. Hence these variables are the most highly correlated.

b. The angle between V3 and V2 is approximately 270° (moving clockwise). Table 16.3 shows that this corresponds to a correlation of 0.

c. The angle between V5 and V3 is approximately 210°, which corresponds to a correlation of –0.87.

SAQ 16.2

a. An oblique solution is a table of factor loadings in which the factors are not at right angles, but are themselves correlated together.

b. A factor loading is the correlation between a variable and a factor.

c. The factor structure matrix is a table showing the correlations between all variables and all factors.

d. An orthogonal solution is a table of factor loadings in which the factors are all uncorrelated (i.e. at right angles to each other).

e. A factor pattern correlation matrix is a table which shows the correlations between all of the factors in a factor analysis. For an orthogonal factor analysis, all of the correlations between factors will be 0 (as they are independent). For oblique solutions, the correlations will be values other than zero.

SAQ 16.3

The eigenvalue associated with a factor is the sum of the squared loadings on that factor, calculated across all of the variables. The communality of a variable is the sum of the squared loadings on that variable, calculated across all of the factors.

a. The communality of variable 2 is $0.98^2 + 0^2 = 0.9604$. The communalities of variables 3, 4, 5 and 6 are likewise 0.82, 0.7325, 0.9604 and 0.7325, respectively.

b. The eigenvalue of factor 2 is $0.10^2 + 0.0^2 + (-0.10^2) + 0.85^2 + 0.98^2 + 0.85^2$, or 2.4254.

c. As there are six variables, factor 2 accounts for 0.4042 of the variance between them.

d. The worked example in the text shows that factor 1 accounts for 0.423 of the variance. As the factors are orthogonal, factors 1 and 2 combined account for $0.43 + 0.4042 = 0.834$ of the variance between the variables.

SAQ 16.4

a. To tackle this question, you can see from Table 16.3 that the angle which corresponds to a correlation of −0.867 is either 150° or 210° and for 0.5 the angle is 60° or 300°. (Why two possibilities for each? Well, it depends if you move clockwise or anti-clockwise when calculating the angles between the factor and each variable.) If these are plotted, the only two possible sets of lines that will represent these correlations are as follows. (It does not matter if you have drawn the figure rotated in some other direction: the position of the lines on the page is arbitrary. The angle between the lines is the critical thing.) Note that you cannot put both variables on top of each other at an angle of 150 or 270° to the factor, for then the angle between them would be zero which corresponds to a correlation of 1.0 not the value of 0.5 shown in Table 16.5.

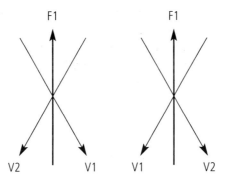

b. Changing the correlations mean that the angles between the variables and the factor change to 30° and 330°, as follows.

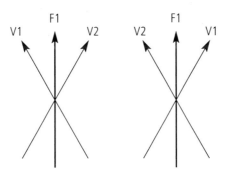

c. Reversing all of the loadings between the variables and a given factor in effect causes the factor to have a correlation of −1.0 with its previous position. Table 6.3 shows that this corresponds to its pointing in the opposite direction (180°) to its previous position. Large negative correlations between a variable and a factor imply that the factor points away from the variables **281** which have the largest correlation with it. Reversing the signs of all of the correlations reverses the direction of the factor so that it passes through the cluster of variables.

SAQ 16.5

Answers to SAQ 16.5

a. The principal components model assumes that performance on the test is determined by just geographical knowledge (plus some random error; a child who knows only 20 facts about Austria may be lucky enough to see 15 of these appear on the test paper, whereas another who knows 100 facts may see just five of them represented in the test).

b. The factor model accepts that performance on the 20-item test will be influenced by geographical knowledge, random error plus specific variance: that is, some children will have better (or worse) knowledge about Austria than you would expect, given their performance on other geography tests.

c. Random errors of measurement: some children will guess correctly (their score will be over-estimated) and some will guess incorrectly (their score will be underestimated).

d. Specific variance: these children may be able to draw on their holiday memories, and so will know more than the rest of the class.

e. Specific variance: it is possible that fishing magazines may contain articles about fishing in Austrian rivers or lakes, and if so children who have read these may have a better knowledge of these aspects of Austrian geography than one would expect.

f. Random error. Some of the wrongly-marked answers will be correct, and some incorrect and so guessing will not systematically increase children's performance.

g. Specific variance, as children who missed the classes may not know some of the information, and may therefore not perform to their normal level.

h. If incorrect guessing was not penalised, children who guessed answers (rather than leaving them blank) would have a higher score, as some of the guesses will probably be correct. Guessing, rather than leaving items blank, would affect specific variance – children who guess achieve better scores than they should.

References

Allport, G. W. and Odbert, H. S. (1936). Trait names: a psycho-lexical study. *Psychological Monographs 47*, whole issue.

Carroll, J. B. (1993). *Human Cognitive Abilities: A Ssurvey of Factor-analytic Studies*. Cambridge: Cambridge University Press.

Child, D. (2006). *The Essentials of Factor Analysis* (3rd edn). London: Continuum.

Eysenck, H. J. (1953). The logical basis of factor analysis. *American Psychologist 8*, 105–14.

Howell, D. C. (1992). *Statistical Methods for Psychology* (3rd edn). Belmont, CA: Duxbury.

Lorenzo-Seva, U. and Ferrando, P. J. (2006). FACTOR: a computer program to fit the exploratory factor analysis model. *Behavior Research Methods 38*(1), 88–91.

Stamm, B. (1995). Personal communication.

Tabachnick, B. G. and Fidell, L. S. (2001). *Using Multivariate Statistics* (4th edn). Boston, MA: Allyn & Bacon.

Performing and interpreting factor analyses

Background

While Chapter 16 gave an overview of the basic principles of factor analysis, it deliberately omitted some of the detail needed either to perform factor analyses or to evaluate the technical adequacy of published studies. Many journal articles that employ factor analysis are so technically flawed as to be meaningless, so it is vital that one should be able to identify (and discount) such studies when reviewing the literature.

Recommended prior reading

Chapter 16.

Introduction

Although it is quite possible to perform exploratory factor analyses by hand, and older texts such as Cattell (1952) provide detailed instructions for doing so, such exercises are best suited to the enthusiast (or masochist) who has several weeks to spare. The calculations involved are lengthy and repetitious, so are best performed by computer. Most of the main statistical packages contain good exploratory factor analysis routines that run analyses in minutes rather than hours, the time taken to perform an analysis being roughly proportional to the cube of the number of variables. Confirmatory factor analyses (which will be described towards the end of this chapter) require specialized packages and analyses can sometimes take hours to run.

Exploratory factor analysis

No matter whether the analysis is being performed using an abacus or a supercomputer, there are eight basic stages involved in performing an exploratory factor analysis, each of which is discussed in the following sections:

- Stage 1. Ensure that the data are suitable for factor analysis.

- Stage 2. Decide on the model – factor analysis or component analysis.

- Stage 3. Decide how many factors are needed to represent the data.

- Stage 4. If using factor (rather than component) analysis, estimate the communality of each variable.

- Stage 5. Produce factors giving the desired communalities (factor extraction).

- Stage 6. Rotate these factors so that they provide a replicable solution ('simple structure').

- Stage 7. Optionally compute factor scores.

- Stage 8. Optionally perform hierarchical analyses, if appropriate.

One of the problems with factor analysis is its power. The computer programs used will almost always produce an answer of some kind and by trying to analyse the data using many different techniques, taking out different numbers of factors and concentrating on different subsets of variables, it is possible to pull something semi-plausible from the most ghastly study. One occasionally encounters journal articles in which the technique has clearly been used in a desperate attempt to salvage something from a poorly designed experiment. Indeed, there are some areas of the discipline, such as personal construct psychology, in which such practice is the norm. Thus it is vital that those who use the technique or read the literature should have an understanding of the design and execution of factor analytical studies. Nowhere is the computer scientists' maxim of 'garbage in, garbage out' more appropriate than in factor analysis, so the present chapter begins with a look at the types of datum which may usefully be factor analysed.

Suitability of data for factor analysis

Not all data can be factor analysed. Factor analysis may be appropriate if the following criteria are fulfilled.

All of the variables in the analysis are continuous – that is, measured on at least a three-point interval scale (such as 'yes/?/no', coded as 2/1/0). One cannot normally factor analyse *categorical* data that form a nominal scale, such as colour of hair (black/brown/red), country of residence, voting preference or occupation. It is sometimes possible to choose codes for categorical data that will convert them into some kind of interval scale that can legitimately be factored. For example, support for a communist party may be coded as '1', for a social democratic party as '2', for a conservative/republican party as '3', and for a right-wing party as '4'. These numbers form a scale of 'right-wingness', which could legitimately be factored.

A problem arises with *dichotomous* data – that is, scores that can assume one of only two values. These are often encountered during analysis of responses to test items (1 = 'yes', 0 = 'no', or 1 = 'correct answer', 0 = 'incorrect answer'). When dichotomous items are correlated together, the correlation can only approach 1.0 if both of the test items have similar difficulty levels. Thus a small correlation can suggest that either:

- there is no relationship between items of similar difficulty, or

- the two items have widely differing difficulties.

Thus factor analysis of the usual Pearson product moment correlations between dichotomous items tends to produce factors of 'item difficulty', as only items of similar difficulty levels can possibly correlate together and form a factor. Other items that measure the same construct but that have very different difficulties will, because of this, show low loadings on the resulting factor. However, it is remarkably difficult to circumvent this problem using the standard statistical packages, which offer no alternative to the use of Pearson correlations. Other types of correlation coefficient that avoid these problems are available and Chambers (1982) gives a useful if somewhat technical précis of the literature. The legitimacy of factoring these coefficients is still a matter for debate (Vegelius 1973), although plenty of people routinely do so. In short, life is made very much easier if one can simply avoid using dichotomous data altogether.

All the variables are (approximately) normally distributed, with outliers properly identified and dealt with; see, for example, Tabatchnick and Fidell (1989: Chapter 4). Skewed data can be transformed if necessary; see, for example, Tabatchnick and Fidell (2001) or Howell (2001).

The relationships between all pairs of variables are approximately linear, or at any rate not obviously U-shaped or J-shaped.

The variables are independent. The easiest way to check this is to go through all of the formulae and ensure that each measured variable affects no more than one score that is being factor analysed. If individuals produce scores on four test items, it would be permissible to create and factor new variables such as:

(score 1 + score 2) and (score 3 + score 4)
or (score 1 + score 2 – score 3) and (1 – score 4)
but not (score 1 + score 2 + score 3) and (score 1 + score 4)
or (score 1) and (score 1 + score 2 + score 3 + score 4)

as in the last two cases, one of the observed test scores ('score 1') affects two of the variables being factored.

It is not possible to factor analyse all the scores from any test where it is impossible for a person to obtain an extremely high (or extremely low) score on *all* of its scales (known as 'ipsatized tests'), as all the scales of such tests are bound to be negatively correlated. Advocates of these tests claim that it is possible simply to drop one of the scales before factoring. However, the interpretation of the results will be affected by the (arbitrary) choice of which scale to omit.

The correlation matrix shows several correlations above 0.3. If all the correlations are tiny, then one should seriously question whether any factors are there to be extracted. If the correlations are small because of the use of tests with low reliability, it may be appropriate to correct for the effects of unreliability as shown by Guilford and Fruchter (1978) among others. Likewise, if poor experimental design led to data being collected from a group of restricted range (e.g. ability scores being obtained from a sample of university students rather than from a sample of the general population), it might be appropriate to correct the correlations for this using the formula of Dobson (1988) before factor analysing. However, such pieces of psychometric wizardry should be used with caution and are really no substitute for sound and thoughtful experimental design.

The Bartlett (1954) test of sphericity tests the hypothesis that all of the off-diagonal correlations are zero and it is routinely computed by packages such as SPSS. However, the test is very sensitive to sample size and minuscule correlations between variables from a large sample will lead the test to indicate that factor analysis is appropriate. It is much safer just to look at the correlation matrix.

Missing data are distributed randomly throughout the data matrix. It would not be wise to factor analyse data where a proportion of the sample omitted to take complete blocks of items. For example, some subjects may have taken tests A, B and C. Others may have taken tests A and C only and others may have taken only tests B and C. Because of this, it would not be legitimate to factor analyse these data, although several statistical packages will do so without a murmur.

The sample size is large. Experts vary in their recommendations, but factor analysis should not be attempted if the number of subjects is less than 100. Otherwise the correlations computed from this sample of people will differ substantially from those that would have been obtained from another sample, giving unreplicable results that are not good approximations of what the **285** relationship between the variables really is in the population. It used to be thought that it is also necessary to relate sample size to the number of variables being analysed. For example, Nunnally (1978) advocates that there should be at least ten times as many cases as variables. More recent studies, such as those by Barrett and Kline (1981) and Guadagnoli and Velicer (1988), show that, as long as there are more subjects than variables, the ratio of subjects to variables is not as important as absolute sample size and the size of the factor loadings. Thus if the factors are well defined (e.g. with loadings of 0.7, rather than 0.4), one needs a smaller sample to find them. If the data being analysed are known to be highly reliable (e.g. test scores, rather than responses to individual items), it should be possible to relax these guidelines somewhat. However, attempts to factor analyse small sets of data (such as repertory grids) are doomed to failure, as the large standard errors of the correlations ensure that the factor solution will be both arbitrary and unreplicable.

Self-assessment question 17.1

A colleague is studying the mathematical skills of a sample of 100 11-year-old children as part of her project work. She has collected data on 120 test items, each of which she has scored as being answered correctly or incorrectly. She has also coded the county of residence for each person, and is keen to factor analyse all of these responses in order to (re)discover the basic dimensions of mathematical ability and to investigate any differences in these dimensions from county to county What advice would you offer her?

Factor analysis vs. component analysis

One school of thought maintains that factor (rather than component) analysis should never be used because of the difficulty in estimating communalities – the estimation of factor scores also turns out to be surprisingly tricky. The second school of thought maintains that, as the factor model is *a priori* much more likely to fit the data, any attempt to estimate communalities is better than none. The principal components model, they would argue, is simply inappropriate when applied to test items and other data which one would expect to contain unique variance. Interested readers should see Velicer and Jackson (1990) for more detailed discussion of this topic.

Tests for the number of factors

Several tests have been developed to help analysts to choose the 'correct' number of factors. These tests require careful consideration – one cannot rely on computer packages to make this important decision, as most of them (e.g. SPSS) use a technique that is known to be flawed and fail to incorporate some of the more useful tests. Determining the number of factors to be extracted is probably the most important decision that one has to make when conducting a factor analysis. A faulty decision here can produce a nonsensical solution from even the clearest set of data. There is no harm in trying several analyses based on differing numbers of factors and in using several different tests to guide the choice of factors.

The first guides are theory and past experience. One may sometimes want to use factor analysis to ensure that a test is performing as expected when used within a different culture, patient group or whatever. Confirmatory factor analysis can be used for this purpose (see later), but if exploratory factor analysis is preferred, the previous results can be used to guide one in deciding how many factors to extract. If a (technically adequate) factor analysis of a test in the USA revealed seven factors, any attempt to factor analyse the tests in another culture should at least consider the seven-factor solution.

Theory and past practice are all very well, but most factor analyses are truly exploratory in nature. The researcher will often have no good theoretical rationale for deciding how many factors should be extracted and previous studies will sometimes be so technically flawed as to be useless. There are a number of other tests that can be used in such circumstances, all of which seek to determine the number of factors that should be extracted from a correlation matrix. The problem is that few of them have been implemented in the computer packages likely to be encountered by non-expert users. Second, the various techniques do not always yield consistent results. One test may point to six factors, another to eight and previous research to nine! In circumstances such as this, it is safest to consider a number of solutions and check them for psychological plausibility. Users should also consider whether:

- Increasing the number of factors increases the 'simplicity' of the solution (such as decreasing the proportion loadings in the range of −0.4 to 0.4). If increasing the number of factors does little or nothing to increase the simplicity of the solution, it is arguably of little value.

- Any large correlations between factors emerge when performing oblique rotations. These can indicate that too many factors have been extracted and that two factors are trying to pass through the same cluster of variables. Correlations between factors larger than around 0.5 could be regarded as suspect.

- Any well-known factors have split into two or more parts. For example, if myriad previous studies show that a set of items form just one factor (e.g. extraversion), yet they seem to form two factors in your analysis, it is likely that too many factors have been extracted.

The Kaiser–Guttman criterion

One of the oldest and simplest tests for the number of factors is that described by Kaiser (1960) and Guttman (1954) and known as the 'Kaiser–Guttman criterion'. It has the advantage of being very straightforward. One simply performs a principal components analysis on the data, extracting as many factors as there are variables, but without performing an operation known as 'rotation' (to be discussed later). The eigenvalues are calculated as usual by summing the squared loadings on each component. One then simply counts how many eigenvalues are greater than 1.0 – this is the number of factors to be used.

There are many problems with this technique, the most obvious being its sensitivity to the number of variables in the analysis. As each eigenvalue is simply the sum of the squared factor loadings, if the number of variables is large, so too will be the eigenvalue. A test for the number of factors should really give the same result whether or not there are four or 40 variables representing each factor and the Kaiser–Guttman test manifestly will not do so. Furthermore, Hakstian and Mueller (1973) observed that the technique was never intended to be used as a test for the number of factors. Because it is extremely easy to implement automatically, most statistical packages will perform a Kaiser–Guttman test by default. It should *always* be overridden.

The scree test

The scree test, devised by Cattell (1966) is also conceptually simple. Like the Kaiser–Guttman criterion, it is based on the eigenvalues of an initial unrotated principal components solution. **287**

However, it draws on the *relative* values of the eigenvalues and so should not be sensitive to variations in the number of variables being analysed. Successive principal components explain less and less variance and so the eigenvalues decrease. The scree test is based on visual inspection of a graph showing the successive eigenvalues, such as that illustrated in Figure 17.1. This graph should be plotted as accurately as possible, using graph paper or a graph-plotting package. The accuracy of plots produced by some statistical packages is inadequate for this purpose.

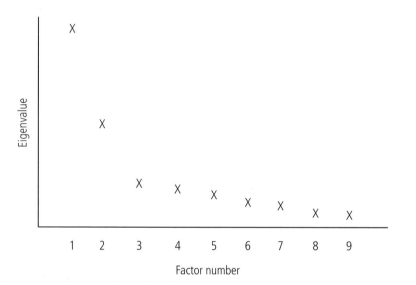

Figure 17.1 Scree test showing eigenvalues from an unrotated principal components analysis of nine variables. The graph indicates that two factors should be extracted.

The basic idea is simple. It is clear that the points on the right-hand side of Figure 17.1 form a straight line, known as a 'scree slope'. It is possible to put a rule through these points and to determine how many eigenvalues lie well above this line. This number of factors should then be extracted. Thus Figure 17.1 depicts a two-factor solution. Further examples of the interpretation of scree tests are given in the literature (Cattell 1966, 1978; Cattell and Vogelman 1977). Several popular texts on factor analysis describe the scree test incorrectly, by asserting that the number of factors corresponds to the number of eigenvalues above the scree line *plus one*. They would thus advocate extracting three factors from our earlier solution. It is not obvious where this confusion arose, as Cattell's papers and 1978 book are quite clear on the matter: '[T]he last real factor is that before the scree begins' (Cattell and Vogelman 1977).

One problem with the scree test is that it does rely on subjective judgement and may sometimes have several possible interpretations, particularly when the sample size or the 'salient' factor loadings are small (Gorsuch 1983). Sometimes more than one clearly identifiable straight scree slope is found. In such cases, one simply looks for the eigenvalues that lie above the leftmost scree slope. An automated version of the scree test has been developed by Paul Barrett and may be downloaded from the internet.

Self-assessment question 17.2

Suppose you performed a factor analysis and discovered that the first ten eigenvalues were 11, 8, 5, 3.5, 2.5, 1.12, 1.08, 1.02, 0.9 and 0.8. Plot a graph to determine how many factors the scree test and the Kaiser–Guttman criterion would indicate.

Parallel analysis

Simulation studies show that parallel analysis is the most accurate way of determining the correct number of factors to extract (Velicer, Eaton, Fava, Goffin and Helmes 2000; Zwick and Velicer 1986) provided that the data being analysed are measured on a continuous scale or a Likert scale with more than two values (Tran and Formann 2009). Now that computers are powerful enough to enable its use, it should be the method of choice. The basic principle is quite simple. It involves checking whether each of the eigenvalues that emerges from a principal components analysis is larger than you would expect by chance.

Suppose that you gather data on ten variables and 100 people and factor analyse the results (but without rotating the factors). The factor analysis program will produce a list of eigenvalues, as many eigenvalues as there are variables.

Now perform another factor analysis, but rather than using the data that you have collected, just analyse random data (again using ten variables, 100 people). You could literally just type in numbers at random into the computer program that you use for factor analysis. Then run the factor analysis again, based on this random data. You would expect the correlations between these random variables to be roughly zero – although some will be a little larger than zero and some smaller than zero by chance. (The size of your sample will affect how close to zero they are: with a small sample, you might find that some correlations are as large as 0.3 or as small as −0.3; with a large sample few if any will be above 0.1 or less than −0.1.) This approach, generating lots of sets of data and seeing what happens when you analyse them in a particular way, is known as Monte Carlo analysis.

It should hopefully be obvious that if all the correlations are zero, no factors are present in the data. In this case, then you would expect each of the eigenvalues to be 1.0 (just take this on trust or try factor analysing a correlation matrix containing zeros yourself to check). So factor analysing the correlation matrix of random numbers and looking at the size of each of the eigenvalues will give you an idea of how large the first, second, third etc. eigenvalues typically are if there are, in reality, no factors present in the data.

The problem is that we have only looked at one set of random data – and, of course, correlations (and eigenvalues) will vary depending what set of random numbers we typed in. So it is necessary to repeat the factor analysis many times – a thousand times, for example – to get an idea how large the eigenvalues typically are: a statistician would say that you find the 'sampling distribution' of the eigenvalues. Then you simply work out the average size of the first eigenvalue, the second eigenvalue etc. by averaging across all 1000 analyses. You also find the 95% confidence limit: that is the value of each eigenvalue that is only exceeded on 5% of the 1000 trials. We call this the *critical value*.

That is all there is to performing parallel analysis. You just look at the first eigenvalue from your analysis of the real data and compare it to the critical value from the random data. If the real eigenvalue is larger than critical value for the first eigenvalue from random data, you conclude **289** that there is at least one factor in the real data and repeat the process for the second, third, fourth factors etc. – until one of the eigenvalues is smaller than the corresponding critical value.

For example, Table 17.1 shows all ten eigenvalues calculated from the factor analysis of ten random variables and 100 participants. Suppose that when you analysed *real* data based on ten variables and 100 participants, you found that the first few eigenvalues were 2.9, 1.63, 1.27, 1.14 and 0.97. How many factors are present in these data? To answer this question using parallel analysis, simply look at the critical values in the final column of Table 17.1 and compare them to those obtained for real data. You can see that the first eigenvalue from the real data (2.9) is larger than the critical value for the first eigenvalue in the table (1.68), so it is unlikely that you would get such a large eigenvalue by chance (i.e. by factor analysing random data). You would thus conclude that there is at least one factor in your data. Likewise the second eigenvalue (1.63) is bigger than 1.47, so there are at least two factors present. The third eigenvalue (1.27), however, is smaller than the critical value of 1.31: it is therefore quite possible that a third eigenvalue as large as 1.27 could have arisen by chance. So you would conclude that there are just two factors present.

You should be concerned about where the numbers in Table 17.1 came from. I did not spend weeks typing 1000 sets of random numbers (each involving ten variables and 100 participants) into an SPSS spreadsheet and performing 1000 factor analyses, laboriously tabulating the results. Several computer programs and websites (search for 'parallel analysis') have been created to produce these tables. It is just necessary to specify the number of variables and participants in your real data and the number of replications to be performed and the program or website will produce a table such as that shown in Table 17.1 within seconds. This may be used to determine the

Eigenvalue number	Average eigenvalue from analysis of 1000 sets of random data	Critical value based on 95% confidence limit: only 5%, or 50, of the random eigenvalues were larger than value shown
1	1.53	1.68
2	1.36	1.47
3	1.23	1.31
4	1.12	1.20
5	1.02	1.09
6	0.93	1.00
7	0.84	0.91
8	0.75	0.82
9	0.66	0.74
10	0.56	0.64

Table 17.1 Eigenvalues obtained from factor analysing 1000 random correlation matrices based on ten variables and 100 participants

appropriate number of factors, as shown here. It is then necessary to analyse your 'real' data using your favourite statistical package and specify that it should extract this number of factors (rather than using the default test).

One word of warning. The critical values for the eigenvalues depend on the number of variables and the number of participants in the factor analysis. The values shown in Table 17.1 will only be correct should you want to find the number of factors present when analysing ten variables and have gathered data from 100 participants. It will be necessary to produce your own version of this table for every set of real data that you need to analyse.

An easier way of performing a parallel analysis may be to use a software package such as Lorenzo-Seva and Ferrando (2006). This program generates the table of simulated eigenvalues automatically and will use the parallel analysis method to extract the appropriate number of factors. It is one of the very few programs that will also perform the MAP test, mentioned in the next section.

Other techniques

The MAP test (Velicer 1976) is another fairly accurate technique for estimating the appropriate number of factors (Zwick and Velicer 1986). Software to perform Revelle and Rocklin's (1979) 'Very Simple Stucture' test for the number of factors can also be downloaded free from the internet. Other techniques of interest include reliable component analysis (Cliff and Caruso 1998) and there are others, too.

Estimation of communalities

The communality of a variable is the proportion of its variance that can be shared with the other variables being factor analysed. In the case of component analysis, it is assumed that this is potentially 100% – that is, that the correlations between variables are entirely attributable to common factor variance and measurement error. In the case of factor models, it is further assumed that each variable has some amount of reliably measured variance that is 'unique' to that variable – and so cannot be shared with any of the other variables in the analysis. This is the variable's 'unique variance', so in factor analysis models the variables' communalities are in general less than 1.0, because of the 'unique variance' associated with each variable.

The estimation of communalities is a process that worries factor analysts, as there is no easy way of checking that one's estimates are correct. Sometimes the procedures used lead to ridiculous estimates of communalities, such as those that are larger than 1.0 ('Heywood cases'). Indeed, the problems associated with this can drive many analysts to use the simpler component model.

Different techniques for factor extraction differ in the way which the communalities are estimated. The simplest is principal-factor analysis, in which communalities are first of all estimated through a series of multiple regressions, using all of the other variables as predictors. Since the communality is defined as the proportion of a variable's variance that can be shared with the other variables in the analysis, it has been claimed that this gives the lower bound for the communality – the smallest value that the communality could possibly have, although a paper by Kaiser (1990) challenges this view. Many packages (such as SPSS principal axis factoring) then modify these values several times through a process known as 'iteration', until they become stable. Unfortunately, however, the theoretical rationale for repeated iteration is dubious and there is no guarantee that it will produce sensible estimates of the true values of the communalities. It **291** is also possible to specify the communalities directly and some packages allow users to choose other values, such as the largest correlation between each variable and any other. Maximum likelihood estimation arguably tackles the communality problem in the most sensible way. That said, it rarely seems to matter much in practice which technique one uses.

Factor extraction

There are a number of techniques available for extracting factors, all with different theoretical backgrounds. Most statistical packages offer users a choice between principal-factor analysis, image analysis (also known as 'Kaiser's second little jiffy'), maximum likelihood analysis, unweighted least squares ('MINRES') and generalized least squares. Most of these techniques have their own individual methods of estimating communalities. In practice, given the same number of factors and communality estimates, all methods will usually produce results that are nearly identical.

However, we must now admit that the previous chapter oversimplified the way in which factors are moved through the clusters of variables. In practice, this is a two-stage process. First, the factors are placed in some arbitrary position relative to the variables, and then another procedure (called *factor rotation*) is used to move the factors through the clusters of variables.

All these techniques for factor extraction therefore place the factors in essentially arbitrary locations relative to the variables. Typically, the factors are positioned so that each successive factor is placed:

- At right angles to previous factors.

- In a position where it 'explains' a substantial proportion of the variance of the items (i.e. where its eigenvalue is large).

Figure 17.2 shows the correlations between four variables V1 to V4. It can be seen that V1 and V2 are highly correlated, as are V3 and V4. Inspection of the figure shows that a two-factor solution would be sensible, with one factor passing between V1 and V2 and another between V3 and V4. However, the initial extraction does not place the factors in this sensible position. Instead, the first factor passes between the two clusters of variables, rather than through the middle of either of them. All the variables will have moderate positive loadings on this factor. The second factor is at right angles to the first and has a positive correlation with V3 and V4 and a negative correlation with V1 and V2. In neither case does a factor pass through the middle of a pair of highly correlated variables.

Factor rotation

Factor rotation changes the position of the factors relative to the variables so that the solution obtained is easy to interpret. As was mentioned in Chapter 6, factors are identified by observing which variables have large and/or zero loadings on them. The solutions that defy interpretation are those in which a large number of variables have 'mediocre' loadings on a factor – loadings of the order of 0.3. These are too small to be regarded as 'salient' and used to identify the factor, yet too large to be treated as if they were zero. Factor rotation moves the factors relative to the variables so that each factor has a few substantial loadings and a few near zero loadings. This is another way of saying that the factors are rotated until they pass through the clusters of variables, between V1 and V2 and between V3 and V4 in Figure 17.2, for example.

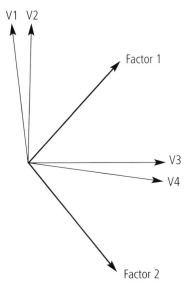

Figure 17.2 Typical position of the two factors relative to four variables following factor extraction.

Thurstone (1947) was probably the first to realize that the initial position of the factor axes was arbitrary and that such solutions were difficult to interpret and harder to replicate. He coined the term 'simple structure' to describe the case in which each factor has some large loadings and some small loadings and likewise each variable has substantial loadings on only a few factors. His 'rules of thumb' are neatly summarized in Child (1990: 48).

Table 17.2 demonstrates how much easier it is to interpret rotated rather than unrotated factor solutions. The unrotated solution is difficult to interpret, as all of the variables have modest loadings on the first factor, while the second factor seems to differentiate the 'mathematical' from the 'language' abilities. After rotation, the solution could not be clearer. The first factor looks as if it measures language ability (because of its substantial loadings from the comprehension and spelling tests), while the second factor corresponds to numerical ability. The eigenvalues and communalities of the variables are also shown. This indicates that, during rotation, the communality of each variable stays the same, but the eigenvalues do not.

	Unrotated		Rotated (VARIMAX)		h²
	Factor 1	**Factor 2**	**Factor 1**	**Factor 2**	
Comprehension	0.40	0.30	0.50	0.00	0.25
Spelling	0.40	0.50	0.64	0.00	0.41
Addition	0.40	−0.40	0.13	0.55	0.32
Subtraction	0.50	−0.30	0.06	0.58	0.34
Eigenvalue	0.73	0.59	0.68	0.64	1.32

Table 17.2 Unrotated and rotated factor solutions

One crucial decision has to be made when rotating factors. Should they be kept at right angles (an 'orthogonal rotation') or should they allowed to become correlated (an 'oblique rotation')? Figure 17.3 shows clearly that an oblique rotation is sometimes necessary to allow the factors to be positioned sensibly relative to the variables. However, the computation and interpretation of orthogonal solutions is considerably more straightforward, which accounts for their popularity.

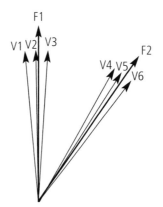

Figure 17.3 Six variables and two correlated factors.

Kaiser's (1958) VARIMAX computer program is the overwhelmingly popular choice for orthogonal rotations and many computer packages will perform it by default. For those who are interested in such detail, its rationale is quite straightforward. Table 17.3 shows the *squares* of each of the loadings of Table 17.2 (squaring is performed to remove the minus signs, if any). The bottom row of Table 17.3 shows the variance (the square of the standard deviation) of these four squared loadings. You will see that, because some of the loadings in the 'rotated' matrix were large whereas others were small, the variance of the squared rotated loadings is much greater than the variance of the loadings in the unrotated solution (0.041 and 0.034, as opposed to 0.002 and 0.006). Thus, if the factors are positioned so that the variance of the (squared) loadings is as large as possible, this should ensure that 'simple structure' is reached. And this (with a minor modification which need not concern us here) is how the VARIMAX program operates. It finds a rotation that MAXimizes the VARIance of the (squared) factor loadings.

	Unrotated		Rotated	
	Factor 1	**Factor 2**	**Factor 1**	**Factor 2**
Comprehension	0.160	0.090	0.250	0.000
Spelling	0.160	0.250	0.410	0.000
Addition	0.160	0.160	0.017	0.302
Subtraction	0.250	0.090	0.003	0.336
Variance of squared loadings	0.002	0.006	0.038	0.034

Table 17.3 Squared loadings from Table 17.2 to demonstrate the principle of VARIMAX rotation

Oblique rotation is more complicated. The first problem is in detecting whether a rotation has reached simple structure. You will recall that the 'factor structure matrix' shows the correlations between all the variables and all the factors. In Figure 17.3, it is clear that, although each factor passes neatly through a cluster of variables, because the factors are correlated it is no longer the case that each variable has a large loading (correlation) with just one factor. Because the factors are correlated, the correlations between V1, V2 and V3 and factor 2 are not near zero. Likewise, although V4, V5 and V6 will have a massive loading on factor 2, they will also have an appreciable correlation with factor 1. This means that the factor structure matrix can no longer be used to decide whether simple structure has been reached.

Another matrix, called the *factor pattern matrix*, can be calculated for this purpose. It does not show *correlations* between the variables and the factors – indeed, the numbers it contains can be larger than 1.0. Instead, it shows regression weights. Thus it can be used to determine whether simple structure has been reached. For the data shown in Figure 17.3, the factor pattern matrix would resemble the VARIMAX-rotated entry of Table 17.2. (In the case of orthogonal rotations such as VARIMAX, the correlation between the factors is always zero and so there are no correlations between factors to correct for. Hence the numbers in the pattern matrix are the same as the numbers in the structure matrix.)

Alarmingly, opinions are divided as to whether the factor structure matrix or the factor pattern matrix should be interpreted in order to identify the factors, or to report the results of factor analyses. For example, Kline (1994: 63) states that 'it is important ... that the structure and not the pattern is interpreted', yet Cattell (1978: Chapter 8) and Tabatchnick and Fidell (1989) hold precisely the opposite view. Brogden (1969) suggests that if the factor analysis uses well-understood tests but the interpretation of the factors is unknown, then the pattern matrix should be consulted. Conversely, if the nature of the factors is known, then the structure matrix should be consulted. Brogden's justification for this position seems to be sound.

Readers may wonder how one would ever be able to identify a factor, but not the variables which load on it. However, this is possible. For example, a selection of behavioural or physiological measures may be correlated and factored. Factor scores might be computed for each person and these may be correlated with other tests. If a set of factor scores shows a correlation of 0.7 with the subjects' scores on a reputable test of anxiety, it is fairly safe to infer that the factor measures anxiety. Alternatively, a few well-trusted tests may be included in the analysis to act as 'marker variables'. If these have massive loadings on any of the rotated factors, this clearly identifies the nature of those factors.

Several programs have been written to perform oblique rotations and Clarkson and Jennrich (1988) and Harman (1976) discuss the relationships between the various methods. Techniques such as Direct Oblimin (Jennrich and Sampson 1966) are among the more useful. Almost all such programs need 'fine tuning' in order to reach simple structure (Harman 1976), usually by means of a parameter controlling how oblique the factors are allowed to become. This is set by default to a value which the program author rather hoped would be adequate for most of the time. Using this value blindly is a dangerous, if common, practice. Harman suggests performing several rotations, each with a different value of this parameter, and interpreting that which comes closest to simple structure. The Index of Factorial Simplicity (Kaiser 1974) is a statistic that shows how well a solution has reached simple structure; unfortunately, its values are rarely computed by statistical packages or reported in the literature. It is important because if the factor solution has not reached simple structure, the results are unlikely to replicate in another sample of people.

Factors and factor scores

Suppose that one factor analyses a set of test items that measure some mental ability, e.g. the speed with which people can visualize what various geometric shapes would look like after being rotated or flipped over. Having performed a factor or component analysis on these data, one might find that a single factor explains a good proportion of the variance, with many of the test items having substantial loadings on this factor. It is possible to validate this factor in exactly the same way as one would validate a test (as discussed in Chapter 15). For example, one can determine whether the factor correlates highly with other psychological tests measuring spatial ability, measures of performance, etc. However, in order to do this it is necessary to work out each person's score on the factor – their 'factor score'.

One obvious way of calculating a factor score is to identify the items that have substantial loadings on the factor and to simply add up each person's scores on these items, ignoring those with tiny loadings on the factor. For example, suppose that response times to only four items were factor analysed and that these had loadings of 0.62, 0.45, 0.18 and 0.90 on a factor (after rotation). This suggests that items 1, 2 and 4 measure much the same construct, whereas item 3 measures something rather different. Therefore, it would be possible to go through the data and average each person's response times to items 1, 2 and 4 only. Thus each person would obtain a 'factor score', which is a measure of the speed with which they can solve the three items with substantial loadings on the factor. Another way of looking at this is to say that each person's scores are 'weighted' using the following numbers – 1, 1, 0 and 1. A weight of '1' is given if the factor loading is thought to be substantial (above 0.4, for example), a weight of -1 would be given if the variable has a loading less than -0.4, and a weight of zero corresponds to a small, insignificant factor loading. Thus a person's factor score can be calculated as:

$$1 \times RT_1 + 1 \times RT_2 + 0 \times RT_3 + 1 \times RT_4 \quad \text{or} \quad RT_1 + RT_2 + RT_4$$

where RT_1 to RT_4 are the response times to items 1 to 4, respectively. The 'weights' (the 0s and 1s) are called 'factor score coefficients'. If each person's factor scores are calculated, they can be correlated with other variables in order to establish the validity of this measure of spatial ability.

While this technique for calculating factor scores is sometimes seen in the literature, it does have its drawbacks. For example, although items 1, 2 and 4 all have loadings above 0.4, item 4 has a loading which is very substantially higher than that of item 2. That is, item 4 is a very much better measure of the factor than is item 2. Should the weights – the 'factor score coefficients' – reflect this? Rather than being 0s and 1s, should they be linked to the size of the factor loadings? This approach clearly does make sense and factor analysis routines will almost invariably offer users the option of calculating these factor score coefficients – one for each variable and each factor. Having obtained these, it is a simple matter to multiply each person's score on each variable by the appropriate factor score coefficient(s) and thus to calculate each person's 'factor score' on each factor. Most computer packages will even do this calculation for you.

For completeness, I ought to mention that factor score coefficients are not applied to the 'raw' scores for each item, but to the 'standardized' scores. Consider item 1. If a person has a response time of 0.9 second to this item, whereas the mean response time of the rest of the sample to this item is 1.0 second, with a standard deviation of 0.2 second, the response time of 0.9 second would convert to a standardized value of or −0.5. It is this value, rather than the original value of 0.9 second, that is used in the computation of factor scores.

The actual mechanics of the calculation of the factor score coefficients need not concern us here. Good discussions are given by Harman (1976: Chapter 16), Comrey and Lee (1992: Section 10.3) and Harris (1967) for those who are interested. Whereas it is a straightforward matter to compute factor scores when principal components analysis is used, the problem becomes much more complex in the case of any form of factor analysis. Here there are several different techniques available for calculating factor scores, each with its own advantages and disadvantages. Bartlett's method is one of the better ones (as argued by McDonald and Burr 1967) and is available as an option on many factor analysis packages.

Self-assessment question 17.4

Suppose that a personnel manager factor analyses applicants' scores on a number of selection tests. How might she use this analysis to decide which tests no longer predict how well employees will perform?

Hierarchical factor analyses

When one performs an oblique factor rotation, the factors obtained are generally correlated. The 'factor pattern correlation matrix' describes the angles between the factors. This matrix of correlations between factors can *itself* be factor analysed – that is, the correlations between the factors can be examined and any clusters of factors identified. This is what is meant by a 'second-order' or 'second-level' factor analysis (factoring the correlations between the variables being the 'first-order analysis'), and researchers such as Cattell have made considerable use of the technique. An example may illustrate the usefulness of the method.

Chris McConville and I once wondered what the basic dimensions of mood might be (1992). We accordingly factor analysed the correlations between over 100 mood items and extracted and obliquely rotated five first-order factors, corresponding to the basic dimensions of mood to discussed in Chapter 12. We then factor analysed the correlations between these first-order factors and discovered that four of these five first-order factors correlated together to form a second-order mood factor called 'negative affect'. The fifth mood factor had a negligible loading on this factor. Thus there was a hierarchy of mood factors as shown in Figure 17.4.

If there are plenty of second-order factors and these show a reasonable degree of correlation, it would be quite legitimate to factor the correlations between the second-order factors to perform a third-order factor analysis. The process can continue either until the correlations between the factors are essentially zero or until just one factor is obtained.

A problem inherent in these hierarchical analyses is that it can be remarkably difficult to identify or conceptualize second- and higher-order factors. Whereas first-order factors can be tentatively identified by inspecting the items with substantial loadings, the second-order factor matrix shows how the first-order factors load on the second-order factor(s). Because of this, it can be quite difficult to identify the second-order factors. For example, what would one make of a factor

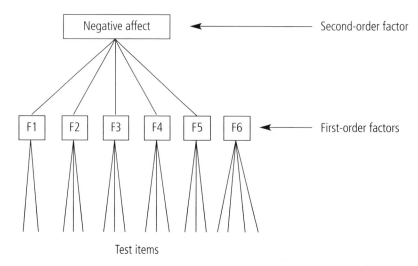

Figure 17.4 Example of hierarchical factor analysis. (After McConville and Cooper 1992b.)

that seemed to measure the primary abilities of spelling, visualization and mechanical ability? It would be much easier to see what was going on if a dozen or so variables could be shown to have large loadings on a second-order factor, rather than trying to interpret the second-order factor in terms of just a couple of large loadings from first-order factors.

Several techniques have been devised to overcome this problem. They all relate second- and higher-order factors directly to the observed variables (Schmid and Leiman 1957). In the example given earlier, the second-order factors would be defined not in terms of the primary factors (spelling, visualization, mechanical ability, etc.), but in terms of the *actual variables*. McConville and Cooper (1992) give an example of this technique in practice. None of the standard factor analysis packages includes the Schmid–Leiman technique, but packages such as EQS and LISREL (described later) can perform similar analyses.

A second problem with these analyses concerns measurement error. Sometimes several quite different positionings of the first-order factors are almost equally satisfactory so far as the criterion of meeting simple structure is concerned. However, the more or less arbitrary choice of one such solution will have a powerful effect on the correlations between the factors and hence the number and nature of the second-order factors. Factor analyses should be performed with above average care if hierarchical solutions are to be produced.

Factor analysis in matrix notation

This section is only intended for readers who have some background in matrix algebra. Factor analysis can be expressed simply in matrix notation; indeed, this is how all the statistical packages compute their solutions. Suppose n variables are administered to a large sample of people. The correlations between these n tests may be represented by a matrix R which has n rows and n columns ('rank n'). We decide to extract m factors. The factor matrix, F, therefore has n rows (variables) and m columns (factors). The aim of factor analysis is simply to find a factor matrix, F, such that:

$$R \approx FF'$$

where F' indicates the transpose of F and $\approx$ means 'approximates'. For example, if there are four variables and two factors, if you multiply the two matrices on the right-hand side of the following equation, you will find that they roughly approximate the correlation matrix. The more factors there are, the better the approximation will be:

1	.10	.20	.60		.03	.90					
.10	1	.60	.30	$\approx$	.89	.11	$\cdot$	.03	.89	.88	.19
.20	.60	1	.20		.88	.11		.90	.11	.11	.87
.60	.30	.20	1		.19	.87					

The problem is that an infinite number of factor matrices, F, give equally good approximations: for example, try multiplying the following matrix by its transpose and comparing the result to the approximation shown earlier:

$$F = \begin{matrix} .66 & .62 \\ .71 & -.55 \\ .71 & -.53 \\ .75 & .48 \end{matrix}$$

Factor rotation provides one way of choosing between these alternatives, by identifying the one factor matrix that best meets the 'simple structure' criterion.

Confirmatory factor analysis

A complete treatment of this topic is beyond the scope of this text. The purpose of this section is merely to mention that the technique exists and to give an example of its usage. Whereas exploratory factor analysis seeks to determine the number and nature of the factors that underlie a set of data through rotation to simple structure, confirmatory factor analysis (as its name suggests) tests hypotheses or rather it allows the user to choose between several competing hypotheses about the structure of the data. For example, suppose you were interested in using a questionnaire to measure attitudes to eating. On reviewing the literature, you might find that one piece of previous research claims that ten of the 20 items form one factor, the remaining ten items form another factor and that these factors have a correlation of 0.4. Another piece of research with the same test might indicate that all 20 items of the test form a single factor. It is vitally important to know which of these claims is correct. The first will lead to two scores being calculated for each person, while the second will produce only one score. Confirmatory factor analysis can be used to determine which of these competing models is most appropriate for the data.

It is possible to specify either factor analytical or principal components models for confirmatory factor analysis. However, almost all studies are based on factor models, where the communality of each variable is estimated. Indeed, it is possible to perform hierarchical factor analyses and to test a huge range of models using the technique. Good descriptions of confirmatory factor analysis and its parent technique, structural equation modelling, are given in Long (1983), Loehlin (2004 [my favourite]) and in Chapters 12 and 13 of Comrey and Lee (1992), among others. Kline (1994) and Child (1990) offer simpler introductions to the subject.

299

A number of computer programs have been written to perform confirmatory factor analysis. The best known is LISREL, written by Karl Jöreskog, the statistician who devised the technique. EQS (Bentler 1989) is another program that is arguably simpler to use than LISREL and one called is MX is freely downloadable.

Confirmatory factor analysis views the basic data (test scores, responses to test items, physiological measures, etc.) as being brought about or caused by one or more factors (often known as 'latent variables'). Thus a set of equations can be drawn up, each showing which factor(s) are thought to influence which variable(s).

For example, suppose we postulate two factors – general intelligence (g) and test anxiety ('TA'). Also suppose that the scores on a test, Test 1, are influenced by both of these factors – but more by general intelligence than by test anxiety. We can represent this by a simple equation, such as:

$$\text{Test } 1 = 0.8 \times g + 0.1 \times \text{TA} + \text{unique variance}$$

The numbers 0.8 and 0.1 show the size of the relationship between the variables and each factor – the factor loadings. Each of these numbers can be:

- specified directly, as a number (as in our example)

- estimated by the computer program

- or set equal to other values that are then all estimated. For example, one could specify that all of the tests are affected by test anxiety to an equal but unknown extent. (This option can be problematical in practice.)

In confirmatory factor analysis, one normally draws up an equation for each variable, showing which factor (or factors) are thought to influence scores on this variable – although not normally the *size* of the loadings. Any factor loadings that are not specified are assumed to be zero. It is also necessary to specify that the variance of each factor is 1.0. The computer program then estimates the best possible values for each of the loadings and also computes statistics showing how closely the postulated structure fits the actual data. It is common practice to try out several different models and to choose the one which gives the best fit – that is, which is best supported by the data.

Loehlin (2004) gives a good discussion of how to interpret the various indices of goodness of fit. While these measures of goodness of fit are useful for choosing between competing models, they are not particularly effective for working out the absolute goodness of fit of a particular model. That is, the technique cannot easily determine whether or not a pattern of factors and factor loadings is found in the data, but can be useful in deciding which of three competing models is the most appropriate.

It is common practice to represent the relationships between the variables, common factors and unique factors by means of a diagram called the 'path diagram'. An example should make this clear.

Ignoring the numbers, Figure 17.5 shows two factors, F1 and F2, each of which is thought to influence some observed variables (V1 to V6). You will notice that V4 is influenced by both of the factors and the other variables are influenced by just one of them. Also shown are the unique variances of each variable (U1 to U6). Each of the lines linking a factor to an observed variable has an arrow at one end, indicating that the factor is presumed to cause a particular observed score (rather than vice versa). The curved line between F1 and F2 represents a correlation – factor 1 and factor 2 may be correlated. Thus this diagram corresponds to an oblique factor solution.

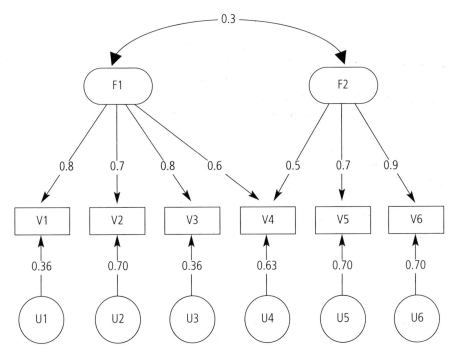

Figure 17.5 Path diagram showing how two correlated factors (F1 and F2) influence the value of six observed variables (V1–V6). The variables' unique variances (U1–U6) are also shown.

The numbers on each of the lines represent the factor loadings (in the factor pattern matrix) or, in the case of the curved line, the correlation between these factors. Some of these values might have been specified by the user at the start of the analysis. More usually, however, all of the numbers will have been estimated by the program. Thus the path diagram in Figure 17.5 corresponds to the factor pattern matrix shown in Table 17.3.

Several other plausible path diagrams can be drawn up on the basis of theory or previous research and each can be tested in order to determine how closely it fits the data. In this way, the researcher can choose between various competing theoretical models. However, there are some risks involved in the use of these techniques. It is all too easy to embark on a 'fishing trip', modifying a model over and over again in order to improve its goodness of fit, regardless of its psychological plausibility. Indeed the programs encourage this practice by suggesting those parts of the model that need modification. However, the computer program knows nothing about psychology or the theory of factor analysis and will frequently suggest something nonsensical, such as allowing the unique variances of different variables to become correlated. Such a model may fit the data from a particular sample wonderfully well, yet make little psychological sense (and be unlikely to replicate in other samples). However, whenever there is a need to choose between competing theoretical models, confirmatory factor analysis can prove to be a very useful tool.

The account given here has been deliberately simplified and readers who intend to use the technique should in particular ensure that they understand from other sources:

- that analyses are usually performed on covariances, rather than correlations, and

- what is meant by the 'identification' of a model.

Summary

Factor analysis is a tremendously useful technique for clarifying the relationships between a number of interval-scaled or ratio-scaled variables. It can be applied to all such data – from physical and physiological measures to questionnaire items. This chapter has described how to perform a technically sound factor analysis and has highlighted some common errors that occasionally creep into published papers. Finally, it has introduced confirmatory factor analysis as a useful technique for choosing between various competing factor analytical models.

Suggested additional reading

This has been largely indicated in the text. The books by Child and Kline are the simplest, but those by Gorsuch and Comrey are also fairly accessible to non-mathematicians.

Answers to self-assessment questions

SAQ 17.1

There are problems with this proposal, the most obvious one being that 'county of residence' is not an interval-scaled variable. When the numerical codes were being allocated, it was entirely arbitrary whether a '1' referred to Cornwall or Cumbria, so the codes do not represent a scale of any kind. Therefore they must be excluded from the factor analysis. (To check for differences in mathematical ability between counties you could suggest that your colleague calculates factor scores on each of the factors and then performs an analysis of variance using 'county' as the between-subjects factor.)

The other problem is that there are more variables being analysed than there are people in the sample. Thus although the number of subjects is greater than the 'magic' number of 100, these data are not suitable for factor analysis. You could suggest that your colleague collects some more data so as to increase the sample size to at least 150. You could usefully warn her about the problems inherent in factoring dichotomous data such as these – where the only possible answers are 0 or 1 – and if the items are found to differ drastically in their difficulty values (the proportion of individuals answering each item correctly), you could consider consulting the literature for alternatives to the Pearson correlation which are suitable for factor analysis.

Finally, you could usefully check with your colleague that the children were given plenty of time to attempt all of the test items and ask whether the items that were not attempted have been coded as being answered incorrectly or given a special code and treated as missing data. If items that were not attempted are given the same code as 'incorrect answer' (e.g. '0'), it is clear that problems can arise if not all of the children managed to finish the test in the time allocated. The items towards the end would appear to be more difficult than they really are, simply because only a few children managed to reach them. In circumstances such as these, it might be better just to analyse the first 50 items (or whatever), in which case there is no need for your colleague to collect any more data, as the sample of 100 would be adequate for this number of items.

SAQ 17.2

Five and eight. You should probably extract five factors, given that the scree test has been found to perform better than the Kaiser–Guttman technique.

SAQ 17.3

Simple structure is a measure of the extent to which each factor passes through a cluster of variables. Let us suppose that the factors are being kept at right angles – an orthogonal rotation. If the rotation has reached simple structure, each factor will have few sizeable correlations (above 0.4 or below –0.4) with some variables, and correlations close to zero (e.g. ±0.1) with the rest. There should be very few medium sized correlations, in the range of ±0.1–0.4. Similarly, when the rows of the factor matrix are examined, each variable should have a large loading on only one or two factors. The position is much the same for oblique rotations (where the factors are not kept at right angles), except that the 'factor pattern matrix', is used to assess the simplicity of the solution, does not contain correlations between the variables and the factors, although it is interpreted in the same way.

Since the initial position of the factors relative to the variables is essentially arbitrary, different researchers would report quite different results if rotation to simple structure were not carried out. It is thus important for ensuring that factors can be consistently identified across several different studies.

SAQ 17.4

The factor analysis will show the nature and the extent of the overlap between the test scores and will probably produce several factors measuring personality and/or ability. Scores can be calculated for each applicant on each of these factors ('factor scores') and each of these factor scores can be validated in precisely the same way that tests are validated, as described in Chapter 4. For example, the applicants could be followed up and their factor scores correlated with measures of productivity or with supervisors' ratings of performance. Alternatively, analysis of variance may be used to determine any differences in factor scores between various groups of employees, e.g. those who are later promoted or those who leave.

If some of the factor scores do seem to be useful in the selection process, the tests that have high loadings on the factors in question could usefully be retained. Those which do not load on any of the useful factors could probably be dropped from the assessment battery.

References

Barrett, P. and Kline, P. (1981). The observation to variable ratio in factor analysis. *Personality Study and Group Behavior 1*, 23–33.

Bartlett, M. S. (1954). A note on multiplying factors for various chi-square approximations. *Journal of the Royal Statistical Society (Series B) 16*, 296–8.

Bentler, P. M. (1989). *EQS Structural Equations Program Manual*. Los Angeles: BMDP Statistical Software Inc.

Brogden, H. E. (1969). Pattern, structure and the interpretation of factors. *Psychological Bulletin 72*(5), 375–8.

Cattell, R. B. (1952). *Factor Analysis*. New York: Harper & Bros.

Cattell, R. B. (1966). The scree test for the number of factors. *Multivariate Behavioral Research 1*, 140–61.

Cattell, R. B. (1978). *The Scientific Use of Factor Analysis in Behavioral and Life Sciences*. New York: Plenum.

Cattell, R. B. and Vogelman, S. (1977). A comprehensive trial of the scree and KG criteria for determining the number of factors. *Journal of Educational Measurement 14*(2), 289–325.

Chambers, R. G. (1982). Correlation coefficients from 2 x 2 tables and from biserial data. *British Journal of Mathematical and Statistical Psychology 35*, 216–27.

Child, D. (1990). *The Essentials of Factor Analysis* (2nd edn). London: Cassell.

Clarkson, D. B. and Jennrich, R. I. (1988). Quartic rotation criteria and algorithms. *Psychometrika 53*(2), 251–9.

Cliff, N. and Caruso, J. C. (1998). Reliable component analysis through maximizing composite reliability. *Psychological Methods 3*(3), 291–308.

Comrey, A. L. and Lee, H. B. (1992). *A First Course in Factor Analysis* (2nd edn). Hillsdale, NJ: Erlbaum.

Dobson, P. (1988). The correction of correlation coefficients for restriction of range when restriction results from the truncation of a normally disributed variable. *British Journal of Mathematical and Statistical Psychology 41*, 227–34.

Gorsuch, R., L. (1983). *Factor Analysis* (2nd edn). Hillsdale, NJ: Erlbaum.

Guadagnoli, E. and Velicer, W. F. (1988). Relation of sample size to the stability of component patterns. *Psychological Bulletin 103*(2), 265–75.

Guilford, J. P. and Fruchter, B. (1978). *Fundamental Statistics in Psychology and Education* (6th edn). Tokyo: McGraw-Hill Kogakusha.

Guttman, L. (1954). Some necessary and sufficient conditions for common factor analysis. *Psychometrika 19*, 149–61.

Hakstian, A. R. and Mueller, V. J. (1973). Some notes on the number of factors problem. *Multivariate Behavioral Research 8*, 461–75.

Harman, H. H. (1976). *Modern Factor Analysis* (3rd edn). Chicago: Chicago University Press.

Harris, C. W. (1967). On factors and factor scores. *Psychometrika 32*, 363–79.

Howell, D. C. (2001). *Statistical Methods for Psychology* (5th edn). Belmont, CA: Duxbury.

Jennrich, R. I. and Sampson, P. F. (1966). Rotation for simple loadings. *Psychometrika 31*(3), 313–23.

Kaiser, H. F. (1958). The VARIMAX criterion for analytic rotation in factor analysis. *Psychometrika 23*, 187–200.

Kaiser, H. F. (1960). The application of electronic computers in factor analysis. *Educational and Psychological Measurement 20*, 141–51.

Kaiser, H. F. (1974). An index of factorial simplicity. *Psychometrika 39*, 31–6.

Kaiser, H. F. (1990). On Guttman's proof that squared multiple correlations are lower bounds for communalities. *Psychological Reports 67*(3), 1, 1004–6.

Kline, P. (1994). *An Easy Guide to Factor Analysis*. London: Routledge.

Loehlin, J. C. (2004). *Latent Variable Models: An Introduction to Factor, Path, and Structural Equation Analysis* (4th edn). Mahwah, NJ: Erlbaum.

Long, J. S. (1983). *Confirmatory Factor Analysis: A Preface to LISREL*. Beverley Hills, CA: Sage.

Lorenzo-Seva, U. and Ferrando, P. J. (2006). FACTOR: a computer program to fit the exploratory factor analysis model. *Behavior Research Methods 38*(1), 88–91.

McConville, C. and Cooper, C. (1992). The structure of moods. *Personality and Individual Differences 13*(8), 909–19.

McDonald, R. P. and Burr, E. J. (1967). A comparison of four methods of constructing factor scores. *Psychometrika 32*, 381–401.

Nunnally, J. C. (1978). *Psychometric Theory* (2nd edn). New York: McGraw-Hill.

Revelle, W. and Rocklin, T. (1979). Very simple structure: an alternative procedure for estimating the optimal number of interpretable factors. *Multivariate Behavioral Research 14*(4), 403–14.

Schmid, J. and Leiman, J. M. (1957). The development of hierarchical factor solutions. *Psychometrika 22*(1), 53–61.

Tabatchnick, B. G. and Fidell, L. S. (1989). *Using Multivariate Statistics* (2nd edn). New York: Harper & Row.

Tabatchnick, B. G. and Fidell, L. S. (2001). *Using Multivariate Statistics* (4th edn). New York: Harper & Row.

Thurstone, L. L. (1947). *Multiple Factor Analysis: A Development and Expansion of the Vectors of Mind*. Chicago: University of Chicago Press.

Tran, U. S. and Formann, A. K. (2009). Performance of parallel analysis in retrieving unidimensionality in the presence of binary data. *Educational and Psychological Measurement 69*(1), 50–61.

Vegelius, J. (1973). *Correlation Coefficients as Scalar Products in Euclidean Spaces* (No. 145). Uppsala: University of Uppsala, Department of Psychology.

Velicer, W. F. (1976). Determining the number of components from the matrix of partial correlations. *Psychometrika 41*(3), 321–7.

Velicer, W. F., Eaton, C. A., Fava, J. L., Goffin, R. D. and Helmes, E. (2000). Construct explication through factor or component analysis: a review and evaluation of alternative procedures for determining the number of factors or components. In *Problems and Solutions in Human Assessment: Honoring Douglas N. Jackson at Seventy*. New York, NY: Kluwer Academic/Plenum.

Velicer, W. F. and Jackson, D. N. (1990). Component analysis versus common factor analysis: some issues in selecting an appropriate procedure. *Multivariate Behavioral Research 25*(1), 1–28.

Zwick, W. R. and Velicer, W. F. (1986). Comparison of five rules for determining the number of components to retain. *Psychological Bulletin 99*(3), 432–42.

18 Constructing a test

Background

This chapter is included for two reasons. First, it is possible that readers may at some stage want to develop their own scale and so it seems appropriate to offer some guidelines on how items may be constructed and assembled into a reliable scale, although I argue against this and explain why I think there are already far too many tests in psychology. Second, it shows why it is not possible to assemble a set of items and assume that they form a reliable and valid scale and offers some insights as to how tests may be constructed without the use of factor analysis.

Recommended prior reading

Chapters 1, 14, 15, 16 and 17.

Introduction

This chapter is included in case readers are either interested to learn how tests are constructed or feel the urge to develop their own scale to measure some personality or ability trait. Please do not do so! In my experience, most students who decide to construct a scale do not appreciate how much work is involved in developing, refining and validating it.

Many readers will have encountered tests that are quite different from those that have been described in this text. Social psychologists, in particular, measure several dimensions of personality that seem to be quite different from the traits that were discussed in Chapters 4 and 5 and readers may wonder why I have not yet discussed locus of control, self-esteem and the like. The problem is that most of these tests are simply not very satisfactory. Some (e.g. measures of locus of control) do not appear to measure a trait at all, but are situation-specific (Coombs and Schroeder 1988). Some involve items that are so similar that they form a 'bloated specific' – a traits that appears simply because all of the items in a scale are paraphrases of each other (see Chapter 15 for an example). Worse still, when the items are factored, they often fail to form a single scale. Many (if not most) of these tests measure *mixtures* of several distinct personality traits, which, as we saw in Chapter 15, makes their interpretation almost impossible.

In the unlikely event of my becoming a dictator, my first edict would be as follows: *It is a penal offence for any psychologist to publish any scale if more than 70% of the reliable variance of that scale can be predicted by existing tests.* In other words, I feel strongly that any new test must be shown to tap some aspects of personality or ability that are really rather different from any combination of traits that we already know and understand. Otherwise, tests will simply proliferate. One scale will measure two parts extraversion and one part neuroticism, while another will measure two parts extraversion and one part psychoticism. Enormous theories will be built up around these personality dimensions and then someone will have the bright idea of correlating the two tests together and (because they both measure extraversion to some extent) the correlation will be large and positive. Ripples of excitement will run through the journals, reputations will be made and yet more complicated theories will spring up to explain what seems rather obvious to us simple-minded psychometricians.

However, there must be something wrong with this description, since most psychologists take exactly the opposite view and the proliferation of tests continues – even though the evidence often suggests that this is really not a good idea. Consider tests measuring self-esteem – a widely used concept in social psychology. There is evidence (summarized in Kline 1999) that tests claiming to measure 'self-esteem' really just tap a mixture of anxiety (or neuroticism) and extraversion. Since it is difficult to imagine why any psychologist would want to measure a mixture of two quite distinct traits in a single test, the continued use of these scales has always rather baffled this author. It is quite permissible to combine scores from several different scales, e.g. by adding together individuals' standardized scores on tests measuring extraversion and neuroticism if there is a need to identify extraverted neurotics. The point is that, by doing this, test users are forced to become aware of what traits are really being assessed, rather than building elaborate theories on what are wrongly believed to be entirely novel aspects of individual differences.

Despite these dire warnings, it is useful to know the merits (and drawbacks) of several techniques for developing scales, so that one can understand and evaluate the merit of published tests. All these apply to tests that measure traits and that are generously timed (so each person has time to attempt all of the questions). This latter point is important, since if very restricted time limits are imposed, the last items will always appear to be difficult, solely because many candidates will not have attempted them.

Writing test items

Obviously, writing the items is *the* crucial step in designing a test. If the items are poorly written, then no amount of psychometric wizardry will be able to produce a reliable and valid scale. Kline (1986) has given some commonsense 'rules of thumb' for writing and I shall draw on this work in the next three sections. You may well also like to re-examine your professional association's guidelines for the construction and use of psychological tests, which may resemble those shown in Appendix B.

Problems arise when developing ability scales that are designed to be used with very restricted time limits. Since some candidates may not reach the items at the end of the test, it is very difficult to estimate the difficulty of those items, which becomes confused with the candidates' speed of answering. It is better to administer the test with unlimited time at the development stage and to impose time limits when putting together the final version.

General principles

The main points to be kept in mind when writing items are as follows:

- The items should be properly sampled and should tap every single aspect of the concept. An arithmetic test should not be based solely on 'addition' problems. A depression inventory should enquire about behaviours (e.g. disturbed sleep and eating habits) as well as feelings. It may be advisable to draw up a list of the main 'facets' of the phenomenon to be assessed and write equal numbers of items to tap each facet. For example, a teacher may decide to assess arithmetical ability on the basis of ability to perform long division, long multiplication, **307** geometry/trigonometry, solution of simultaneous equations, finding roots of quadratic equations, differentiation and integration. It may often be necessary to conduct a literature search (or examine diagnostic manuals such as the *Diagnostic and Statistical Manual of Mental Disorders* (DSM-IV) to ensure that you have a full and complete understanding of the topic that is to be assessed.

- Decide on the population with which the test is to be used before writing the items. Items in an ability test designed to select between graduates would obviously need to be harder than one designed for use with the general population. A personality test targeted at adolescents should bear in mind that their vocabulary will be restricted.

- The test should be long enough to ensure that it covers all aspects of the topic and is reliable. As a rule of thumb, you may wish to start with at least 30 items and reduce these down to a list of no fewer than 20 items, although if there are many facets you may well need more.

- Items should be short and clear.

- Check words using a dictionary to ensure that an item does not have several possible interpretations. One personality questionnaire used to include the item 'do you enjoy gay parties?', meaning 'lively'.

- Each item should assess only the trait that it is designed to measure, so items should be written so that the responses are unlikely to be affected by individual differences in vocabulary, by social desirability, any other similar sources of systematic bias or by any other traits.

- The cultural appropriateness of each item should be carefully considered. This will typically include the implicit knowledge required to understand (or solve) the problem. In the arithmetic test example, the teacher assumes that all children will be able to add, subtract, multiply and divide and to understand the order in which arithmetic operations are performed in equations, etc.

- It is important to ensure that the items are logically independent. In the case of personality tests, check that if a logically consistent person answers any item in a particular way, then this does not 'force' them to give any particular answer to any other item(s) – that is, no two items should mean the same thing. In the case of ability tests, you should never base one item on the answer to a previous item such as 'item 1: what is 2 + 3?', 'item 6: what is the answer to item 1 multiplied by 4?'.

- It is very easy to produce a scale with a high level of reliability by paraphrasing the same item several times, but this is artificial, since the items are not being properly sampled from the domain of interest. Therefore I would urge item writers to examine every possible pair of items and check that the way a person answers one item does not force him or her to answer any other item in a particular way, other than through the influence of the trait that the test is designed to measure.

Items for ability tests

- Decide on the response format, e.g. free response (2 + 2 = ?) or multiple choice (2 + 2 = (a) 4, (b) 22, (c) 5, (d) 3) and, if a multiple choice format is chosen, decide how many alternatives should be offered. There should be at least four alternatives in order to reduce the effects of lucky guessing.

- Write an equal number of items for each facet, taking care to construct good, plausible distractors (possibly based on an analysis of common errors from an earlier, free-response pilot version of the test if using a multiple-choice format). Ensure that the items in each facet appear to span a similar and appropriate range of difficulty.

- Make sure that you are not tempted to test the trivial just because it is easy to do so. For example, if you were designing a test to assess students' statistical ability, the easiest type of item to write would concern formulae and definitions, e.g. 'what is the equation for calculating the sample standard deviation from a set of data?' The problem is, of course, that the instructor *should* be interested in testing how well students *understand* and can *apply* the concepts – repeating definitions parrot fashion is rarely what is wanted. The driving test provides another good example. I can remember learning and reciting stopping distances, although the examiners never seemed to check that candidates knew what those distances actually looked like when they were driving.

- If the test is to be timed, then it is necessary to carry out a pilot study to choose an appropriate time limit.

- Ensure that the instructions for the test are brief, clear and unambiguous. They should cover how to solve the problems, how to record the chosen answer, whether or not to guess if unsure of the answer and should specify the time allowed.

- Ensure that there are several practice items and that the answers to these are given before the main test, so that test takers can check that they understand what to do.

Gulliksen (1986) is an excellent, non-technical paper on the assessment of abilities and attainment. It considers several other forms of test items and makes vital reading for anyone interested in constructing tests in this general area.

Items for personality tests

- The first step is to decide how you want respondents to answer your questions – there are several popular formats. The test may present statements with which people agree, are neutral or unsure or disagree, e.g. 'I lie awake at night worrying about the day's events'. You might also consider adding 'strongly agree' and 'strongly disagree' to the list, but do not use any more than seven categories. If you are using this type of scale, *always* use words such as 'agree/?/disagree' on the questionnaire and not just numbers. Statistical problems can arise if less than three categories are used (see Chapter 8 and Appendix B). With this type of item, try to keep to an odd number of choices, since this ensures that there is a central, neutral answer that test takers like. Alternatively, the test may give several possible answers, e.g. 'in the last week, my worries kept me from falling asleep immediately on (a) no days, (b) 1 or 2 days, (c) 3 or 4 days (d) 5 or more days'.

- Try to write items that are clear, unambiguous and require as little self-insight as possible. Wherever possible, you should refer to behaviours rather than to feelings, as in the second example in the previous paragraph.

- Ensure that each item asks only *one* question. For example, do not use a statement such as 'I sometimes feel depressed and have attempted suicide', since extremely depressed people who have not (quite) got round to attempting suicide would have to disagree with it, which is presumably not what is intended.

- Try to avoid negatively phrased items such as 'I dislike students: yes/?/no', since choosing 'no' requires the participant to interpret a double negative.

- Try to avoid questions asking about frequency or amount. Instead, refer to specific rather than general behaviour. Instead of asking 'do you read a lot?', try asking 'how many books have you read for pleasure in the past month?' – or, better still, 'list the books that you have read for pleasure in the past month' (which may reduce socially desirable responses).

- Try to ensure that about 50% of the items in each facet are keyed so that a 'yes/strongly agree' response indicates a high score on the trait and the others are keyed in the opposite direction. For example, 'I generally fall asleep at night as soon as the light is turned off' would be scored so that 'strongly disagree' indicated anxiety.

- If you *must* ask about something socially undesirable, consider phrasing the item from another person's point of view, e.g. 'some people might describe me as mean' rather than 'are you mean?'

- It is wise to ensure that the instructions ask respondents to give the first answer that springs naturally to mind, rather than looking for hidden meanings.

- Draft instructions so that participants are clear about what you want them to do, whether they should answer all questions, whether there is a time limit.

Item analysis

- Having compiled a draft test, it is necessary to ensure that all of the items measure the same construct before proceeding to check that the test is reliable and valid. In order to do this, the test should be administered to a large ($n > 200$) sample of people, similar in nature to the individuals who will ultimately use the test. For example, if a test is to be used to select graduate applicants for a particular organization, it would be appropriate to try out the test with undergraduates, but not with 16-year-old pupils in a comprehensive school (because of their different academic background) or pensioners (because of their different age). Using smaller samples is most unwise, for, as Nunnally (1978) shows, the estimate of reliability that is calculated from a sample of data is only reasonably close to its true value when samples of 200+ are used.

- The responses are then scored. In the case of ability tests, this will typically involve giving one point for a correct answer and zero points for an incorrect response or an omitted item. In the case of Likert-scaled items (e.g. strongly agree/agree/neutral/disagree/strongly disagree), the response is converted to a number indicating the strength of the response. Suppose the scale was supposed to assess squeamishness and someone wrote 'disagree' to the item 'I feel physically sick at the sight of blood'. Strongly agreeing with this item would gain five points (since a five-point scale is used), so 'disagree' gets two points. These scored items would then normally be entered into a computer package such as SPSS. And yes, you do need to enter the score for each individual item – not the total score.

- The next stage is to examine the mean score for each of the items, together with its standard deviation. In the case of an ability test (where a correct answer is awarded one point and an incorrect answer is given zero points), the mean score indicates the difficulty of each item. A mean score of 0.95 would indicate that 95% of the sample gave the correct response to an item.

In the case of personality tests, the mean score shows the extent to which individuals tend to agree or disagree with statements. As a general rule of thumb, it would be undesirable to have *too* many very easy or very difficult items in the test, so if more than about 10% of items have mean scores above 0.8 or below 0.2, it would be prudent to consider removing some of them.

> **Self-assessment question 18.1**
>
> Why is it not advisable to have too many very easy or very difficult items in a test?

Examine the standard deviation for each item. This shows the level of individual differences found in participants' responses to it. For example, if an item has a standard deviation of zero, everyone has answered it in the same way and the item is therefore clearly not tapping any kind of individual differences and should be removed from the scale. (When items are scored using a two-point scale, such as correct/incorrect, the standard deviation is linked directly to the mean, as readers who have studied the binomial theorem should be able to verify. This step should be skipped in such cases.)

Although checking the items' means and standard deviations is a necessary first step, this cannot reveal the questions in the test that are flawed in content. For example, suppose that one item in a personality test used language that was too difficult for the participants to understand, so causing them all to guess an answer. Another item might be badly affected by 'social desirability'. We shall mention four techniques of *item analysis* for identifying items that, for whatever reason, simply do not measure the same thing as the other items in the test.

When using any of the four techniques described later to eliminate items from the test, it is important to try to ensure that the test retains approximately equal numbers of items in all of its facets (as described earlier). Suppose, for example, that a teacher started off by writing five items in each of seven facets of mathematical attainment: long division, long multiplication, geometry/trigonometry, solution of simultaneous equations, finding roots of quadratic equations, differentiation and integration. Item analysis will remove some of the 35 items (those that are too easy, too hard or which simply do not seem to work), but it would clearly be unfortunate if the analysis led to the removal of *all* the long division items and *all* the long multiplication items, since the teacher believes that these are two important components of the pupils' mathematical attainment. Item analysis is an art as well as a science and when removing items it is important to try to ensure that approximately equal numbers are left in each of the facets.

Methods of test construction

Constructing tests by criterion keying

Suppose that we are asked to construct a psychological test to select aeroplane pilots – the goal is to develop a test whose total score will be able to predict the pilots' final score on their training course and which may therefore be used to identify applicants who are likely to perform poorly on this course. Having no clear idea of what may be appropriate personality and ability characteristics for this application, we might put together a vast questionnaire consisting of 600 items that we hope will measure all of the main abilities and personality traits that can be assessed. But which ones actually predict pilot performance?

Suppose that the draft version of the scale has been administered to several hundred trainees. The most obvious way of identifying the good (i.e. predictive) items in the test is to validate each item directly against the criterion. For example, suppose that at the end of their training, each trainee pilot is awarded a mark of between 0 and 100, indicating their overall level of performance in the pilot training course. Surely the item analysis process would simply involve correlating the trainees' scores on each of the items in the test with their scores on the training course. Items that have substantial correlations would appear to be able to predict the criterion and those that do not would be dropped from the test.

This procedure, which is known as *criterion keying*, has been used in the construction of several well-known scales, including the Minnesota Multiphasic Personality Inventory , the MMPI and MMPI-2 (Graham 1990; Hathaway and McKinley 1967) and the California Psychological Inventory (Gough 1975), the scales of which can supposedly discriminate between various clinical groups. *Do not use this method of item analysis*. As Nunnally (1978) reminds us, it has several fatal flaws.

First, it is very likely to produce scales that have very low reliability – that is, scales containing items that measure a number of different things. For example, suppose that success in the pilot training course depended on mathematical ability, mechanical ability, spatial ability, low neuroticism and extraversion. If criterion keying were to be applied to a large sample of items, it would produce a scale that measured a mixture of all these things. Second, it is rarely possible to identify a *single* criterion to be used when selecting items. For example, consider my post, which involves lecturing in individual differences and psychometrics, research, writing and editing books, writing research papers, taking tutorials, administration (e.g. planning courses), marking essays and examination papers, coordinating certain laboratory activities, supervising PhD students and a host of other activities. Which one of these should be used as the criterion against which my performance should be judged? If they are to be averaged in some way, how many scientific papers or how much course planning are equivalent to one book? If one criterion is used, one particular set of predictive items will be identified – if another criterion is chosen, the chances are that quite a different selection of items will be indicated. The third point is a little more statistical. In order to select the 'best' items by criterion keying, one correlates responses to particular items with the criterion – if the test consists of 400 or so items (as does the MMPI), then one calculates 400 correlations. Without going into details, if large numbers of correlations are being calculated, we would expect several of the correlations to be appreciably larger than their true (population) values. In other words, some of the items that we select by this procedure are unlikely to work for other groups of applicants. Finally, this procedure gives us no real understanding of *why* the test works – it is completely atheoretical. Without an understanding of what psychological constructs are being measured by the 'useful' items, it is impossible to tell whether the test is likely to be useful in other applications (e.g. for selecting air-traffic controllers) and it becomes very difficult to 'fix' the test if it suddenly stops predicting performance. For all these reasons, criterion keying should be avoided.

Constructing tests by factor analysis of items

Psychologists such as Cattell advocate the use of factor analysis to construct tests, although others (e.g. Nunnally 1978) have identified some problems with this approach. Here the correlations between the (scored) items are factor analysed, and the factor(s) that emerge are tentatively identified on the basis of their loadings on the rotated factors, as described in Chapters 16 and 17.

When putting together a set of items to measure one particular construct, we would of course *hope* that just one factor will emerge and that all of the variables will have large loadings (in the same direction) on that factor. In practice, there may be more than one factor and some variables may not have loadings above 0.4 on *any* factor and so should be dropped. This method of constructing scales simply involves identifying and retaining those items that have a substantial loading on the main factor(s).

Constructing tests using classical item analysis

We have left the easiest technique of item analysis until last. You will recall that high reliability is generally thought to be an excellent feature of a test. It therefore seems sensible to try to estimate the extent to which each of the items in a test correlates with individuals' 'true scores', which, you will recall, are the scores that each individual would have obtained had he or she administered all items that could possibly have been written to measure the topic. If we somehow identify items each of which has a substantial correlation with the true score, when we add up individuals' scores on these items, the total scores on the test are bound to show a substantial correlation with the true score. This is, of course, another way of saying that the test has high internal consistency reliability. Thus if it is possible to detect items that show appreciable correlations with the true score, it is also possible to choose those items that will produce a highly reliable test.

The problem is that we can never measure individuals' true scores. However, there is one piece of data that can be shown to approximate to this, namely, the individual's total score on all of the items in the test. Thus classical item analysis simply correlates the total score on the test with the scores on each of the individual items. Consider, for example, the data shown in Table 18.1, which represent the responses of six people to a five-item test (where a correct answer was scored as 1 and an incorrect answer as 0), together with each person's total score on the test. The row marked '*r* with total' simply correlates the responses to each of the items with the total scores on the test. You may wish to check one or two of these so that you can see how they have been calculated. Here Item 4 appears to be the best measure (that is, it correlates well with the total score) while Item 3 is the worst. It is probable that dropping Item 3 will improve the reliability of the scale.

	Item 1	Item 2	Item 3	Item 4	Item 5	Total
Person 1	1	0	1	1	1	4
Person 2	0	1	1	1	0	3
Person 3	0	0	1	0	0	1
Person 4	0	0	1	0	0	1
Person 5	0	1	0	1	1	3
Person 6	1	0	1	1	0	3
r with total	0.63	0.32	−0.20	0.95	0.63	
Corrected *r* with total	0.11	0.22	−0.48	0.87	0.50	

Table 18.1 Hypothetical data for item analysis

The correlations between each item and the total score are as close as we can get to estimating the correlation between each item and the *true* score, so it seems sensible to drop those items that have low correlations with the total score – keeping a careful eye on which facet of the trait is measured by a particular item and ensuring that the items that are left contain approximately equal numbers of items from each of the facets. Thus while the item analysis procedure involves removing an item which has a low correlation with the total score at each stage, this will not always be the very lowest correlating item.

There is one obvious problem associated with correlating items with total scores and this is the fact that each item *contributes* to the total score, so we are to some extent correlating each item with itself. In order to circumvent this difficulty, we usually base the item analyses on 'corrected item–total correlations', or the 'Guilford-corrected item–total correlations', which are simply the correlations between each item and the sum of the *other* remaining items. In the present example, Item 1 would be correlated with the sum of Items 2, 3, 4 and 5. Item 2 would be correlated with the sum of Items 1, 3, 4 and 5, and so on. Other techniques for performing such corrections have been proposed, but may create as many problems as they solve (Cooper 1983).

Each time an item is eliminated, the reliability of the test (alpha) should be recalculated. As items that have low correlations with the total score are eliminated, the value of alpha will rise. As more and more items are removed, the value of alpha will eventually start to fall, since it depends on both the average correlation between the items and the number of items in the test. Of course, removing a 'poor' item boosts the average correlation between the remaining items – but it also shortens the test. Items are successively removed (on the basis of a consideration of their corrected item–total correlations and the facets from which they originate) until the test is short, well balanced and highly reliable.

One annoying feature of this method of analysis is that it is not possible simply to look at the table of corrected item–total correlations and decide from this precisely which items should be eliminated. This is because each person's total score will inevitably change each time an item is dropped and consequently each of the correlations between the remaining items and the total score will also change. Therefore it is necessary to decide which item to drop, recompute the total scores and recompute all the remaining item–total correlations, as well as recomputing alpha at each stage. But such analyses can be performed relatively painlessly using the SPSS Reliability procedure or similar – or even a spreadsheet.

Self-assessment question 18.2

a. What can factor analysis alone reveal about the structure of a test?

b. In classical item analysis, why is it necessary to recompute all the item–total correlations after removing an item?

c. Name four problems associated with constructing tests by criterion keying.

Next steps

The test constructor's task is far from finished once the item analysis has been completed. Instructions (and possibly answer sheets) should be refined and example items should be developed and checked before the revised (shorter and hopefully more reliable) test is given to another sample of about 200 individuals and its reliability and factor structure rechecked. Its validity should also be established at this stage (e.g. by construct validation) as described in Chapter 15. In the case of ability tests, the amount of time that individuals take to complete the test should be noted and a decision taken as to what time limits (if any) should be imposed. A test manual should be prepared showing the results of these analyses, the administration instructions, the marking scheme and as much evidence as possible that the test is reliable and valid.

Summary

This chapter has covered some basic principles of item writing for both ability tests and personality tests. Item analysis has been introduced as a procedure for detecting and eliminating items that are inappropriate and that detract from the test's reliability and/or validity. Four techniques for performing item analysis have been discussed, namely criterion keying, factor analysis, item response theory and classical item analysis. Major problems have been identified in the all-too-common technique of criterion keying and factor analysis and/or classical item analysis are recommended for producing short, reliable and potentially valid scales.

Suggested additional reading

Gulliksen (1986) is still essential reading for anyone who is interested in the assessment of abilities or educational attainment. Most and Zeidner (1995) and Spector (1992) are also well worth reading.

Answers to self-assessment questions

SAQ 18.1

If the test contains many very easy or very difficult items, you will not obtain very good discrimination between the individuals in the sample. The trait that the test supposedly measures is probably normally distributed (that is, the frequency diagram is bell-shaped). If your test contains many difficult items, then it is drawing fine distinctions between the high ability participants (of whom there are relatively few in the sample). If it contains plenty of very easy items, then the test is drawing fine distinctions between the low ability participants (but there are also few of them). You would normally want to discriminate between the great majority of individuals in the sample, and this implies having plenty of items that discriminate well in the $p = 0.2$ to $p = 0.8$ range, since these are the items that discriminate between most members of the sample.

SAQ 18.2

a. Factor analysis can show how many distinct constructs are measured by a set of items – other techniques *assume* this is just one. Sometimes a set of items can measure two quite highly correlated but distinct abilities, e.g. fluid and crystallized ability, and indeed Cattell (1971) claims that these two factors can be found when factor analysis is used to examine tests that were constructed using classical item analysis.

b. Every time an item is removed, each person's total score changes and so all the other items' correlations with this total score will *also* change.

c. The test will have a very low (probably zero) reliability, as it will almost certainly measure a mixture of traits. The arbitrary choice of which criterion to measure will greatly influence the items that make up the test. Because so many correlations are calculated between the test items and the criterion, some of these correlations will be seen as significant purely by chance. Likewise, some items that *should* be included will not be. It is also very atheoretical – having constructed the test, we have no real understanding of *why* it works or what it measures.

References

Cattell, R. B. (1971). *Abilities, Their Structure, Growth and Action*. New York: Houghton-Mifflin.

Coombs, W. N. and Schroeder, H. E. (1988). Generalized locus of control: an analysis of factor-analytic data. *Personality and Individual Differences 9*, 79–85.

Cooper, C. (1983). Correlation measures in item analysis. *British Journal of Mathematical and Statistical Psychology 32*, 102–5.

Gough, H. G. (1975). *The California Personality Inventory*. Palo Alto, CA: Consulting Psychologists Press.

Graham, J. R. (1990). *MMPI-2: Assessing Personality and Psychopathology*. New York: Oxford University Press.

Gulliksen, H. (1986). Perspective on educational-measurement. *Applied Psychological Measurement 10*(2), 109–32.

Hathaway, S. R. and McKinley, J. C. (1967). *The Minnesota Multiphasic Personality Inventory Manual (Revised)*. New York: Psychological Corporation.

Kline, P. (1986). *A Handbook of Test Construction*. London: Methuen.

Kline, P. (1999). *The Handbook of Psychological Testing* (2nd edn). London and New York: Routledge.

Most, R. B. and Zeidner, M. (1995). Constructing personality and intelligence instruments: methods and issues. In D. H. Saklofske and M. Zeidner (eds), *International Handbook of Personality and Intelligence*. New York: Plenum.

Nunnally, J. C. (1978). *Psychometric Theory* (2nd edn). New York: McGraw-Hill.

Spector, P. E. (1992). *Summated Rating Scale Construction*. Newbury Park, CA: Sage.

19 Problems with tests

Background

This chapter introduces some problems that can affect scores on tests of ability and personality – background, attitudes to taking tests and so on. In particular, it considers the claim that psychological tests are biased against members of minority groups, beginning with a look at the nature of test bias and techniques for detecting it in tests.

Recommended prior reading

Chapters 14 and 15.

Introduction

It is undeniable that psychological tests have a public image problem, since grave doubts have been expressed in both the popular press and the psychological journals about the 'fairness' of various psychological tests. For example, Kamin (1974) drew the attention of a generation of psychologists to the way in which some early ability tests were used to identify 'feeble-minded' immigrants to the USA during the 1920s and argued passionately that any attempt to assess individual differences was and is unfair and discriminatory. And, in the case of those early tests, Kamin was completely correct. Rather than being tests of abstract reasoning, these tests included items assessing factual knowledge about the American culture (e.g. knowledge of past presidents). It is unsurprising that immigrants (many of whom could not even read or speak English, far less have a knowledge of the culture of a nation on the other side of the globe) failed to show their true ability on these tests. The tests were unfair to members of these cultures in that they grossly underestimated their true potential.

When tests systematically underestimate or overestimate the true scores of groups of individuals, they are said to be *biased* against (or in favour of) certain groups. Thus the IQ tests that Kamin cites were, without doubt, biased against all those who did not speak English fluently and/or had little knowledge of the American way of life. Members of these groups achieved scores on these tests that did not reflect their full potential. Note, however, that bias was found in this case because of the way in which the test was used – someone, somewhere, selected an inappropriate test for this particular application. The test used in this example might have been perfectly adequate for other uses in school and occupational psychology, where language difficulty was not a problem. Hence it is important to appreciate that bias can creep into an assessment procedure because of a flawed choice of an otherwise perfectly satisfactory test, although tests themselves can also be at fault.

When we considered reliability theory in Chapter 15, each person's score on a test was assumed to have some measurement error associated with it. According to this model the square root of the reliability of the test is a close approximation to the correlation between an individual's score on the test and their 'true score' on the trait being assessed. The crucial assumption made there is that measurement error is essentially random. If an individual took several tests measuring the same trait, one might overestimate their scores slightly, another might underestimate their score slightly, but, on average, the tests would provide accurate estimates of the person's ability. In this chapter, we shall instead consider systematic errors of measurement – the type of measurement error that will consistently overestimate some individuals' true scores and underestimate the true scores of others. The immigration test will grossly underestimate the intellectual ability of certain well-defined groups of applicants (those who cannot read English and know nothing of American culture). It is not difficult to think of more subtle items that also show bias, particularly in knowledge-based tests, e.g. 'how many players are there in a netball team?', 'what is the ratio of flour to fat in shortcrust pastry?', 'what is the purpose of a camshaft?' and 'what is the ratio of cement to sand for bricklaying mortar?'

It is not only trivial knowledge questions that can be affected by such forms of measurement error. When children are being assessed by educational psychologists, is it possible that the gender/age/race of the psychologist will affect their performance on the test? How about the test taker's motivation to perform well? It is clearly vital to ascertain whether any of these variables *can* influence children's performance, otherwise the abilities of some children may be over- or underestimated. The remainder of this chapter will mention some of these sources of measurement error, point to their implications and suggest how they can be detected.

The finding that some groups achieve different scores on some psychological tests has serious implications for those who use such tests as part of a selection procedure. The use of these tests will clearly lead to group(s) with the lower mean scores on the test being underrepresented in the workforce. This has led some bodies to abandon the use of psychological tests as part of a selection procedure, preferring instead to select suitably qualified individuals at random. While random selection is likely to select individuals who are representative of all applicant groups, it is manifestly unable to choose the best person for the job. Since ability tests often have validity coefficients of the order of 0.4, this could imply that organizations will simply not employ the most able applicants.

It is therefore probably best not to discard psychological tests altogether, but to appreciate the (sometimes subtle) issues raised by group differences and test bias when using or interpreting the results of psychological tests, although some authors such as Rust and Golombok (2009) take a more pessimistic view.

It is not just membership of certain sociocultural groups that can affect test scores. Several psychological or behavioural characteristics that are completely unrelated to what the test measures can also affect scores, particularly on personality tests. These are often known as 'response sets' or 'response biases', and efforts must be made to minimize their effects when designing or using tests. The most common is social desirability – the tendency to present oneself in a good light.

External bias in tests

What Kamin omits to mention in his discussion of ability tests is that the problems inherent in the immigrant screening programme would have been recognized if and when the tests had been validated. If scores on the tests had been correlated with subsequent criteria (e.g. annual income, school performance of children), it seems inevitable that the uselessness of the tests would quickly have become obvious. For example, follow-up studies might have shown a relationship such as that shown in Figure 19.1, which illustrates the (hypothetical) annual income of immigrants (denoted by circles) and second-generation Americans (denoted by crosses) 10 years after IQ testing, as a function of their scores on the IQ test.

In Figure 19.1 you will notice that most immigrants (circles) had very low scores on the IQ test – their scores are to the left of the graph. The crosses represent the second-generation Americans and it is clear that there is a substantial correlation between IQ test score and income for these individuals only. The figure shows the 'line of best fit' to the data for the second-generation Americans, calculated using a statistical technique called regression analysis. This allows one to predict subsequent income from the IQ test scores of the second-generation individuals. It is merely necessary to find the point on the x axis that corresponds to a person's score on the IQ test and move vertically upwards until one meets this regression line. The individual's estimated income can then be read off the y axis at this point.

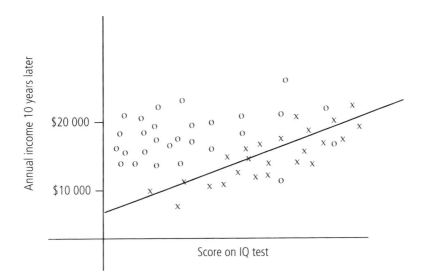

Figure 19.1 Hypothetical links between scores on an IQ test and income 10 years later for two groups of individuals.

If the test were fair to the immigrants, you might expect the same underlying relationship to apply. That is, if IQ is important in determining subsequent income (as seems to be the case in the second-generation group), then the low IQs of the immigrants would imply that they will subsequently earn relatively little. The immigrants' scores should lie close to the same regression line as that of the majority group. You can see that this is far from being the case. Immigrants who have low scores on the IQ test tend to earn far more than would be expected on the basis of a regression analysis and, if you consider the immigrant group alone, you can see that there is virtually no correlation between their scores on the IQ test and their subsequent income – which is hardly surprising given that the IQ test is meaningless for members of this group.

The first graph produced in answer to self-assessment question 19.1 demonstrates a very important principle. Here, there is a clear group difference in IQ scores (circles score lower), but members of this group also *earn* less. This suggests that there is a genuine difference in the IQ scores of the circles and the crosses, for while the circles achieve low scores on the IQ test, this graph (unlike Figure 19.1) shows that the IQ test does not appear to *underestimate* their potential.

The important lesson to learn from this is that *the presence of group differences does not necessarily imply that a test is biased*. This point cannot be made too strongly – it is fundamental and almost universally agreed by measurement specialists (Berk 1982; Jensen 1980; Reynolds 1995). Test bias implies that test items are too difficult for members of certain groups *for reasons that are unrelated to the characteristic being assessed* – for example, because items in an IQ test require an ability to read and write English assume cultural knowledge that a recent immigrant simply will not possess. It is possible that there will be genuine differences between the abilities of different groups. For example, there is a substantial literature on sex differences in educational attainment.

If regression lines between test scores and criterion performance are the same for two groups, then it does not matter if there are differences in the mean scores of the groups. Bias can be inferred when different groups follow different regression lines (differing in either slope or height) or when the scores of members of some groups fall further from the regression line than the scores of members of other groups (i.e. there is a lower correlation with the criterion). Using a test of low reliability automatically produces a larger spread of scores on either side of the regression line, so it is also sensible to check that the reliability of the test is similar in both groups.

Several psychologists are intensely interested in group differences (generally racial differences) in personality and ability, which some regard as genuine effects and not attributable to bias of any kind. Thus we read that the Japanese tend to have above average spatial ability skills compared to Europeans and that black Americans tend to have lower scores on IQ tests than white Americans. The lack of references to these papers is deliberate because, personally speaking, I cannot see the academic appeal of this area. Even if there *are* clear differences between groups, it is not entirely obvious why they have arisen. Do the Japanese have better skills because they eat more fish, because their educational system develops such skills more than in the west, because of genetic differences or because they had to hunt for food during the ice age and so there was natural selection for this characteristic (although, strangely, not for running fast)? These have all been offered as explanations for the group differences and it is not easy to test any of these hypotheses (particularly the last one). It is also easy to become obsessed with group differences and to forget that individual differences *within* groups of people far outweigh the relatively small differences *between* groups of individuals. The political dangers of a doctrine of group differences, racial inferiority and the like can hardly be overlooked.

Skin colour and gender nevertheless do appear to have a strange fascination for some psychologists. Applied psychologists also have to be aware of the implications of group differences in ability when using selection tests. For although I argued earlier that group differences need not necessarily imply that a test is biased, the legal system takes the opposite view and adopts what Kline (1993) calls the 'egalitarian fallacy'. It *assumes* that all ethnic and gender groups must have the same underlying levels of all abilities and that, if tests suggest otherwise, there must be something wrong with the tests. Those using tests for selection, guidance and placement are therefore obliged to ensure that their tests reflect few group differences.

Self-assessment question 19.2

Earlier in this chapter it was stressed that it is wrong to infer that a test is biased merely because it shows group differences. Suppose that you administer a test in order to select applicants for a particular job, find that a particular test predicts job performance quite well (r = 0.3), but discover that male applicants score appreciably lower than female applicants (e.g. half a standard deviation lower):

a. What would happen if the test were used in its present form?

b. What non-psychological factors might account for the observed difference in performance between the two genders?

c. What steps might you take?

Internal bias in tests

The type of bias already discussed is known as 'external bias', since it examines the relationship between test scores and some external criterion. However, it is not necessary to have an external criterion to detect bias in a test, for it is possible that a test may contain just a few items that are demonstrably biased against one or more groups – that is, they are substantially more difficult for members of some groups than others. Several techniques have been developed to detect such 'internal bias' and Berk (1982) and Osterlind (1983) provide an excellent discussion of these issues. I shall only mention one approach: these days most attempts to detect bias in tests relies on a technique called item response theory, which is beyond the scope of this text.

Suppose that many people complete an ability test and that each response is scored as correct or incorrect. These individuals may be classified as members of one or more groups (e.g. according to gender and ethnic origin). To keep matters simple, we shall just concentrate on gender differences and will assume that the test consists of 50 items. It is possible to perform a mixed-model (one-between-and-one-within) analysis of variance on the item scores, using 'gender' (two levels) as the between-subjects factor, and 'item' (30 levels) as the within-subjects factor. That is, we treat the responses to all 30 items in the test as different levels of a single within-subjects factor. The ANOVA table resulting from this analysis will show:

- the significance of the 'item' effect
- the significance of the 'group' effect
- the significance of the 'group × item interaction'.

The 'item' effect tests whether all of the items in the test have the same difficulty level. They will almost certainly not be equally difficult, so it can usually be guaranteed that this term will be very significant indeed. This term is of no interest whatsoever for detecting bias.

The 'group' effect tests whether males and females tend to have the same average score on the test items. This is of no great interest either, although the presence of substantial group differences will be a problem if one intends to use the test for selection or placement.

The 'group × item interaction' term is the really interesting one. If this effect is statistically significant, it implies that some items are easier for members of one group than for members of the other group – that is, some items are biased. It is possible to find out precisely which items are implicated by plotting the interaction, testing simple effects, etc. The items can then be removed from the test. Thus the presence of a significant group × item interaction can indicate that some test items are problematical.

One difficulty with this approach is, of course, that the statistical power of the procedure affects the significance of this interaction. In practice, this means that if the analysis is performed on a small sample of individuals, it is unlikely to detect subtle degrees of bias. However, if the analysis is performed on samples of many thousands of individuals, any test will show a statistically significant (albeit small) degree of bias. For the sake of completeness, I ought to acknowledge that there are known to be some problems with this approach, as has been mentioned by Osterlind (1983) among others, although in my view (and experience), it can show up seriously biased items.

I believe that it is advisable to consider internal (item) bias whenever developing or using a test. Suppose, for example, that a 40-item test consisted of 20 items that were much easier for females to process than for males and 20 items that were much easier for males to process than females. If one merely looked for a significant difference in the total scores of the two groups, it is quite possible that none would be found, as the items that are difficult for men are easy for women and vice versa. Thus it is quite possible for a test to be riddled with biased items, yet for the analysis of group differences or regression analyses of the type shown in Figure 19.1 to give the scale a clean bill of health. It is only by going down to the level of test items that one can really see what is going on and identify items that could usefully be removed from the scale. Many other techniques have also been developed for detecting bias in tests: see for example Osterlind (1983) and Reynolds (1995).

Response styles

Response styles (also known as 'response biases' or 'response sets') plague tests assessing personality, mood, motivation and attitudes. When people are asked to report their behaviour of express an opinion using a questionnaire, the way in which people respond is not entirely determined by the trait that the test hopes to measure. For example, it is well known that individuals are more likely to agree with statements than to disagree with them – a tendency that is exploited to the full by unscrupulous market researchers. Suppose that you asked a carefully selected sample of the population 'do you intend to vote for the present government in the next election?' and found that 55% said that they did. Then suppose you asked another sample of people 'do you intend to vote for one of the opposition parties in the next election?'. You might naively expect that, on the basis of the first survey, about $100 - 55 = 45\%$ of the population would answer 'yes'. In fact, the proportion is likely to be considerably higher, just because people seem to be more willing to say 'yes' than 'no' *whatever the question may be* (Cronbach 1946). This is known as the response set of *acquiescence*.

This finding has some fairly unpleasant implications for personality testing. It means that any personality scale – a scale of anxiety, for example – whose items are all scored in the same direction (so that a response of 'yes' or 'strongly agree' to each item produces a high score on the test) will be influenced by acquiescence. Individuals' scores will be a little higher than they should be because of this tendency to agree with statements – everyone would appear to be a little more anxious than they actually are. This in itself may not appear to be too much of a problem. If it were possible to estimate that, on average, each person's score was two points higher than it should be because of this response set, it would be a simple matter to deduct this amount from each individual's score. In practice, there would be no need to bother doing so, since the correlations between the test scores and other things would be unaffected by deducting a constant from each person's score. So what is the problem?

The real difficulties arise if there are individual differences in this response set of acquiescence. Perhaps some individuals have a strong tendency to agree with statements, whereas others are completely immune from doing so. This is what is so dangerous, since if individuals' scores on the anxiety test are influenced by both anxiety and their tendency to agree, it is clear that the test will overestimate the anxiety scores of the acquiescent individuals, while being completely accurate for low acquiescent people. This is why most personality tests contain items that are scored in both directions. If about 50% of the items are phrased so that agreeing with a statement implies a high score on the trait (e.g. 'I suffer from "nerves"') and the remainder are phrased the opposite way round (e.g. 'I am calm and relaxed most of the time'), then acquiescence will have little effect. When the test is scored, any tendency to acquiesce will cancel itself out. Tests that are *not* constructed in this way should be viewed with suspicion.

Social desirability is another response style that can affect the way in which people answer test items. It is the tendency to show oneself in a good light and to deny any behaviours or feelings that may be socially unacceptable. Items relating to swearing, being mean, being aggressive, having a sense of humour, being honest, being hard working and being intelligent are among those that may be influenced by this response style. It is a particular problem when personality tests are used for personnel selection – anyone with a modicum of intelligence is likely to realize that it is probably not a good thing to admit to experiencing hallucinations, being dishonest or having a 'slapdash' attitude when filling in a personality questionnaire while applying for a job.

It is not difficult to measure social desirability. It is possible to ask raters to scrutinize items in personality questionnaires and to decide how much each item is affected by social desirability. Where there is good agreement between raters, then it is highly probable that social desirability will affect the way in which the item is answered. Edwards (1957) carried out this experiment and observed that there was a substantial correlation between ratings of the social desirability of test items and the way in which they were answered. People tended to answer items in a socially desirable way.

As with acquiescence, this raises severe difficulties only if we assume that some people are more swayed by social desirability than others when filling in personality questionnaires. Unfortunately, it is rarely possible to use the same solution for social desirability (balancing the test items so that some socially desirable responses tend to increase the score on the trait, while others decrease it). Can you think of a test item that measures anxiety where the 'anxious' response is also more socially desirable than the 'low-anxiety' response? Instead, it is common practice to try to eliminate highly socially desirable items from personality questionnaires as they are being developed.

323

Individual differences in the tendency to give socially desirable responses can be measured using the Crowne–Marlowe scale (Crowne and Marlowe 1964), so a group of individuals can be given this questionnaire along with the questionnaire that is being developed *in the context in which it will be used*. If any items in the questionnaire are strongly influenced by social desirability, the responses to these questions will correlate substantially with individuals' scores on the Crowne–Marlow scale. If the items are little affected by social desirability, the correlations will be trivial. Thus it is possible to identify which items are strongly affected by social desirability and so consider eliminating or rephrasing them during the process of test construction.

The way in which people use Likert scales can also be influenced by other features of their makeup. A typical Likert scale might invite someone to circle one of the numbers from 1 to 5, where a rating of 1 implies that they 'strongly disagree' with a statement and a rating of 5 that they 'strongly agree' with it. Some years ago, Paul Kline, Jon May and I were interested in developing an 'objective test' to measure authoritarian attitudes. We suspected that authoritarian types tended to see the world in 'black and white' terms, free from any doubt or ambiguity. Therefore we postulated that when presented with a 5-point rating scale they would circle plenty of 1s and 5s, but rather few of the middle points compared to control groups, which is exactly what we observed (Cooper, Kline and May 1986). So here is another personality trait that influences the way in which people use any Likert scale.

Self-assessment question 19.3

Name some variables that may affect performance on personality tests.

Factors that affect performance on ability tests

It should go without saying that the conditions under which the test is administered are likely to have a massive effect on test performance, particularly in the case of ability tests. Testing large groups of nervous people in an overcrowded, stuffy room with a high level of background noise is a fairly obvious recipe for disaster, as is *any* deviation from the test instructions, practice examples or time limits. However, in this section we shall consider some other psychological characteristics of individuals that can also influence the way in which they approach ability tests.

A person's motivation with regard to any test is likely to affect their performance. Encouraging even young children to perform well can lead to significant increases in their scores on ability tests compared to control groups (Brown and Walberg 1993). Cultural factors have also been suggested as important influences in test performance. If a child believes that he or she is unlikely to perform well on a test, then it is possible that he or she *will* perform poorly so as to conform to a stereotype (Steele and Aronson 1995). It has also been suggested that the social psychology of the testing situation is important, and that the age, sex, level of anxiety and level of warmth of the individual may influence their scores. However, as Cronbach (1994) concludes, there is remarkably little evidence of any consistent differences. Neither do black children perform better at ability tests when the psychologist is black rather than white (Jensen 1980; Sattler and Gwynne 1987).

There is also a massive literature on the psychology of test anxiety and its effect on performance; there is an international society for the study of the subject and there have even been tests of anxiety designed for particular subject areas such as mathematics or sport, as well as generalized test anxiety (Spielberger 1980), although there is little convincing evidence (in my view) that test anxiety is really any different from 'normal' state or trait anxiety. High levels of test anxiety do seem to be associated with lowered performance on many tests of attainment (Schwarzer, van der Ploeg and Spielberger 1989), but arguing causality from this seems to be dangerous. It could be that high anxiety results from the (correct) appraisal that one is not going to perform at all well. For, as we mentioned in Chapter 4, the literature shows rather small correlations between trait anxiety and general ability.

Practice effects and coaching can also improve test performance under some circumstances, but a distinction must be made between interventions that are designed to change the levels of the *trait* and those that are specific to one particular *measuring instrument*, as discussed in Chapter 10. Interventions designed to improve levels of traits pose no great ethical problems, yet attempts to improve performance on one particular test are undoubtedly unfair to candidates who lack the inside knowledge of how the test works that would enable them to choose appropriate strategies or who lack the money to undertake coaching. Neither are the benefits enormous. In the case of the Scholastic Aptitude Test (a test used to select students for colleges in the USA), it is not entirely clear whether the time and energy devoted to learning the 'tricks of the test' would not be better spent taking a course to improve one's mathematical ability or some other area of academic weakness (Evans and Pike 1973). The fundamental point is surely that psychological tests should not be so well publicized that would-be candidates can gain useful knowledge in this way. All the necessary information should surely be given to all candidates during the test instructions.

Those who argue that such problems mean that ability tests should be cast out into the psychological wilderness, along with phrenology and animal magnetism, overlook two points. First, if these effects were all important, then ability tests would not be able to predict any criterion behaviours. As we have seen, the evidence suggests that, despite these issues, ability tests *can* make a useful contribution here. Second, they ignore guidelines for 'good practice' in test administration. The instructions for virtually all tests stress that the examiner should use his or her interpersonal skills to make participants feel as relaxed and unthreatened as possible, to motivate children to perform their very best and so on. Moreover, virtually all tests include several test items that familiarize candidates with the types of problem to be presented, the use of the answer sheet and so on. Thus, in practice, most candidates should be made to feel relaxed and motivated and will get some practice prior to the main testing session.

In addition, several organizations now offer candidates the opportunity to pretest themselves. For example, the Northern Ireland Civil Service runs an exemplary selection system that involves sending applicants a detailed sample of psychometric test items so that they can try these out for themselves before attending the psychometric assessment procedure (an additional benefit being that individuals who score very poorly on the self-administered tests may choose not to apply, thereby reducing costs).

Summary

This chapter has considered some problems with psychometric testing and, in particular, the concept of *bias* – which is poorly understood both within and without the psychological community. We have also briefly considered some other variables that can influence performance on tests of ability and personality and commented on their importance and implications for testing practice.

325

Suggested additional reading

Jensen's (1980) book *Bias in Mental Testing* is, in my view, one of the most interesting psychometrics books ever written. It contains excellent sections on the nature of test bias and its detection and can be heartily recommended. Reynolds (1995) is also excellent. Two elderly chapters by the late P. E. Vernon are still well worth reading – Chapter 20 of Vernon (1979) and Chapter 12 of Vernon (1963) and once again, Cronbach (1994) and Rust and Golombok (2009) have thoughtful discussions of the influence of anxiety, motivation and the various response sets on performance, as do several occupational psychology texts.

Answers to self-assessment questions

SAQ 19.1

1.

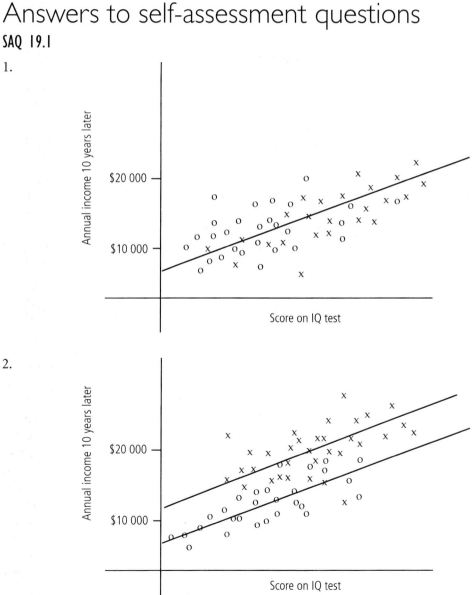

2.

SAQ 19.2

a. The test will select more females than males into the organization.

b. It is important to remember that applicants for a particular job do not form a random sample of the population. Factors such as geographical location of the business, the nature of competing businesses, *perceived* chances of employment, the structure of a divided education system, emigration, family traditions of employment, etc. can all interact with ability to produce rather distorted samples. For example, if there is a popular major employer in the same geographical area that takes large numbers of high-IQ female employees, other businesses may end up taking applicants who were rejected.

c. Plot the graph of criterion performance vs. test performance for both groups and check that the two lines have similar heights and slopes. Also check the reliability of the test within each group, and check for signs of internal bias. Remove biased items if any are found and recompute the validity coefficients. Consult the literature to discover whether others have reported similar results using the same test against similar criteria. If all else fails, consider trying another test.

SAQ 19.3

Apart from the personality trait that the test seeks to measure, responses will be influenced by social desirability, acquiescence and extreme responding/conservatism, although other variables (such as the individual's perception of the *reason* for testing) might also be important.

References

Berk, R. A. (ed.) (1982). *Handbook of Methods for Detecting Test Bias*. Baltimore, MD: Johns Hopkins University Press.

Brown, S. M. and Walberg, H. A. (1993). Motivational effects on test scores of elementary students. *Journal of Educational Research 86*, 133–36.

Cooper, C., Kline, P. and May, J. (1986). The measurement of authoritarianism, psychoticism and other traits by objective tests: a cross-validation. *Personality and Individual Differences 7*(1), 15–21.

Cronbach, L. J. (1946). Response sets and test validity. *Educational and Psychological Measurement 6*, 475–94.

Cronbach, L. J. (1994). *Essentials of Psychological Testing* (5th edn). New York: HarperCollins.

Crowne, D. P. and Marlowe, D. (1964). *The Approval Motive*. New York: Wiley.

Edwards, A. L. (1957). *The Social Desirability Variable in Personality Research*. New York: Dryden Press.

Evans, F. R. and Pike, L. W. (1973). The effects of instruction for three mathematics item formats. *Journal of Educational Measurement 10*, 257–72.

Jensen, A. R. (1980). *Bias in Mental Testing*. New York: Free Press.

Kamin, L. J. (1974). *The Science and Politics of IQ*. Harmondsworth: Penguin.

Kline, P. (1993). *The Handbook of Psychological Testing*. London: Routledge.

Osterlind, S. J. (1983). *Test Item Bias*. Beverly Hills, CA: Sage.

Reynolds, C. R. (1995). Test bias and the asessment of intelligence and personality. In D. H. Saklofske and M. Zeidner (eds), *International Handbook of Personality and Intelligence*. New York: Plenum.

Rust, J. and Golombok, S. (2009). *Modern Psychometrics: The Science of Psychological Assessment* (3rd edn). New York: Routledge/Taylor & Francis.

Sattler, J. M. and Gwynne, J. (1987). White examiners generally do not impede the intelligence test performance of black children. *Journal of Consulting and Clinical Psychology 50*, 196–208.

Schwarzer, R., van der Ploeg, H. M. and Spielberger, C. D. (eds). (1989). *Advances in Test Anxiety Research* (Vol. 6). Amsterdam: Swets & Zeitlinger.

Spielberger, C. D. (1980). *Preliminary Professional Manual for the Test Anxiety Inventory*. Palo Alto, CA: Consulting Psychologists Press.

Steele, C. M. and Aronson, J. (1995). Stereotype threat and the intellectual test performance of African Americans. *Journal of Personality and Social Psychology 69*, 797–811.

Vernon, P. E. (1963). *Personality Assessment: A Critical Survey*. London: Methuen.

Vernon, P. E. (1979). *Intelligence, Heredity and Environment*. San Francisco: W. J. Freeman & Co.

20 Conclusions

This book has covered a wide range of theories and methodologies, from classical psychoanalysis to factor analysis by way of the main trait theories of personality and ability – proof indeed of the wide range of skills necessary both to understand and to evaluate other people's research and to begin to *use* the techniques in earnest. For I hope that by now some of the interesting issues in individual differences research will be obvious.

Generally agreed issues

Although new techniques of exploratory factor analysis are still being developed, there is now some agreement that the technique can produce replicable factor structures, given decent-quality data, which was a matter of some debate in the 1970s. Although some authors have claimed to produce alternative models of ability (e.g. Johnson and Bouchard 2005), there is concern that these may arise because the tests that were factor analysed were not sampled broadly: if one administers many visualization tasks, for example, one can pretty well guarantee that a broad second-order factor of visualization will be found. There is a need for better tests for the number of factors and an even more urgent need for those tests that *do* exist to be incorporated into the main computer packages.

There is thus fairly good agreement about the structure of personality, with extraversion, neuroticism and a choice between agreeableness/conscientiousness and psychoticism being found consistently although a recent paper (De Raad et al. 2010) suggests that only three personality factors – extraversion, agreebleness and conscientiousness – emerge cleanly in all cultures. There is also a good level of agreement about the structure of ability *as it is traditionally visualized*, although Sternberg's widening of the concept needs to be taken into account. Educationalists swear by Gardner's model of multiple intelligences, although psychologists who are familiar with the literature in this area will question whether all the 'intelligences' are (a) all cognitive, as the term is usually used and (b) different from some of the second-order abilities identified through factor analysis. Evidence now seems to be coming in demonstrating that Gardner was simply incorrect in asserting (without evidence) that the intelligences are uncorrelated.

Process models have, of course, had to wait for some consensus structural model to emerge – one can hardly investigate the processes that seem to underpin personality and ability if there **329** is no general agreement about the precise nature of the main dimensions. Thus most process models are fairly rudimentary and significant new developments are reported in the journals every month. The correlations between measures of ability and reaction time measures, inspection time, etc. seem solid. The exciting research relates g and personality to brain physiology and cognition, for example cortical thickness and grey matter density in the case of g. Likewise studies that try to determine whether the correlation between (say) g and inspection time (IT) indicates that IT determines g, whether g determines IT, or whether a set of genes influence both variables are extremely valuable.

The evidence that both personality and ability have a substantial genetic basis seems to be solid and this work also shows that the influence of the shared environment on adult personality and general ability is very small indeed, a finding that seems to me to have some rather interesting implications for the validity of certain personality theories that stress the importance of the family for adult development. It is possible that some minor personality factors or abilities may be influenced by these, but g, E and N most certainly are not.

My experience of marking undergraduate examination papers shows that very often students believe that behavioural genetics is a technique used by right-wing reductionists with a political agenda who are keen to show that social factors are unimportant. Nothing could be further from the truth. If the family environment were all important, and genetic influences were trivial, these analyses would show it. It is an empirical fact that the influence of genetic makeup is often rather larger than one would expect – the methodology is not biased towards this finding. Good science may not produce the answers that we would wish to see.

Clinically oriented psychologists find that repertory grid techniques, Q-sorts, etc. are therapeutically useful, although it is sometimes difficult to see how the techniques can be validated. Unfortunately, academic psychologists seem to have rather lost sight of the benefits of repertory grid techniques. For as well as their use in personality psychology and knowledge elicitation (when extracting knowledge from expert humans as part of developing expert systems for computerized decision making), repertory grids can be useful for any application where a person's idiosyncratic view of complex stimuli is needed. For example, when exploring how people categorize pictures (experimental aesthetics – pictures are the elements and people are shown three pictures at a time and asked to generate a construct). Or odours (perceptual psychology). Or people (social psychology).

There is general agreement that psychoanalysis is an ineffective form of therapy and that most, if not all, of Freud's theories are untestable. The lingering fascination felt for these theories in other disciplines leads on to some interesting debates about whether the definition of 'truth' (in terms of experimental verification) used throughout psychology is, indeed, the only criterion against which a theory should be evaluated.

Finally, there is good agreement about the way to construct (and validate) scales measuring traits.

Controversial issues

Anything to do with psychoanalytical theory or unconscious mental processes is regarded as highly controversial and it must be said that many attempts to validate aspects of Freud's theories do not provide strong, replicable results, possibly (but not necessarily) because psychoanalytical concepts are so very difficult to operationalize. Work on the unconscious processing of threat-related stimuli looks to be one of the least disappointing areas of research, but little there is very little good-quality research currently being undertaken in this area.

Findings with regard to the relationship between EEG/AEP (electro-encephalogram and auditory evoked potential) measures and personality and general ability has been a disappointment, with results sometimes *suggesting* links in the postulated directions, but apparently being influenced by many other variables. The several failures to replicate the Hendricksons' results represent a rather severe blow to neural theories of ability, although quite why high temporal consistency of the AEP (which is, surely, what is implied by the 'string measure') was important in the first place seems to have been the subject of rather less attention than one would have expected. McRorie and Cooper's research into the relationship between reflex latency and intelligence does, however, seem to show that speed of neural processing can predict intelligence – as long as synaptic transmission takes place.

Gardner's model of abilities and Goleman's notion of emotional intelligence have generated a huge amount of publicity and interest in the popular press, education departments and (heaven help us) in government ministries. Both were accepted as fact in the complete absence of supporting evidence. Indeed, it is only recently that it has been possible to assess either of the concepts: how can you possibly evaluate something that you cannot measure? It is possible that they may be of some use, although the results that are now available seem to suggest that the questionnaire measures of emotional intelligence really just measure the old, familiar personality traits, while I know of no evidence to support Gardner's claims that he has discovered several completely uncorrelated dimensions of ability. Instead, his findings appear to simply back up what was already known about the hierarchical structure of ability.

Another issue of concern is the role of language in ability tests. There is always a concern that the items in some ability tests may be difficult because only those with well-developed language skills can perform well on them: those with weaker skills (such as a limited vocabulary) may not understand what is required, or the meaning of individual items. Johnson and Bouchard (2005) have analysed correlations between test scores and found that rather than forming the usual fluid and crystallized intelligence, as suggested by Carroll, Cattell, Horn and others, there seem to be broad spatial and verbal factors (plus a memory factor). That said, I have major reservations about this work, as their battery of tests comprised so many spatial tests that a higher order spatial factor is hardly surprising: the authors may not have randomly sampled the primary mental abilities. However, this model needs to be explored further.

There is one issue that may perhaps influence the conclusions drawn from those behavioural–genetic studies involving twins, but which does not seem to feature large in the literature. Sets of twins share a uterine environment, but there are quite important differences between the environments enjoyed by identical and non-identical twins. For example, identical twins often share the same placenta (and sometimes the same amniotic sac) whereas dizygotic twins do not. If the uterine environments of identical twins are more similar (in terms of equality of nutrition, etc.) than the uterine environments of dizygotic twins, and if these factors also strongly influence adult intelligence, then it is possible that the reason why identical twins resemble each other so closely in adulthood is not down to genetic similarity at all, but similarity of the uterine environment. That said, other studies that do not involve twins at all (e.g. those that examine similarities in the abilities of different family member or of similarities between adopted children and their adoptive and biological parents) tend to show similar results to twin studies, so perhaps this is not a major issue after all.

331

The subject of test bias is widely misunderstood, even in the psychological community, with many colleagues inferring bias from the presence of group differences. Group differences in ability are highly controversial, the right-wing argument appearing to go along the following lines:

- some racial groups perform less well than others on ability tests

- intelligence has a substantial genetic component

- therefore some groups are genetically inferior to others.

The last statement does not follow logically from the first two. Just because within-group differences have a substantial genetic component it does not follow that between-group differences have any genetic component at all.

The Bell Curve (Herrnstein and Murray 1994) caused considerable controversy when it appeared, much of it ill informed. However, there is some agreement that, while the *data* presented there (linking IQ to a variety of social behaviours) may be legitimate, some of the political and social recommendations may not be. There are also some problems with the statistical analyses in this book: Cooper (1999) shows that while the data analysed there suggest moderate to strong links between general ability, educational qualifications and earnings, the size of the relationships with other variables is generally tiny.

Some comments on the method of psychometrics have recently caused something of a stir. Michell (1997a, 1997b) argued that all tests used in psychology are fatally flawed because they do not have an equal unit of measurement. Unlike rulers, balances and so on, there can be no guarantee that the interval between being neutral and 'agreeing' with a statement is the same size as the interval between 'disagreeing' and 'strongly disagreeing' with it. Yet this is what we assume whenever a Likert scale is used. Could this be one of the reasons why personality tests seem to be much weaker predictors of behaviour than ability tests, for which the measurement problems may be less pronounced?

Under-researched issues

The whole area of mood and motivation does seem rather neglected and there is not even much consensus on the structure of mood. A *vast* number of variables seem to affect mood level (including cognitions, scanning and the appraisal of stress), which means that experiments in this area will need to control for a large number of potentially confounding variables. Once this is coupled with the possibility of the measurement process (long questionnaires!) influencing the very moods that are being assessed, it is clear why mood research is so difficult.

The finding that many simple-minded 'motivation' questionnaires (such as those measuring (achievement motivation) seem to measure personality rather than anything as dynamic and fluctuating as true motivation is really rather a blow to this area and it would seem that research into the nature and structure of interests and the 'payoffs' of various interests in terms of goal fulfilment really would repay some serious attention, even if it only involved an attempted replication of some of Cattell's work in this field. Cattell's work is now very dated indeed and I feel somewhat embarrassed at having to include it: I do so because he is one of the few theorists to appreciate that there is more to motivation and its assessment than responses to simple inventories (such as achievement motivation questionnaires) can offer. That said, there are some more recent theories of motivation which may turn out to be useful (Bernard, Mills, Swenson and

Walsh 2005; Parks and Guay 2009), the first of which has also led to a questionnaire (Bernard, Mills, Swenson and Walsh 2008), although I do not think that there is enough evidence in yet to allow either theory to be properly evaluated.

Conclusions

The scientific study of individual differences has changed enormously in the last 30 years. There is now some measure of agreement between researchers about the main dimensions of personality and ability, making the search for process models possible and readers will gather that there is still much to do – psychometricians do not yet have the measure of man.

References

Bernard, L. C., Mills, M., Swenson, L. and Walsh, R. P. (2005). An evolutionary theory of human motivation. *Genetic Social and General Psychology Monographs 131*(2): 129–84.

Bernard, L. C., Mills, M., Swenson, L. and Walsh, R. P. (2008). Measuring motivation multidimensionally: development of the assessment of individual motives – questionnaire (AIM-Q). *Assessment 15*(1), 16–35.

Cooper, C. (1999). *Intelligence and Abilities*. London: Routledge.

De Raad, B., Barelds, D. P., Levert, E., Ostendorf, F., Mlacić, B., Di Blas L. et al. (2010). Only three factors of personality description are fully replicable across languages: a comparison of 14 trait taxonomies. *Journal of Personality and Social Psychology 98*(1), 160–73.

Herrnstein, R. J. and Murray, C. (1994). *The Bell Jar: Intelligence and Class Structure in American Life*. New York: Free Press.

Johnson, W. and Bouchard, T. J. (2005). Constructive replication of the visual–perceptual–image rotation model in Thurstone's (1941) battery of 60 tests of mental ability. *Intelligence 33*(4), 417–30.

Michell, J. (1997a). Quantitative science and the definition of measurement in psychology. *British Journal of Psychology 88*, 355–83.

Michell, J. (1997b). Quantitative science and the definition of measurement in psychology – reply. *British Journal of Psychology 88*, 401–6.

Parks, L. and Guay, R. (2009). Personality, values, and motivation. *Personality and Individual Differences 47*(7), 675–84.

Appendix A

Correlations

[See also Liebetrau (1983).]

Suppose that each person in a sample produces two scores, which might be scores on psychometric tests, test items or whatever. We often want to know the extent to which the two scores are related. A correlation coefficient – sometimes known as the Pearson correlation coefficient after its inventor, Karl Pearson – is a number between −1.0 and 1.0 that indicates the extent to which these two variables overlap and the direction of this relationship.

A correlation of 0 indicates that a high score on one variable is associated equally often with high, medium and low scores on the other variable. A scatter diagram shows individuals' scores on one variable plotted as a function of their scores on the other variable. The scatter diagram in Figure A1.1 shows a correlation of approximately zero.

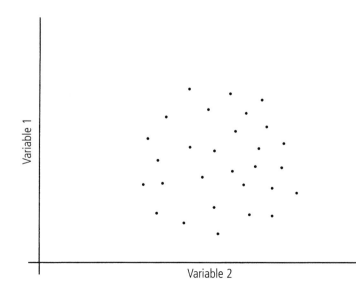

Figure A1.1 Scatter diagram showing a correlation of zero.

A correlation of 1.0 or −1.0 would indicate that if one of each person's scores is known, it is possible to predict the other one exactly. That is, the two variables are precisely proportional to each other. Figure A1.2 shows the scatter diagram for such a correlation.

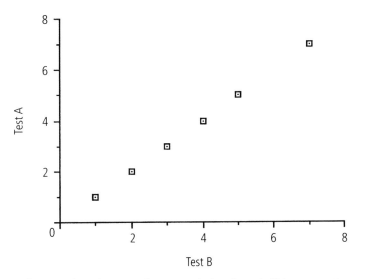

Figure A1.2 Scatter diagram showing a perfect correlation ($r = 1.0$) between two variables.

This is an example of a perfect positive correlation, where 'perfect' means that all of the points lie *exactly* on a straight line and 'positive' means that a person who has a high score on Test A also has a high score on Test B. A negative correlation would mean that a high score on Test A would be associated with a low score on Test B, so the points would lie on a line that slopes from top left to bottom right.

In this example, you can see that each person's score on Test A is exactly equal to their score on Test B. So if a person's score on one of these two tests were known, it would be a simple matter to work out what their score was on the other test. As the correlation is perfect (1.0), we would expect this prediction to be completely accurate.

Perfect correlations simply do not exist in real life. Even if the underlying relationship is 'perfect', each of the observed scores will be contaminated by measurement error, since no test has perfect reliability or validity. In our example, imagine that each of the points was moved a small, arbitrary distance up/down (corresponding to measurement error on Test A) and left/right (corresponding to measurement error on Test B). Figure A1.3 shows what the resulting scatter diagram would look like.

Although there is still a strong tendency for high scores on Test A to be associated with high scores on Test B, this relationship is no longer perfect. So now knowing someone's score on one of the tests would only allow us to make a rough estimate of their scores on the other test, as the scores do not fall on a perfect straight line.

Question

To obtain a perfect positive correlation, is it necessary for one variable always to be equal to the other?

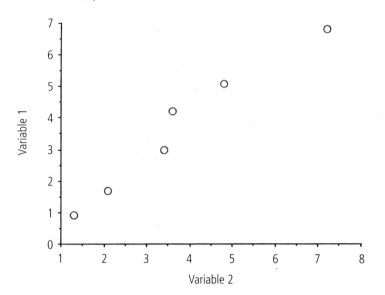

Figure A1.3 Scatter diagram showing a large positive correlation between two variables.

The answer is no, as shown in Figure A1.4. Here you can see that there is again a perfect correlation between the two sets of variables. That is, they all lie exactly on a straight line. However, the variables most certainly are not equal (in fact, the equation linking them is 'Score on Test A = 3 × score on Test B × 2'. Thus a perfect correlation just shows that two variables are perfectly linearly related – not that they are identical.

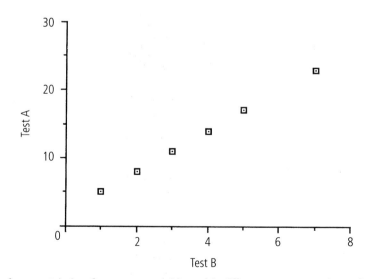

Figure A1.4 Perfect correlation from two variables with different means and standard deviations.

Suppose that when two tests, A and B, are given to a large sample of people, their scores on this test are found to have a correlation of 0.4. Try to work out whether this correlation would (a) rise, (b) fall, (c) change in some unpredictable way or (d) stay exactly the same if, instead of calculating the correlation from the raw data, you first:

a. multiply each person's score on Test A by 6, leaving their score on Test B unaltered

b. subtract 20 from each person's score on Test A, leaving their score on Test B unaltered

c. multiply each person's score on Test A by 2 and subtract 9 from their score on Test B

d. square each of the values of Test A, leaving their score on Test B unaltered.

If the answers are not obvious, you should try to settle this matter empirically. Using your favourite statistics package, define two variables, Test A and Test B. Then invent some scores on these two tests from half a dozen hypothetical students – use any numbers you like. Having done this, calculate the correlation between Test A and Test B and then modify the values of Tests A and B as just described. Recalculate the correlation at each step.

You should have found out that the correlation does not change at all when you:

- alter the mean level of either or both of the variables (by adding or subtracting a constant, e.g. 20, to either or both of the scores)

- alter the standard deviation of the scores on either of the variables (by multiplying or dividing test scores by a constant, e.g. 6).

However, when you perform any other operation (such as squaring or taking logarithms) the correlation will change. It will *probably* decrease if there were a fairly linear relationship between the two untransformed variables.

The first two properties of the correlation (insensitivity to the mean or the standard deviation of either distribution of scores) are necessary, since scores on tests:

- Have an *arbitrary zero point*. A raw score of 0 on a test of mechanical reasoning does not imply that a person has no mechanical reasoning ability whatsoever. If one person scores 20 on such a test, this does not imply that they have four times the ability of someone who scores 5. The scores form an *interval scale*, rather than a *ratio scale*.

- Have an *arbitrary scale of measurement*. A scale having 20 items scored as 'number of items correctly answered' will produce scores that are about twice as high as a test consisting of ten such items (assuming that each test contains items of similar difficulty). The correlation between the two tests logically should not be affected by the number of items in each test and/ or the range of scores – and the exercise shows that this is indeed the case.

Thus correlations are very well suited for showing the relationship between scores on tests, as they are not affected by the mean or standard deviation of the scores on either of the scales.

It is possible to test whether a given correlation is significantly different from zero, from another value or indeed from another correlation coefficient. We are usually interested in determining whether a correlation is significantly different from zero – that is, whether the data show that high **337** scores on one variable tend to be associated with high (or low) scores on another variable. Any good statistics book will give details of how to do this.

The importance of r²

A statistical significance test merely shows whether the correlation that is computed from a particular sample is too large to have arisen purely by chance. It does not say how important it is. When large samples of people are tested, even tiny correlations (e.g. r = 0.06) can be statistically significant: in other words, large enough to convince us that the correlation in the population is probably not zero.

r² is known as the *coefficient of determination*. It shows the percentage of the variance of one variable that can be predicted from the other. Thus if the correlation between two variables is 0.7, 49% of the variance of one variable can be explained by the other. The remainder is due to other variables and/or random error. In the previous example, a correlation of 0.06 explains only 0.0036 of the variance of the other. We can be confident that a relationship exists (because of the large sample size) but it is certainly not large enough to be useful for anything! When calculating a correlation, it is always worthwhile mentally squaring it. For example, if a battery of selection tests shows a correlation of 0.5 with job performance, this implies that it explains about a quarter of the variance in job performance.

Correlation and causality

A correlation need not imply that one variable causes the other. There would be a substantial correlation between the number of television sets and the number of bottles of wine sold each year between 1960 and 2001. This does not imply that purchasing a television makes one drink wine or that drinking wine makes one purchase a television. Rather, they both reflect social trends.

Correlations and group differences

One has to be very careful when calculating correlations between sets of data that show group differences. For example, suppose that you perform a survey, notice in passing that there are large sex effects on some of the variables, but proceed to use them in a correlation. This is a very common, very dangerous practice. To see why, plot a scatter diagram showing the test scores three males and the three females in Table A1.1.

It is clear that there is a huge positive correlation between the variables for the males and a similarly large positive correlation within the female sample. However, when all the data are plotted together, because there is a massive difference between the male and female means on the variables, there is a huge *negative* correlation between the two variables (r = −0.98)! So when there are differences in the means between several groups, it is very dangerous indeed to calculate a correlation from the raw data. Instead one should standardize the scores of each of the groups. For each person, subtract their group mean from their score and divide by the group standard deviation. So the first male would obtain a score of $\frac{3-4}{1}$ on Test A (as you should verify: the mean of 3, 4 and 5 is 4 and the SD is 1). Likewise the first female's score on Test A would be $\frac{20-21}{1}$ (mean 21, SD 1). This will bring both variables to the same mean and standard deviation.

Gender	Test A	Test B
Male	3	25
Male	4	26
Male	5	28
Female	20	2
Female	21	4
Female	22	5

Table A1.1 Hypothetical data showing the danger of calculating correlations where there are significant group differences

Dichotomous data

There are a few special cases of the correlation coefficient of which you should be aware. One common case involves one variable which is continuous (e.g. a test score) and another which is dichotomous (i.e. which can only assume one of two values). Dichotomous variables are fairly common in psychology. Responses to test items may be coded as 'correct/incorrect' or responses such as 'true/false' or 'agree/disagree' may be correlated together. They will often be coded as 0/1, although in fact any two numbers can be used. When a dichotomous variable is correlated with a continuous variable, the correlation coefficient is often known as the *point-biserial correlation*. It is calculated in precisely the same way as the usual Pearson correlation – it just has a different name for historical reasons. (The biserial correlation is different and best not used.) A common use of the point-biserial correlation is when correlating responses to individual test items with other variables – the test items being coded as correct (1) or incorrect (0).

When two dichotomous items are correlated together (again using the usual formula for a Pearson correlation), the correlation is sometimes known as the *phi coefficient*.

Both point-biserial and phi coefficients are problematical, because correlations between variables can only be 1.0 under rather special circumstances. Instead of representing just the amount of overlap between two variables, the point-biserial and phi coefficients are also influenced by the difficulty levels of the two dichotomous items. An example will make this clear. Table A1.2 shows individuals' responses on two dichotomous items and the numbers denoted by a, b, c and d show the number of individuals falling into each of the cells of the table.

		Response to Item 1		
		Correct	**Incorrect**	**Total**
	Correct	a	b	a + b
Response to Item 2	**Incorrect**	c	d	c + d
	Total	a + c	b + d	a + b + c + d

Table A1.2 Responses to two two-valued (dichotomous) variables

A perfect positive correlation will imply that $b = c = 0$ – that is, everyone who answers Item 1 correctly also answers Item 2 correctly and everyone who fails Item 1 also fails Item 2. This is possible only when the proportion of individuals who answer Item 1 correctly is exactly the same as the proportion who answer Item 2 correctly, as you may care to verify. Phi can equal 1.0 only if the means of the two distributions are identical.

The same problem affects the point-biserial, only more so. It is mathematically impossible to obtain a point-biserial correlation larger than about 0.8, under the very best circumstances (which is when 50% of the values of the dichotomous variable are 1 and the 50% are 0). As this mean of the dichotomous variable shifts away from 0.5, the maximum possible point-biserial falls to 0.7 (mean = 0.2 or 0.8) and 0.6 (mean = 0.1 or 0.9). Nunnally (1978) has provided full diagrams showing this effect.

This creates problems when interpreting correlations. A small correlation could come from two variables that just happen not to be particularly strongly correlated together or from two variables that have very different distributions and so *cannot* correlate substantially. Because of this, other forms of correlation have been developed to analyse dichotomous data. The tetrachoric correlation coefficient is not affected by the different distributions of the variables and so should probably be calculated instead of phi for the analysis of dichotomous data. However, it is tedious to compute and packages such as SPSS will not do it for you. See Rae (1997) for more information.

References

Liebetrau, A. M. (1983). *Measures of Association*. Newbury Park, CA: Sage.

Nunnally, J. C. (1978). *Psychometric Theory* (2nd edn). New York: McGraw-Hill.

Rae, G. (1997). On the derivation of Camp's tetrachoric correlation approximation. *Educational and Psychological Measurement 57*, 631–6.

Appendix B

Code of Fair Testing Practices in Education: prepared by the Joint Committee on Testing Practices

The Code of Fair Testing Practices in Education states the major obligations to test takers of professionals who develop or use educational tests. The Code is meant to apply broadly to the use of tests in education (admissions, educational assessment, educational diagnosis and student placement). The Code is not designed to cover employment testing, licensure or certification testing or other types of testing. Although the Code has relevance to many types of educational test, it is directed primarily at professionally developed tests such as those sold by commercial test publishers or used in informally administered testing programmes. The Code is not intended to cover tests made by individual teachers for use in their own classrooms.

The Code addresses the roles of test developers and test users separately. Test users are people who select tests, commission test development services or make decisions on the basis of test scores. Test developers are people who actually construct tests, as well as those who set policies for particular testing programmes. The roles may, of course, overlap, as when a state education agency commissions test development services, sets policies that control the test development process and makes decisions on the basis of the test scores.

The Code has been developed by the Joint Committee on Testing Practices, a cooperative effort of several professional organizations that has as its aim the advancement, in the public interest, of the quality of testing practices. The Joint Committee was initiated by the American Educational Research Association (AERA), the American Psychological Association (APA) and the National Council on Measurement in Education (NCME). In addition to these three groups, the American Association for Counselling and Development/Association for Measurement and Evaluation in Counselling and Development and the American Speech-Language-Hearing Association are now also sponsors of the Joint Committee.

This is not copyrighted material. Reproduction and dissemination are encouraged. Please cite this document as follows.

Code of Fair Testing Practices in Education. (1988) Washington, DC: Joint Committee on Testing **341**

Practices. (Mailing Address: Joint Committee on Testing Practices, American Psychological Association, 1200 17th Street NW, Washington, DC 20036, USA.)

The Code presents standards for educational test developers and users in four areas:

- developing/selecting appropriate tests

- interpreting scores

- striving for fairness

- informing test takers.

Organizations, institutions and individual professionals who endorse the Code commit themselves to safeguarding the rights of test takers by following the principles listed. The Code is intended to be consistent with the relevant parts of the Standards for Educational and Psychological Testing (AERA, APA, NCME 1985). However, the Code differs from the Standards in both audience and purpose. The Code is meant to be understood by the general public, it is limited to educational tests and the primary focus is on those issues that affect the proper use of tests. The Code is not meant to add new principles over and above those in the Standards or to change the meaning of the Standards. The goal is rather to represent the spirit of a selected portion of the Standards in a way that is meaningful to test takers and/or their parents or guardians. It is the hope of the Joint Committee that the Code will also be judged to be consistent with existing codes of conduct and standards of other professional groups who use educational tests.

Developing/selecting appropriate tests

Test developers should provide the information that test users need to select appropriate tests.

Test users should select tests that meet the purpose for which they are to be used, and that are appropriate for the intended test-taking populations.

Test developers should:
- Define what each test measures and what the test should be used for. Describe the population(s) for which the test is appropriate.

- Accurately represent the characteristics, usefulness and limitations of the test for their intended purposes.

- Explain relevant measurement concepts as necessary for clarity at the level of detail that is appropriate for the intended audience(s).

- Describe the process of test development. Explain how the content and skills to be tested were selected.

Test users should:
- First define the purpose for testing and the population to be tested. Then select a test for that purpose and that population based on a thorough review of the available information.

- Investigate potentially useful sources of information, in addition to test scores, to corroborate the information provided by tests.

- Read the materials provided by test developers and avoid using tests for which unclear or incomplete information is provided.

- Become familiar with how and when the test was developed and tried out.

- Provide evidence that the test meets its intended purpose(s).

- Provide either representative samples or complete copies of test questions, directions, answer sheets, manuals and score reports to qualified users.

- Indicate the nature of evidence obtained concerning the appropriateness of each test for groups of different racial, ethnic, or linguistic backgrounds who are likely to be tested.

- Identify and publish any specialized skills needed to administer each test and to interpret scores correctly.

- Read independent evaluations of a test and of possible alternative measures. Look for evidence required to support the claims of test developers.

- Examine specimen sets, disclosed tests or samples of questions, directions, answer sheets, manuals and score reports before selecting a test.

- Ascertain whether the test content and norm group(s) or comparison group(s) are appropriate for the intended test takers.

- Select and use only those tests for which the skills needed to administer the test and interpret scores correctly are available.

Interpreting scores

Test developers should help users to interpret scores correctly.

Test users should interpret scores correctly.

Test developers should:
- Provide timely and easily understood scores reports that describe test performance clearly and accurately, and also explain the meaning and limitations of reported scores.

- Describe the population(s) represented by any norms or comparison group(s), the dates the data were gathered and the process used to select the samples of test takers.

- Warn users to avoid specific, reasonably anticipated misuses of test scores.

- Provide information that will help users to follow reasonable procedures for setting passing scores when it is appropriate to use such scores with the test.

Test users should:
- Obtain information about the scale used for reporting scores, the characteristics of any norms or comparison group(s), and the limitations of the scores.

- Interpret scores, taking into account any major differences between the norms or comparison groups and the actual test takers. Also take into account any differences in test administration practices or familiarity with the specific questions in the test.

- Avoid using tests for purposes not specifically recommended by the test developer, unless evidence is obtained to support the intended use.

- Explain how any passing scores were set and gather evidence to support the appropriateness of the scores.

- Provide information that will help users to gather evidence to show that the test is meeting its intended purpose(s).

- Obtain evidence to help show that the test is meeting its intended purpose(s).

Striving for fairness

Test developers should strive to make tests that are as fair as possible for test takers of difference races, gender, ethnic backgrounds, or different handicapping conditions.

Test users should select tests that have been developed in ways that attempt to make them as fair as possible for test takers of different races, gender, ethnic backgrounds, or handicapping conditions.

Test developers should:

- Review and revise test questions and related materials to avoid potentially insensitive content or language.

- Investigate the performance of test takers of different races, gender and ethnic backgrounds when samples of sufficient size are available. Enact procedures that help to ensure that differences in performance are related primarily to the skills under assessment, rather than to irrelevant factors.

- When feasible, make appropriately modified forms of tests or administration procedures available for test takers with handicapping conditions. Warn test users of potential problems in using standard norms with modified tests or administration procedures that result in non-comparable scores.

Test users should:

- Evaluate the procedures used by test developers to avoid potentially insensitive content or language.

- Review the performance of test takers of different races, gender and ethnic backgrounds when samples of sufficient size are available. Evaluate the extent to which performance differences may have been caused by the test.

- When necessary and feasible, use appropriately modified forms or administration procedures for test takers with handicapping conditions. Interpret standard norms with care, in the light of the modifications that were made.

Informing test takers

Under some circumstances, test developers have direct communication with test takers. Under other circumstances, test users communicate directly with test takers. Whichever group communicates directly with test takers should provide the information described below.

Test developers or test users should:

- When a test is optional, provide test takers or their parents/guardians with information to help them to judge whether the test should be taken, or if an available alternative to the test should be used.

- Provide test takers with the information they need to become familiar with the coverage of the test, the types of question formats, the directions, and appropriate test-taking strategies. Strive to make such information equally available to all test takers.

Under some circumstances, test developers have direct control of tests and test scores. Under other circumstances, test users have such control. Whichever group has direct control of tests and test scores should take the steps described below.

Test developers or test users should:

- Provide test takers or their parents/guardians with information about rights test takers may have to obtain copies of tests and completed answer sheets, retake tests, have tests rescored, or cancel scores.

- Tell test takers or their parents/guardians how long scores will be kept on file, and indicate to whom and under what circumstances test scores will or will not be released.

- Describe the procedures that test takers or their parents/guardians may use to register complaints and have problems resolved.

Note: The membership of the Working Group that developed the Code of Fair Testing Practices in Education and of the Joint Committee on Testing Practices that guided the Working Group was as follows:

Theodore P. Bartell	John J. Fremer	George F. Madaus	Nicholas A. Vacc
John R. Bergan	(Co-chair, JCTP and	(Co-chair, JCTP)	Michael J. Zieky
Esther E. Diamond	Chair, Code Working	Kevin L. Moreland	(Debra Boltas and
Richard P. Duran	Group)	Jo-Ellen V. Perez	Wayne Camara
Lorraine D. Eyde	Edmund W. Gordon	Robert J. Solomon	of the American
Raymond D. Fowler	Jo-Ida C. Hansen	John T. Stewart	Psychological
James B. Lingwall	Carol Kehr Tittle	(Co-chair, JCTP)	Association served as
			staff liaisons)

Additional copies of the Code may be obtained from the National Council on Measurement in Education, 1230 Seventeenth Street NW, Washington, DC 20036, USA. Single copies are free of charge.

Subject Index

Author Index